THE BOOKS OF
SAMUEL
VOLUME TWO

Also by Cyril J. Barber

Nehemiah and the Dynamics of Effective Leadership
Judges: A Narrative of God's Power
Ruth: A Story of God's Grace
The Minister's Library, Volume 1
The Minister's Library, Volume 2
The Books of Samuel, Volume One

THE BOOKS OF
SAMUEL
VOLUME TWO

THE SOVEREIGNTY OF GOD ILLUSTRATED
IN THE LIFE OF DAVID

CYRIL J. BARBER

An Expositional Commentary
on Second Samuel

LOIZEAUX
Neptune, New Jersey

The Books of Samuel, Volume Two
© 2000 Cyril J. Barber

A Publication of Loizeaux Brothers, Inc.,
A Nonprofit Organization
Devoted to the Lord's Work and to the Spread of His Truth

Unless otherwise stated, all translations and paraphrases of Scripture in this book are the author's. The chapter and verse divisions cited in parentheses correspond to those found in most English Bibles (and not to the Masoretic Text). Scripture citations without an accompanying reference to a book of the Bible are all from Second Samuel.

In this book occasional references are made to the Apocrypha of the Old Testament. These are to show the usage of a particular word or to draw the reader's attention to some tradition or belief. Neither the author nor the publisher equate the Apocrypha with the canonical Scriptures, even though some Bibles have the Old Testament Apocrypha in them.

The Hebrew letter that appears on the title page and also encloses each chapter number is the first letter in the Hebrew spelling of *Samuel.*

Library of Congress Cataloging-in-Publication Data

Barber, Cyril J.
The books of Samuel: the sovereignty of God illustrated in the lives of Samuel, Saul, and David / Cyril J. Barber.
Includes bibliographical references and index.
ISBN 0-87213-027-4 (volume 1)   ISBN 0-87213-029-0 (volume 2)
1. Bible. O.T.   Samuel—Commentaries.   I. Bible. O.T.   Samuel.
English. Barber. 2000. II. Title.
BS1325.3.B37   2000
222'.4307—dc20   94-337

Printed in the United States of America
10 9 8 7 6 5 4 3 2 1

To

Stephen C. Bradley,

a faithful servant of Jesus Christ.

CONTENTS

FOREWORD

Here is a commentary on 2 Samuel that seeks to combine careful scholarship with the practical application of Biblical truth. Behind every twist and turn in Israel's history is a sovereign God who orchestrates events so that His purposes will be fully accomplished.

Cyril Barber is convinced that the books of Samuel were written not to display the horror of David's sin of murder and adultery (though that painful lesson is clearly evident), but rather to demonstrate God's faithfulness in raising up prophets, priests, and kings to move history toward the coming of Christ. The central focus of this commentary is to show that the sovereign God weaves His own historical patterns alongside human failure and sins. In fact, the faithfulness of God is always seen more clearly against the backdrop of the unfaithfulness of mankind.

I've known Cyril since the days he organized and directed the Dallas Seminary book room. Already then he was a walking encyclopedia of bibliographic information. He not only knew the titles and authors of hundreds of books (if not thousands) but also their content. All of us have benefited from his book *The Minister's Library* and other works from his prolific pen (or personal computer).

Some people will read this commentary for the exegetical light it sheds on 2 Samuel. Others will seek personal applications and find help in the great lessons that can be learned from the mistakes and successes of the past. All who read it will derive a new appreciation for the work of God in human history.

I should warn you that this commentary challenges familiar interpretations and looks at the events of 2 Samuel through a different set of glasses. But precisely for this reason I wish it a wide distribution.

May God help all of us to understand His ways better.

Erwin W. Lutzer,
Senior Pastor
The Moody Church, Chicago, Illinois.

INTRODUCTION

Have you ever thought about the way some of our traditions are perpetuated? Peter Drucker tells the story of five British freshmen cadets who were on a gunnery range for the first time. Their instructor showed them how to load a cannon and then commissioned four of them to fire off some shells. One cadet adjusted the level of the barrel in keeping with the coordinates given him, two others carried and loaded the shells, and a fourth closed the chamber and fired the cannon. The fifth cadet, however, felt like a spare part.

Not having had experience with the "speak only when spoken to" rule, he asked the officer in charge of the detail, "What am I to do, sir?"

A volley of expletives punctuated the answer, but it boiled down to replacing any of the men should he be injured or killed.

Again the plebe protested, "But in these days of modern warfare, if the unit should sustain a direct hit, we'd all be killed."

This produced the reply, "Look, @#$%, here we do things by the book. The book says there are to be five of you assigned to each unit, and if you count carefully you will find that there are five of you assigned to this unit. Now the sooner you learn to do as you're told and not ask @#$% questions, the better off you will be!"

But the question stuck in the instructor's mind so he respectfully asked his superior officer the reason for the fifth man in the gunnery crew.

"I don't know," was the reply. "That's the way we've always done it!"

This career officer was likewise puzzled, so he asked the colonel in charge of the training school, reminding him that he had once been a student of the man who had written the manual. Feeling as if he had been backed into a corner, the colonel promised to look into it. Try as he might, though, he could not remember why they had always had five men assigned to each detail when it was plain that they needed only four. Finally, he told his aide to locate the author of the manual.

The aide finally located the retired general, now well advanced in years, in a retirement home. A call was put through and the general was called to the phone. With many apologies for intruding on the general's "valuable time," the colonel reminded his former mentor that he had once studied under him. Then he explained the reason for the call.

"Yes I remember writing the manual. You mean they are still using it? I can't for the life of me remember why we needed five men, but..." There was a long pause. Then finally, as the veteran recalled long forgotten facts, he said: "To hold the horses. Yes, that's right. The fifth man was to hold the horses!"

THE THEME OF 2 SAMUEL

We have our traditions too. As with those in the military academy, we sometimes perpetuate what we believe to be the teaching of Scripture because we were taught it by a revered man of God. And we are grateful for his contribution. We owe much to the stalwarts of the faith who amid times of severe conflict stood firmly for what they believed. Each generation, however, needs to reexamine, and reaffirm its own beliefs, standing ready to request an explanation for some of the teachings that have been handed down to them.

The Traditional Approach

Most of us, when we were in Sunday school or taking a religion course in college, were told that 1 Samuel recorded the transition of Israel's government from a loose tribal federation to a united kingdom. And in many popular textbooks and study Bibles we are informed that 2 Samuel hinges on David's sin with Bathsheba. Part one (we are told) looks at David's triumphs, and part two looks at the trials that came in the wake of his affair with Uriah's wife.

These outlines are so neat and easy to remember that many of us have accepted them as sacrosanct. Unhappily, this has resulted in our missing the point of what God wishes *to reveal about Himself.* In reality, the "books" of Samuel form a unit. There is no arbitrary division separating one from the other and necessitating a specific theme for 1 Samuel and separate one for 2 Samuel. Dr. William G. Blaikie wisely observed:

> Let us bear in mind all along that the great object of these books [of Samuel], as of the other historical books of Scripture, is peculiar: *it is not to trace the history of a nation*, in the ordinary sense, *but to trace the course of Divine revelation*, to illustrate God's manner of dealing with the nation whom He chose that He might instruct and train them in His ways, that He might

train them to that righteousness which alone exalteth a people, and that He might lay a foundation for the work of Christ in future times, in whom all the families of the earth would be blessed.[1]

I do not wish to rehash my discussion of the theme of these canonical writings that was included in my *Introduction* in volume 1. Rather I want us to consider carefully the *unity* or *continuity* of these books. Dr. David M. Gunn's words are most apropos.

Reading the Second Book of Samuel as a separate book is rather like reading a single chapter in an episodic novel. The story makes sense but keeps directing us beyond itself to its larger context. In the case of 2 Samuel, that context is the great story of God and Israel—its origins, nationhood, and eventual removal from the land—told in Genesis through 2 Kings.[2]

He continues:

Second Samuel belongs to the part of the story that recounts Israel's nationhood in the promised land and its attempt to adapt religious and political institutions to changing circumstances.... The story is not just Israel's story, however, it is also God's. Above all, it is about Yhwh's attempt to maintain or recreate a relationship of loyalty between [Himself] and [His] people....

The story of David's rise, woven into the story of Saul, finds fulfillment in the story of kingship in 2 Samuel. In turn, just as the account of Saul's end dovetails into 2 Samuel, so the account of David's death dovetails into the beginning of 1 Kings, which continues the story of monarchial Israel.[3]

Confirmation of the Theme

We may confidently see the theme of 2 Samuel as *God's sovereignty in establishing the throne of His anointed.* Irrefutable support for such a belief comes from a very ancient source. Ethan the Ezrahite wrote:

Once You spoke in a vision to Your godly ones,
And [You] said: "I have given help to one who is mighty;
I have exalted one chosen from the people.
I have found David My servant;
With My holy oil I have anointed him,
With whom My hand will be established;

My arm also will strengthen him.
The enemy will not exact usury from him,
Nor the son of wickedness afflict him.
But I shall crush his adversaries before him,
And strike those who hate him.
My faithfulness and My lovingkindness will be with him,
And in My name his horn will be exalted.
I shall also set his hand on the sea,
And his right hand on the rivers.
He will cry to Me, 'You are My Father,
My God, and the rock of my salvation.'
I also shall make him [My] first-born,
The highest of the kings of the earth.
My lovingkindness I will keep for him forever,
And My covenant shall be confirmed in him.
So I will establish his descendants forever,
And his throne as the days of heaven"
           (Psalm 89:19-29. See also Psalm 78:65-72).

The emphasis on *I* and *My* and what God promised to do for David cannot be ignored. Ethan's words, however, were written after David's death. They look beyond David's lifetime to Christ's reign and the Millennial Kingdom that He will establish. In the resurrection, David is to have a place that will fully conform to all that Ethan prophesied in his psalm.

Further proof comes from the writer of 2 Samuel.[4] He pointed out how the Lord continued to help David as he fought against all his enemies:

Now there was a long war between the house of Saul and the house of David; and David grew steadily stronger, but the house of Saul grew weaker continually (3:1).

And David became greater and greater, for Yahweh of Hosts was with him (5:10).

And David realized that Yahweh had established him as king over Israel, and that He had exalted his kingdom for the sake of His people Israel (5:12).

And Yahweh helped David wherever he went (8:14*b*).

OUTLINE

An outline of the book is suggested by the recurring statements: "Now it came about after..." (1:1), "Then it came about afterwards..." (2:1), "Now it came about when..." (7:1), "Now it came about that..." (8:1), "Now it was after this..." (10:1), and "Now it was after this...(13:1). Subdivisions commence with 11:1 and 15:1.

In broad strokes, therefore, we can outline the book as follows:

* The Sovereignty of God in Preparing the
  Way for a New Dynasty, 1:1-27

* The Sovereignty of God in Establishing
  the Kingdom, 2:1–6:23

* The Sovereignty of God in Instituting
  the Davidic Covenant, 7:1-29

* The Sovereignty of God in Expanding
  the Kingdom, 8:1–12:31

* The Sovereignty of God in Sustaining
  the Kingdom, 13:1–20:26

* An Appendix, 21:1–24:25

The sections beginning with 11:1 and 15:1 introduce subordinate trends within the section dealing with the expansion of David's empire.

THE IMPORTANCE OF THE COVENANT

Instead of chapters 11–12 (David's adultery and the aftermath) being the fulcrum upon which the book turns, *God's sovereignty in establishing the kingdom* is the climax (see chapter 7), where the Lord enters into a covenant with David and promises to establish his dynasty for ever. This is preceded by an account of the consolidation of David's empire and the establishment of Jerusalem as his capital (5:1–6:23). Following the assurance that David will have an enduring dynasty, we are prepared for an account of his different conquests (8:1–10:19).

The Gracious Character of the Covenants

All of God's covenants were essentially gracious. They were established quite apart from human merit. It is true that, in the twenty or more years following David's affair with Bathsheba and the murder of Uriah, David encountered certain problems (13:1–20:26), but these difficulties illustrate how God sovereignly sustained David and his kingdom in accordance with His covenantal promise. The Lord preserved the throne for David from all who would wrest it from him. These chapters, therefore, treat the threats to the throne as fulfilling a twofold purpose: (1) Showing the greatness of God's grace and forgiveness; and (2) showing us the inviolability of God's promise.

Those preachers and teachers who loudly proclaim that David had a character defect that incapacitated him from further effective leadership show their arbitrary interpretation of the events of chapters 11–12 by ignoring other passages of Scripture that contradict their theory (e.g., Psalm 51, especially vv. 12-13, 17). Furthermore, far from setting David on the shelf as someone disapproved for further service (cf. 1 Corinthians 9:27), God's blessing continued to rest upon him. This is confirmed when we compare Scripture with Scripture. Consider, for example, Abraham's eulogy.

> And Abraham breathed his last and died in a good old age, an old man and satisfied with [life]; and he was gathered to his people (Genesis 25:8).

Such praise is reserved for those whose righteous deeds have earned for them special recognition. Now read what Scripture records of David:

> Now David...died in a good old age, full of days, riches...and honor...(1 Chronicles 29:28).

The point is obvious. Once David had confessed his sin, God forgave him. With forgiveness came restoration to a position of favor. Certain personal consequences did follow his sinful acts, but we commit a grievous error if we fail to see how God, in His sovereign grace, continued to prosper David. It is an unfortunate part of human nature that we tend to focus upon people's sins rather than upon God's forgiveness. And when we allow our weakness in this area to color our interpretation of Scripture we not only delude ourselves but we mislead others as well.

The Relationship of the Covenants

The benefits of approaching 2 Samuel as a continuation of 1 Samuel's record of God's sovereignty are underscored by the way this continuity builds upon the Abrahamic Covenant (Genesis 12:1-3, 6-7; 13:14-17; 15:1-21; 17:1-14; 22:15-18; etc.).

The Abrahamic Covenant is foundational to the other Biblical covenants.[5] It is also essential to a proper understanding of Old Testament history from the period of the patriarchs to the time of Christ.[6] This covenant formed the basis upon which the Palestinian Covenant was built (Deuteronomy 29:2—30:20), and in accordance with God's progressive revelation, the Davidic Covenant of 2 Samuel 7 was likewise founded upon it. In the course of time, long after the reign of David, God would again reveal His will to the prophet Jeremiah, and the Abrahamic Covenant would then be seen to undergird the blessings of the New Covenant (Jeremiah 31:31-34).

In order of importance, therefore, the Davidic Covenant is of infinitely greater significance than any other single event recorded in 2 Samuel!

Some important issues need to be acknowledged if we are to see the events of 2 Samuel within the context of the times. These include: (1) The transitional nature of chapter 1 and the events that followed David's move to Hebron; (2) an assessment of the nature and extent of David's kingdom during the early part of his reign; and (3) a consideration of the divine/human element that led up to the consolidation of David's kingdom. These issues will be discussed at appropriate places in the exposition of the text.

Most of us find it easy to identify with David *before* he became king. We, too, have experienced times of hardship and adversity. We admire David's example and receive encouragement from his life. We also find instruction in his psalms. But most of us experience difficulty identifying with him once he had become king.

The point goes beyond our inability to identify with the "rich and famous." If we are honest with ourselves, those of us who will never become president or CEO of our company or be appointed chairman of the board may secretly envy those who, under the hand of God, have received such an honor. So to relate better with David, we would do well to take our eyes off the "honor" and see in David's rise to power the dangers to which those in such positions are particularly prone.

This, however, does not give us licence to ferret out David's supposed sins where Scripture is silent on any wrongdoing. His strengths and weaknesses will be discussed as each passage comes under scrutiny. And being aware of the imbalance others have demonstrated, we will attempt to achieve a more moderate balance.

* * * * *

Readers will again find that I have provided my own translation of the Masoretic (Hebrew) Text. With so many versions available (all of which, to some extent, paraphrase Biblical idioms), I have made available a literal rendering so as to bring out as far as possible exactly what was said and done. I am aware that my translation does not read with the fluency of style of many modern versions; but what I have sought to provide does *not* replace the work of others. It does, however, provide a basis of comparison.

Occasionally reference has been made to other translations. These have generally been identified as follows: AV = Authorized (King James) Version; NASB = New American Standard Bible; NIV = New International Version; and NKJV = New King James Version.

As the notes at the end of this book will show, I have made use of a variety of sources. I regret, however, that J. P. Fokkelman's study of the life of King Saul and the rise of David (scheduled for volume 2 of his four-volume study) had not been released when I completed the manuscript on 1 Samuel. In addition, his projected volume 3 (intended to cover the consolidation of David's kingship) had likewise not been published when I finished this manuscript. In writing this book, I have had access only to volume 1, treating 2 Samuel 9–20 and 1 Kings 1–2.

Likewise, Joyce Baldwin's commentary on 1 and 2 Samuel was unavailable to me during the writing of 1 Samuel. I have made use of her work, however, in this study of 2 Samuel.

Robert Polzin's *Samuel and the Deuteronomist*, covering 1 Samuel, came out about a year after I had finished my study of 1 Samuel and was already immersed in a consideration of the text of 2 Samuel.

And neither of Anthony F. Campbell's volumes on *1 Samuel* and *2 Samuel*, projected for inclusion in the *Forms of the Old Testament Literature* series, have so far made their appearance. I am sure that serious students of Scripture will benefit from these works.

Finally, in the years following my completion of *Ruth: A Story of God's Grace*, a need arose that necessitated my selling approximately nine thousand volumes from my library. I no longer have access, therefore, to some important lexicons, grammars, and other studies that I had used in earlier expositions.

In conclusion, I wish once again to express my sincere appreciation to my counselees who have graciously allowed me to give brief synopses of their experiences. These, as will readily be seen, have been used to illustrate some aspect of the Biblical text. In each case the identity of the person, as well as relatives and friends, has been protected. My indebtedness to them is very real!

Finally, I would like to thank my good friend, Dr. Erwin W. Lutzer, senior pastor of the Moody Memorial Church, Chicago, Illinois, for setting aside the time to read the manuscript and write the Foreword.

Cyril J. Barber
October 1, 1991

LIFE'S TRANSITIONS

2 Samuel 1:1-27

A few years ago, my pastor phoned to ask me if I would teach a Sunday school class for a particular group of people in the church. They ranged in age from their early thirties to late fifties and were in need of some specific help.

I enquired about the curriculum and was told that there was none–I would have to develop my own. I tried to decline, but my pastor sounded urgent and so at last I agreed. Having had experience tailoring courses to the unique needs of doctoral students, I decided to do the same with this Sunday school group.

We spent our first gathering getting to know one another. I introduced myself and, to break the ice, I told of some of the crises and struggles I had faced. Then I asked them to share something about themselves and explain why they had decided to participate in this unusual kind of class. Here are a few of the situations they were going through:

- Lauren's husband, Ron, had recently served her with divorce papers. Divorce was something she had strenuously resisted as long as Ron had remained at home. Now Lauren was awash in the conflicting crosscurrents of her emotions.

- Joe had been a professional football player. Last season he had sustained an injury and spent the rest of the year on the bench. Now, in spite of a doctor's "clean bill of health" and his protests that he was ready to play, he had been terminated. He was filled with anger and resentment.

- Irene and her children had recently moved to the Greater Los Angeles area from Philadelphia. Tom, her husband, had promised to come with the furniture and other household items as soon as he sold the house. The house had been sold, but her husband had not arrived.

She traced accident reports, but none led to Tom. In her anguish, Irene finally had to admit that Tom had opted for a "poor man's divorce." But this left her and the children without income and facing the bitterness of his deceit and rejection.

• Larry was struggling with the untimely death of his only son. His wife and daughters had turned from the Lord, and he was left alone with his doubts and the unanswered questions that flooded his mind. He frankly admitted that this was the most painful experience he had ever had to endure.

• Harry joined the class a week after it began. He came because he thought the discussion of different issues might help him. He had been given "early retirement" by his company and now, no matter how hard he tried, he could not find a job. The story was always the same: "Your credentials are impeccable; your work history is excellent; but, quite frankly, we're looking for a younger man."

The fact that the law forbade such discrimination made no difference. Harry was left to spend his days answering ads and making phone calls. Even his friends began avoiding him. He had begun to feel rejected, useless, and unwanted.

Others in the class were likewise trying their best to cope with the hurts and challenges of their lives. All seemed to be *in transition.* Now that I knew each person's situation, I was able to develop a curriculum that would attempt to meet their felt needs. As the weeks went by we spent time studying what the Bible has to say about the *transitions of life,* including the one David faced when he returned to Ziklag. But, someone will ask, "What practical value is there in this story for me? So David returns to Ziklag. There he is told of Saul's death. Later he settles in Hebron. So what? I fail to see in these stories anything that is even remotely relevant to me and the problems I face."

It is true that the story centers on David. But as we examine his circumstances, we will find that he faced an important transition. Saul was dead, but David did not know this. And while David had been anointed king by Samuel fifteen or more years earlier, as he viewed the ruins of Ziklag and considered the predicament facing him and his men, the throne of Israel seemed to be very far away. He was in a difficult *transitional phase* of his life.

Because all of us go through many transitions (some of which will be mentioned later on in this chapter), we have much to learn from David's experience.

OVERVIEW OF THE TRANSITION PROCESS

Transitions generally fall into three identifiable and progressive stages:

- An *ending*, in which a facet of life as we know it (e.g., a relationship, a job, an investment, a place of residence, etc.) comes to a close. This generally involves four phases: disengagement, disidentification, disenchantment, and disorientation.

- A *neutral zone*, in which we may experience bewilderment, hopelessness, and helplessness, while becoming painfully aware of our powerlessness and of the disintegration of our plans.

- A *new beginning*, accompanied by the realization that, in spite of our doubts and uncertainties, God has been working in and through our circumstances to bring about His purposes in our lives.

It will be easy for us to see in this chapter *the sovereignty of God in preparing the way for a new dynasty*. This, however, was not as clear to David. He did not know what was happening. He could see God's hand in separating him and his men from the Philistines (1 Samuel 29:3-8). But Saul had been consistently successful in battle, and if he should somehow gain the victory over Israel's enemies, what would the future hold for him and his men? Could they continue to rely upon the protection of Achish?

The dismissal of David and his men from the Philistine army represented an *ending* (even though they were not aware of it at the time). Then, in 2 Samuel 2, we read of David being crowned king over the people of Judah. This was a *new beginning*. In between, however, was the *neutral zone*, in which he felt the full weight of the frustration of his plans compounded by an inability to make sense of what was happening to him. In this respect he must have felt as we often do when we face life's disruptions.

With this brief overview, let's take a closer look at the different stages through which we pass.

Endings

Dr. William Bridges, in his book *Transitions: Making Sense of Life's Changes*, writes:

> Considering that we have to deal with endings all our lives, most of us handle them very badly. This is in part because we misunderstand them and take them either too seriously or not seriously enough. We take them too seriously by confusing them with finality—that's it, all over, never more, finished! We see them as something without sequence, forgetting that in fact they are the first phase of the transitional process and a precondition of self-renewal. At the same time we fail to take them seriously enough. Just because they scare us, we try to avoid them.[1]

In David's experience, we notice first the place of disengagement. An ending came when he was forced to leave the field of battle and return to Ziklag. The event, however desired and prayed for, happened suddenly. The rejection by the "lords of the Philistines" was unforeseen. David's dismissal involved packing up and going home (1 Samuel 29:7,10-11).

Life has many such endings: leaving home for college, the breakup of a marriage, a death in the family or the loss of a close friend, leaving one job for another, moving to a new city or state, facing the "empty nest," having to endure a debilitating illness, and even retirement. Willingly or unwillingly we are separated from the past–from activities and routines, relationships, roles, and responsibilities that were important to us. And with disengagement an inexorable process of change begins.

Second, the breaking of old connections is accompanied by disidentification, or a loss of self-definition. How much of this David felt with his demotion is hard to determine (cf. 1 Samuel 28:2-3; 29:8). His relationship with the Philistines had always been tenuous, and with the rejection of him and his men, he must have felt vulnerable.

A greater sense of disidentification came over him when he returned to Ziklag and found the city in ruins (1 Samuel 30:1-5). He and his men had lost everything that was dear to them, and they had no assurance that in time they would recover what had been taken.

God sometimes allows us to experience this kind of uprooting. But while we think only of the immediate present, the Lord, in His infinite wisdom, is preparing us for something new. For David and his men, it would be a move to Hebron.

We need this part of the process because old things may stand in the way of our following God's will. And while we may be thankful that He does not always deal with us in the same dramatic way He did with David, the process He chooses nonetheless accomplishes His purpose. The more we are tied to our old identity, the more surely He will need to pry us loose from it. We need to be on guard, therefore, against letting some cherished goal stand in the way of our doing His will.

Third, when separated from the old and familiar, we often feel as if we are in limbo. We are caught between two worlds: the subtle ties of assumption and expectation no longer fit our new circumstances, and neither do our former skills and abilities. As we find ourselves increasingly unable to cope with what is happening, we become disenchanted. It is then that many either resist the process of change (and give way to depression) or passively give in. Both are false approaches to life's transitions and lead ultimately to despair.

Perhaps David's men felt some of this, for they vented their anger on David and blamed him for what had happened. They even spoke of stoning him (1 Samuel 30:6). Several days later, however, when their families had been restored to them, they were in a festive mood. Then they give him a kingly title by referring to the spoils of war as "David's spoil" (1 Samuel 30:20). But we do not read of them beginning to rebuild their houses. Some may have started, but the text is singularly silent as to any organized building project. It seems as if they sensed that something else was going to happen, so they waited.

David's approach to this period of his life gives us an example of a healthy way to deal with unwanted transitions. He acted in his integrity. He honestly admitted how he felt (he was deeply distressed but "strengthened his hand in Yahweh his God," 1 Samuel 30:6*b*). He also sought the will of God (1 Samuel 30:7; 2 Samuel 2:1. Note the word "Then..." in both instances). He made the Lord his trust!

But how did David and his men handle the many questions that would naturally course through their minds? How had the battle gone? Had God, in His grace, given Saul another remarkable victory? Had Saul and his sons survived the conflict? If, however, the battle had gone against Israel, were the royal family now captives of the Philistines? Should they send out spies to find out what had happened? And if Saul and his sons were captives, should they try to rescue them?

Each man would also have to wonder about the fate of his extended family still living in their ancestral homes. What about their parents, brothers and brothers-in-law still living in their homes in Israel? Were they alright? And their sisters? What of them? Had they been carried off as part of the spoils of war to be sold into slavery?

Periods of transition are difficult to bear. Time hangs heavily on our hands. Our doubts multiply. We are naturally concerned about the future. Skills or techniques for getting along that worked for us before now seem to be inadequate. And if we resort to their use, our activity only results in failure and increasing frustration.

It is at this juncture that many of us wish to return to the past— a former employer or friend or region of the country. But when these doors close, the darkness of disillusionment settles on us. What this indicates is that the stage of disenchantment is well advanced. Only as we work through it will we be able to go on to the next phase.

Finally, as if to add to our misery, there comes disorientation. We feel our situation is hopeless. The solution to our problem(s) eludes us. We give up our plans for the future. We don't know what to do. Our efforts to find something meaningful and fulfilling end in failure. We secretly entertain the fear that our former confidence or vivacity or happiness has become like old clothes stored in some disused trunk in the attic. In reality, for those of us who are Christians, this process can be the Lord's way of bringing us to place our confidence unreservedly in Him.

There is evidence of disorientation in David's forgetting the answers given him by the Amalekite (cf. 1:8,13). His grief on hearing of the death of Saul and his sons from the mercenary may have caused him to overlook certain details. And the forced marches of the last two weeks (to Aphek and back and then into the desert to reclaim what had been stolen) may have left him tired in body, mind, and spirit. This general disorientation, though, extended to his men as well. From what we are able to deduce from the text, none gave serious thought to the future. They appeared to be waiting on David for directions; and in truth, he did not know what to do.

The Neutral Zone

Dr. Bridges describes this period of the transitional process as "a moratorium from the conventional activity of everyday existence... [to a time of] attentive inactivity and ritualized routine."[2] Many whom I have counseled have experienced frustration as their lives appear to be marked by a lack of productivity. But many also have drawn closer to the Lord during this period. Those who have placed their trust in the Lord may have resumed a study of the Bible that had been relinquished years earlier for reasons that no longer appear relevant. And they may also have toned up their prayer life.

As circumstances run their course, these people come to a place in which they surrender their all to the Lord. This process of dying to their own will makes possible the slow, inner renewal of their spirits so that they begin seeking the mind of Christ (see Romans 12:1-2).

I have often suggested to people in this kind of situation that they keep a journal or diary in which they write down what happens or does not happen during the course of a day, and also, more importantly, record *how they felt about it*. In this way they are able to try and identify their varied emotions.

This simple strategy helps them understand (at least in retrospect) something of God's dealings with them in what might otherwise be an apparent wasteland phase of their lives. It also helps them assess what they really want out of life. These tentative desires or faltering aspirations then need to be surrendered to the Lord.

A New Beginning

Following a time of reflection, and aided by a daily meditation upon some passage of God's Word, there comes a clearer sense of the purpose of life. As William Bridges has shown,

> In the transitional process we come to beginnings only at the end. It is when the endings and the time of fallow neutrality are finished that we can launch ourselves anew, changed and renewed by the destruction of the old-phase and the journey through the [neutral zone].[3]

New beginnings are not always clearly defined at the time they occur. David's rise to prominence gives evidence of several stages or "new beginnings." These are recorded in the early chapters of 2 Samuel.

In addition, instead of waiting for external signs that would point the way to the future, he sought counsel directly from the Lord (2:1).

It is well for us to realize that, during these times of transition, God's guidance may not be blazed in neon lights on some skyscraper saying Yes or No. We are more likely to experience intuitively the leading of the Holy Spirit as He says to us, "This is the way, walk in it" (Isaiah 30:21. See also Psalms 25:9,12; 27:11). But let us remember that our success at the beginning of a new phase of our lives directly relates to our cooperation with the *process* that has brought about the change.

Dr. Bridges summarizes the truth about the transitions through which we all pass:

> New beginnings are accessible to everyone, and everyone has trouble with them. Much as we may wish to make a new beginning, some part of us resists doing so as though we were making the first step toward disaster. Everyone has a slightly different version of these anxieties and confusions, but in one way or another they all arise from the fear that real change destroys the old ways in which we established our security.[4]

From David's experience of a painful transition we learn many important things about ourselves. And as we consider what the inspired penman wrote, we will see more clearly the connection with the past as well as the way in which, in the providence of God, He used these events to prepare David for the future.

OUTLINE

This chapter can be outlined as follows:

*The Sovereignty of God in Preparing the Way
for a New Dynasty (1:1-27)*

- Report of the Battle (1:1-10)
- Response to the News (1:11-12)
- Retribution on the Unrighteous (1:13-16)
- Requiem for the Dead (1:17-27)

THE SOVEREIGNTY OF GOD IN PREPARING THE WAY FOR A NEW DYNASTY (1:1-27)

Report of the Battle (1:1-10)

With Saul now dead, Israel is leaderless. The people who already know the outcome of the battle are bewildered. Because it takes time for word to spread to the major cities, those farther away from the scene of battle might not learn of the Philistine victory until the victors are seen coming to loot their homes. And even when Abner will want to make Ishbosheth king, there will still be a further lapse of several weeks before the elders of the people and the leading citizens can assemble for his coronation. Meanwhile, David is in the southern city of Ziklag, far removed from these activities and cut off from the usual sources of information.

The actual events of this chapter require little comment. They describe the story of how word of Saul's death is brought to David. The purpose of the writer—subtly interwoven into the events of this chapter—seems to be to make clear that David played no part in Saul's demise. His approach also serves secondarily to defend David's right to the throne and vindicate his appointment, first as Judah's king, and then as king over all Israel.[5]

Drs. Herbert Alleman and Elmer Flack have shown that the news of Saul's death could not have reached David before the arrival of the Amalekite. Instead, the report was received when David and his men were apparently resting after the exertion of the past two weeks.[6]

The mercenary[7] who seeks out David in Ziklag announces by his disheveled appearance that he is the bearer of bad news.[8] The fact that he looks like a mourner does not mean that he was personally grieving for Saul. He is merely following the custom of his times and intimating that he shares the grief he feels sure will be experienced by those to whom he brings the news.

The Amalekite's attitude also implies that he recognizes David as the new king (cf. 2:8-10), and so he gives David Saul's diadem (or coronet) and forearm bracelet. He does this in order to ingratiate himself to David. His expectation is that he will then be suitably recompensed for his supposed loyalty (4:10).

The story he tells conflicts with the information presented in 1 Samuel 31:3-6 (cf. 2 Samuel 1:6-10). The fact that he knows of Saul's request to his armor bearer, namely, that he kill him, may indicate that the Amalekite was close enough to the king to overhear the brief conversation. It seems evident, however, that he deliberately distorted the truth to serve his own ends.[9]

The Response to the News (1:11-12)

On hearing of the death of Saul and his sons, David and those who are with him immediately give expression to their grief (cf. 13:31). Their worst fears have been realized. They show their sorrow by lamentation, weeping, and fasting.[10]

We might have expected David to mourn only for Jonathan, his closest friend. David, however, grieves for Saul as well. The past ten or more years, during which time Saul has been his implacable enemy, are forgotten. He mourns for a life that is now ended; one that had been so full of promise!

The loyalty of David and his men to their people must not be ignored. They express their sorrow (as the chronicler notes) for the "house of Israel."[11] Though compelled to become the vassals of Achish, their true identity has always been with God's people. "Now," as Joyce Baldwin explains, "there is no need to make a pretense of having deserted the Philistines."[12]

Retribution on the Unrighteous (1:13-16)

After the mercenary has concluded his story, he waits. All about him are weeping. It is only later, when David has partly recovered from his grief, that his eye falls on Saul's diadem[13] and bracelet.[14] He calls the young man to him. Expecting to receive his reward, the Amalekite comes forward.

"Where are you from?" David inquires.

"I am the son of an alien,[15] an Amalekite," is the reply (1:13).

Those who had taken up residence within the borders of Israel were obliged to adhere to the nation's God-given laws. Dr. Kyle McCarter rightly observes:

> The sojourner (*gēr*) was neither a native nor a foreigner in legal status, but he had some of the privileges and responsibilities of each. He was a resident alien, accepted and protected by the community among whom he lived more or less permanently but by whom he was regarded finally as a foreigner.... Pertinent here is the fact that a sojourner, even in cultic and ceremonial matters, was not exempt from the laws of the community or the penalties prescribed by them (Lev 24:22; cf. 20:2; 24:16; etc.).[16]

David then asks,

> "How is it that you were not afraid to stretch out your hand against Yahweh's anointed?" (1:14).

As a resident, the Amalekite could not plead ignorance of the law. He had assumed that David would feel as he himself would have felt if the situation were reversed. He judged David by his own standard. His object was to show how great a service he had rendered David.

Seldom has heartless selfishness more completely overreached itself. Instead of a reward, the impious and self-confessed murderer earns his own punishment.[17] Calling one of his young men, David says:

"Go, fall on him."

As the young man approaches the Amalekite with his drawn sword in his hand, David pronounces sentence:

"Your blood is on your own head, for your mouth has testified against you."

And the young man strikes him down and he dies.

This may appear to us as a harsh method of righting a wrong, particularly since the Amalekite had evidently lied about what took place on Mount Gilboa. However, what is clear to us was not clear to David. He acted on the information given him by the Amalekite. And regardless of how we may view David's actions (from our vantage point nearly three millennia later), his conduct is loooked upon with favor by the people of Israel. It was also one more evidence that he had not participated in Saul's death nor rejoiced in the late king's demise.[18]

Requiem for the Dead (1:17-27)

David's lament for Saul and Jonathan is a eulogy without rival in Near Eastern literature.[19] He does not want these great men to be forgotten, and so he instructs that the song he has composed be taught to the people. In keeping with his request, it is written in the *Book of Jashar*[20] (see also Joshua 10:12-13). The sentiments he expresses show a heart rising above bitterness and resentment, revenge and self-seeking. His words highlight Saul's and Jonathan's strengths. All who sing it are able to reflect upon what was noble and praiseworthy in the lives of these great men.

> Tell it not in Gath,
>   Proclaim it not in Ashkelon,
> Lest they rejoice,
>   The Philistine maidens,
> Lest they exult,
>   The heathen girls.[21]

Great strength of feeling resonates in these lines. Though the heavy clouds of war and oppression still hang over the land, David's patriotism shines like a bright star in a darkened sky. He feels keenly the disgrace of his people and wishes to silence even the legitimate happiness of their enemies. Furthermore, any who might look for a hint of the thought that "Saul had it coming to him," will find that such sentiments are missing from the elegy. What rises up is the enormity of the people's loss.[22]

Then, as if to involve the land itself in mourning for the fallen, David writes:

> Ye hills of Gilboa
>   And lofty uplands,
> Let there be no dew
>   Nor rain upon you;
> For there was disgraced
>   The warrior's shield,
> The shield of Saul
>   With oil unanointed.
>
> From the blood of the slain,
>   From the entrails of warriors,
> The bow of Jonathan
>   Never retreated,
> Nor the sword of Saul
>   Returned empty.[23]

The "beauty of Israel" had fallen on Mount Gilboa. Such a loss was unparalleled in the history of David's people. That is why he and those with him in Ziklag fast. A national tragedy should be accompanied by national mourning. And as the land had been given them by God, let the land enter into their sorrow.

> Saul and Jonathan,
>   Beloved, delightful,
> In life they were comrades,
>   In death were not parted;
> Swifter they than eagles,
>   Stronger than lions.
>
> O maidens of Israel,
>   Weep ye for Saul,
> Who was wont to clothe you in scarlet,
>   Who decked your garments
> With golden ornaments!
>   How have the warriors fallen
> In the midst of the battle![24]

So far David has sung of Saul *and* Jonathan. Now, there is a change. He cannot finish without a special lamentation for his friend.[25] With eloquent pathos he describes his own loss.

The gazelle of Israel
Is slain on thy heights;
I grieve for thee,
My brother Jonathan,
For sweeter wast thou
Than the love of women.[26]
How have the warriors fallen.
And the weapons of war been lost![27]

Words expressing such emotion need no amplification. To add anything is to weaken their effect. It is sufficient for us to see the heart of David owning his and the nation's loss, grieving over the passing of his father-in-law, and reminding the people of all that was best in the characters of Saul and Jonathan.

And so the chapter ends.

RETROSPECT AND PROSPECT

The chief purpose of the writer seems to have been to highlight David's integrity and exonerate him from the kind of suspicion that could so easily gain a foothold, especially in a land where the transmission of information was dependent upon word of mouth.

As we have noted, communication between towns and villages was slow and, at best, partial. Many might never know that David and his men had been dismissed from the field of battle. And with people so prone to believe the worst, they might elaborate on any shred of evidence to support their theory that David had in some way engineered Saul's defeat.

Furthermore, from the plethora of events that the Biblical writer might have cited, he chose only those that prove conclusively that David had acted with uprightness of heart. He had played no part in Saul's death and, in fact, had acted in an exemplary manner when news of the Philistine victory was brought to him.

David's integrity stands in marked contrast to those Christian leaders of our day who have caused the name of Christ to be impugned by the media and blasphemed in our places of business. By comparison, David's honesty may be seen in his reaction to the news of the battle, his prompt actions to redress a national wrong, and his transparent emotion as he grieved for those who were dear to him.

REWARD OF PERSEVERANCE

Throughout the story we see David acting uprightly. It would have been easy for him to resort to human ingenuity and gather about him a council of his mighty men. They could then discuss what needed to be done. Instead, as difficult as it was to wait, that is what he did. In the "neutral zone" of his transitional experience, we find him open and transparent about his emotions.

Honesty in Expressing Our Feelings

Someone has said, "The past is valuable as a guidepost, but dangerous as a hitching post." This is especially true in a transitional phase. I have encountered this often among the recently divorced, among men and women whose employment has been unjustly terminated, or among the growing number of elderly who retire and then feel as if society has set them on a shelf.

For example, Lauren came to see me the week after our class at the church began. She was obviously distraught. Receiving the divorce papers from her husband had renewed the trauma she had experienced when he first told her he was leaving. She slumped into a chair. It seemed as if she was weighed down with grief and a sense of failure. We talked a long time about what had happened.

Finally, I asked her to tell me honestly how she felt—to put into words her emotions. She couldn't. Several weeks later the hurt was still there, but her perspective had begun to clear.

"I feel betrayed and humiliated and angry when I think of Ron sleeping with that woman. I seems as if all I held dear in our relationship has been violated by his infidelity. I have lost what was precious to me, and a feeling of depression presses down like a heavy weight on my chest. And, yes, I'm angry. And I feel fear too. I'm concerned about the future. How will I cope? What effect will all this have on the children? Will I ever find happiness again? Will I ever be able to trust anyone again? What will become of me?"

Whenever we face an *ending*—whether of a marriage, a working relationship, or of our supposedly "productive years"—each of us feels as if we have crossed some kind of threshold. Grief over relationships severed, depression from an acute sense of loss, mental and emotional confusion, and also bewilderment (*What will I do now?*) have to be owned in the cold light of reality.

Then comes the need to learn how to let go, to relinquish what was so much a part of our life, and to face our fears. As Christians, we can honestly commit the future to the Lord (1 Peter 5:7). He is sovereign. What is important is not whether we will be as successful or financially well set as before but how we honor the Lord during this difficult time.

Being honest about the positive and negative aspects of our life is also necessary. We need to face maturely the questions that keep gnawing away in our minds: "What was it that led up to——? To what extent might I have contributed to it? How may I replace negative attitudes and ways of dealing with people with positive ones? And are there any vocational skills which I should develop?"

Resisting the process of change is futile. What we can all look forward to are the results that come after plowing up the fallow ground (see Jeremiah 4:3; Hosea 10:12). As a result of all that we have experienced, we will be better prepared for what lies ahead!

Making Impartial Decisions

But what of the numerous decisions that must be made? It's hard to make the right decisions when we are emotionally distraught. Scripture shows David in the decision-making process. What should be done for/to the Amalekite who brought the news of Israel's defeat? David obtained the relevant facts and then made his determination in accord with the teaching of God's Word.

Applauding the Deeds of Others

When we have been wronged, it is not easy to overlook or forgive the hurts others have inflicted on us. In David's elegy for Saul and Jonathan he avoided dredging up the past. Rather, his truly great spirit shone through. He composed a song, literally a lament, by which his own generation as well as those to come would be reminded of the greatness of Israel's first king.

Praise comes hard to some people. They find it difficult to commend others. Some, of course, use flattery as a means to manipulate people and obtain their own ends. But as we take a closer look at David's eulogy, we note that he emphasized the accomplishments of Saul.

In life, when we praise the good works of others we encourage them without feeding their egotism. Conversely, the good things we say about others never give them as much lasting pleasure as the pain caused by our corrosive criticism. This tells us that the glow of praise dims quickly and must be continually replenished.

David survived the transitional phase of his life because he was a man of integrity. Likewise, our integrity and trust in God are our only safe guides when we, too, face the inequities of life and do not know what the future holds.

FULFILLMENT OF GOD'S PROMISE

2 Samuel 2:1–3:1

Off the rugged coast of Scotland lie the Orkney and Shetland islands. From the air they look like giant stepping-stones into the North Sea. These islands face the full fury of gales that blow in from the Atlantic. As a result, portions of the western coastline of most of them have eroded over the years into towering lines of stubborn cliffs. The most impressive of these jagged barriers is on the island of Hoy.

Over time, as the wind and the waves battered the coastline, a giant monolith was slowly separated from the surrounding area. This rugged pinnacle, called "The Old Man of Hoy," towers 450 feet above the rubble, which is covered twice a day by the onslaught of the incoming tide. At high tide it resembles a lighthouse in the sea.

Several years ago I watched a documentary on television that related the attempt of some seasoned mountaineers to climb to the top of "The Old Man of Hoy." Many of them had climbed other, more notable summits like Mount McKinley and Mount Hood, or the Jungfrau and the Matterhorn, or different peaks in the Himalayas and the Alps. Yet they found that this small but sheer rock challenged their resources and demanded all their skill.

At the end of two days, when the tired climbers stood on the small, bald dome of this pinnacle, they admitted that the difficulties of the climb were such that success had never been assured.

Watching the documentary impressed upon me anew the truth that appearances are deceptive and that past accomplishments do not automatically guarantee new achievements. David was certainly aware of this when he became king over Judah. The extent of King Saul's empire had shriveled like a dried leaf.[1] The northern tribes were under Philistine domination. This was not true, however, of those Israelites living in Transjordan. Nor does it appear to have been true of those in Judah. But this did not make the task David faced—of uniting the men of Judah and administering the people in the south—any easier. He still confronted unique difficulties that demanded of him all of his skill. The smallness of the territory he governed was no measure of the formidable obstacles that lay before him.

OUTLINE

The last chapter dealt with the way in which the Lord removed Saul from the throne. This chapter begins the next phase in the fulfillment of God's promise. In it we see *the sovereignty of God in establishing the kingdom (2:1–6:23)*. God not only set David on the throne, He safeguarded his rights to independent kingship. We may outline 2:1–3:1 as follows:

The Sovereignty of God in Establishing
the Kingdom (2:1–6:23)

- God's Guidance and a New Beginning (2:1-3)
- God's Promise and an Offer of Conciliation (2:4-7)
- God's Will Thwarted by Human Ambition (2:8–3:1)

This theme of the sovereignty of God in establishing David's kingdom will be continued in the next two chapters.

The writer sets the events of this chapter off from the preceding with the words, "And it came to pass after this...." Some expositors have called this literary device a "recurrent transition-marker." As pointed out in the Introduction, this statement marks the natural divisions and subdivisions of this book (see 7:1; 8:1; 10:1; 13:1; and 15:1).

THE SOVEREIGNTY OF GOD IN ESTABLISHING THE KINGDOM (2:1–3:1)

God's Guidance and a New Beginning (2:1-3)

David knew that God had anointed him to be Israel's king, but for more than fifteen years he seemingly had been driven further and further from realizing God's will for his life. With Ziklag now in ruins, he may have wondered, Is this the time the Lord is going to make me the leader of His people?

To ascertain God's will, David inquires of Him, "Shall I go up to one of the cities of Judah?"

And Yahweh says to him, "Go up."

David then narrows his request: "Where shall we go up?"
And the Lord replies, "To Hebron" (2:1).

We are not told how David discovered God's directive. It could
have been through Urim and Thummim (Exodus 28:30; Leviticus 8:8)
or the casting of lots (1 Samuel 14:37-42; 23:9-11; 30:7-8; 2 Samuel
5:19,23) or by means of the ephod or through prophetic utterance (1
Samuel 28:6; 2 Samuel 7:2-17). In this instance most scholars prefer
the method of casting lots, and there is much in favor of such a conclusion. In a matter as important as this, however, it seems as if David
may have obtained guidance from God with the help of Abiathar the
priest who had come to him at Keilah with an ephod (1 Samuel 22:20-
23; 23:9).

Hebron (cf. Numbers 13:22) was a city of antiquity situated nineteen miles south-southwest of Jerusalem.[2] This royal city had earlier
been known as Kiriath-arba (Judges 1:10), a name which may have
meant "city of four-quarters"—with each quarter being governed by
one of Anak's sons.

It was also a city hallowed by its associations with the patriarchs.
Abraham and Sarah had lived near there and been buried in the Cave
of Machpelah close to Hebron's ancient walls (Genesis 13:18; 23:19;
25:9-10; 35:27). According to Genesis 49:31-32, Jacob had buried Leah
in the cave next to the bodies of Abraham and Sarah. Then, before
he died he gave instructions that his body was to be entombed in
this ancestral site (Genesis 49:29-30; 50:1-13). And when the land was
settled, Caleb, of the tribe of Judah, had wrested Hebron from the
hands of the mighty sons of Anak.

But what of David's vassalage to Achish? Many able students of
God's Word believe that David had to obtain permission from the
Philistines[3] before he could leave Ziklag and settle in Hebron. This is
unlikely, even though Achish may still have regarded him as his
liegeman.

Saul's defeat had not given the Philistines the right to exercise
their rule over all Israel. When David learned of the rout of Israel's
army, the victorious Philistines had not yet returned to their cities.
They were engaged in plundering Israeli towns and villages. When
they did return to Philistia several weeks of religious festivals and
feasting would follow before they would again take an interest in
matters as mundane as the relocation of David and his men. Even
then the most they would have done was to tell Achish to keep an
eye on him. And if Achish still regarded David as his vassal, this may
explain why the Philistines left him alone.

It is more likely, therefore, that when David (and the approximately two thousand people with him) went to Hebron,[4] he would only explain his actions to Achish if called upon to do so.

One question, however, burns its way into our minds: How did the people of Hebron receive David and his followers?

Certain authorities believe that the words "go up" have a military connotation (see Judges 1:1; 2 Samuel 5:17,19), and in certain contexts this is true. Accordingly, they feel that David and his men took over Hebron by force.[5] They believe that the sentiments of the people toward the outlaw were the same as Nabal's (see 1 Samuel 25:10,14), particularly since he had recently gone with the Philistines to war against his own people.

We need to remember, though, that David never lifted his hand against the Israelites. He would rather have lived in exile than do such a thing. The words "go up," then, most likely refer to the steady ascent from Ziklag to the mountain range on which Hebron is situated. In addition, in an age when news sometimes took several days or even weeks to reach different cities, we have no sure knowledge that David's journey to Aphek was known to the elders of Judah. One thing they would know about was the attack of the Amalekites (1 Samuel 30:1), for these wily Bedouin of the desert had ransacked the cities in the "Negev of Caleb" (1 Samuel 30:14). They would also know of David's victory over the raiders, for David had sent them part of the spoils of war (1 Samuel 30:26-31). We feel safe, therefore, in rejecting the view that David took over Hebron by force.

Settling his men and their families throughout the cities in the Negev, may have posed a problem. It is likely that David showed respect for the leaders of his people and requested permission to settle in their cities. He and his followers then selected places in which to live or land on which to build their homes, and as quickly as possible established a healthy rapport with the people. In time the residents would be glad to have David's men augment their militia, for this would give them added protection against Arab attacks on their villages.

With the resettlement completed, David waits for God to reveal the next step in His will.

The author, having emphasized the importance of guidance and having mentioned the new center of David's activity, now turns his attention to the importance of family unity. David and his two wives, Ahinoam[6] and Abigail,[7] also moved to Hebron. Though they did not know it, this would be their home for the next seven and a half years. They would not have to move about as before. Perhaps now they could give thought to having children.

God's Promise and an Offer of Conciliation (2:4-7)

How long it takes for men of Judah to decide to make David their king is not revealed. As word of Saul's defeat spreads through the villages to the south, the people realize they are now leaderless. They probably also fear they will be powerless to resist if the conquering Philistines try to seize their land, live in their cities and villages, and annex their grazing land. Who among them is able to lead them against the Philistines and prevent such encroachments?

It should be noted that the people of Israel in general, and those in Judah in particular, had for many years been disgruntled with Saul's administration. Only the tribe of Benjamin remained loyal to Israel's first king. Whatever may have been the general view of David's association with the Philistines, the consensus now[8] is that for better or worse he is the only one who can inspire the people to stand against their enemies. Furthermore, in the present upheaval, they can not rely upon help from the northern tribes.

They decide, therefore, to break away from their brethren in the north and appoint their own leader. And David is the only logical candidate. Accordingly, the men of the different towns and villages approach him with the request that he become their king. He assents, and they anoint him king over Judah.

In accepting the throne, it is likely that David confers upon the people of Judah a greater honor than they bestow upon him. The text specifically omits all mention of David being crowned. He does not use Saul's diadem, for he does not see himself standing in the line of Saul. The kingdom he controls is very small. The problems that face him are out of all proportion to the size of his realm. Furthermore, the people of Judah are notoriously known for their vacillation and, in the past, have been easily intimidated by the superior numbers of their enemies (cf. Judges 15:9-13). All this makes the task David faces even more difficult.

In retrospect, we see clearly God sovereignly leading David and establishing him in Hebron. And because God's sovereignty includes freedom of choice, we note that in spite of disagreements or misgivings, and acting (from a human point of view) with complete liberty, the leaders of the people of Judah choose David as their king. They seat him on some rough-hewn throne, perhaps little more than a seat with a skin or colored cloth thrown over it, and proclaim him their king.[9] His enthronement is not a lavish, gala function, but rather a modest affair conducted with little if any fanfare.

As we reflect on these events, let us note that God often directs our attention away from the glitter and pageantry of our dreams to the reality of living in a fallen world. Like David, we must depend on the inner assurance that we are in God's will. In the long run, this is preferable to receiving the accolades that come from others.

Also note that in this sequence of events there is an absence of human effort. David did not campaign for the honor of becoming king. Instead, he waited patiently for the Lord, and in God's good time He brought about His purpose for His people. In doing so, He also fulfilled His promise to David.

The Biblical writer moves without a transition from David's ascension to the throne to his first act as Judah's new king (2:4b-7). Because we are not given the identity of the people who informed him of the courageous act of the men of Jabesh-gilead,[10] we are left to conclude that they may have been the same people who had so recently made him their king.

Upon hearing of their bravery, David immediately sends his first ambassadors to their city. The message they carry is one of commendation and conciliation.

> "Blessed [are] you of Yahweh [in] that you have done kindness (i.e., shown *hesed*, acted 'loyally') toward (lit. with) your lord, with Saul, [in] that you have buried him. And now, may Yahweh do with you (i.e., deal with you) in kindness and truth; and I also will do good to you because you have done this thing" (2:5-6).[11]

It should be noted that, in David's invitation for the people to join forces with him, there is respect for their autonomy. He knows that, with the Philistines controlling the highlands and valleys of central Canaan, he will need the help of all the tribes if he is to expel them from Israel's borders. If the leaders of Jabesh-gilead can be persuaded to join forces with him, perhaps other towns will follow.[12]

But Abner, Saul's general, has other plans. It is difficult to determine exactly when he makes Ish-bosheth,[13] Saul's son, king over Israel. There is every probability that a gap of several weeks (perhaps even a few months) intervenes between the events of verses 7 and 9. If this reconstruction of the passing of time is correct, then David's men arrived in Jabesh-gilead before Ish-bosheth's inauguration.

Even so, the elders of this Gadite city would have known of Abner's plans, for Saul's general would have sent out messengers to the different centers advising them of his intentions, and Jabesh-gilead would have been one of the first cities to be informed of his plans.

In responding to David's invitation, the elders adopt a politically expedient posture. As was found in 1 Samuel 11, they are not noted for their courage. And in keeping with this same spirit, they now choose *not* to identify themselves with David and, as a result, lose a valuable opportunity.

In this respect, David's experiences are fully in accord with life. The Bible is true in all it portrays. Issues of expediency and human insecurity often cause delays that lead to further difficulties.

Many of us have been taught from the pulpits of our churches that if we are in God's will, everything will fall into place—the wind will always be at our backs, and life will always run smoothly. Consequently, many sincere Christians are dismayed when they encounter opposition. It is then that certain outspoken members of the community, by referring to Psalm 66:18, will try to "encourage" them by saying, "There must be some unconfessed sin in your life, and that is why the Lord is with holding His blessing."

Such teaching has become widespread. What these proponents of Scripture ignore are the verses that follow verse 18. Unfortunately their spiritual naivete may result in devout believers becoming discouraged, struggling with false feelings of guilt, and even doubting God's guidance and lovingkindness toward them. To be in the will of the Lord, as David was, virtually guarantees opposition.

Most people to whom we relate will not act in ways that further the work of the Lord. So we must contend with human frailty on the one hand and human ambition on the other. And both of these may be compounded by misguided zeal and faulty theology. So let's be prepared for opposition. It will be found in those men and women who are determined to keep their positions of authority while requiring that others abide by the decisions they make. We must persevere in doing good, as David did, and in time God will bring His will to pass.

God's Will Thwarted by Human Ambition (2:8–3:1)

A Rival King (2:8-11). Meanwhile in the north, as soon as Abner has the elders of the people behind him, he takes Ish-bosheth,[14] Saul's youngest son, and crowns him king over Israel. The scene of his coronation is Mahanaim in Transjordan.

The language used to describe Abner's actions makes it plain that he, and not Ish-bosheth, is the real power in Israel. But was he acting in good faith or merely seeking his own ends?

At first Abner's motives seem altruistic. Those involved in the proceedings might well assume that he was still loyal to Saul and that maintaining the Saulide dynasty was the wisest policy. Abner was also one of the nation's heroes. The people, therefore, might conclude that he would surely continue to wisely and beneficially influence the young monarch.

What we read in the next chapter (note 3:9 and 18) indicates clearly that Abner was activated by unworthy motives. He knew God's choice was David, yet he took a course of action diametrically opposed to what he knew was right. And he has many followers even today. In business and industry, law and government, medicine and human resource management, entertainment and the arts, and especially in education, people will deliberately formulate plans, make policy, engage in activities, or teach material with scarcely a thought to the ethical ramifications of their actions. The result is a moral breakdown that has brought our nation to a position of spiritual and ethical bankruptcy.

By contrast, the message David sent to the people of Jabesh-gilead was God-centered and affirming. He was conciliatory. His message revealed a desire for unity. Instead of trying to punish those who had served King Saul, he wanted to show them his favor. To confer such distinction on them was kind and forgiving, and presented to all the evidence of the grace of God in his life.

A Pivotal Contest (2:12-17). As we compare verses 12-17 with 4*b*-7, we find that the well-meaning efforts of David to ward off strife and bring the people together, are frustrated. Dr. William G. Blaikie writes:

> Unmoved by the solemn testimony of God, uttered again and again through Samuel, that He had rejected Saul and found as king a man after His own heart; unmoved by the sad proceedings at Endor, where, under such awful circumstances, the same announcement of the purpose of the Almighty had been repeated; unmoved by the doom of Saul and his three sons on Mount Gilboa, where such a striking proof of the reality of God's judgment on his house had been given; unmoved by the miserable state of the kingdom, overrun and humiliated by the Philistines and in the worst possible condition to bear the strain of civil war, Abner insists on setting Ishbosheth [on the throne] and endeavors to make good his claims by the sword.[15]

The word *wayyese'*, "to go out" (2:12), is a military term and implies a planned military operation. Abner, at the head of a strong contingent, proposes to invade the tribe of Judah and bring the people under the rule of Ish-bosheth.[16] Since he now knows of David's rulership over Judah, he believes David must also be aware of Ish-bosheth's coronation. Joab,[17] with an inferior force, intercepts Abner at Gibeon,[18] just outside the borders of Judah and approximately five and a half miles north of Jerusalem. A large reservoir thirty-seven feet in diameter separates the two forces. There the contest described in these verses takes place. It is a gruesome scene.

Dr. Roland deVaux, in his book *The Bible and the Ancient Near East*, has shown that single combat to decide an issue has had its adherents in both ancient and modern times. When Abner proposed that twelve of the best young men (*hanne'arim*, professional soldiers) from each side should compete in a tournament or duel (2:14), it was with the intent that the victors would gain the victory for their side.[19]

It was widely believed that the will of the gods (or, as in the case of Israel, God) would be known by the outcome. This was, therefore, a pivotal contest, and the right to rule the (united) kingdom would then go to the one whose men were successful.

The number twelve has been thought to represent the twelve tribes of Israel. In this context, however, it is better to look on it as the number of completeness.

Abner, of course, feels assured of success. He chooses strong and resolute men from the tribe of Benjamin. They are loyal to the memory of King Saul and quite possibly fear David's wrath if they lose the contest and become the subjects of the one whom they have persecuted. (This, as we have seen, was a false belief. David bore no malice toward any of the followers of Saul).

The contestants square off against each other in a field adjacent to the pool. Each man chooses an opponent. Then, like sumo wrestlers beginning a match, they spring forward, eager to grasp either the hair or the girdle[20] of their adversary. By gaining a firm hold they can keep their enemy off balance and prevent him from using his dagger effectively. Furthermore, with one's antagonist off balance, it is then much easier to position oneself to thrust a dagger into his midsection. (A relief from *Tell Halaf*, Biblical Gozen, shows soldiers in the posture described here[21]).

The contest between Abner's and Joab's forces is indecisive, for each man kills his adversary. As a result, the field where the battle has been waged is called *ḥelqat haṣṣūrîm*, "the field of daggers [or rocks]." This may have been because the ground was very stony or because the daggers were of sharpened flint.

A Senseless Death (2:18-23). When all the combatants have killed each other, the men under Abner's command flee for their lives. This is unexpected, for they greatly outnumbered Joab's small force.

Pursuing them are the sons of Zeruiah, David's older sister (1 Chronicles 2:16; or perhaps his half-sister, 2 Samuel 17:25). Since they are never identified by the name of their father, we are left to conclude that Zeruiah was the dominant person in the home. Two of her sons, Joab and Abishai, are seasoned warriors (1 Samuel 26:6-8). The third is Asahel, most likely the youngest member of the household.

Dr. A. F. Kirkpatrick refers to him as "a mere stripling,"[22] but this is not altogether accurate, for in 1 Chronicles 27:7 we learn that Asahel was a general over a contingent of men. He was also old enough to have a son named Zebadiah who assisted him. Though younger than Joab and Abishai, he is not inexperienced in warfare.

Asahel is fleet of foot, and Josephus preserves a tradition that he could outrun a horse[23] (see 1 Chronicles 12:8; Proverbs 6:5).

From what is presented in these verses it appears as if Asahel was determined to make a name for himself. Perhaps he felt that he had stood for too long in the shadow of his brothers. So when he sees Abner running as fast as he can toward the desert that separates him from the River Jordan and safety, he takes off after him.[24] Abner is remarkably fit for his age, and it is only with difficulty that Asahel begins to overtake him.

When Abner hears a runner behind him, he takes a quick look over his shoulder. It is Asahel. He has no desire to kill Asahel and so encourages him to turn aside and acquire spoils of war from someone else.

> "Turn to your right or to your left, and take hold of one of the young men for yourself, and take for yourself his spoil" (2:21).

It is significant that Abner uses three imperatives—"turn aside," "capture," and "take"—in an effort to dissuade Asahel from following him. They have the force of implied commands. But the warning goes unheeded.

In verse 22 Abner again speaks to Asahel.

> "Turn aside from following me. Why should I strike you to the ground? How then could I lift up my face to your brother Joab?"

This imperative statement, "Turn aside...," is followed by two interrogatory clauses, "Why should I strike you to the ground?" and "How then could I lift up my face to your brother Joab?"

Abner plainly does not fear Asahel. Some Bible scholars have inferred from Abner's words that he was unwilling to kill Asahel because he would then incur blood-guiltiness.[25] Joab would then be compelled to play the role of the "avenger of blood."

This is an unlikely interpretation, for blood shed in war was not looked upon as murder (see 2:28-30; 1 Kings 2:5; 31-33). Most likely,

Abner's primary concern has to do with the possibility of future dealings with Joab. He may already have felt the first inklings of eventual defeat, for his superior force was being resoundingly beaten by Joab's smaller band of warriors. Looking to the future, therefore, and realizing that one day he might have to negotiate peace with David, he could see how Asahel's death might stand in the way of an amicable agreement.

Asahel refuses to listen, and Abner is compelled to strike him with the blunt end of his spear. Such is the speed of Asahel's forward movement that he is impaled on it[26] (2:23).

During the time Asahel has been chasing Abner, the men of Judah have continued to pursue Abner's men. As they come to the place where Asahel's body lies in a pool of blood, they pause, stunned by the manner of his death. Then they continue with their rout of the men of Israel.

A Call for Peace (2:24-29). By nightfall the men of Judah have forced Abner and the remnants of his fighting force to take refuge on the slopes of the hill of Ammah. The exact location of this site is unknown, and the repeated reference to it seems to intimate that it was not a well-known place.[27]

Abner and his men know that they have been soundly defeated. Not being prepared to surrender, Abner tries to gain an advantage through diplomacy.

> "Shall the sword devour forever? Do you not know [Joab] that it will be bitter in the end? How long will you refrain from telling the people to turn back from following their brothers?" (2:26).

To this Joab replies,

> "As God lives, if you had not spoken, surely then the people would have gone away in the morning, each from following his brother" (2:27).

Abner is more adept at diplomacy than Joab. He bases his plea for peace upon familial ties. The people of Israel and Judah were all descendants of Jacob. This made them "brothers."

But he omitted all mention of the fact that he was the one who had flaunted these ties when he invaded the land to subject the people of Judah to his rule. He also blamed Judah for perpetuating hostilities when he was plainly the aggressor.

Joab's response shows that he has allowed himself to be swayed by Abner's argument. He fails to assert the rights of the king whom he represents. And because he does not confront Abner with his wrongdoing, Abner will continue to harass Judah (3:1).

Joab also reveals the vacuous nature of his Godward relationship. In taking an oath, "As God lives," he does not use the covenant name for the Lord, *Yahweh*—the divine name that united the sons of Israel together and constituted them a nation—but *'Ĕlōhîm*, "God." This would seem to indicate that, as with many professing believers today, his relationship with the Almighty was a matter of convenience.[28]

In answering those who assert that Joab's later assassination of Abner was an act of blood-vengeance, let it be noted that in acceding to Abner's request, Joab does not insist that he remain behind so that they can settle the issue. He does not challenge Abner to a duel. Instead, he blows the trumpet, giving the signal for hostilities to cease.

Not trusting Joab, Abner and his men journey all that night through the Arabah.[29] In the gray light of early dawn, they cross the River Jordan, and by noon they reach Mahanaim. No hero's welcome is given them. Their faces tell the story. They have been trounced.

What were Abner's thoughts as he prepared to give his report to Ish-bosheth? We do not know. He appears to have been supremely confident in his own abilities and may have rationalized the situation to the king as coaches do when their team has suffered a devastating loss: "Well, we'll beat 'em next time."

A Significant Victory (2:30-32). Joab and his men likewise leave the scene of battle. They take a route toward Hebron that passes by Bethlehem, the home of Zeruiah. There they bury Asahel in the family tomb. Then, journeying south, they reach Hebron as the sun's first rays begin to dispel the dark shadows from the ridges of the central highlands.

The outcome of the battle is recorded in the number of soldiers killed. David lost only twenty men (including Asahel). However, three hundred and sixty of Abner's finest lie dead in their tracks.

These statistics show that Abner must have moved to attack Judah with a large force. He probably brought sufficient men with him to later divide up and take charge of the villages of Judah to quell any resistance.

The accuracy of the description of these events reflects the observations of an eyewitness. The details of the story also show that, in spite of Israel's superior numbers, the Lord is with David!

THEN AND NOW

Several important thoughts from this passage impress themselves upon us.

The Importance of Guidance

We hear much today about "finding God's will." Many books have been written on the subject, and most courses on "discipleship" include instruction in "how to know God's will." In spite of this, many of us have difficulty making the right decisions.

Conceptually, the process is simple. It is based on our abiding in fellowship with Him (Psalm 32:8. See also Psalm 34:15-16). As we read God's Word and come across specific commands or injunctions, we should put them into practice in our lives. As Dr. John R. W. Stott once remarked, "Every imperative [in Scripture] should be treated as a supreme command."[30] By obeying the teaching of God's Word, we engage in a process that brings us into conformity to His revealed will.

But what of those times when we face the kind of decisions David faced? How can we know what the Lord would have us do?

The habit of living under the authority of Scripture makes it easier for us to discern God's will in specific situations. As the late Dietrich Bonhoeffer wrote in his *Letters and Papers from Prison*, "We should find God in what we do know, not in what we don't."[31]

This is where a knowledge of God's Word becomes indispensable. Today we cannot consult the Urim and Thummim or ascertain the will of the Lord by casting lots. We can be assured of His leading as we commit ourselves and our decisions to Him, asking Him to lead us (1 Peter 5:7; Psalm 55:22). And implied in this is our obedience to the things He has already revealed to us.

The Significance of the Home

In addition to knowing and doing God's will, we need to be sensitive to the fundamental issues of life. David had an entire tribe to organize. The despondent people needed to be energized with a will to be free. It would have been easy for him to neglect his wives (2:2; 3:2-5). But he did not.

Perhaps the clearest indication that David did not take Hebron by force is found in the fact that Ahinoam and Abigail accompanied him there. He never took his wives into battle. And there, in Hebron, the first of his sons was born.

The importance David placed on the home should not be overlooked. We, today, perhaps largely as a result of our technological advances, find ourselves engulfed in difficulties that threaten to destroy the natural and God-given enjoyment that should be ours as we "rejoice in the wife of our youth" (Ecclesiastes 9:7-9).

One of the great blessings of marriage is that it should get better as we get older. Too many couples, however, place their children in the center of their lives. They forget that marriage is permanent, while children are with us temporarily. We should not neglect the little ones whom an all-wise Father has entrusted to our care, but it is unspeakably tragic if they take preeminence over the cultivation of the husband-wife relationship.

In giving counsel to women, Ruth Bell Graham has said: "The best advice I can give to unmarried girls is to marry someone you don't mind adjusting to. God tailors the wife to fit the husband, not the husband to fit the wife."[32]

We may be sure Ahinoam and Abigail did this.

But what counsel is there for men? Let them remember that with all the pressures that daily bear down upon them, they must not forget to love, honor, and protect those with whom they are in covenant.

The Value of Right Attitudes

As we build on the need for guidance and the centrality of the home, let us also take note of the value of kind words. In David's message to the people of Jabesh-gilead, he blended grace with the sincere desire that their actions receive God's richest reward. He also assured them of his intent to deal with them in friendship. And when he invited them to be the first to join forces with him, he nonetheless respected their autonomy and left the decision to them.

How different from the attitude of some people in authority today. They have mastered the art of manipulation and will often use guilt as a motivator or promise more than they can deliver. Sufficient to say that it is our attitude that influences people for good or ill. To be able to act as David did, we need to be confident in our standing before the Lord, content with what He has given us, and inwardly assured that He will work out His plan in His own time.

The Fact of Opposition

Finally, we need to learn from David's experience how to face opposition. He did not have an unrealistic ideal of what things would be like when he became king. And he did not think of himself as being out of the will of God because a coalition from the tribes to the north came to attack him. He had learned from experience to expect opposition.

Some people thrive on opposition, others resist it. Some face it boldly, others see it and conclude that they must have sinned in some way and incurred God's displeasure. Difficulties, however, come upon all of us, particularly when we are doing God's will.

A good friend of mine, Dr. Stuart Orr, specializes in turning around failing companies. I have had the privilege of working with Stuart, and his attitude impresses me. He always seeks to ascertain the will of God before taking on a new client or a new responsibility. Then, no matter how adverse the conditions, he will respond with words like, "The Lord has led us and blessed us in so many ways, I cannot imagine that He is not in this and will not work things out." And time and again God has done so.

The Apostle Paul knew what opposition was like. His whole life was full of it. When he wrote his second letter to Timothy, he said:

> For God has not given us a spirit of timidity, but of power and love and discipline. Therefore do not be ashamed of the testimony of the Lord...but join me in suffering for the gospel according to the power of God (2 Timothy 1:7-8; see also v. 12).

> Be strong in the grace that is in Christ Jesus.... Suffer hardship with me, as a good soldier of Christ Jesus (2 Timothy 2:1, 3).

> But realize this that in the last days difficult times will come.... Just as Jannes and Jambres opposed Moses, so [there will always be those who] oppose the truth...(2 Timothy 3:1, 8; see also v. 12).

And finally, as he concluded his admonition to his young protege, he said:

> I have fought the good fight, I have finished the course, I have kept the faith (2 Timothy 4:7).

Like Paul, David faced violent, virulent opposition. The Biblical writer records that a long war dragged on between the house of Saul and the house of David; and David grew steadily stronger, but the house of Saul grew continually weaker (3:1). God did not prevent Abner from working against David, but He used the opposition to consolidate the people of Judah behind their newly appointed king.

A NEW START AND A RAY OF HOPE

PART ONE

2 Samuel 3:2–5:5

Literature is replete with examples of human strength and weakness. In few instances has the tension between the strong and the weak been presented more clearly than in E. M. Forster's book *A Passage to India*. Here's a thumbnail sketch of the story:

Mrs. Moore, who lives in England, wishes to see her son, Ronnie, before she dies. To do so, she makes a journey to India in the company of Adela, who is unofficially engaged to Ronnie.

Mrs. Moore is from the upper middle-class. She is educated, articulate, self-assured, and financially independent. Adela, by contrast, has led a sheltered life and is secure only in company of those who give her a measure of emotional support. And Ronnie, who would not have achieved success as an attorney in his homeland, has been made a magistrate in India and is very much aware of the power he wields over others.

The social life of the English-speaking whites in India revolves around "The Club." Membership means acceptance, and provides a sense of belonging. To have that membership revoked is to be deprived of virtually all social contact with one's peers.

The key to understanding the interplay between strength and weakness in the story lies in a discussion that takes place between Mrs. Moore and Ronnie at "The Club" one hot, sunny afternoon. The ill-concealed contempt shown the Indians, who wait on and entertain the whites, repulses Mrs. Moore to the point where she expostulates with Ronnie:

Mrs. Moore: "This is one of the most unnatural affairs I have
                ever attended."
Ronnie: "Of course it is unnatural...."
Mrs. Moore: "I do not see why you all behave so unpleasantly
                toward these people."
Ronnie: "India isn't a drawing room. We're out here to do
                justice and keep the peace. Do you want me to
                sacrifice my career and lose the power I have
                for doing good in this benighted country?"
Mrs. Moore: "Good? And speaking about power, the whole of
                this—[this] entertainment, is an exercise in
                power and the subtle pleasures of personal
                superiority. God has put us on earth to love and
                help our fellow man."
Ronnie: "Yes, mother."[1]

The most abject example of subservience is found in the attitude
and conduct of Dr. Aziz. Though anxious to please those who control
his country, deep down he resents their presence!

Dr. Aziz is befriended by Richard Fielding, the principal of Government College. Fielding understands the interplay between strength
and weakness, and he has taken a position at the lowly Government
College in order to help those who want to learn and advance as far
as their abilities will take them.

But where does Adela fit into all of this? As has already been observed she feels secure only in the presence of others who advise or
protect her. One day Adela decides to go cycling on her own. She is
anxious to see more of the country, and not only those parts selected
for her by her host. Her wandering takes her through a rural area
where she finds an old sign pointing down a path leading to a disused temple.

The temple had been built in honor of Shiva, god of love. And there,
carved into the stones that make up the temple, are representations
of people in various coital positions. All of a sudden Adela feels emotions awaken within her that cause her emotional confusion. She is
both fascinated by what she has seen and fearful of the sensations
she is experiencing. Unnerved, she hastens back to the place where
she is staying and the security of those whose culture she shares.

Some time later, Mrs. Moore and Adela are taken by Dr. Aziz to the
caves in the Marabar Hills. Inside one of the caves the self-assured
Mrs. Moore suffers from claustrophobia. The darkness frightens
her. She also finds disconcerting the sweaty bodies of the natives

pressing all around her. Adding to her discomfort is the strange sound of a wind rushing toward her (when in reality there is no movement of air in the cave at all).

Feeling suddenly very weak and vulnerable, she turns and pushes her way through the crowd toward the small half circle of light that is barely discernable above the heads of the people in the cave. Only in the open is she able to regain control of her emotions.

Adela also shows her weakness when the social structure that makes up so much of her security is suddenly removed. At Mrs. Moore's suggestion, Dr. Aziz takes her higher up the hills to some other caves. At one part of the climb Adela is forced to accept his hand to help her over a rough part of the path. This arouses in her the same kind of emotions she experienced at the temple. Not knowing how to respond she goes alone into one of the caves when Dr. Aziz' back is turned. Far from helping her regain her composure, the experience heightens her anxieties. Loosing all reserve, she runs down the steep slope cutting herself on thorn bushes in her haste to get back to Mrs. Moore.

At the bottom of the slope Adela is met by the officious wife of the Viceroy who immediately assumes the worst and tells all those present that Dr. Aziz had attempted to rape Adela. And Adela is too weak and too confused to contradict her.

All the members of "The Club" pronounce Dr. Aziz guilty before he even comes to trial. Richard Fielding dissents and his membership in the club is immediately revoked.

At the trial, however, Adela is led to recount the events as they actually occurred. Dr. Aziz is acquitted, but Adela is now *persona non grata* in the eyes of her fellow-countrymen. She escapes the embarrassment by going home on the first boat on which she can book a passage.

The ordeal through which Dr. Aziz has passed has had an effect upon him. His anger over the injustices he has suffered has caused him to reject the vaunted superiority of those in authority. He now no longer thinks of himself as inferior to them and emerges from the ordeal stronger in himself than he was before.

All of this reminds us of the wise words of Dr. Paul Tournier: "No one is exempt from conflict which can strengthen a man as well as overwhelm him.... All [conflicts] are both useful in the reactions they arouse in us, and harmful in the cowardly defeats and proud victories to which they lead."[2]

Our last chapter closed with a reminder that while David continued to grow stronger, the house of Saul became weaker and weaker.

Now, in 2 Samuel 3:2–5:5 we see the continued interplay between these extremes.

SUBTLE REMINDERS

In the events leading up to David being made king over Israel, we cannot help but note the Biblical writer's oscillating emphasis between strength and weakness. Here are a few of the more obvious examples:

> And David grew steadily stronger, but the house of Saul grew continually weaker (3:1*b*).

> Abner was making himself strong in the house of Saul (3:6*b*).

> And [Ish-bosheth] could no longer answer Abner a word, because he was afraid of him (3:11).

> And Ish-bosheth sent and took [Michal] from her husband [a show of strength]...but her husband went with her, weeping [but powerless to withstand the king's command]... (3:15-16).

> David said: "I am weak today...and these men, the sons of Zeruiah, are too powerful for me" (3:39).

> Now when Ish-bosheth...heard that Abner had died in Hebron, his hands dropped (i.e., he lost the will to go on), and all Israel was disturbed (4:1).

The contrast between strength and weakness ultimately comes down to our estimation of what constitutes personal success or failure. This is three-dimensional and may best be conceptualized by three separate though interlocking circles. Each circle represents one of the following ways of assessing success or failure: (1) Information about ourselves—filtered through our perceptions, thoughts, and beliefs—has a direct bearing upon what we assume constitutes success or failure for ourselves as individuals; (2) data received from other people—feedback by which they evaluate our success or failure; and (3) standards or principles by which we believe God judges us as to our success or failure.

Because we cannot be absolutely assured of accuracy, even in self-assessment, it is best to treat our impressions of and about ourselves as tentative. We can then refine our thinking as new knowledge or experience enlarges our understanding.

OUTLINE

In this section of 2 Samuel we take another look at *God's sovereignty in establishing the kingdom of His anointed (2:1–6:23)*. In our last chapter we noted how He set David upon the throne of Judah and safeguarded his rights to independent action (2:1–3:1). Now we will see how His sovereignty was exercised so as to secure for David an enduring dynasty and bring "all Israel" to Hebron to anoint him king. The broad strokes of the present passage (3:2–5:5) may be outlined as follows:

- The Commencement of a New Dynasty (3:2-5)
- The Continuation of an Old Problem (3:6–4:12)
- The Culmination of God's Promise (5:1-5).

As we shall see, the Lord will gradually bring His plans for His people to fruition. Not everything will happen at once. And while we may not always be able to discern the reason for the delays, the fact remains that He is sovereign and will bring everything to pass in His good time.

THE COMMENCEMENT OF A NEW DYNASTY (3:2-5)

No children had been born to David during his outlaw years. Now that he is settled in Hebron, the writer presents us with practical evidence of God's blessing upon his house. In a very real sense we have here the beginning of the Davidic dynasty. As Joyce Baldwin has shown,

> Already during David's reign in Hebron the state archives contained records of those who might qualify as heirs to his throne. Some born later in Jerusalem are listed in 2 Samuel 5:13-16 (cf. 1 Chronicles 3:1-19).[3]

Certain writers,[4] however, have interpreted these verses in light of neo-Victorian standards of ethics. They have wrongly accused David of breaking the seventh commandment. Without question, it is God's desire for one man and one woman to live together in a unique and lasting relationship (namely, marriage. See Genesis 2:18-25;

Mark 10:6-9). But this same God, in the Law that He gave from Sinai, permitted Israelites to have more than one wife (see Exodus 21:10. See also Deuteronomy 21:15-17). Responsibility for taking additional wives rested on the shoulders of the individual.[5]

What the Biblical writer intends to show in these verses is the Lord's blessing upon His servant (see Psalm 127:3).

Many of the same preachers and writers who accuse David of multiple acts of adultery also indict him for being a weak, indulgent father who did not set his children a proper example. With all of the pressures of administration now resting upon his shoulders, and with his subordinates lacking experience, it would have been easy for David to neglect his family. But he did not do so. He was aware of the fact that the children of today become the leaders of tomorrow. To neglect them is to mortgage the future. The evidence of Scripture is that David spent time with his children.

Let us listen in on what he said to them, and let us take note of the kind of instruction he gave them.

> "Come, [my] sons, listen to me;
> I will teach you the fear (i.e., reverence) of Yahweh.
> Who [is] the man who desires life,
> Loving [many] days to [that he may] see good?
> Keep your tongue from evil,
> And your lips from speaking guile.
> Depart from evil and do good;
> Seek peace and pursue it.
> The eyes of Yahweh [are] upon the righteous;
> And His ears [are open] to their cry"
> (Psalm 34:11-14).

Years later, Solomon would say:

> "When I was a son to my father,
> Tender and the only [son] before (i.e., in the sight of) my mother,
> Then he taught me and said to me,
> 'Let your heart hold fast my words;
> Keep my commandments and live;
> Get wisdom, get understanding;
> Do not forget [her], and stretch not away from
>   (i.e., do not depart from) the words of my mouth.
> Do not forsake her and she will keep (or guard) you;
> Love her and she will watch over you'"
> (Proverbs 4:3-6).

All the Biblical evidence at our disposal indicates that David was a good father.[6] He did not allow the press of many external concerns to detract from his involvement with and instruction of his children.

Unfortunately, this is just what some of us may not do. We come home from work late, we are tired, and our children may already be in bed. Our contact with them may be limited to weekends. Let us learn from David the importance of the home and pledge to ourselves that, no matter how great the pressures of our work may be, we will not neglect our wives and those young lives whom the Lord has entrusted to our care.

THE CONTINUATION OF AN OLD PROBLEM (3:6–4:12)

The scene now shifts to Mahanaim. There the picture is vastly different from the one of domestic satisfaction that David enjoys. The pressure of repeated failure is causing tension for Ish-bosheth[7] and Abner (3:1). And there is no intimation in the text that the Lord is building a dynasty for Ish-bosheth.

Dissension Weakens the Northern Kingdom (3:6-11)

Abner has begun to think of his weak and vacillating nephew as an impediment to the fulfillment of his personal plans.[8] And Ish-bosheth, who has seen his uncle assume more and more authority, feels increasingly ill at ease. He finds himself a puppet in Abner's hands. But all the authority Abner assumes does not result in victory over Judah. Both Ish-bosheth and Abner are learning the painful lesson that "unless the Lord builds the house (or kingdom), they labor in vain who build it" (Psalm 127:1).

A hostile confrontation erupts when Ish-bosheth accuses Abner of taking Rizpah,[9] Saul's concubine, into his bed. Whether Ish-bosheth, in his immaturity, accuses his uncle of having done so without sufficient proof cannot be determined. Taken at face value, Abner's protestations of innocence seem to indicate that he had not had sexual relations with Rizpah. Yet people such as Abner are often masters in the art of deception (see 3:25),[10] and so the issue remains unresolved.

The basis of Ish-bosheth's charge is a most serious one. To take a king's wife or concubine[11] is to tacitly lay claim to the throne (cf. 16:20-23; 1 Kings 2:22ff.).

Abner is furious when Ish-bosheth accuses him of adultery. He loses control of himself and blurts out:

"[Am] I a dog's head of (lit. to) Judah? Today I deal [with] kindness to the house of Saul your father, to his brothers and to his friends, and have not given you into David's hand; but you charge against me sin [with] this woman" (3:8-9).

His opening statement, "Am I a dog's head of Judah?"[12] is an arresting one. Attempts to explain it have been both ingenious and interesting. Some have sought to draw a parallel between the semi-domesticated dogs of antiquity with their sexual promiscuity and Abner's alleged action. Others have used an analogy based on 2 Kings 6:25 to explain the statement. Their reasoning goes like this: As a donkey's head was the least useful part of its body, so they reason Abner was saying in effect, "Am I a worthless dog from Judah and useless to you? You should treat me with greater deference on account of all that I have done for the nation of Israel."[13]

Regardless of the meaning of this enigmatic expression, Abner unwittingly shows his contempt for Judah—the tribe from whom the Lord had predicted Israel's kings would come (Genesis 49:8-12).[14]

But he is not finished. From his next words we deduce that he has sensed for some time that he has been fighting a losing battle. In his anger he now gives expression to a thought that in a less heated moment he might have stifled or else introduced with greater tact. The Hebrew text is difficult to translate and may be paraphrased as follows:

"So may God do to Abner, and add to it, if, as Yahweh has sworn to David, I do not do this for him; to cause the kingdom to pass over from the house of Saul, and raise up the throne of David over Israel, and over Judah, from Dan even to Beersheba" (3:9-10).

Abner's words are treasonous, but Ish-bosheth is powerless to either arrest him or prevent him from carrying out his plan (3:11). Dan[15] is the northernmost outpost of Israel, and Beersheba[16] is the southernmost border town, twenty-three miles southwest of Hebron.

Abner's statement also shows his contempt for and defiance of Ish-bosheth. And the fact that he did not retract his words when his anger cooled shows that he had no real loyalty to the northern tribes. His only discernible commitments were to himself. He knew that war with Judah was inevitable, and when the fighting was over, he wanted to be on the winning side.

Diplomacy Strengthens the Southern Kingdom (3:12-16)

It would appear as if Abner loses no time in making good on his threat to unite the tribes under David. In advising David (via a messenger) of his intentions, he asks rhetorically: "To whom does the land really belong?" (3:12a).

His words have been assumed by some Bible scholars to indicate to David that he, Abner, was the real power in Israel. Others, however, believe that they were a clumsy form of flattery and imply: "The land really belongs to you, David."[17] What is obvious is that Abner wants David to guarantee him some important position (perhaps general of his armies), and that is why he says, "Make your covenant with me" (3:12b).

David and Abner, of course, are well acquainted. During the years when David had himself been a general in Saul's army and was a member of the king's council, he had met with Abner at each new moon when Saul entertained his cabinet (1 Samuel 20:18, 25-29). Later, during David's outlaw years, Abner had accompanied the king on at least one expedition to capture David. In spite of the betrayal of David's position by the Ziphites, David, on a never-to-be-forgotten night, had spared Saul's life. And Abner had been an unwilling witness of his magnanimity (1 Samuel 26:1,14-16).

Abner's message contains no trace of contrition or humility. Rather, there is evident in his words, "Look, my hand shall be with you, to bring about all Israel to you," the attitude of one who believes that he is talking with an equal. The people of Israel do not matter to him. Those who have died under his command during the civil war he instituted were mere pawns in a game. His only real interest is the advancement of his own ambitions.

But this raises an important question: to what extent should David now trust a man who had deliberately opposed the known will of God (cf. 3:9), set Saul's son on the throne, and now propose a transfer of loyalties?

Abner greatly erred in his assessment of David. David probably sensed that there was no word of regret in Abner's offer. Nor was there any remorse for having plunged the nation into a civil war. He, therefore, answers Abner judiciously. With diplomatic skill he first encourages him, then he asserts his authority, and finally he lays down a preliminary condition to any talk of union:

> "I will make (lit. cut) a covenant with you; but one thing I ask of you, namely, you will not see my face except you first bring Michal, the daughter of Saul, when you come to see me" (3:13).[18]

We admire David's firmness. By compelling Abner to bring Michal to him, he will be able to test the genuineness of his offer. And once Michal is with him, he will be able to efface the slight put upon him by Saul.

We may confidently assume that David had often grappled with the problem of how to have Michal restored to him. Only now that there appears to be a weakening in the north can he demand her return. He also realizes that as much as he desires to have her with him for the love he has for her, her presence in Hebron will serve a secondary purpose. Those loyal to Saul will be more inclined to switch their allegiance, knowing that in Saul's daughter they have a friend at court.

Many devout Christians suffer from severe conniptions over the thought of David taking Michal from her second husband. In support of their disapproval they cite Deuteronomy 24:1-4 and Jeremiah 3:1. They then reaffirm their previous opinion of David as an adulterer and state that he was a more righteous man during his outlaw years than he was after he became king.[19]

Others, to excuse David for what they believe to be poor conduct, claim that he was the product of his times. They point out that, inasmuch as polygamy was expected of monarchs and rich people, he was doing what was socially acceptable for a person in his position. To have many wives was a sign of wealth and power. But these advocates of toleration betray their "holier than thou" attitude when they go on to state that *we* do not have a plurality of wives today because *we* have proved monogamy to be preferable.[20]

Monogamy is preferable to polygamy because it is what God has designed, not because we have found it to be better. If social mores become the basis for approval or disapproval of different practices, then divorce can be said to be preferable to an unhappy or unfulfilling marriage because so many people within our society are opting for it.

To properly understand this passage we need to keep the facts surrounding Michal's being given to Paltiel clearly in mind (see 1 Samuel 25:44). It was with a view to hurting David that Saul gave his daughter in marriage to one of his friends. And Michal had no power to withstand her father's wishes.

We also need to remember that David and Michal had never been divorced. And the *mohar*, or bridal price, David had paid for her had never been returned to him.

But how are we to understand his demand for her return? What is presented still appears to go against the teaching of Scripture.

There is a logical and consistent approach to these verses that interprets them in light of the culture and laws of the times and removes all opprobrium from David's actions. The law codes of the ancient Near East cite certain cases where a married woman could be given to someone else. If, for example, her husband went away on business or to war (where, presumably, he was captured) and did not return, his wife could be given in marriage to another. Should he eventually return, he could take her back even though she may have borne children to her second husband.[21]

When Saul forced David into exile he did not expect him to return or ever be able to reclaim Michal. Acting within the law, he gave her to Paltiel in marriage. Michal did not commit adultery when given to Paltiel, for she had no power to withstand her father's wishes. And neither she nor David were involved in adultery when David took her back, for they had never been divorced.

Biblical support for this view may be gleaned directly from the text. First, when David (perhaps not trusting Abner) sent a message to Ish-bosheth reinforcing his request and requiring Ish-bosheth's endorsement of his reunion with Ish-bosheth's sister, Saul's son complied. He never questioned David's rights. Nor did he offer any valid grounds for refusing David's request (3:14-15).

Second, Paltiel raised no objection, as would have been expected if he had been treated unjustly. All we are told is that he followed along behind the procession weeping until told by Abner to return.[22]

And finally, no hint is given by the Biblical writer of any disapproval on the part of God or the people. Rather we read that "everything the king did pleased the people" (3:36*b*). They would not have approved of his actions if adultery had been involved![23]

Once Michal is ensconced in Hebron, Abner sets about making good his promise to David (i.e., "to bring all Israel over to him," 3:12*b*). He first visits with the elders of each tribe. This may have involved sitting with each group during negotiations, answering questions, and persuading them of the viability of his plans. Then, after months of negotiation, and en route to Judah, he visits with the people of Benjamin, Saul's own tribe. More so than with any of the other tribes, he knows that they will need to feel a part of the proposed union.

Eventually they all agree; and "with the votes counted" (as we would say today), he makes his way to Hebron (3:20-21).

The meeting between David and Abner goes so well that at the end of the negotiations they celebrate the success of Abner's efforts with a banquet.[24] After this, the chronicler records no less than three times that David sends Abner away in peace (3:21-23).

Abner leaves Hebron with the intention of gathering the whole congregation of Israel together so that they may solemnly ratify the appointment of David as their king. Through his efforts he has rendered great service to the nation. At last he enjoys the exhilaration of success. What this shows us is that even when ungodly people do what God wants done, He may prosper and bless their cause.

Disagreement Delays the Establishment of the United Kingdom (3:22-39)

David's meeting with Abner had taken place while Joab was on a raid. The people of Israel were constantly at war with the nations to the south of their border as well as to the east and west. Not waiting for the Bedouin of the desert or the Amalekites to gather their forces (cf. 1 Samuel 30:14), it was deemed to be the better part of wisdom to attack them first. The "spoils of war" were a major source of the people's income.

On Joab's return to Hebron from a successful raid (3:22), courtiers who are uneasy over David's new alliance with Abner tell Joab all that has transpired during his absence.

Before we move on to discuss Joab's reaction to Abner's visit, we need to take careful note of something in the text. We are told that Joab returned to Hebron with "the servants of David and Joab" (3:22). Apparently the pressures of administration forced David to remain in Hebron. Joab must have used this to elevate himself to a position on a par with David in the army. The fact that David did not like this arrangement may be deduced from his willingness to have Abner replace Joab.

Without requesting an audience with the king, or even asking to see David in private, Joab bursts into the throne room and demands to know what agreement has been reached. In his anger, and as David's nephew, he does not talk with David as his king or even as his equal, but rather treats him as an inferior. And he doesn't stop there. He continues to blurt out words of angry denunciation. The court recorder must have had difficulty keeping up with the torrent of accusations and abuse. Here is what he wrote:

> "What have you done? Look, Abner came to you! Why [is] this, [that] you sent him away, and he is already gone? You know Abner the son of Ner, that he came to deceive you, and to know your going out and your coming in, and to know all you are doing" (3:24-25).

An angry man is always right in his own eyes, and Joab is plainly angry. His *what* question (in which he demands an explanation) is followed by one beginning with *why*—plainly putting David on the defensive.

Before Joab had come in to see him, David may have been feeling euphoric. Inwardly, he may even have been praising God for finally bringing about the union of the tribes. Joab, by contrast, feels threatened by Abner. His assumption and attitude reveal his weakness. His reaction is typical of someone who feels threatened by another.

Joab, of course, was out of line in scolding David. If David answered him, his reply is not recorded. What is more likely is that Joab stormed out of the council room intent upon doing what he believed was necessary in order to preserve his position in the kingdom. His thoughts were of himself, not of what was best for the nation. And so he institutes a plan that in effect places him above the crown.[25] Unknown to David, he sends a messenger after Abner, most likely requesting in the king's name that he return to Hebron.

The messenger overtakes Abner at the well of Sirah, a couple of miles north of Hebron;[26] and Abner, and those who are with him, fearing nothing, respond to what they believe to be a royal summons.[27]

As they approach the gates of the city, Joab takes Abner aside as if to tell him privately why the king has recalled him. As the two of them step away from the crowd, Joab stabs Abner in the stomach. And as life flows from Abner's body, Joab lets him fall to the dust at his feet.

Abner's men are probably dissuaded from avenging the death of their leader by the presence of a suitable number of Joab's men who have been positioned around the gate of the city. And because Abishai knew of Joab's plot, he is implicated in Abner's murder (3:30).

The explanation Joab gives to excuse the murder of Abner is that he was avenging the death of his brother Asahel (2:17-18).[28] But Abner had killed Asahel in wartime, and the concept of the "redeemer of blood" (Numbers 35:9-34; Deuteronomy 4:41-43; 19:1-13) did not apply to deaths that occurred during a war. In reality, Joab was afraid of being replaced by Abner, and so assassinated him.[29] In this we see the dark side of ambition.

When David hears that Abner has been killed by Joab, he immediately declares himself and his kingdom (*mamlākā*, "king-ship") innocent of all wrong doing. He then lays a very solemn curse on Joab (3:29).[30] The penalty is to involve him and his family. The essence of the malediction is that Joab and his descendants will constantly succumb to disease, war, and famine. The phrase "one who has a discharge" (3:25) refers to someone being perpetually unclean and barred from worship in any of Israel's sanctuaries. The same would be true of a leper. One who "takes hold of a distaff" implies a man, so

limited in his physical abilities, that he is relegated to doing the work
of a female slave or servant. Those of Joab's descendants able to go
to war will die on the battlefield. And the rest will beg for bread.

While David leaves Joab's punishment in God's hands, he is the
one who is now angry. He commands Joab to take part in the official
ceremony to bury Abner, instructing him to lead the procession to
the burial site. He wants the people to know that his mourning over
the loss of a "leader and a great man" (3:38) is real. Since Joab had
caused Abner's death, it would not be appropriate for him to wear
sackcloth[31] or to follow the bier as a mourner. David and his attendants, however, are attired in sackcloth, and they follow the bier on
which the body of Abner lies. As they do so, they give suitable expression to their grief.

David even composes a short elegy in Abner's honor (3:33-34). In
it he states that Abner's hands were not bound or chained so that he
could not defend himself; but as one falls before the wicked (a direct
reference to Joab), so he had fallen.

After Abner's burial, courtiers encourage David to have something
to eat. He refuses. This demonstrates to all that his grief over Abner's
death is genuine (3:35).[32] The people take note of it, and it pleases
them to know that the king had neither sanctioned nor condoned
what had been done.

David is incensed that Joab, for personal reasons, ignored the good
of the people. In contrast, Abner had succeeded in bringing an end
to the civil war. But Joab thought only of himself and the possibility
of losing his position of power in Judah. David also realizes, however, that he is powerless to oppose Joab, for Joab has the army
under his control and might easily lead a coup. That is why he says
to his trusted advisors,

> "And I today [am] weak, though anointed king; and these men,
> the sons of Zeruiah, [are] too hard (i.e., strong) for me. May
> Yahweh repay the doer of evil (lit. the evil) according to his evil
> (i.e., his wickedness)" (3:39).

We are surprised to see evidence of David's weakness. Earlier
in his life he had killed a lion and a bear. He had also felled Goliath.
But standing up to those forces was one thing, holding in check a
relative as volatile and devious as Joab was something entirely
different.

David may not have liked the present division of responsibility.
Joab never kept him informed of his movements or told him what he
was doing. He played by his own rules and made life difficult for

David. And while David realized that the militia were developing a loyalty to Joab, he nonetheless was compelled to go along with the present arrangement.

It is a sign of a good leader when he can admit his weaknesses, and in this chapter we see David in an invidious position. In his favor, however, is the fact that he has a realistic view of himself.

SUCCESS AND FAILURE

As each person in *A Passage to India* had both strengths and weaknesses, so here. Those about whom we have been reading provide us with an unvarnished picture of these all-too-human characteristics. No utopian ideal is held forth. Rather we see flesh and blood individuals grappling with the same kind of dilemmas we face today. We can learn from them in at least three areas.

Secrets of Strong Families

Children need and deserve to receive from their parents *involvement, modeling*, and *instruction*. All three are necessary; remove any one of them and the process will fail. Though David was busy setting up and administering his kingdom, this did not prevent him from spending quality time with his children.

Drs. Nick Stinnet and John DeFrain, in their book *Secrets of Strong Families*, identify six important qualities found in strong families:

Commitment. Members of strong families are dedicated to promoting each other's welfare and happiness. A high premium is placed upon family unity.

Appreciation. Members of strong families show appreciation for each other. And they do it often.

Communication. Members of strong families have good communication skills.

Time. Members of strong families spend large quantities of quality time with each other.

Spiritual wellness. Whether they attend places of worship or not, strong family members have a deeply ingrained sense of the presence and power of God in their lives and a belief system that gives them strength and purpose.

Coping ability. Members of strong families are able to keep stress in perspective and look upon crises as opportunities for further growth.[33]

Each one of us can promote these qualities in our homes. In some families a lot of change may be needed. But the results of our perseverance will be an increase in their *"HQ"* (Happiness Quotient) that will significantly enrich the lives of all concerned. David, we know, spent time with his children, and we may be sure he and they enjoyed these times of togetherness.

Plans of Strong Leaders

Abner and Joab shared a lot in common. They were both proud and selfish. Their lives were destructive of those who were closest to them. Each wanted power, and neither cared how it was obtained.

Abner was smarter than Joab. But he was not smart enough to know his limitations. He had forfeited his honor for the sake of personal gain. Then, to try and recover some of his losses, he proposed that David make his covenant with him. He did not understand that the greater the power the more dangerous the potential for its abuse.

Abner's nemesis, Joab, did not realize the dangers that were already gathering around his exercise of power. It has been said that the more power a person acquires, the less he or she knows. Powerful people are often totally insulated by their subordinates. They tell them only what they think their superior wants to hear or what will support their previous decisions. It was thus with Joab. His servants told him of Abner's visit but not of its purpose. And Joab acted predictably.

Like Abner, Joab was ruthless and devious. Power had intoxicated him. He knew what he wanted and how to get it. He had military power, but not moral capacity to contain it. As a result, in a strange way he was both powerful and powerless. He also knew how to keep what he had won or been given, but his paranoia caused him to see in Abner a dangerous competitor. He perceived Abner to be a threat to his well-being, and so he took immediate steps to dispose of the unwanted competition.

Joab did not realize that the lust for power was rooted in his weakness, not his strength. As a consequence, he did not see that his animosity toward Abner was merely a reflection of his own insecurity. And lacking a strong Godward orientation, he was no stronger than his passions.

Integrity of Strong Leaders

In this interplay between the strong and the weak, David freely confessed his weakness. He was honest with himself and with those whom he had admitted to his confidence. He did not pretend that he had the situation under control when he knew full well of Joab's growing power base.

David also brought his vulnerability and imperfection before the Lord. His psalms frequently make mention of the powerfulness of his enemies. And realizing his limited ability, he cast himself upon the Lord and made Him the source of his strength.

What we find in David is the way weaknesses, by a strange paradox, can be turned into strengths. Like a kite rising against the wind, David mounted each crisis with his confidence in the Lord, and the result was that he grew with each new challenge. He did not live in an ideal environment, nor was his task an easy one. He faced complexities and pressures that are similar to the ones we face today. We can learn from his honesty and prayer life how to handle the setbacks and detours that are a part of life.

Above all, David was a man of integrity. His subjects knew they could trust him, and they loved him for it. His goal was God's greater glory, and this preserved him from some of the pitfalls of power.

4

A NEW START AND A RAY OF HOPE

PART TWO

2 Samuel 3:2–5:5

An old story told me as a child by my grandmother reminds me of Ish-bosheth. A timid mouse once lived near a lion's lair. Each evening, as the lion set out in search of his prey, he would roar so loudly it seemed as if the trees of the forest would tremble.

The mouse was greatly impressed with the lion's strength and secretly wished that he, too, could roar like that.

One day, instead of the usual intimidating roar from deep within the lion's chest, all the mouse heard was a low moan coming from inside of the cave. Being curious, he peered cautiously into the cave, where he saw the lion lying down, trying to extract a thorn that had broken off in his paw. His teeth were too large, and it was plain that he could not succeed.

The mouse offered his sympathies and asked if there was anything he could do to help. With teeth that were smaller and sharper than the lion's, the tiny rodent was able to gradually draw out the thorn.

When the job was done, the lion asked if there was anything he could do in return.

"Yes," replied the mouse. "You could teach me to roar the way you do."

The lion showed the mouse how to fill his lungs with air and then let it out in a mighty roar. The mouse followed the lion's instructions carefully and, to his amazement, uttered a roar that surprised a few of the animals in the glen. Then, feeling very proud of his accomplishment, he returned to his hole near the lion's lair.

But he remained a mouse!

CONTINUATION OF AN OLD PROBLEM (3:6–4:12)

This story illustrates in a humorous way what Ish-bosheth did when he rebuked Abner for having taken his father's concubine into his bed. He "roared like a lion," but at heart he remained the same weak, vacillating person he had always been. And he was powerless to stop Abner from trying to persuade the leaders of Israel to join forces with David (3:12-21). However, just when Abner's plan appeared to be succeeding, he was cruelly and maliciously murdered by Joab (3:26-27).

Despair Hastens the Capitulation of the Northern Kingdom (4:1-12)

Assassination of a King (4:1-8). The text creates a graphic picture of events in the northern kingdom as news is brought to Ish-bosheth of Abner's murder. He immediately loses all confidence (*wayyirpū yādāyw*, "his hands hung loose, his courage flagged").[1] The text reads:

And [when] the son of Saul heard that Abner [was] dead in Hebron, his hands dropped; and all Israel was terrified (4:1).

The paralysis felt by the king spreads to the tribes under his nominal control. "All Israel" becomes troubled. They realize that Saul's son has been a mere puppet in the hands of his uncle.[2] And while the majority of the people do little more than lament the precarious situation they are in, two leaders from Saul's own tribe decide to take matters into their own hands. They are Baanah and Rechab, the sons of Rimmon the Beerothite. Their village is about nine miles north-northeast of Jerusalem.[3]

The writer is most anxious for his readers to realize that David did not instigate the events that are about to be recorded, so he specifies as clearly as possible the names of the real culprits (4:2, 5, 6, 9). To further insure that there is no confusion, he also names their father and the place of their residence (4:2b-3).[4]

Baanah and Rechab are seasoned warriors. They had most likely trained under Saul and had seen battle in a variety of places (cf. 1 Samuel 14:47-48). Both have risen through the ranks to become captains. And when Saul broke the covenant with the Gibeonites, their family had been among those that received a grant of land from the king.[5]

Now these men not only plan the assassination of Saul's son, they also carry it out themselves. Apparently, they do not want to leave anything to chance.

With 2 Samuel 4:4 we come to a slight digression. Some scholars ignore this kind of phenomenon and believe that verse 4 gives evidence of insertion by a later editor. But it is unnecessary to postulate such an addition to the text. It seems certain that the Biblical writer deliberately digressed to tell of another of Saul's "sons" who could have ascended his throne—namely, his grandson, Mephibosheth.[6]

Mephibosheth had met with a tragic accident seven years earlier when news reached Gibeah of Saul's defeat by the Philistines (1 Samuel 31:3-6). Mephibosheth's nurse had wisely taken precautions to safeguard his life. She knew that the Philistines would kill off all descendants of the late king. Unfortunately, in her haste to leave the palace, she dropped him. Perhaps his ankles became dislocated as a result of the fall. Whatever the cause, he had become permanently lame in both feet.

The point being made by the writer is that Mephibosheth, though an heir, is totally unfit to lead the people of Israel.

Following this brief reference to Mephibosheth the writer resumes his story. To do so he engages in a certain amount of repetition (cf. 4:2 and 5ff.).

Rechab and Baanah (the order of their names is now reversed to show that Rechab, the younger brother, is the one who takes the lead) enter the house of Ish-bosheth in the heat of the day. In accordance with the usual custom, people take a siesta at midday. They rest until the sun begins to decline in the west and a cool breeze springs up.

Exactly how the brothers gain access to Ish-bosheth's bedroom without being challenged by the guard is difficult to determine.[7] The text of verses 6 and 7 poses some interpretative problems, and these have caused many biblical scholars to conclude that the Masoretic (Hebrew) Text is defective. In looking for help, they have resorted to the Septuagint (the earliest translation of the Hebrew text into Greek). There they have read:

> And behold the porter of the house winnowed wheat, and he slumbered and slept; and the brothers Rechab and Baanah came unobserved into the house. Now Ish-bosheth was sleeping on the bed in his chamber: and they smote and killed him, and took off his head: and...they went all night by the western road.[8] And they brought the head of Ish-bosheth to David.

Here, for comparative purposes, is a translation of the Masoretic (Hebrew) Text. The difficulties posed by its seemingly unnecessary repetitions are obvious:

> And they came to the middle of the house, bringing wheat; and they struck him (i.e., Ish-bosheth) in the belly; and Rechab and his brother Baanah escaped. And they entered the house, and he (i.e., Ish-bosheth) was lying on his bed in his bedroom; and they struck him and killed him, and took his head; and they took his head and went the way of the Arabah all the night, and brought Ish-bosheth's head to David in Hebron...(4:6-7).

While we do not prefer the Septuagint over the Masoretic Text—because it is only a translation and not a copy of the original, and in some places contains inaccuracies—in this instance it does help us understand what may have taken place.[9]

Execution of Two Murderers (4:9-12). Bringing before David Ish-bosheth's severed head, the two brothers tell David what they have done. They also remind the king of how Saul had persecuted him. Then they piously gloss over their infamy by assuring David of their loyalty. They confidently assert that as a result of their actions the Lord is furthering His cause:

> "Yahweh has avenged my lord the king this day of Saul and of his seed" (4:8).

In spite of the evidence in the text, some critics persist in claiming that David had instigated Ish-bosheth's murder. Like a drama on TV, they portray the killers hastening to their master to receive their reward. David, these critics believe, was caught on the horns of a dilemma. To distance himself from the fallout that was sure to follow the death of Ish-bosheth, he had his henchmen, Rechab and Baanah, executed. In this way he was able to maintain before the people his protestations of innocence.

Such a view distorts the teaching of Scripture. David's response to the words of Rechab (who spoke for himself and Baanah) is to emphatically denounce their act. He had neither sought their help nor would he now take delight in their news.

We gain some intimation of the intensity of David's feelings by the oath he takes.

> "[As] Yahweh lives, who has redeemed my life from all distress,

when one spoke to me, saying, 'Look, Saul [is] dead,' and he
was in his own eyes as a bearer of good news; then (lit. but) I
seized him and killed him in Ziklag which [was] the reward (lit.
for a reward) that I gave him. Indeed, when wicked men have
killed a righteous man in his [own] house [and] on his [own]
bed, even now should I not seek his blood at (lit. from) your
hand and burn (i.e., remove) you from the earth" (4:9*b*-11).

Although the crime had been committed in Israel, outside of David's
jurisdiction, David knows that he is Yahweh's representative to the
nation. In this capacity he does not hesitate to pronounce sentence
upon the sons of Rimmon. The illustration he cites by way of legal
precedent is of the Amalekite who had brought him news of Saul's
death (1:2-16). That man claimed he had killed Saul to put an end to
his suffering (1:10). In his case there might have been extenuating
circumstances (1:9). But in the case of the murderers of Ish-bosheth,
they had confessed to killing him in his sleep (4:11). There were no
extenuating circumstances.

Ish-bosheth is not said to have been the Lord's anointed, even
though he had been made king (cf. David's own anointing, 1 Samuel
16:13). But he was an innocent man. By contrast, his murderers were
wicked men who were guilty of premeditated murder.[10]

With the sentence pronounced, David commands his men to take
Rechab and Baanah to a place of execution.[11] After that their hands
(that had been so quick to shed innocent blood) and feet (that were
so swift to carry the news) are to be cut off and their bodies are to be
hanged on a tree by the side of the pool in Hebron.[12] This is a public
place frequented by all who come to draw water. The sight of these
men will serve to dissuade others from contemplating similar courses
of action.

At dusk the bodies are cut down and thrown into the valley (outside the city walls) that serves as the city's garbage dump. A fire[13]
that burns there continuously will in time consume their remains
(cf. Deuteronomy 21:22-23). In this way, and in accordance with
David's decree, the names of Rechab and Baanah will be "removed"
from the earth.

The head of Ish-bosheth is then placed in the tomb of Abner.

David is now left without a rival to the throne. While Baanah and
Rechab had formulated and carried out their scheme independent
of the Lord, at no time was God in a quandary over what to do. He is
sovereign and makes even the evil that men do contribute to the
outworking of His plans.

THE CULMINATION OF GOD'S PROMISE (5:1-5)

From a human point of view, David had waited a long time for God to fulfill His promise and make him the "shepherd" of His people, Israel. Now, with each new event, it appears as if the day is drawing nearer when he will be crowned king.

Looking back over the past few years there have been setbacks. Abner's selfishness had led to the crowning of Ish-bosheth and a delay in the appointment of David as king over all Israel. And even after Abner had experienced a change of heart and was intent upon uniting the tribes, Joab's pride had put an end to Abner's plans on the very eve of their coming to fruition. Now, the precipitous actions of Rechab and Baanah result in a further delay.[15] Though these postponements have been unfortunate, we do not find David chafing under them. Instead, he behaves wisely and patiently waits for God's promise to him to become a reality.

In due time, and after careful deliberation, the rulers (*šōbĕṭê Yiśrā'ēl*, a select group of men, most likely comprising some of the more learned elders, with special powers delegated to them that exceed their normal authority) come to David in Hebron. They appeal to him to become their king. Their petition has three parts. It is based (1) upon ties of kinship (cf. Deuteronomy 17:15); (2) David's proven worth as a military leader (1 Samuel 18:13b-14,30; 19:8); and (3) God's designation of him as the one who is to be His prince over His people (cf. 2 Samuel 3:9-10).[16]

As we look at these specifics, we will find that the circumstances facing David were far from ideal. Those intent upon securing his aid were not spiritual giants who understood the ways of the Lord and were anxious to see the nation of Israel fulfill its destiny. They had only one real goal: freedom from Philistine oppression.

But how can they persuade David to become their leader? Let's carefully consider their words.

The first part of their petition is based on their blood relationship: "Look, we [are] your bone and your flesh" (5:1).

To us this seems like a blunt way of raising the subject of David's kingship. We would certainly have expected them to subordinate their wishes to the will of God. The delegation, however, is more concerned with the Philistine threat than with God's will.

They then remind him that in the past "when Saul was king over us, you were the one who led Israel out and in" (5:2a).

Under Saul, David had proved himself to be a capable leader. Though young, he had been at the head of Israel's armies, and his achievements were still remembered by those who had then rejoiced in his victories. Now they need him again so that he can lead their militia and lift the burden of servitude that lies so heavily upon them.

The third reason is the most important of all, yet worldly-minded men do not always place God first in their lives. They are likely to include some mention of the Almighty because they think it might impress us and enable them to get what they want.

So it is with these leaders. They conclude their remarks with a pious comment: "And Yahweh said, 'You will shepherd My people Israel, and you will be a ruler over Israel'" (5:2*b*).

It is not to the credit of these Israeli leaders that this reason is cited last. Had it been their first concern, then it would have brought all other matters into perspective. But why, we may ask, if God's will was so plain, had they neglected to carry it out? Ought not a spirit of repentance to have brought them to their knees in confession? And did not their past history (i.e., the era of the Judges) teach them that their problems were the result of their neglect of the will of the Almighty?

The leaders of the people give no indication that they are aware of spiritual realities. They show no sign of remorse for the seven long years of civil war. All they want is for David to renew his exploits against their enemies.

In this respect they were like many Christians today who desire God's blessing yet fear that if they acknowledge His sovereignty He will demand more of them than they are willing to give. They prefer, therefore, to maintain their autonomy and give the Lord only a tertiary place in their lives.

Following this opening statement, there is a discussion of mutual concerns. David has the opportunity of assessing their sincerity, and they are able to talk about any lingering concerns they may have had over the assassinations of Abner and Ish-bosheth. In addition, and if asked, David could also have given them a satisfactory explanation of the reasons for his flight to Gath and subsequent residence in Ziklag. Occasion, therefore, was given for open dialogue so that any lingering lack of trust in him could be explored and confidence reestablished.

With everyone satisfied, David makes a covenant[17] with them before the Lord, and they anoint him king over Israel (5:3). The covenant is most likely based upon the "shepherd" duties that will characterize his relationship toward them. And they respond by swearing their allegiance to him. David's public anointing confirms his private consecration by Samuel twenty-two to twenty-five years earlier (1 Samuel 16:6-13).

Before drawing this section to a close, we need to consider briefly the absence of malice on the part of David. His sufferings under Saul had been prolonged and painful. The leaders of Israel, who came to him in Hebron, seemed indifferent to the hurts he had suffered. What is implicit in the account is that David bore no grudge toward the house of Saul. It is evident that he had forgiven those who had wronged him.

In those instances where others have wronged us and have not asked for our forgiveness, we can still pardon the offender by giving up to the Lord our desire for revenge or just retribution. When this is done, we can maintain a healthy (though judicious) relationship with them without compromising our convictions.

In Hebron, with all issues amicably resolved, God's will for His people comes to pass. David is able to look back on the years of trial, so crowded with difficulties and sufferings, perplexities and dangers, and mark how God had delivered him from all his fears. This must have reinforced his confidence in the Lord for, in spite of the opposition that had been raised against him, the Lord had orchestrated events so that at last David was securely ensconced on the throne. In gratitude to the Lord for all that He had done, David's supreme desire is to serve Him faithfully to the end of his days. His song of praise, once he was alone, was:

> "O Yahweh, truly I am Your servant; I am Your servant, the son of Your handmaid; You have loosed my bonds. I will offer to You the sacrifices of praise, and will call on the name of Yahweh" (Psalm 116:16-17).

The Biblical writer, who is able to look back over David's entire reign, then closes with a summary statement:

> At Hebron [David] reigned over Judah seven years and six months, and in Jerusalem he reigned thirty-three years over all Israel and Judah (5:5).

David had not yet captured the Jebusite fortress of Jerusalem. The writer of this history, knowing what will happen, takes this opportunity to summarize the total length of his reign.

PRACTICAL CONSIDERATIONS

As we reflect on the contents of 4:1–5:5 we take note of three important principles:

- **The folly of self-seeking.** For many years following Israel's defeat by the Philistines, Ish-bosheth and the elders of Israel had made their own plans. In doing so, and much like politicians today, they had left God out of their deliberations. Their actions illustrate for us the truth that disobedience to the known will of God leads to frustration and eventual failure.

- **The certainty of retribution**. Rechab and Baanah succeeded in carrying out their scheme to murder Ish-bosheth, but they also suffered the just consequences of their deed. While the best laid plans may succeed for a time, all of us ultimately reap what we sow.

- **The trustworthiness of God's promise**. God's promises are sure. We should wait patiently for them (Psalm 27: 14). In accordance with His sovereign will, He will bring to pass all He has said and fulfill all His promises to us.

The Folly of Self-seeking

Counselors and psychologists are confronted with a seemingly endless line of people who are hurting because of some decision they made years earlier. I spent many years as a pastoral counselor, and I can personally attest to this. The following story is only one of many I could relate.

Karen had married Zac even though she knew he was not a Christian. During their courtship, she had been swept off her feet. Zac was the life of every party, and she was the envy of her peers. She secretly relished overhearing her friends refer to her as "Zac's girl." She was exuberant when they were together. And she couldn't imagine life without him!

Karen had grown up accustomed to having her own way, and she was convinced that she would be able to "win Zac for the Lord." Now, years later, Zac (so his friends say) is still fun to be around, but he is seldom seen with Karen. With the birth of each of their children, he has become more and more distant. Karen has tried to draw him into her life, but has done so in all the wrong ways.[18] She resents having to stay home and look after their daughters while he takes off to have a good time. Now, in her early forties, her expectations of happiness have died. She feels cheated. Zac comes home to eat and sleep. The only thing they share in common is their address.

Scripture assures us that the pathway of the disobedient is hard (Proverbs 13:15). We often ignore this warning until it is too late. But we cannot sin with impunity. Ish-bosheth and most of the people in Israel knew that David was God's designated ruler, but they chose to turn their backs on this fact to pursue their own selfish ends. And they suffered grievously as a result.

Today sin is made to look appealing and satisfying. It is excused under the guise of self-realization or self-fulfillment or self-actualization. Few ever see the end result of deliberate disobedience to the known will of God. And if Biblical Christianity is appealed to, it is either mocked or seen as something inhibiting. The truth is we reap what we sow, and when we sow to the wind we reap the whirlwind (Job 4:8; Hosea 8:7; Galatians 6:8*a*).

The Certainty of Retribution

One of the awesome truths of the Bible is that of retribution in kind. Jacob lied to his father, Isaac, and in time his sons lied to him (Genesis 27:19-23 and 37:30-35). Repeatedly in the book of Psalms we are told that the wicked, who metaphorically have "dug a pit in which to capture the righteous," fall into their own trap (see Psalms 9:15; 35:7-8). Those who wrongfully accuse the righteous will one day find themselves arraigned before a righteous Judge, and there will be none to help them (Psalms 37:14-15; 64:2-8. See also Psalms 28:3-4; 37:32-33; 71:4-5, 12-13).[19]

Rechab and Baanah plotted the death of Ish-bosheth, but each knife thrust only brought them closer to their own demise. Yet, instead of taking warning from what happened to them, people in all walks of life think that they can sin and get away with it. They think that because they prosper for a time, the Lord has either not taken account of their sins or else has forgotten about it (see Psalm 10:11).[20]

Frank, whom I counseled only briefly, illustrates this point. He came from a home in which he received little or no love and where his every achievement was subjected to critical scrutiny. As he grew to adulthood he began to manifest the same traits as his parents. He was often harsh and demanding. Those who worked under him knew the sting of his acerbic tongue.

Frank never married. Perhaps it was for the best. He alienated people in the church he attended and seemed happiest when he was hiking in the Rockies with his dog. He loved the outdoors and as the years passed he hiked along most of the trails from Colorado to Canada.

Frank's boss and some other businessmen who took an interest in him recommended some weekend seminars on human relations. He never went.

As he grew older, he became more and more of a recluse. At work people avoided him. The only person he ever saw was his widowed mother. She prepared dinner for him each Sunday. But even with her he had little to say. He would go over to her cottage, eat, and then make some excuse for leaving early.

Frank became prematurely old. With the passing of the years, he became more and more of a loner. Then his dog died. His mother did not know about this until he failed to come for dinner on Sunday. Fearing that something had happened to him, she called a friend and asked to be driven to her son's condominium.

Her knocks and calls brought no response. She then called the police and they broke in. Passing through the living room to the kitchen, she noticed that across a small patio the door to the garage was slightly ajar. The smell coming from the garage should have told her what had happened, but she was too concerned to notice it. She thrust open the door to find Frank hanging by an electric light cord from a beam with a chair on its side near the wall.

In designing our personalities, God built in a need for companionship. Frank, however, had turned away from his friends and those who wanted to help him. As he grew older life held less and less for him. His only consolation was his dog. When he died, Frank had nothing to sustain him or to relieve his loneliness. In the end he reaped what he had sown.

The Trustworthiness of God's Promise

There is, however, a bright side to our story of David. God's faithfulness is seen as a beam of golden sunlight to encourage him when the going is rough. And this is of encouragement to us when the circumstances of our life requires that we persevere in doing what is right regardless of outward circumstances that are often the exact opposite of what we expected or prayed for (Psalm 119:107, 149,156).

The fact of God's faithfulness is illustrated for us in the life of Donna. Before Dave married Donna he told her that he felt called to the ministry. Donna was delighted, for this confirmed to her his commitment to Christ. She had always wanted to marry a strong Christian, and the more time she spent with Dave the more he seemed to be the answer to her prayers.

Dave and Donna were married, and after a brief honeymoon they packed up their worldly possessions and headed for seminary. The studies were hard, and in his second year Dave's interest in them and the ministry began to decline rapidly. Donna suggested that they seek help, and they consulted with the chaplain. But after a few visits Dave refused to go.

Before the end of the semester, Dave dropped out of school. Then he told Donna he no longer loved her and wanted a divorce. Donna was devastated and went to her pastor. He suggested that she contact me. We tried hard to forestall the divorce, but nothing we did could shake Dave's resolve. I saw them separately and together, and it was evident that he had developed a hatred for her that was difficult to understand.

Eventually the divorce was granted and, as Dave and Donna were leaving the courtroom, he took her aside. He felt relieved and wanted to talk. He explained that he had only married her and begun theological studies because he was afraid of his homosexual desires. He believed that if he was married and training for the ministry, they might go away. When they did not, he became increasingly frustrated. Each time Donna had wanted them to make love, it had exacerbated the way he felt. And as his studies became less and less rewarding, his anger grew. Ultimately he had only one desire and that was to be free. As he and Donna parted, he wanted her to know that the failure of their marriage was not her fault.

Donna poured out her frustration and anger with tears that seemed to have no end. In later sessions she asked many hard questions, particularly about God and His love for her and why, if He is sovereign, had He not stopped her from marrying Dave. She also asked why He had not answered her many fervent prayers. My attempts to encourage her must have seemed very inadequate. In time she returned to the home of her parents and lived with them until she found a place of her own. I lost contact with her and often wondered how I might have been of more or better help.

About five years passed. Then in the mail one day I received a letter. I recognized the handwriting but was baffled by the name of the sender: D. Hamstead.

When I opened the letter, I found that it was from Donna. She had remarried. She told me of her long struggle to maintain her faith in a God whom others (myself included) had assured her really cared for her. Slowly her depression had lifted. As she began to feel better, she had begun taking part in events at her church. There she had met a young man named Jack Hamstead. At first she had refused his invitations to go out for coffee after the evening service, but after a while she had relented. Then they began going to different functions together.

Their relationship slowly grew to the point where she had begun to consider if she might possibly remarry.

To make a long story longer, at the time she decided to write to me, they had been married for two years. Jack was everything she had ever wanted in a man, and she was happier than she had ever been before. She was also expecting their first child in about five and a half months.

God is trustworthy. He is true to His word. He does not always fulfill our expectations, but those who faithfully follow Him experience, as David did, the eventual fulfillment of His promises.

QUEST FOR A USABLE FUTURE

2 Samuel 5:6-25

What is your idea of success? If asked for a definition, what elements would you include?

People in all walks of life have their opinion. One wise wag said, "Success is being able to hire someone to mow the lawn while you play tennis for exercise."

Another claimed, "Success consists of getting up just one more time than you fall down."

The president of a large corporation to whom I addressed the question observed, "The way to be successful is to do whatever work you are doing well; then you will be picked to do some other job that is not being done well."

A university president remarked: "Success, real success in any endeavor, demands more from an individual than most people are willing to give—but not more of what they are capable of giving."

And a colleague of mine noted, "Successful people are not necessarily the most gifted. They are hard working. In time their perseverance pays off in what others call 'success.'"

In our last chapter we saw David's long obedience in the same direction culminate in his coronation. His many years as an outlaw, to which were added seven-and-a-half years spent amid internal conflicts and external strife, might have seemed to him to have been time wasted, years lost, with nothing to show for them but the hardships he had endured.

David, however, knew the discipline of delay. He had dreamed of his sons as plants growing to maturity and of his daughters as corner pillars adorning the palace. He had also envisioned God's blessing upon the people so that their garners would be full of wheat and their flocks and herds so fruitful that they would cover the hillsides (Psalm 144:12-13). Reality, though, had compelled him to face the remorseless postponement of his plans for the reorganization of the kingdom. There had been what seemed like an interminable civil war, and his designs for applying the Word of God to the governance of the people had been put on hold for so long that his ideas had lost their freshness.

Now, at last, the civil war is over.[1] The events in Hebron have proved beyond question the faithfulness of God. But the Lord has done more than bring the kingdom to David. He has sovereignly orchestrated all of the circumstances of David's life to prepare him for the task of shepherding His people.

SETTING AND OUTLINE

The verses that make up the remainder of this chapter bring to an end the Biblical writer's account of David's rise to power. *The Lord, God of Hosts* has not only set His king upon the throne of His people, but He has also secured him there in spite of strong external opposition. Now, those who had opposed His will (e.g., Abner and Ishbosheth) are dead, and in 5:6-21 we see David successfully capturing Jerusalem, enjoying the benefits of a friendship that will last him the rest of his life, rejoicing in his growing family, and repulsing two Philistine invasions.

Here is an outline of this section:

- Establishing a New Capital (5:6-10)

- Building a New Palace (5:11-12)
  Digression: New Heirs to the Throne (5:13-16)

- Defending the New Empire (5:17-25).

In all that David undertakes he is successful. But what do these events teach us about the true nature of success? The brevity with which they are recorded is astonishing. The climax (as far as the chronicler is concerned) is reached when David is elevated to rulership over *all* Israel. Few details are given of the taking of Jerusalem, the building of David's palace, the mothers of his sons, and his wars with the Philistines.

While the analysis of the passage appears simple, problems in the text require the expositor's careful attention. For the most part (and to leave the material in this chapter unencumbered by too many explanations and discussions of technical data) these issues have been treated in the endnotes. These discussions are important, however, for they illustrate the difficulties of accurate interpretation and the dangers that await those who are either too dogmatic or too simplistic in their understanding and approach.

We begin with the conquest of Jerusalem.

ESTABLISHING A NEW CAPITAL (5:6-10)

In this section the focus of attention shifts from the coronation in Hebron to the establishment of a new capital in Jerusalem.

> Now the king and his men went up to Jerusalem against the Jebusites,[2] the inhabitants of the land (5:6a).

We may be sure that David inquired of the Lord what he should do. This had been his first act after his return to Ziklag (2:1), and we may be certain that he did not proceed to Jerusalem without explicit direction from "the Lord of Hosts."

Earlier in Israel's history God had indicated that when His people were settled in the land, He would "put His name" in one of the cities (see Deuteronomy 12:5,11,14,21). So far none had been designated. The way David proceeds in this chapter and the next seems to intimate that the Lord had revealed His will to him. The fact that Yahweh might so singularly honor David should not surprise us. He had seen in him a man after His own heart (Psalm 78:70-72; Acts 13:22), and as His representative on earth it was to be expected that He would make His wishes known to him.

Once God's will is known, David carries it out promptly.

The Importance of the City (5:6a)

The name Jebus occurs here and in two other places in the Bible (Judges 19:10-11; 1 Chronicles 11:4). It is obviously a shortened form of Jerusalem. Jebus was a very ancient city, and had at one time been ruled by Melchizedek (see Genesis 14:18; Hebrews 5:6; 7:1).

Long before David selected Jebus for his capital, it had been a city of great importance for its location at the crossroads of Canaan. When Joshua had divided up the land, he had assigned this territory to the tribe of Benjamin (Joshua 18:28). Inasmuch as it lay on the border between Benjamin and Judah, it was attacked first by the men of Judah (Judges 1:8). They defeated the Jebusites but did not possess the city, for it belonged to the Benjamites.

This gave the Jebusites time to repossess it, and when the men of Benjamin wanted to live in it they could not dislodge them from their stronghold (Judges 1:21). As a consequence, the Jebusites retained possession of this well-protected, strategically located city. And such were the improvements they made to the fortifications that it became virtually impregnable. Later on, when a coalition of Benjamin and Judah attacked the city, they failed to take it (cf. Joshua 15:63).

Politically, administratively, and economically, Jerusalem was a most advantageous place from which to rule a kingdom. Its position within the territory of Benjamin, yet close to the tribe of Judah, made it an excellent site from which to bind together the two royal tribes. The people of Benjamin would feel conciliated, and the leaders of Judah would not feel alienated.

Jerusalem was also virtually in the middle of the land given by God to His people Israel. As Dr. Arthur P. Stanley has shown,

> It was on the ridge of the backbone of hills, which extend through the whole country from the desert to the plain of the Esdraelon. Every traveller who has trod the central route of Palestine from north to south, must have passed through the table-land of Jerusalem.[3]

In addition, the position of the city was unrivaled militarily. It stood on a rocky plateau surrounded on three sides by steep ravines that formed a natural fortress. As later history showed, Jerusalem was virtually unassailable.[4]

David's capture of this strategically located city is first described summarily (5:6b-7) and then specifically (5:8-9).

The Capture of the City (5:6b-9)

David and those who have been with him throughout his wilderness years[5] make the short journey of approximately nineteen miles to Jerusalem, intending to attack the city.[6] The Jebusites, however, mock them. David and his band are relatively few in number, and the walls of the city are high. So secure do the Jebusites feel that they taunt David by saying,

> "You shall not come in here, but the blind and the lame shall turn you away" (5:6b).

This statement is typical of the pre-battle boasting and reviling that we read about in the annals of the kings of this period, and it isn't surprising that David, in his reply, goes one further. He equates the Jebusites with the blind and the lame.[7]

Josephus, in his *Antiquities of the Jews*, claimed that the Jebusites actually put the blind and the lame around the walls to show to David how confident they were of their city's invincibility.[8]

To the Jebusites' consternation, David quickly and easily succeeds in capturing their citadel. It is accomplished so rapidly that the Jebusites are taken completely by surprise. In fact, the Biblical writer does not record fighting of any sort. And having established that David took the city (5:6b-7), he then shares with his readers a brief account of how it was done.

Unfortunately for us there are certain ambiguities in the text and a lack of consensus on the part of Bible scholars on how to resolve them. These difficulties center in the meaning of the word *ṣinnôr*, sometimes translated "water shaft," but also translated in a variety of other ways as different translations readily reveal.[9] The only other instance of the usage of this word is in Psalm 42:7 where it has the meaning of "cataracts" or "waterfalls."

During wartime, Jerusalem drew its water supply from a shaft that connected the city with the Gihon Spring in the Kidron Valley. Natural ledges in the limestone rock made it barely possible for a person to climb up to the city. Early in the nineteenth century, Sir Charles Warren engaged in some excavations of the city of Jerusalem. He came across an almost sheer tunnel by which people within Jerusalem could let down buckets into the spring and so were assured of water during times of seige. At great personal risk, Sir Charles climbed this difficult and dangerous shaft, proving that it was just possible for the city to be entered by this means.[10]

And this is the most likely explanation of how David and his men gained access to the citadel, and why the city fell without a lengthy seige.

Other translations of *ṣinnôr* include "grappling iron," "scaling hook," or "fortress." Scholars who propose such meanings believe that either the walls were scaled using these implements or David used these weapons to climb up the tunnel leading from the Gihon Spring into Jerusalem. To add to the confusion of interpretation, the Septuagint renders *ṣinnôr* as "dagger."[11] None of these ideas provide certain evidence as to how David and his men were able to enter the city unopposed. The most likely explanation is that they did what Charles Warren did—only two millennia earlier when it was much easier because the limestone ridges were not as worn.

Once inside the city David's men capture the fortress. But what happened to the Jebusites? Were they expelled, exterminated, or allowed to "peacefully coexist" with the new king?

In the absence of any specific statement in the text, most modern

scholars advocate coexistence. Some of the Jebusites may have remained. One of them was Araunah, who was possibly a proselyte (cf.
2 Samuel 24:16). It is preferable to conclude with Josephus that the
Jebusites (excluding a few proselytes) were expelled.[12]

The Fortification of the City (5:9)

At last David is in a position to take up permanent residence in
Jerusalem. In honor of his victory, Jebus is called "the city of David."
By choosing it as his capital, David establishes his headquarters in a
place that transcends tribal loyalties. The healing of the wounds
caused by Saul's misadministration can now begin.

But Jerusalem needs attention. The foundations need to be secured. The place called *the Millo*, possibly referring to the "supporting terraces" of the hill inside the city wall, has to be reinforced.
Archaeologists have found evidence of such buttressing both before
and after the time of David.

This done, the new king can turn his attention to other matters.

Summary (5:10)

The writer of this narrative is careful to remind his readers that, in
the final analysis, David's success must only be attributed to the good
hand of the Lord upon him. In other words, real success is synonymous with God's blessing. It is quite apart from material wealth.

The term *Yahweh 'ĕlōhe ṣĕbāʾôt*, "the LORD, the God of Hosts,"[13]
recalls to mind 1 Samuel 1:3-8. This term has as its root the idea of
God's sovereignty over all things. David has been borne along and
given success by the God whose heavenly messengers are always at
His command (Psalm 103:20ff.; Daniel 7:10; Hebrews 1:14).

The chronicler then provides his readers with two indications of
God's further blessing upon David: (1) an example of foreign poten-
tates seeking his favor; and (2) a posterity who will insure that his
dynasty continues after his death.

BUILDING A NEW PALACE (5:11-12)

Equipment and Personnel (5:11)

To illustrate David's growing reputation, God's inspired penman
mentions an embassy from Hiram, the powerful king of Tyre,[14] that
comes to Jerusalem. These ambassadors most likely come to

congratulate David on his accession to the throne of his people and his success in defeating the Jebusites. In their actions they also prefigure those who, during the reign of Christ on the earth, will come to Jerusalem bringing Him gifts (Psalms 68:29*b*; 72:8-11; Isaiah 60:5; 61:6).

Tyre was one of the two great cities of Phoenecia. It was known for its maritime trade and the fine buildings of cedar that skilled craftsmen had erected. Israel had been appraised of Tyre's defenses (Joshua 19:29), for Phoenecia lay on the border of the tribe of Asher.

To court the favor of King David was a wise move on the part of Hiram. Tyre was dependent upon Israel for its supplies of wheat and oil and trade from the merchants of the cities of the Tigris-Euphrates River Valley. These traders could embark from Tyre and sail to western ports, thus avoiding months of arduous travel over robber-infested terrain.

Dr. John Bright, in his *History of Israel*, and Professor A. A. Anderson, in his scholarly commentary on *Second Samuel*, raise a question concerning Hiram's age and service to both David and Solomon. They believe that David reigned from 1000-961 B.C. They further point out that Hiram helped Solomon with plans for building the Temple. Since Hiram reigned from 969-936 B.C., they conclude that this delegation from Hiram was not sent until *late* in David's reign.[15]

In actual fact, David began his reign in Judah in 1011 B.C., and he reigned over all Israel from 1004-971 B.C. The "Hiram" mentioned in this passage must have been either the father or the grandfather of the king of Tyre who helped Solomon (see 1 Kings 5:1-12,18). For a son or grandson to bear the name of his father or grandfather was common among the people of antiquity (see Luke 1:59-61).

The cedar logs[16] that Hiram sends to David were cut on the slopes of Lebanon, floated down to Joppa on barges, and then hauled overland to Jerusalem (see 2 Chronicles 2:16). Cedar wood is particularly hardy and highly prized for building purposes, and its strength and resistance to decay are often alluded to in Scripture (see Psalm 92:12; Ezekiel 31:3; Amos 2:9). Because the Israelites were a pastoral people, they were unskilled in building palaces or temples. Hiram's offer of assistance, therefore, was most propitious.

Summary (5:12)

David sees in the friendship of Hiram and the success that is attending his efforts on behalf of the people unmistakable proof of God's favor. As Matthew Henry pointed out,

[David's] kingdom was established.... He that made him king established him...(Psalm 139:21-28). Saul was made king, but not established; David was established king...[and] was exalted in the eyes of both friends and enemies. Never had the nation of Israel looked so great or made such a figure as it began now to do.... David perceived by a wonderful concurrence of providences to his establishment and advancement, that God was with him. *Many have the favour of God and do not perceive it, and so want the comfort of it: but to be exalted to that and established in it, and to perceive it, is happiness enough.*[17]

DIGRESSION: NEW HEIRS TO THE THRONE (5:13-16)

The birth of sons to David listed in these verses spans the thirty years of his reign in Jerusalem. What is important for us to notice is that David did not suddenly add numerous wives and concubines to his harem. His *seraglio* was small when compared with surrounding monarchs, sheiks, and emirs. Solomon, in taking so many foreign wives, did disobey the command of the Lord (cf. Deuteronomy 17:17 and 1 Kings 11:1-3). But those who charge David with doing so show their ignorance of his culture and times.

Only seventeen sons were born to David during the thirty years of his reign in Jerusalem (with four coming from the same wife[18]). This is a paltry figure when compared with the number of Gideon's offspring or Ahab's progeny (Judges 8:30; 2 Kings 10:1,6) and the large families of some of the leaders who had preceded David as God's theocratic representatives (Judges 12:9,13-14).[19]

DEFENDING THE NEW EMPIRE (5:17-25)

The First Attack (5:17-21)

The Philistines had apparently been tolerant of David while he ruled in Hebron and may still have regarded him as their vassal (even though there is no proof that David paid tribute to them). But when all Israel proclaims him as their king, they realize that he is honor bound to expel them from the cities they have lived in since defeating King Saul on the slopes of Mount Gilboa.

Having great respect for David's prowess, the entire Philistine force converges on the Valley of Rephaim.[20] They intend to divide David's territory in two unequal portions, force David to return to Hebron, and in this way make it impossible for him to govern the northern tribes. Such a strategy will also enable them to place Judah under tribute. The Valley of Rephaim, therefore, is strategically suited to their purpose.

Had the Philistines been successful, David would not have been able to rule effectively. The battles mentioned in this chapter, therefore, were of the utmost importance.[21]

Most authorities are of the opinion that the first attack took place *before* David captured the city of Jerusalem. They offer as "proof" the belief that the Philistines "went in search of David" and did not go up directly to Jerusalem.

These difficulties can be answered easily and without rearranging the implied chronology of the passage. It was David's taking of the citadel of Jerusalem that provoked the Philistine attack upon him. If David had still been in Hebron, the Philistines would have known exactly where to find him.

As soon as David learned of the invasion, he took inventory of the situation. He realized that he had insufficient time to rally *all* Israel behind him, and he and his men were ill-prepared to withstand a long seige. Furthermore, with the Philistines in the Valley of Rephaim, they had the advantage of position.

David, therefore, left Jerusalem and made his way to a *mĕṣōdā*, "strong-hold"—possibly the Cave of Adullam—where his initial intent may have been to engage in guerilla warfare and thus nullify the Philistines' advantage. Such warfare would also neutralize to some extent their superior manpower. And, as far as our story is concerned, the Philistines, on learning from the local inhabitants that David had left Jerusalem, began looking for him because they had no idea where he had gone.

By making the base of his operations a stronghold such as the caves of Adullam, David achieved two additional things: (1) he caused the Philistines concern for their own cities and towns and villages, for he was now nearer to them than they were and could easily attack these virtually defenseless places; and (2) he prevented the Philistine move eastward, for they could only divide his land in half by dividing their own forces.

In facing this supreme challenge of his rulership, David inquires of the Lord what he should do: "Shall I go up against (lit. to) the Philistines?" (5:19*a*).

He may have had in mind a surprise raid on their camp, a hit-and-run maneuver. And Yahweh responds, "Go up, for I will certainly give the Philistines into your hand" (5:19*b*).

This was a test of David's faith. The Lord had told him to attack the combined Philistine armies with only six hundred men (see 1 Samuel 23:13; 27:2; 30:9). The army that had invaded his land represented the might of Philistia which seven-and-a-half years earlier had defeated the army of Israel under King Saul. Yet David obeys. His trust in Yahweh is implicit. His approach is to attack the enemy base camp. The tents and other gear will give his men a slight advantage.

The victory Yahweh gives exceeds David's wildest dreams. His force breaks through the enemy's ranks like rushing water breaching a barricade. And the Philistines are completely routed.

The Biblical writer then contrasts the power of God with the power of the Philistine gods. The Philistines abandon their gods in the Valley of Rephaim and run as fast as they can back to their cities. Their idols are then taken as trophies of war (cf. 1 Samuel 19:16) and are later burned (1 Chronicles 14:12). The victory has shown the men of Israel that these creations of man's hands are "no gods" when compared with the Lord of glory.

The Second Attack (5:22-25)

After the first invasion, David raises a levy of thirty thousand fighting men from "all Israel" (6:1). These are ready in case the Philistines launch another attack.

The Philistines are not easily dissuaded from their hostile intentions. They determine to break David's power before he can threaten their trade monopoly in the narrow stretch of land that links the lucrative commerce of Egypt with the wealth of the Tigris-Euphrates River Valley. They reevaluate their plan and determine that the Valley of Rephaim is still the best location for an attack.

In their second attempt to gain the upper hand, they once more invade Israel and take up their positions on ground that favors them. And David is again forced to leave Jerusalem and make the Cave of Adullam the base of his operations.

As he considers his position in light of the Philistine threat, David inquires of the Lord what he should do. He could easily have relied on the strategy that had worked the first time. Being a godly man, however, and realizing that he is only God's regent to govern His people, he asks God for instructions. And Yahweh says to him,

> "You shall not go up [frontally against the Philistines]; circle around to their rear and come to them in front of the weeping trees.[22] And it shall be, when you hear the sound of marching in the tops of the trees, then you shall strike for then Yahweh shall go out before you to strike the army of the Philistines" (5:24).

God's message is clear. This time there is to be a surprise attack. And David obeys. He is not presumptuous. He acts in complete reliance upon the Lord.

The *baka*, "weeping trees," have been variously identified as balsam trees or mulberry trees or even aspen trees.[23] "Balsam" is the traditional Jewish interpretation for the Hebrew *baka*, "crying, weeping," describes what happens whenever a balsam tree is cut or torn in any way. Sap oozes from the breach made in the bark, making it appear to weep.

The command of the Lord requires David's complete obedience. It is always easier for us to follow a plan that has worked before. But this is not always God's way. His command to David requires patience, for David and his men are to wait until they hear the sound of marching in the tree tops.

Many commentators have offered ingenious explanations for the disturbance the men heard that night. No natural phenomenon could have caused such a sound. The wind might produce a rushing noise, but not the methodical march of innumerable feet. What David and his men heard was designed by God to give them assurance. Yahweh, the Lord of the Heavenly Armies, was going out before them to strike the army of Philistia.

David and his men do exactly as the Lord has commanded them. At the appropriate time they attack quickly and decisively. The rout of the Philistines is complete. They flee from Geba[24] all the way to Gezer.[25] And from this time onward the Philistines make no serious attempt to attack Israel.

By these actions the Lord showed that He had put His hand upon David and that He would secure the throne of His anointed (cf. Psalm 20)!

Some scholars believe that the exploits of David's "mighty men" took place at this time (cf. 23:8-12; 1 Chronicles 11:11-14). On either of these occasions, Jashobeam might have killed the three hundred Philistines mentioned in 1 Chronicles 11:11, but it is unlikely that the other acts of valor occurred during these wars. The setting of these remarkable feats does not fit these invasions.

OF RISKS AND REWARDS

Success is something we all desire, yet few of us can define it. Inwardly, we often connect success with the satisfying of our wants; however, as soon as these have been met, other desires arise. Unless we recognize what is happening, our lives will be filled with discontent and an endless striving after the wind.

Playing to Win

While David succeeded in capturing Jerusalem, what was reinforced upon his conscious mind was that the Lord was blessing him
(5:10). Others had tried to take the citadel only to fail, and yet it fell
to him within a single night. The Lord alone could have given such
success.

With the capture of Jerusalem behind him, David could begin to
restore Israel's sagging fortunes. The Philistines had to be driven
from the land. Moab, Zobah, Syria, Edom, and Ammon in turn flexed
their muscles against him. On each occasion, however, the Lord gave
him the victory over his enemies.

What, then, was the secret of his success?

The key lies in the psalms David wrote during this period. In them
we find that he had developed a strong, internal God-consciousness.
He had come to see the Lord of glory as "God Most High"—a name
implying His sovereign authority over all things (e.g., Psalm 47:2).
He alone has the right to be worshiped (Psalm 50:14). And He alone
is able to answer prayer (Psalm 57:2-3). In Psalm 91 we find that He is
the believer's *Shelter* in times of trial, *Refuge* when all seems to be
going wrong, *Fortress* when facing opposition, and *Deliverer* from
danger.

So with his Godward relationship secure, David could concentrate
on doing the Lord's will. As a result, wherever he went the Lord prospered him (7:1*b*).

Setting the Pace

The second area in which we see David's success is in the friendly
relations he was able to establish with other kings (cf. 1 Samuel 22:3-
4; 27:10; 29:9-10). Hiram sent an embassage to David, and he and
David became lifelong friends.

To the ancient Greeks and Romans, friendship was the most valuable of human possessions. They believed it to be the crown of life.
By contrast, we today have many acquaintances, but few if any real
friends.

Christ placed His stamp of approval on friendship when He said,
"No longer do I call you servants; for a servant does not know what
his master is doing; *but I have called you friends*, for all things that I
have heard from My Father I have made known to you" (John 15:15,
emphasis added).

We tend to confuse acquaintances with friends. But this is surely
an error as the following chart makes clear. We may have many

acquaintances, but during a lifetime we may have only two or three good friends.

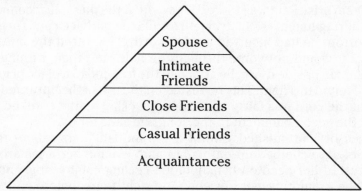

I have been blessed with good friends. Unfortunately, because I have lived in several countries, some of them reside in different parts of the world. But separation has not dulled my appreciation of them. Their friendship still ranks among my most cherished possessions.

The Blessing of the Lord

A third area in which we see David's success is in the area of his family. Children, we are told, are the heritage of the Lord (Psalm 127:3). The blessing they bring was impressed upon my wife and me when, for our thirty-fifth wedding anniversary, we decided to go somewhere we had never been before. We chose the Tahitian archipelago.

We were warned by our travel agent not to go in June because it was winter in the southern hemisphere. We had little choice in the matter and found that the first two weeks of June were, in reality, the most ideal time to visit the islands.

The Tahitian people are very friendly, and we spent an idyllic two weeks in this part of the Pacific. We also learned a lot about Americans! While on the island of Moorea, we were told that the Tahitians think Americans are "the hardest working people in the world, who enjoy life the least."

As we watched the natives, so poor (because they have no real natural resources) and yet so happy, we learned once again that true happiness comes from relationships!

Each evening the hotel staff entertained the guests. A variety of tribal dances and singing took up most of the time after dinner. One elderly man named Paul played the role of a stand-up comic. He was all smiles as he told of his wife, children, and grandchildren.

A couple of days later we went for a picnic on an atoll (or *motu*, as the Tahitians call these small, flat, generally uninhabited islands). To our surprise Paul was there. He provided the musical accompaniment during lunch. His instrument? A plastic garbage can. Through the bottom he had inserted a thick cord. He knotted the one end so that it would not come through the hole; and then, turning the garbage can upside down, he attached the free end to a piece of metal he had found in a field. This he rested on the rim of the upturned can so that the cord was fairly taut. Then, plucking on the cord, he provided the accompaniment to the songs he sang for us.

When he had finished, one of his granddaughters (about three years of age) climbed up on his lap and, placing her arms around him, rested her head on his shoulder. Feeling comfortable and secure, she promptly went to sleep. And right there, before our eyes, we saw true contentment. Paul was happy to have his little girl close to him, and she was content to sleep in his arms.

Paul is a happy man. He derives his contentment from his family and friends and his work at the hotel (Ecclesiastes 3:12-13, 22*a*; 9:9).

David too loved his children, and it is reasonable to believe that his sensitive heart was gladdened as his sons and daughters climbed over him, tousled his hair, and asked innumerable questions.

Leading—or Being Led?

Finally, we consider the significance of the Philistine invasions. Twice they attacked Israel, and twice they were repulsed. The first time David faced them he had only his loyal band of six hundred followers. The next time their ranks had been augmented with thirty thousand warriors. The victories he won were seen as being given to him by "God Most High."

Of importance to us as we assess the dynamics of success is the fact that David never ran ahead of the Lord. He asked for guidance and was quick to obey. He did exactly as the Lord commanded him.

And what was his reward? The delight of knowing that the Lord was fulfilling His purpose in and through him.

Real success is not a matter of satisfying our wants or desires. It comes from the joy we receive when our hearts are in conscious agreement with God and we are experiencing the blessings of fellowship with our family and friends.

THE IMPORTANCE OF OBEDIENCE

2 Samuel 6:1-23

General Bull Moose was a colorful cartoon character of a generation or two ago. His decisions could be summed up in the brief statement, "What's good for General Bull Moose is good for the country."

Each morning millions of Americans would open their newspapers to the "funnies" to find out what new mess the General was in. As a result of his one-dimensional style of reasoning he blundered from one *faux pas* to another without ever realizing that he was trying to do the right thing in the wrong way.

General Bull Moose has many followers. A mother, for example, may still want to influence and control the lives of her grown children. Her motives may be altruistic, but she fails to realize that her plans are construed as interference by her sons and daughters and their spouses.

An employer may have "gut feelings" about what needs to be done, but he may only impede the progress of his staff by his insistence on following procedures that became dated with the Edsel.

Only recently I learned of a church in Illinois that had fired its pastor. Everyone had liked him. He preached well and was genuinely concerned about the well-being of his flock. And the church had grown under his leadership.

The board, however, was comprised of influential businessmen who had built their companies into mega-corporations with worldwide interests. These men reasoned that if they had been eminently successful in the secular sphere, then why not apply these same principles to the church. They developed a forward-looking philosophy. They had a five-year plan that included radio and television programs, and a ten-year plan that anticipated educating missionaries and placing them in every country of the world.

These men felt that the pastor was an impediment to their plans because he did not agree with their procedures. So they did what large corporations are prone to do: they got rid of him. And with him out of the way, they felt sure that nothing could now hinder the implementation of their ideas. They would soon be *the* example of a vibrant evangelical church–a model for the rest of the world.

There was a fly in the ointment, however, and it was made up of the congregation. They became disgruntled with the authoritarianism of the board and their many demands. One by one they left. Within a year, those attending services had dropped from a little over two thousand to about sixty-two.

The board had attempted to do the right thing, but in the wrong way.

The same principle holds true for us in all areas of life: Our worship of the Lord, family relationships, the rearing and educating of children, the cultivation of friendships, our involvement in politics–everything. More is needed than good intentions. The right things must be done in the right way if we are to truly honor the Lord in every area of our lives.

OUTLINE

In 1 Samuel 6 we see David making plans to bring the Ark up to Jerusalem. God had revealed to him that Jerusalem would be the place in which He would put His Name.[1] The Ark of the Covenant was intimately connected with the presence of God, so it seemed logical to have it ensconced in Jerusalem, where He could be at the center of His people's worship.

As the representative of the Lord of Hosts,[2] David began to implement his plans. These included erecting a tabernacle to receive the Ark and composing a special hymn that he had taught to the Levites. He intended them to sing this psalm of praise as the Ark began its final approach to the gates of the city. All that remained, therefore, was to bring the Ark from the house of Abinadab in Kiriath-jearim (in this chapter called Baale-judah)[3] to Jerusalem, a distance of eight or nine miles. What could be simpler?

The chapter may be divided into three parts:

- A Celebration That Ends in Sorrow (6:1-11)

- A Convocation That Culminates in Blessing (6:12-19)

- Criticism That Eclipses God's Praise (6:20-23)

A CELEBRATION THAT ENDS IN SORROW (6:1-11)

David's first task following his enthronement had been to secure Jerusalem for the Lord. With God's help he had taken the city without the need for a costly, time-consuming siege. More, however, was involved in the capture of Jerusalem than the establishing of a new capital. Later psalmists and prophets would extol her significance and importance:

> [Jerusalem] beautiful in elevation, [and] the joy of the whole earth (Psalm 48:2).

> Thus says the Lord, [even] Yahweh, "This is Jerusalem;
> I have set her at the center of the nations..." (Ezekiel 5:5).

> Jerusalem, that is built as a city that is compact together;...to which the tribes go up to give thanks to Yahweh (Psalm 122:3-4).

> As the mountains surround Jerusalem,
> So Yahweh surrounds His people (Psalm 125:2).

> Yahweh bless you from Zion, and may you see the prosperity of Jerusalem all the days of your life (Psalm 128:5).

Even David seems to have had some intimation that it would one day become the city of the great King, Messiah Himself (cf. Acts 2:30). He appears to have consciously anticipated the time when the Messiah would come, set up His Kingdom, and rule over the nations of the world. To David, the "mountain peaks" of God's prophetic word were clear, but the "valleys" or intervals between one event and the next were not as well defined for him as they are for us today.

So, with the city secure, David's second goal is to unite the tribes by making Jerusalem the center of worship. William J. Deane reminds us that

> the massacre at Nob had left the priestly community in a most depressed state, and although the solemnities of worship were performed in some sort at Gibeon, it was with maimed rites that they were carried on and with no active support.... The Levitical arrangements originally established by Moses had in part become obsolete, and in part were unsuited to the circumstances of the present time.[4]

Conscious of this spiritual interregnum, David wants to restore a true spirit of worship to his people. In reviewing his activities, Dr. William G. Blaikie has this to say about his motives:

> He seeks first the kingdom of God and His righteousness, trusting that other things shall be added unto him. What a contrast to the ordinary rule of public life, and of private life, too! Where shall we find the public men, whose first concern is for the honour of God, and who really believe that the favour of the Highest is the true palladium of their country's welfare?[5]

David, then, decides to unify the nation and enhance the worship of the people by bringing the Ark to Zion. His actions may well be looked upon as a turning point in the history of Israel. As a result of his actions, the worship of the Lord would become the focal point of the people's devotion.

The Greatness of the One Worshiped (6:1-2)

To honor God and also to protect themselves from a possible surprise attack by the Philistines (cf. 1 Samuel 7), David again summons his army of thirty thousand men. They are accompanied by as many of the people, priests, and Levites as wish to participate in this auspicious event (1 Chronicles 13:1-2).

David shows commendable prudence by involving the whole nation in the joyful celebration. He wants them to be a vital part of what is taking place. And the people are to be commended for their willing participation. Their numbers are so great that they line both sides of the path from Kiriath-jearim to Jerusalem. In taking part in this auspicious event they begrudge neither the time nor the trouble nor any expense.

> The joyful spirit in which this service was performed by David and his people is another interesting feature of the [narrative]. Evidently it was not looked upon as a toilsome service, but as a blessed festival,[6] adapted to cheer the heart and raise the spirits. What was the precise nature of the service? It was to bring into the heart of the nation, into a new capital of the kingdom, the Ark of the Covenant,[7]–that piece of sacred furniture which had been constructed nearly five hundred years before in the wilderness of Sinai–the memorial of God's holy covenant with the people, and the symbol of His gracious presence among them. In spirit it was bringing God into the very

midst of the nation...Rightly understood, the service could bring joy only to spiritual hearts; it could give pleasure to none who had reason to dread the presence of God. To those who knew Him as their reconciled Father and the covenant God of the nation, it was most attractive.[8]

The description given of the Ark is arresting. Before any physical features can be alluded to, we read: "which is called by *the Name*" (6:2).

The Hebrew reads "over which (i.e., over the Ark) is called the Name" (cf. Deuteronomy 28:10; 1 Kings 8:43). The "*Name*" stands for the totality of God's person. From above the wings of the cherubim,[9] the Lord looks down on the blood-covered mercy seat. Because of the shed blood, He is able to deal in grace with His people.[10]

The Danger of Spiritual Ignorance (6:3-5)

The best of well-intentioned plans, however, may go wrong, and so it is on this occasion. With misguided zeal "they" (probably the sons or grandsons of Abinadab–Uzzah and Ahio) place the Ark in a new ox-drawn cart made especially for the occasion. Then, taking the path that descends into the short valley that ultimately swings upward toward the mountains on which Jerusalem is built, they lead the procession with David and his retinue following behind.

Apparently, no one questions why Levites are not carrying the Ark as prescribed by the Law (see Numbers 7:9; cf. 3:29-31), and none of the priests or Levites voice any objection. All of this underscores for us the fact that when God's Word is not taught, people become ignorant of His will. They then run the risk of making decisions based upon experience or observation. In this instance, the precedent Uzzah and Ahio may have relied on might have been a pagan one (cf. 1 Samuel 6:7). Uzzah and Ahio wanted to do the right thing; they did it, however, in the wrong way.

For the moment, God tolerates this violation of His explicit command. The people's praise–to the accompaniment of stringed and percussion instruments[11]–is acceptable to Him.

The Consequence of Spiritual Pride (6:6-7)

As the cart carrying the Ark comes abreast of the threshing floor of Nachon, something happens that causes the oxen to stumble.[12] Perhaps a wheel gets stuck on a protruding rock and the cart begins to tip. Whatever happened, Uzzah steps forward to steady the Ark.

> And the anger of Yahweh burned against Uzzah, and God struck
> him down for his irreverence; and he died there by the Ark of
> God (6:7).

To us this seems like a capricious act on God's part. "What had
Uzzah done to deserve this?" we ask.

It may be that, having cared for the Ark for many years, he had
become inwardly proud of the privilege bestowed upon him. And
when the Ark was in danger of falling, his pride caused him to act in
a way that attracted attention to himself. If this is correct, then he
has many followers, for there is nothing like handling sacred things
to make a person act in a superior manner.

As before at Beth-shemesh (cf. 1 Samuel 6:19), where an act of
irreverence toward the Ark had been punished by death, so it is now.
To the popular mind, Uzzah's act appears natural and well-meant.
One of the great lessons Israel had to learn, however, was about the
unapproachable majesty and holiness of the Lord of glory. And here,
in the first step toward the inauguration of a new era of worship, the
death of Uzzah conveys a solemn warning to David and the people.
(In the New Testament the deaths of Ananias and Sapphira offer a
parallel. In both 2 Samuel 6 and Acts 5, a single punishment caused
the people to experience a holy reverence for the Lord.[13])

So the procession stops. The day had started out with the happy
anticipation of Yahweh being enthroned in His city, but it ends in
disaster. And the people, who are more superstitious than they are
God-fearing, come close to losing confidence in their king.[14]

The Need for Spiritual Instruction (6:8-11)

David is understandably angry.[15] Anger arises from feelings of rejection, humiliation, or frustration (and sometimes all three).

As we look back on these events, it is easy for us to sense intuitively David's conflicting sentiments. First, he experienced a feeling
of *rejection*. When everything was apparently going well, God broke
in on the celebration and showed that He was displeased with what
was being done. And David, who had worked so hard to make the
day's activities something his people would remember for years
to come, realized that he had done something wrong. Yahweh had
looked with disfavor upon the execution of his plans, and this
caused him to feel rejected.

Second, David also felt *humiliated*. The crowd that had joined in
so enthusiastically was bewildered. They looked to him for an explanation, and he had none to give them. We all know that, when some

catastrophe strikes, it is the person in charge who is blamed. He is supposed to have been able to prevent it. And David, because of his perceived failure and inability to explain Uzzah's death, felt humiliated.

And finally, David was inwardly *frustrated*. As we have shown, he did not know what had gone wrong or why Uzzah had died. He wanted so badly to have the Ark in Jerusalem. Now it seemed as if all his plans were for nought. And this led to frustration. That was why, perhaps sensing his helplessness, he asked, "How can the Ark of Yahweh come to me?" (6:9*b*). This is the cry of a frustrated man. But David's anger is soon replaced by fear.

The able British Bible scholar, Joyce Baldwin, reminds us that

[David] who had experienced wonderful protection over the years from the Lord his God, and had known unusual intimacy with Him, had to come to terms with the fact that he had overstepped the mark, and presumed upon the relationship while failing to observe the regulations laid down to safeguard respect for God's holiness.[16]

So David became fearful. Fear, when God is the object, is based upon two elements: repulsion and attraction. David was afraid to proceed, so he withdrew. Yet at the same time he longed for the Lord's presence in Jerusalem. Being uncertain what to do, he has the Ark placed in the house of Obed-edom the Gittite.

Gittites were generally from Gath (or some city with Gath in its name like Gath-hepher), and it is possible that Obed-edom was a proselyte. If so, then he stood in a long and noble line of devout and honorable men and women who are mentioned in Scripture–people such as Ittai of Gath or Jephunneh the Kenizite–whose godliness earned them respect.

Other writers believe that Obed-edom was from Gath-rimmon, a Levitical city (Joshua 21:24-26), making him in all probability, a Levite (see 1 Chronicles 15:21; 16:5,38).[17]

Still others are of the opinion that he was from the land of Edom.[18] And then there are those who believe that "edom" was the pagan name for the god '*a-tu-m*, the consort of one of Egypt's gods.[19]

Either of the first two explanations may validly be deduced from the evidence. The latter two are based upon speculation and must be rejected on the grounds that there is insufficient evidence to support them.

Obed-edom is fully aware of what has taken place, yet he welcomes the Ark into his home. Its presence in other places had been the signal for disaster and death (cf. the seven months it spent among the Philistines, 1 Samuel 5:1–6:9; and it's brief stay at Beth-shemesh, 1 Samuel 6:14-20). Yet he does not suffer. Honoring God, he is honored by Him, and a manifest blessing rests upon his house. This led Dr. Joseph Hall to remark, "The God of heaven pays liberally for His lodging."[20]

As we reflect upon the teaching of these verses, one thought stands out: the importance of doing the right thing in the right way.

David, it seemed, had done all he could to honor the Lord and involve the people in worshiping Him. He had planned well. He had included the people in the procession. The joyful spirit of the proceedings augured well for the entrance of Yahweh into Jerusalem. Those who thronged the path believed they were taking part in a never-to-be-forgotten event–one they would tell to their children and grandchildren in years to come.

But the best of plans, like those conceived in the mind of General Bull Moose, can go wrong. There may be some neglect of God's will that results in chaos. As David watched, he saw Uzzah fall dead under the hand of the Most High. And others looked on in stunned amazement.

Those not at the scene would naturally have seen the procession stop. As word spread, the singing would fade, and one by one the lyres and flutes, harps, tambourines and castanets would become silent.

No one knew why Uzzah had died. The passages of Scripture dealing with the transportation of the Ark (like much of the Old Testament today) had not been studied since the people came into the land approximately four hundred and fifteen years earlier (1405 B.C.). They were deemed to be unimportant now that Israel's days of wandering were over. But no portion of God's Word is unimportant. As the apostle Paul pointed out in Romans 15:4,

> For whatever things were written previously, were written for our teaching (i.e., instruction), in order that through patience and through the comfort of the (*graphē*, sacred) writings we may have hope.

How, then, do we handle these setbacks, especially when everyone is watching?

> The failure is doubtless meant as a trial of our faith and humility; and if we wait on God for further light; if we beware of retiring in sullen silence from God's active service, and proudly resolving

to be done with such work for ever, good may come out of the apparent evil; the discipline of disappointment may issue in blessing.[21]

Fortunately, our story does not end on a negative note. David devises a way to bring the Ark of the Covenant up to Jerusalem.

A CONVOCATION THAT CULMINATES IN BLESSING (6:12-19)

During the next several weeks, David's mind must have turned time and again to the Ark and the empty tabernacle in Jerusalem. He may well have been occupied with affairs of state, and this may have prevented him from giving concentrated thought to the appropriate way of transporting the Ark. We may be sure that, after the unfortunate incident outside the threshing floor of Nachon, he thought often on why God had so abruptly shown His displeasure.

The truth may not have come to him immediately. Those who believe that Abiathar instructed him in the correct procedure for carrying the Ark must explain why he took so long to inform the king of the Lord's instructions. Most likely it took time for David to recall what Samuel had taught him. Slowly thoughts came together in his mind. He remembered that long years before he was born, God had instructed Moses and Aaron about the Ark. Then he recalled how it was carried in the desert. Only Levites were to bear this sacred vessel, and they were to do it by means of long poles (Exodus 25:12-14; 1 Chronicles 15:2). Could this be what God wanted him to do now?

The catalyst that motivated David to take the risk came one day when he was told "Yahweh has blessed the house of Obed-edom and all that belongs to him" (6:12*a*).

On hearing this, David responds promptly. He sets in motion the events that will result in the Ark being brought to Jerusalem.

Was he selfish? Did he want God's blessing for himself?

Selfish people have shriveled personalities. They want things for themselves because they believe that possessing them will make them happy. There is no evidence that David falls into this category. A preferable interpretation is to see David as desiring that all Israel be blessed. This view is borne out by verses 17-19. With the Ark in Jerusalem, Israel will once more benefit from having the Lord in their midst.

So David plans an impressive convocation. With "all Israel" assembled (i.e., as many as wish to come, out of all the cities and villages of the twelve tribes), he goes forth to bring the Ark to Jerusalem. He also arranges for the Levites to carry the Ark. As a sign of humility, he takes off his royal robe and places an ephod over his undergarments.[22] In addition, oxen are prepared for sacrifice. As soon as the bearers of the Ark have taken six paces the first of the sacrifices commences.

When the crowd realizes that no one has died under the hand of the Lord, a spirit of happy expectation ripples through the throng. This is heightened by the assurance that past sin has been atoned for, and they give vent to their gladness by dancing before the Ark.[23]

David, too, overflows with joy when he realizes God is not angry but pleased. He dances, leaping and whirling around, with all his might before the Ark. Far from seeing David as undignified, God is well-pleased with His servant's heartfelt praise.

As the procession nears Jerusalem, Michal, David's wife, looks out a window. She sees her husband's energetic dancing in the street and condemns him in her heart for such unkingly actions.

We are left to question what had happened to her over the years to cause her Godward relationship to atrophy to the point of being virtually nonexistent. And what had happened to her since coming to Hebron? Did David's godliness have no effect on her? She had been reunited with him virtually as his queen. In the eyes of the people, all that was needed was for her to bear David a son, and he would have been viewed by all as the successor to the throne of his father.

Alexander Whyte has some interesting comments on Michal's attitude and relationship with her husband.

> Had Michal done that day what any woman with any sense of decency left in her would have done—had she put on her royal garments and set out with David to the house of Obed-edom, how differently for her and for David that day would have ended! For, once on the ground; once surrounded with the assembled people, the magnificent scene would have carried [her] away.... No ambitious woman, and least of all Saul's royal-hearted daughter, could have seen assembled Israel that day without being swept into sympathy with [the people].
>
> But Michal lost her last opportunity that morning. Her proud and unsympathetic temper got the better of her...[She] was left alone with a heart the most miserable in all Israel. Her heart became harder and darker and fiercer as the day went on. Harder and darker and fiercer at David, and at all the ordinances and delights of that day.
>
> And when Jerusalem rang [as the Ark entered the city] Michal stole to her window and saw nothing but David dancing before the Lord. And she despised him in her heart.

As Dr. Whyte continues, he uses the teaching of the New Testament to highlight the importance of compatibility in the home.

> [Let] the wife see that she reverence her husband.... Reverence does not come at a divine command. [It] does not spring up in a day. [It] is the result of long teaching and long training. [It] has its roots in the heart and in the character; and the heart and the character only come and bring forth reverence as life goes on.
>
> [Paul] speaks to all wives, and he expects that all wives who hear it shall lay it to heart. And yet their husbands are in so many things so difficult, so impossible, to reverence. They fall so far short of their young wife's dreams and visions. They are so full of faults, and follies, and tempers, and habits to which no wife can possibly be blind.[24]

Scripture, in turn, calls upon husbands to love their wives, and requires that wives honor their husbands (Ephesians 5:1-2,22,24-25). David's enthusiasm is viewed by Michal with disdain. To her faithless eye, the Ark was little more than a chest of gold, and it seemed of little consequence where it was kept. Her affections were alienated from God and the glory of His presence. She could see none of the grace and love that had mastered her husband.[25] How tragic that, with all of the benefits of a godly spouse, Michal should persist in manifesting the traits that brought her father to an ignominious end.

We will comment further on Michal later in this chapter. For the present let us return to the story of the procession. Perhaps David had composed Psalm 24 in preparation for use on this occasion. If he had, then at a special place along the route the Levites would have begun their antiphonal singing. Everything has been carefully timed. The words of the psalm are worth noting. They must have filled all present with a holy awe.

> The earth [is] Yahweh's and the fullness of it;
> The world, and those who live in it.
>
> For He founded it upon the seas;
> and upon the rivers [He] established it.
>
> Who shall go up into the hill of Yahweh?
> And who shall stand in His holy place?
>
> The [one who is] of clean hands and [is]
> pure of heart;

who has not lifted up guile to his soul,
        and has not sworn in deceit.

He shall receive [the] blessing from Yahweh,
and righteousness from the God of his salvation.

This [is] the generation [of those who] seek Him,
who seek Your face, [O God] of Jacob.
                                                  Selah.

Lift up your heads, O gates;
and be lifted up, O everlasting doors;
and the King of glory shall come in.

Who [is] the King of glory?

Yahweh, strong and mighty!
Yahweh, mighty in battle!

Lift up your heads, O gates,
and [be] lifted up, O everlasting doors;
and the King of glory shall come in.

Who [is] the King of glory?

Yahweh [of] Hosts,
He [is] the King of glory.
                                                  Selah.

With the last strains of the psalm still lingering in the air, the Ark of the Covenant is placed in the tabernacle.[26] It has been a great day. God has been honored by His people's praise.

David then offers sacrifices of thanksgiving and dedication. This done, he turns and blesses the people. Happiness—the joy that comes from being right with God—fills every heart. But David will not let them leave empty-handed. He has arranged for cakes of bread, dates, and raisins to be given to every man and woman present. Then, feeling physically, emotionally, and spiritually refreshed, they all go to their homes.

David, too, is content. It is easy for us to imagine his feelings. Deep within his heart is a mingling of gratitude and satisfaction. Everything has gone according to plan. God's presence is once more in the midst of His people. And with his heart overflowing with thankfulness, he goes to bless his household.

CRITICISM THAT ECLIPSES GOD'S PRAISE (6:20-23)

If the Bible were the product of human authors, this chapter might well have omitted verse 16 and ended with "And David returned to bless his house." Period.

But because the Bible accurately portrays human life, we get to see that, even in King David's household, at least one person is out of sympathy with him. He had not seen Michal at the window of her quarters and so is unaware of her hostile reaction to his activities.

Significantly, the Biblical writer refers to Michal as the "daughter of Saul." This is designed to prepare us for what takes place as David enters the palace.[27] In contrast to David's heart, which is overflowing with praise to the Lord, hers is filled with enmity. She heaps scorn upon him. Her words are steeped in sarcasm.

> "How great was the king of Israel today, who was uncovered today before the eyes of the girl-slaves[28] [of] his servants, as openly as one of the vain ones uncovers himself" (6:20).

Rancor drips from her lips like poison from the fangs of an adder. She implies that the only distinction or honor he had gained was that of a male prostitute in Canaanite religious festivals or some shiftless and homeless individual who has lost all sense of modesty and relieves himself on a street corner. As Matthew Henry so accurately observed,

> Her contempt for [David] and his devotion began in her heart, and it was out of the abundance of her heart that her mouth spoke.[29]

In all probability Michal exaggerated David's supposed immodesty to serve the purpose of her scathing attack. She preferred to see him return home with the sweat and dust of battle, not stripped of his royal robes and worshiping a God no one could see.

David picks up on her nonverbal attitude–an imperiousness that he had perhaps witnessed in his child-bride in Saul's palace at Gibeah, but had now hardened into a calloused and supercilious demeanor–and he addresses this attitude rather than her words. He reminds her that her father became a rejected and dishonored king because he had disregarded and disparaged spiritual realities. He also reminds her that he had been chosen by God as her father's successor because of his devotion to the Lord. And far from looking down on the so-called slave girls in whose eyes he is held in the highest esteem, he values their sincere praise.[30] "And Michal the daughter of Saul had no child to the day of her death" (6:23).[31]

In this way the Lord, whose servant she had deprecated, caused her to be disgraced before David's household and all the people of Israel. He also brought to an end the royal line of Saul. Joyce Baldwin writes:

> In the context, Michal's childlessness implies that from this point on marital relations between her and David came to an end. The relationship between them had irrevocably broken down.[32]

Miss Baldwin has the support of rabbinic opinion.[33] Dr. John Mauchline, however, sees things differently. He believes that conjugal relations with Michal continued, but God deliberately withheld children from her.[34]

While we cannot draw any final conclusion (because Scripture is silent), we do know that the supreme desire of David's heart was to see God honored, and anything that detracted from His honor was lightly esteemed. It seems probable, therefore, that Michal remained in David's harem but without ever again being called to his bedroom.

Husband-wife strife is tragic, especially among those professing to know and follow Christ. Pearl S. Buck, in her book *The Exile*, tells of the differences that separated her parents. They were missionaries to China. Instead of resolving these tensions as believers should, they continued with their work, living together but drifting further and further apart.

> Alone together in the house, alone on the junks, alone plodding side by side through the dusty country roads or along the crowded cobbled streets of cities, there was no talk to be made between them.[35]

Who can measure the pain of such loneliness? God made us for togetherness.

Dr. Alexander Whyte concludes his sermon on David's and Michal's marriage, delivered before the congregation of Free St. George's Church, Edinburgh, Scotland, with the following observations:

Michal is a divine looking-glass for all angry and outspoken
wives…. To understand David and sing his psalms, you must
have come through David's experiences…. The truly noble, the
truly humble, and the terribly lonely man that he was, [he] took
up the taunt of his godless and heartless wife, and wore it as a
badge of honour before the Lord. Yes, he said, it will be as you
say. I will seek and I will find among the poorest and the most
despised of God's people that which my own married wife denies
me at home.

And who can tell how many husbands here are in David's
desolate case? Who can tell how many have to go out of their
own homes to find the finest sympathy and the completest rest
for their hearts? [Let] the wife see that her husband has not to
go abroad to find his best friend.[36]

Apparently, even in Dr. Whyte's day, a wife's caustic tongue could
make her husband feel so rejected that he would be vulnerable to
the first woman who would listen to him. Let wives beware, therefore, of the "creeping separateness" that eventually results in a situation as painful as the one experienced by David and Michal.

A TIMELY REMINDER

With all of our knowledge and sophistication, it is easy to think
we've learned–finally!–how to do the right thing in the right way. But
is this really true? David's experience in bringing the Ark up to Jerusalem illustrates the tragic consequences of doing the most praiseworthy of tasks in the energy and wisdom of the flesh. Whether in our
homes, places of business, or social contacts, we, too, can commit
similar errors.

If we are truly honest with ourselves, would we have to admit that
our attendance at a place of worship has become formal and per-
functory? Have we lost our "first love" for the Lord? Do we perform
our religious duties more out of obligation than delight? Are our
prayers fervent and sincere, or has there crept into our petitions
those repetitions that weary the ear of God?

We may be doing all the right things, but is the wonder of worshiping the Sovereign Lord of the universe missing? How then may we go
about recovering the reverential awe of God that those about His
throne have when they say:

You are worthy, O Lord,
To receive glory and honor and power;

> For You created all things,
> And by Your will they exist and were created
>   (Revelation 4:11).

Or the adoration of those in heaven who sing:

> Thrice holy is Yahweh of Hosts,
> The whole earth is full of His glory (Isaiah 6:3).

However lavish our churches may be, and however splendid the organ music and the choir anthems, when the wonder of God is lost, the soul becomes dry and unresponsive.[37]

One of the most prevalent issues I have seen in counseling couples has to do with the loving protection the husband is to give his wife. His goal is to make her feel secure, significant, and satisfied. Quite often, those having difficulty in this area will remind their wives of their God-given "headship."

But what does "headship" mean?[38] Does his wife feel loved and protected? Is her husband able to provide sufficiently for her so that she is relatively free from care? Or does a codependency situation exist that weakens the structure of the home rather than strengthen it?[39]

Similar problems may arise with the rearing of children. Children need to be loved and provided an environment that is conducive to their growth in all areas of life: personal, relational, physical, and spiritual.[40] Where this is lacking, no amount of cajoling or coercion will produce the desired results.

And what of our schools? We have the finest educational facilities of any country in the world. Why, then, do we graduate so many young people from high school who are functionally illiterate? In addition, what happened in the halls of academia a generation or two ago that resulted in values being omitted from the curriculum? And why is it that students in high school are allowed to intimidate their teachers so that these valued members of the community enter the classroom in fear?

As we consider our social relationships, do we try to build up those whom we meet, or do we assess a given situation to see how we might use it to our advantage? Are our friends and colleagues comfortable in our presence? Do they feel accepted, or is there a subtle play for power as we try to make them conform to our standards or ways of thinking? How well do we keep confidences, honor our word, and show kindness to others without expecting any acknowledgment or word of appreciation?[41]

When confronting the materialism that has so many of us in its grasp, do we find any truth in the statement of Epicurus, the Greek philosopher, that "To whom little is not enough nothing is enough"? How should we view our possessions?[42] And if contentment is not to be found in the comforts and conveniences of affluence, where is it to be sought (Ecclesiastes 3:11-13; 5:18-20; 8:15)?

Are the people whom we elect to govern us men and women of integrity?[43] Have those in office shown by their voting record and accomplishments that they are intent upon representing their constituency, or do they vote in line with the dictates of their party? Furthermore, to what extent do those holding office model for their followers truth, humility, and righteousness (cf. Psalm 45:6b-7a)? Or are they devious, arrogant, and unscrupulous?

Our hospitals rank among the best in the world, and many of them are outfitted with the latest and best equipment. Why, then, do so many nurses say that, after seeing some surgeons perform operations, they would never allow these doctors to operate on them? And why do so many physicians fear entrusting themselves to their colleagues during their final illness?

We could go on and on. To do so would be to belabor the point. The right things have been done in the wrong ways. Only as we follow God's Word can we honor the Lord and do those things that are pleasing in His sight.

SIDELIGHTS ON GOD'S CHARACTER

2 Samuel 7:1-29

A convention of distinguished churchmen was being held in Boston, and the accommodations offered by the local diocese had all been assigned. At the last minute, a bishop was able to clear his schedule and fly to the city to attend the meetings. His plane arrived late at night, so he booked himself into a hotel, leaving a wake-up call for 6:00 a.m. the next morning.

The hotel staff was so impressed that a *bishop* had decided to stay with them that they immediately brushed up on their etiquette. They also woke the manager and told of their distinguished guest. He rose early to insure that the church dignitary would receive every courtesy.

During the early hours of the morning, a severe thunderstorm swept across the city causing a power-outage. Even the telephones were down.

Realizing that it would soon be time to waken his lordship, the manager called the bellhop and instructed him to knock firmly on the bishop's door and then say politely, "It's the boy, my lord. It's time to get up."

The bellhop had never done anything like this before and was over-awed at the thought that he could be of service to a bishop. He paced the lobby with an eye on his watch and carefully rehearsed his lines. A waitress he cared for happened to come in a minute or two before 6:00 a.m. Before hurrying to the restaurant and the candle-lit tables, she asked the bellhop if he would tie the bow of her apron. He happily obliged, and they exchanged a few endearing comments. As she left, he watched her walk across the lobby and did not take his eyes off her until the restaurant door swung closed behind her.

This tete-a-tete had not taken long, but when the bellhop looked at his watch again it was 6:04. He rushed up the three flights of stairs, charged down the passage and skidded to a stop in front of the door to the bishop's suite. Flustered and breathless he pounded on the door and yelled, "It's the Lord, my boy. Your time is up!"

SOME ERRONEOUS VIEWS OF GOD

Many people view God this way. They see Him as a killjoy who constantly interrupts their pleasures and summons them to some task they would rather not perform.[1] To others, God (at least initially) is supposed to be the heavenly counterpart of Western Union. They pray and expect Him to rush to do their bidding. Whatever their need, He is supposed to be there to supply it. And Bible verses, often taken out of context, appear to guarantee His help. Rabbi Harold Kushner, in *Why Do Bad Things Happen to Good People?* has offered a slight variation on this theme. He states that the Jewish people have been taught to address God as "Father," but in their expectations they want Him to act more as a heavenly Grandfather.

But faulty concepts of God create false expectations. A young man I counseled some years ago had asked God for a car. To make sure he would get one, he claimed all the verses he had heard his pastor use while exhorting his congregation to trust the Lord. When the car did not come in the specified period of time, he concluded that God was not trustworthy. He rebelled, refusing to go to Sunday school and church with his parents and sisters, and he quickly turned his back on everything his parents had taught him.

Our felt needs often drive us to our knees. Charles Swindoll, radio pastor of *Insight for Living,* tells of a woman who had listened diligently to a series of sermons he had delivered on faith. She decided to put his words to the test. Feeling unloved and alone, and desperately wanting the comfort and security of a husband and a home, she bought a pair of men's slacks and hung them between the posts at the foot of her bed. Her prayers night and morning were for the Lord to put a man in them.

At the opposite end of the spectrum are people who think of God as an impersonal Creator, far removed from the reality of their situation. He may be transcendent[2] (as theologians teach), but He is not immanent[3] in their experience. This was in part the view of Jean-Paul Sartre. He wrote:

> Man can count on no one but himself; he is alone, abandoned on earth in the midst of infinite responsibilities, without help, with no other aim than the one he sets himself, with no other destiny than the one he forges for himself on earth.[4]

To such people, God and His Word may be likened to some of the professors they had in college. The professor(s) seemed distant and disinterested in those who had signed up for the course. Their class notes, like the Bible, contained some good information, but the data was perceived as dry and irrelevant. Much emphasis was placed upon content, but nothing nourished the soul.

Still others have developed a view of God based on popular assumptions or choruses they've heard. They see God in one of two roles: (1) a heavenly "Magician" who always works through signs and wonders, or (2) the Person they can turn to in trouble, who will always solve their problems. To the former, supposed manifestations of power in church services or special meetings indicate the Lord's presence, and their absence supposedly indicates His absence. To the latter, their theology is encapsulated in the following song:

> The Master can solve every problem,
> The tangles of life can undo;
> There's nothing too hard for Jesus,
> There's nothing that He cannot do.

But what happens if the sovereign Lord of all the universe chooses *not* to work through signs and wonders or does not solve all of one's problems even when His children have asked Him repeatedly? Is their theology sufficiently well-tuned to enable them to *endure, as seeing Him who is invisible*? (cf. Hebrews 11:27 AV).

To rightly understand the nature of God, we need to distinguish truth from error, discern the dangers inherent in half-truths, and formulate a view of Him based on *all* that is taught in Scripture (i.e., the whole counsel of God, Acts 20:27. See also John 8:32; 17:17b). In this regard, what is revealed in 2 Samuel 7 may contain some surprises for us.

STRUCTURE AND OUTLINE OF THE PASSAGE

In this chapter we come to the third division, and *the* climactic chapter of 2 Samuel. The key that alerts us to the fact that we are entering a new phase of the Biblical writer's theme lies in the words, "Now it came to pass..." (7:1a).

This statement, as we have seen in earlier divisions, is the writer's method of indicating a new section. Previously, we saw God sovereignly remove Saul from the throne thus making way for David to become king over His people (1:1-27). Then we noted how His sovereignty was exercised in establishing the kingdom under David

(2:1–6:23). Now we need to pay attention to the circumstances under which David was assured of a continuing dynasty.

When God instituted the Abrahamic Covenant[5] in Genesis 12:1-3, He promised Abraham three things: (1) a *land* as an inheritance, (2) an enduring *seed* who would live in the land, and (3) personal, national, and universal *blessing*.

The *land* part of the covenant was later elaborated on in Deuteronomy 29:1–30:20, in what has come to be known as the Palestinian Covenant.[6] Now, in 2 Samuel 7, we have fresh revelation about the second part of the Abrahamic Covenant, the *seed* portion of the promise.[7] In this chapter, therefore, we see

GOD SOVEREIGNLY INSTITUTING THE DAVIDIC COVENANT (7:1-29).

The chapter may be outlined as follows:

- The Introduction (7:1-3)

- The Revelation of God (7:4-17)
    The Temple of the Lord (7:4-11*a*)
    The Tabernacle of David (7:11*b*-17)

- The Response of His Servant (7:18-29)

The passage begins with an expression of David's sincere desire to build a house (i.e., Temple) for the Lord, followed by Nathan's[8] hearty endorsement of his plan (7:1-3). That night, however, God reveals to Nathan that David is not to build a temple for Him (7:4-7).

Lying latent in these verses is a clear picture of what God is really like. In declining David's offer, He begins by affirming him (note the words "*My servant*" in verses 5*a* and 8*a*). He then corrects him by asking questions (7:5*b*,7). At no time does David feel belittled, demeaned, or rejected.

God's sovereignty is emphasized in statements like "I took you..." in verses 8-14. His immanence is found in His involvement with His people (delivering them from Egypt, accompanying them through the desert in a tabernacle, etc., and leading, caring for, and helping David from his youth to the present hour). His transcendence is hinted at in the title "Yahweh of Hosts" (7:8*a*).

In 7:11*b*-17 Yahweh institutes a special covenant with His servant, promising him that his dynasty will never be replaced. In spite of the clarity of the Biblical narrative, some theologians deny that God entered into a covenant with David.[9] Others, who accept the idea of a covenant, reject the thought that these verses imply an everlasting dynasty. The former point out that the word *covenant* is not found in this passage, while the latter claim that the promises of God to David were fulfilled during the reign of Solomon.[10]

The teaching of Psalms 89:3,20-37 and 132:12 would seem to answer the former charge. And passages of Scripture such as Luke 1:32-33 and Acts 15:16-18 (that came centuries *after* the time of Solomon) would seem to satisfy those who are in doubt about the eternality of God's promise to David (see also Amos 9:11; Isaiah 11:1-9; Jeremiah 23:5 that also were written after the reign of Solomon).

David's response to God's revelation (7:18-29) shows his understanding of what has been communicated to him. His words reveal a humble familiarity with the Lord of Hosts that is astonishing. In his attitude and response he sets before us the goal of true devotion.

THE INTRODUCTION (7:1-3)

This chapter follows closely the theme of chapter 6, even though it may have been separated from the events recorded there by several years. In chapter 6 we saw the Ark of the Covenant being brought up to Jerusalem. Now, with Israel's enemies defeated (and for the present lacking the strength to renew their aggressive behavior), David's thoughts again turn to the Lord. In fact, his opening words seem to echo Moses' charge to the sons of Israel when they were camped on the banks of the River Jordan (see Deuteronomy 12:10-11), and it is possible that he had been meditating upon this portion of sacred Scripture.

From what follows, it is clear that David's heart is full of gratitude to God for the victories He has given him. Being generous by nature, David thinks now of what he can do for the Lord. The contrast between his munificent palace and the resting place of the Ark is sufficient to suggest to him the possibility of building a Temple for the One who has helped him in ways too numerous and too remarkable to mention. Possibly at a banquet held in the palace, with Nathan as an honored guest, the king makes a suggestion: "See now, I am living in a house [of] cedar, but the Ark of God dwells within a tent-curtain"[11] (7:2).

As David reveals more of his desire to build a Temple for the Lord, Nathan, seeing nothing in the king's plan that conflicts with God's revealed will, encourages him to proceed. His response is a wholehearted endorsement of David's plan: "All that is in your heart, go and do, for Yahweh is with you" (7:3).

The evening comes to a happy conclusion, and with the festivities over, the guests depart. Nathan, too, leaves the palace and goes home to a rustic bed and a good night's rest. David also retires, but in all probability he does not sleep. In his mind he begins planning the Temple.

THE REVELATION OF GOD (7:4-17)

The Temple of the Lord (7:4-11a)

Nathan is possibly in a sound asleep when the Lord speaks to him.

> "Go, to My servant, to David, and you shall say: 'Thus says Yahweh, "Will you build Me a house for a dwelling? For I have not dwelt in a house since the day I brought up the sons of Israel from Egypt, even to this day, but I have been moving about in a tent, even in a tabernacle. In all [places] [where] I have gone with all the sons of Israel, [have] I spoken a word with one of the tribes[12] of Israel that I commanded to feed, to shepherd, My people, Israel, saying, "Why have you not built Me a house of cedars?"'"" (7:5-7).

In Hebrew, a writer may emphasize his point in a number of different ways. For example, he may place words he wishes to stress first in the sentence, or at the very end. Or he may repeat phrases. And then there are times when he may use a personal pronoun when one is already a part of the verb. Such a device would not sound right to western ears, but to an easterner it would convey clearly and accurately the thought of the speaker. In the present passage, the following emphatic statements should be noted.

First, "Go and say to...David," implying urgency.

Second, the repetition of the words "My servant" (7:5, 8) underscoring David's favorable standing before the Lord.

Third, the use of emphatic pronouns that stress God's sovereignty. In verses 6 through 14 we note. for example, the frequency of God's use of the personal pronoun *I*:

> "*I* have not dwelt in a house...*I* brought the children of Israel up from Egypt...*I* have moved about...*I* have walked...Did *I* ever speak...*I* took you...*I* have been with you...*I* have made you a great name...*I* will appoint...*I* will set up your seed...*I* will establish his kingdom...*I* will be his Father...*I* will chasten him...."

While the subtleties of Hebrew syntax may be intriguing, we must not loose sight of the way in which God is saying no to His servant. David is not to build the Temple. And this is the message that Nathan takes to David.

In all probability he has to knock loudly on the door of David's palace so as to rouse the sentry. Only when the captain of David's bodyguard is thoroughly persuaded of the urgency of Nathan's visit does he go to inform the king. David, we assume, is still awake. Rising, he pulls on a long robe and goes to his council chamber, where he receives the prophet. And there Nathan dutifully relates to him everything the Lord has said to him.

Note again where God begins. It is with affirmation: "Go...say to *My servant....*"

To be called the "servant of God" is to receive the highest accolade known to people on earth. If David had been seeking honor for himself, he might very well have felt slighted or rejected at being told that he cannot build the Temple. But God says no to him so graciously that he is scarcely aware of being turned down.

But let us not pass from verses 5 and 6 too hurriedly. Further evidence of God's character is found in the way He declines David's offer. He does so by asking questions. He first asks if David is the one to build Him a Temple (7:5). Then He asks if a house for Him to live in is really necessary (7:7). He had not complained of His Tabernacle[13] from the day He brought the sons of Israel out of Egypt, nor had He reproved any of the tribes for not building Him a Temple. By phrasing His refusal in the form of questions, He causes David to reason his way through the issues. As David does so, he begins to think God's thoughts after Him. He then comes to realize that the Lord has something far more significant in mind.

In God's manner of dealing with David, we learn an important fact about Him. He declined David's offer to build the Temple in a context of unconditional love and acceptance. He also affirmed David's worth, and then reminded him of the ways in which He had been with him from his earliest years right up to the present. Instead of feeling slighted or unappreciated, David feels secure in his relationship with the Lord.

In speaking of David's dynasty, God shows Himself knowledgeable of David's fears. The dynasties of his day were precarious at best. Horrible tragedies were often perpetrated on the family of a deceased or deposed monarch. Claimants to the throne were killed without mercy. From these atrocities the Lord promises to spare David and his house.

The Temple though is not forgotten. Unlike some items that today are tabled or become lost "in committee," God says that David's son will build the Temple. Furthermore, Yahweh will enter into a distinct Father-son relationship with him. If he falls into sin, he will be chastened but not destroyed. God's mercy will not depart from him or his house as it did from Saul.

Verses 11*b*-17 do not exhaust the Lord's *ḥesed*,[14] "loving-kindness." In them Yahweh gives David assurance of His continued favor toward him. Furthermore, as Nathan tells the king, word for word, what the Lord has spoken, David comes to understand the magnitude of God's promise. Note verse 16:

> "And your house [shall be] sure (i.e., established), and your kingdom to the ages (i.e., forever) before Me; your throne shall [also] be established to the ages (i.e., forever)."[15]

But how are we to interpret the promise of God to David when Israel's king was removed from his throne in 586 B.C. and the people deported to Babylon?

The idea of a deportation was not something God had failed to foresee. The Almighty was not taken by surprise when Israel's sins required that the nation be punished. It had been a part of the warning the Lord had given His people through Moses centuries before (see Deuteronomy 29:27-28; 30:1-5).

From Matthew 1:1-18 and Luke 3:23-38, we know that accurate genealogical records were kept in the Temple, as well as by different families. Throughout the centuries the line of David was preserved. There had always been someone who could have ascended the throne. Both Joseph and Mary were direct descendants of King David. That was why they had to register in Bethlehem at the time of the census, for they were "of the house and lineage (i.e., descent) of David" (Luke 2:5). And that is why Christ was born in Bethlehem.

Nine months earlier Gabriel had announced to Mary,

> "You shall conceive and give birth to a son, and you will give Him the name Jesus. *He shall be great, and will be called the Son of the Most High. The Lord God will give Him the throne of His ancestor David, and He will be king over Israel for ever; His reign will never end*" (Luke 1:30-33, emphasis added).

The centuries that elapsed without a king sitting on David's throne did not annul God's covenant. His promise was sure. What He promised three millennia ago will one day be fulfilled when Christ will sit on David's throne and rule over the kingdoms of the world.

But how does all this affect our view of God?

If He is the same yesterday, today, and forever (Hebrews 13:8), then we may expect Him to be faithful to His Word. Far from being a harsh, uncaring deity, we find He is full of lovingkindness and faithfulness (see Psalm 86:1-13). While modern caricatures of Him may imply that He delights in stopping us from having fun, in reality He has our best interests at heart. He does not deal with us as our sins deserve but always in terms of His grace.

As we take another look at verses 11*b* through 17, we find that they give us a remarkable picture of God. He is not limited by time as we are. He is also loving and kind. His words show His unconditional acceptance of David, His watchful and tender care for him, and His plans for David's future. While His servant's proposal is turned aside, it is not denied.

It must have been with great gratitude and awe that David learned of God's gracious plans for him and his descendants. His dynasty would be a stable one. And the news that his son, still to come from his loins (1 Chronicles 17:11), would build Yahweh's Temple clearly showed that the Lord had sovereignly set aside the law of primogeniture.

THE RESPONSE OF HIS SERVANT (7:18-29)

On hearing all this, David does not question the veracity of Nathan's words. He accepts them as coming from the Lord. He requires no further confirmation of God's will. Yet he is overwhelmed at the magnitude of the Lord's promise. His emotions tumble over one another as they seek expression. There is thankfulness, delight, gratitude, and praise. God has granted him the unspoken request of his heart (cf. Psalm 37:4) and has done so in ways that far exceeded his fondest dreams.

And the Lord still delights to honor those who serve Him. Often we take a negative response from Him in ways He never intended. We then blindly ignore His numerous blessings that He continues to lavish upon us.

Leaving his council room, David walks through the darkened streets of Jerusalem to the place where he had erected the tent that was to serve as a temporary shelter for the Ark of the Covenant. A group of soldiers assigned to guard him follow at a respectful distance. And perhaps Nathan does too.

On coming to the place where the Ark is, David enters the outer court. Those who have accompanied the king wait outside.

Inside, David sits before the Lord. This is the only instance in Scripture in which a person sat before the Lord and prayed to Him. Yet

David's attitude is not one of familiarity having bred contempt. He is too filled with wonder, love, and praise for such impure or selfish motives. And in this position he pours out his gratitude to God for what He has already done and is still to do. "Who [am] I, O Lord God, and what [is] my house...?" (7:18*a*).

The question is rhetorical. David remembers that he has come from one of the smallest villages of Judah and is the youngest in his father's household. His birth and place of origin are sufficient to cause him to live his entire life in obscurity. Certainly none who were present when he was named would ever have thought that he would one day sit upon the throne of Israel!

He then expresses astonishment at the accumulated evidence of God's past goodness to him: "You have brought me to here (i.e., thus far, to this place)" (7:18*b*).

Through all his formative years–his service as a lowly shepherd, his brief association with the court of Saul, his flight from the king and years as a fugitive–God had been with him. And throughout this period he had come to know the protection and guidance of the Lord of Hosts. All of this is now recalled as God's words through Nathan trigger a kaleidoscope of memories.

But as the realization of God's covenant with him sinks in and is processed through his mind, David gives expression to further praise. The Lord is infinitely more precious to him than all the benefits of a throne and a kingdom. And those who have experienced similar blessings can echo the words of the psalmist:

> Whom [is] there to me (i.e., whom have I) in heaven?
> And besides You I do not desire [anyone] on earth.
> My flesh and my heart waste away;
> God [is] the rock of my heart forever.
> For behold, those [who are] far from You shall perish;
> You have cut off all who go whoring from You.
> As for me (lit. And I), the nearness of God to me [is] my good;
> I have made my refuge in the Lord Yahweh,
> To declare all Your works (Psalm 73:25-28).

Following his expression of wonderment, David contemplates in rapt awe the future:

> "And yet [this] was but little in Your eyes, O Lord Yahweh; for You have spoken also to Your servant of [his (lit. the)] house concerning the future; and this [is] [according to] the law of man, O Lord Yahweh" (7:19).

David marvels at God's condescension. The Lord has accommo-
dated Himself to His servant's perceptions and used a human vehicle (namely, a covenant) to communicate to David what He is about
to do. This heightens David's astonishment, and all he can do is con-
template the outworking of God's plan.

In worship, genuine spiritual sentiments are pervaded with elements of holy awe. In David's experience, what has been revealed to
him evokes intense adoration and gratitude. He continues his praise:

> "And what more can David say to You?...Because of Your word,
> and according to Your heart You have done all this greatness....
> Therefore...O Yahweh God, there is no god except You.... And
> who [is] like Your people, like Israel, one nation in the earth
> that God went to redeem (from Egypt) for Him[self] for a people,
> and to make for Himself a name" (7:20-23).

This reverent recounting of God's past goodness further gener-
ates confidence in the Lord. He does not doubt God's willingness to
perform what He has promised. He shows his acceptance of His words
by saying,

> "And now, O Yahweh God, establish the word You spoke about
> to Your servant...And may Your name be great forever...And
> now, let it please You, and bless the house of Your servant, to
> be forever before You..." (7:25-26, 29).

This is a most appropriate ending to a most remarkable prayer.

INTIMACY WITH GOD

The most impacting image we take with us from this chapter is of
David sitting before the Lord. In childlike trust, he poured out his
heart to the One who was sitting enthroned above the cherubim.

David's attitude was the exact opposite of that of a young man I
met while taking studies in library science at a Roman Catholic college in Illinois. Suspecting that I was not a Catholic, he began the
discussion somewhat defensively: "I am a Catholic, but all I know is
that there is or was a supreme being, and for me he is either (1) a big
clown, or (2) is someone who likes to pick on me, or (3) he went on
vacation and has not come back."

We had a most interesting talk. At the end of it he had begun to
realize that you cannot have a relationship with Someone you don't
know.

The Bible mentions a variety of people who had a personal knowledge of God and a relationship with Him similar to David's. They found Him to be sufficient for their every need. Abraham, for example, was a man of faith. The writer of Hebrews records that he went out from his homeland to a place he knew not. His pilgrimage, however, was a spiritual one, for he was looking for a city whose Builder and Maker is none other than God Himself (see Hebrews 11:8-10).

Deborah lived at a time when her people were oppressed by a powerful ruler. She gave encouragement to all who came to her. On one occasion she stirred up the faith of Barak, Israel's general. Her vision of what God was going to do was so clear to her that she told him of the results before the battle took place. This spurred him on to fulfill in actual fact what the Lord had revealed to her (Judges 4:4-7,14).

Ruth was a proselyte. She came to "trust under Yahweh's wings," and the Lord fully compensated her for her faith in Him (see Ruth 2:11-12).

Samuel, as a young lad, heard God calling him, and it is recorded of him that "he let none of His words fail" (i.e., slip from his mind. See 1 Samuel 3:4-9,19-21).

And so we could go on. The question facing each one of us is, How may we experience God in this way? What must I do to have a relationship with the Lord that enables me to worship Him as David did, in a free and uninhibited manner?

For our encouragement, and before someone comes along and tells us that such intimacy was only for people living in Bible times (and perhaps a few other men and women of God who have been specially called to such a privilege), let us look at Psalm 15. There we read:

> O Yahweh, who shall sojourn in Your Tabernacle?
> Who shall settle in Your holy mountain?
>> He who walks uprightly and works righteousness,
>> And speaks the truth in his heart.
> He does not vilify (or backbite) with his tongue,
> He does not do evil to his friend;
> And [he] does not lift up a reproach against his neighbor.
>> In his eyes the reprobate has been despised,
>> But those who fear Yahweh he honors.
> He has sworn to his hurt, and will not change it.
> His money he did not give at interest;
>> Nor has he taken a bribe against the innocent;
>> He who does these things shall not be shaken forever
>>   (Psalm 15:1-5).

Dr. James I Packer, in his book *Knowing God*, tells of walking one day with a friend who had clashed with some high-ranking officials of his denomination. As a consequence, his hopes of advancement had been effectively smashed on the rocks of ecclesiastical polity. In responding to Jim Packer's words of encouragement, he said: "But it doesn't matter, for I've known God and they haven't."[16]

What does it mean to truly *know God*?

All of us know that it is possible to have grown up in the church, perhaps to have gone to a Christian college and even a seminary, and yet not really know God. Many know a great deal about Him without really knowing Him. And it is also possible for us to have read all the Christian classics that speak of devotion to the Lord and not be able to translate the principles of these books into practice. How, then, may we worship in sincerity and truth as David did?

Certain progressive steps we can all take will eventually lead us into a deeper understanding of, and an enriched fellowship with the Most High.

The Importance of Meditation

First, we need to spend time meditating on the things that God has chosen to reveal to us in His Word, the Bible. I know that many programs are available whereby a person can read the entire Bible through in a year, or three years, or five. Such programs are *not* what I have in mind.

David, as a shepherd, spent time each evening meditating on the things Samuel had taught him. He wisely took these truths and developed them into themes, much the same way we can link Scripture with Scripture to enhance our understanding of a specific facet of Biblical truth. David then used his creativity and further developed these themes into psalms, which were later set to music. Such an exercise took time, concentration, creativity, and effort. His beautiful poems were the result of long meditation. And all the while he was growing in fellowship with the Lord and in a true knowledge of Him.

David continued this same practice during his wilderness years and even after he became king. Meditation on God's revealed truth was his first duty in the morning as well as his last thought at the end of a day (see Psalms 1:2; 16:7; 42:8; 55:17; 57:8-9; 63:6. See also Psalms 77:6; 119:147-48).

Mere Bible reading in and of itself is insufficient. We need to become "rooted and grounded" in the truth (Colossians 2:6-7) if we are to order our way aright (see also Jude 20-21).

The Value of Praise

Second, we need to expand our awareness of what the Bible reveals of God Himself. A careful reading of David's psalms, perhaps highlighting statements that have to do with God's activities or attributes, will certainly place us on the right track and help toward the achieving of our goal.

As we persevere with our thoughtful reading of Scripture, the Lord's ways will gradually become more evident to us. We will also see more clearly His wisdom and power, the uniqueness of the life He gives to every living thing, and come progressively to know how to regulate our lives according to His Word.

In addition, we will find that He is sovereign over all our trials and difficulties. He may not remove the test from us, but He has promised to give us the grace to endure them (1 Corinthians 10:13). We will also come to see in renewed perspective how the grace He gives not only helps us endure the trial(s) but also works in us to test and strengthen us, and to progressively conform us to the image of Christ (2 Corinthians 3:18). And when this happens, we should give Him the praise (Psalm 50:23. See also Psalms 22:22-23; 33:1; 67:3; 109:1; 113:1; 146:1; 147:1; etc.). Praise is an important part of any relationship.

The story of Katelyn, a woman whom I counseled, illustrates this point.

Katelyn came to me following a service one Sunday morning. Her marriage was in a shambles, and she was seriously thinking of leaving Jeremy, her husband. The description she gave of him was not flattering. We talked for a time and then parted. I was scheduled to preach for four weeks while her pastor was on vacation, so I saw her again.

An incidental thought from one of my messages set Katelyn thinking. Instead of constantly criticizing Jeremy, she decided to start thanking God for him. She began by writing down his good qualities. The list wasn't long. Then she added to it as she thought of new traits or abilities. She then thanked the Lord daily for the man He had given her. As she did so, and without her realizing it, she began to undergo a change. And Jeremy noticed (even though he knew nothing of what she had done), and he began responding positively to her. The results were amazing. On my last Sunday there, Katelyn came to me and told of what had happened. Love had been reborn in their relationship and a new day had begun to dawn.

If this is true on the human level, imagine the potential when we begin to thank the Lord for all His goodness to us. The change in us will be surprising, and those about us will notice the difference!

The Cultivation of a Relationship

Third, we often overlook the fact that God wants a relationship with us. He has offered each one of us individual salvation–the free pardon of our iniquities, cleansing from all defilement, and eternal life–if we will only accept by faith the Lord Jesus Christ as our Savior.

His blessings, however, do not end with our salvation. The relationship He wants us to enter into gives us a unique sense of *belonging*. We are now members of His family. We call Him "Father." In the apostle Paul's terminology, we are given the adoption of sons[17] (i.e., we have a standing before Him equal to that of any other mature man or woman of God). We also have access into His presence. He is never too busy to listen to us.

His unconditional acceptance of us makes possible the cultivation of a uniquely intimate relationship with Him. He knows all about us and we can be transparently honest before Him.

This relationship also gives us a unique sense of *worth*. As we consider the price Christ paid for our salvation, we come to appreciate how valuable we are to God (see 1 Peter 1:18). And then, as if that were not enough, we find that He has made us joint heirs with Christ of all the glories of His Kingdom (Romans 8:17).

Our worth no longer depends on what others think or some hard-to-please person's conditional acceptance of us. We know of God's love for us by what He has done for us. We are accepted by Him "in the Beloved" (Colossians 1:13). Our forgiveness, based on the blood of Christ, has also freed us from guilt and shame and the weight of our past sins. And the burden of performance–of proving we are somehow worthy of His love and favor–has forever been lifted from us.

In addition, the Lord has given us the Holy Spirit to empower us. In a word, He enables us or makes us *competent* to handle all the vicissitudes of life. The Holy Spirit also helps us pray, and He works through us so that we can do in His power what we could not do in our own wisdom or strength. He also leads us and gives us discernment so that we can distinguish truth from error. We may not always be "successful" (as the world defines success), but through His indwelling He makes us competent to handle whatever comes our way.

David did not attain to the kind of intimacy with God we find described in this chapter overnight. It was a long process. In 2 Samuel 7, we see the results.

In a book edited by John Woodbridge titled *Renewing Your Mind in a Secular Age*, Dr. Paul Meier describes the process of spiritual growth. After testing seminarians in several different institutions he was able to divide them into three groups: Group A were those with above average mental/emotional health; Group B had average mental/emotional health; and Group C was for those with significant mental/emotional problems.

Dr. Meier found that the one thing which made it possible for a person to move from Group C to Group B and then to Group A was his or her daily meditation upon some portion of Scripture. The books of the Bible are meant to be read from beginning to end, not dipped into and verses lifted out of context to meet some emergency. Paul Meier found that the process of change from one group to the next took about three years.[18]

God, in giving us His Word, has provided the resource needed to improve the quality of our lives. David sets before us the goal of what we may become.

BE STRONG IN THE LORD

2 Samuel 8:1-18

Several years ago some friends from out of state came to visit my wife and me. Wanting to give them a good time, we asked where they would like to go and what they would like to see: "Disneyland? Knott's Berry Farm? Arrowhead or Big Bear Lakes? Laguna or Malibu beaches?"

Top of their list was Universal Studios.

So early one Saturday morning we set out for Universal City and the famous lot where some notable movies have been made. Our guide explained the essence of "flim-flam" (i.e., the use of illusion in making films) and how certain special effects are created.

This knowledge came in handy on the tour when we got caught in the kind of sudden cloudburst seen in movies (we were in a bus, so we did not get wet), watched a flash flood, witnessed a scene from *Battlestar Galactica*, attempted to cross a bridge only to be startled by a thirty foot King Kong who shook it violently, and participated in an 8.3 earthquake while in a subway train station. Later on, as the tour was nearing its end, we passed through the section of the lot where *The Ten Commandments* had been filmed. The waters "parted" to mimic what happened at the time of the Exodus, but while our attention was distracted those to the rear of the bus were startled as the great white shark from *Jaws* came up out of the water behind them and scared them out of their seats and into the aisle.

That tour enabled us to peer behind the scenes of movies and see what gives them their sense of reality.

In contrast to the illusionary world of films, the Bible deals with truths that are often stranger than fiction. In a few instances, it permits us to observe what takes place behind the events of history. On these rare occasions, the veil of time parts and we glimpse a different dimension of reality that otherwise could not be known.

One example of this is found in Daniel 10. Daniel had been praying about a matter for three weeks (Daniel 10:12-14) and, as with us, he was perplexed when his prayer was not answered. Unknown to him, however, was the fact that a spiritual battle had been taking place. God's angelic messenger had been sent as soon as Daniel had begun to pray but he had been prevented from fulfilling his mission by the "prince of the kingdom of Persia." (That this "prince" was a fallen angelic being in the service of Satan becomes evident from what follows.)

The struggle between these two angels—the one good and the other evil—continued uninterrupted for three weeks. It was ended only when the archangel Michael came to the aid of God's messenger (Daniel 10:21; 12:1. cf. Hebrews 1:14; Jude 1:9; Revelation 12:7). Only then was the good angel able to go on his way and meet with Daniel.

When we link this reference with other passages of Scripture like Isaiah 24:21 and 46:1-2 (Bel and Nebo were Babylonian gods); Jeremiah 46:25 and 49:3; Psalm 96:4; and in the non-canonical books of the Apocrypha, Baruch 4:7 and Ecclesiasticus 17:17, we realize that "guardian angels" stand watch over countries as well as individuals (Matthew 18:10). And Satan has mimicked God's plan by appointing powerful archfiends to control, as far as possible, different parts of the world. These demonic beings foment wars and oppose all that is good.[1]

Perhaps this explains what we read about in 2 Samuel 8. God had entered into a covenant with David (ch. 7), promising him an enduring dynasty. This hope was bound up in David and a son who had not yet been born. If David should be killed, then God's promise could not be fulfilled.

From a historical point of view, God's covenant had no sooner been set in motion than kingdoms formerly subdued by David, or else neutral toward Israel, began attacking God's people without provocation (cf. Psalm 83:3-8). They came from all points of the compass. Their rapid rise and concerted efforts seem to indicate that they had been stirred up by some malignant force.

Because such Satanic or demonic activity takes place beyond the realm of our senses, it is easy for us to conclude that it does not exist. From the rare glimpses afforded us in Scripture, however, it is plain that behind the political and social conditions of the world there are angels—good and evil—each with a mission to fulfill. Although we are often ignorant of their work, their activities have a direct bearing on what takes place upon earth.

The much-loved and highly respected Bible teacher, Dr. Ray C. Stedman, has written about our struggle:

In a very real sense those of us who believe in the Lord Jesus Christ are engaged in a battle. But the forces we face are not clothed in flesh; they are not human agencies. Rather, they are the deadly pantheon of spiritual hosts of wickedness, invisible and dedicated to our destruction.

These forces are under the authority of the one who is the Father of lies, the prince of darkness, the Devil himself. Only by recognizing him as real, as the Scriptures clearly declare, can we begin to understand the meaning of life as it really is. Only then can we comprehend the vital necessity of putting on the whole armor of God which, far from being a figure of speech, is, in fact, Christ himself, as he is to us.[2]

But there is need for caution. In applying Biblical truth to life, it is important for us not to go to extremes. As a counselor, I am frequently confronted by people who see in every ache and pain and illness evidence of demonic activity. And pity the poor individual who is afflicted with a bipolar mental disorder or suffering the aftermath of child abuse or experiencing postpartum depression or some other physiological or psychological condition. These hurting people are subjected to exorcisms and a variety of embarrassing rituals. And when these fail to cure the problem, they are thrust out by their would-be helpers as lacking faith or harboring sin in their heart on account of which the Holy Spirit cannot heal their infirmity.[3]

Not every misfortune emanates from the demonic realm. But those that do need to be discerned and treated as such, and it seems as if the sudden onslaught of enemy attacks that we read about in this chapter falls into this category.

BACKGROUND

Though the record of David's battles is easily told, the link between chapters 8 and 9 is not so easily recognized. The opening statement of 9:1 appears strange and seemingly out of place. There is no reasonable cause to explain why David would suddenly desire to show the kindness of God to the house of Saul. Most scholars agree, therefore, that the unhappy events of 21:1-14 took place during the events of chapter 8 and *prior* to David's desire to know if there were any survivors of Saul's household. If this is so, then it means that during these wars David and the people of Israel also had to contend with a famine that grew in severity with each passing year (21:1*a*).

Famines seldom herald their arrival (an exception being a plague of locusts).[4] They most often result from drought. In the beginning, the famine is almost imperceptible. The wise scan the sky for a sign of rain, shake their heads, and tighten their belts. Only after a period of time are the effects of a prolonged drought both seen and felt. And even then farmers still hope that things will be better next year.

Whatever the cause of the famine, the nations that rose against Israel seem to have assessed the situation well. They attacked at the very time when Israel was being weakened internally. Their military strategy also seems to have had as its goal the closing of trade routes.[5] These included "The Way of the Sea" from Egypt through Philistia; "The King's Highway" from the Gulf of Aqaba north through Edom and Ammon; and the main highway from the Tigris/Euphrates valley south through Tadmor and Damascus.

If successful, such actions would effectively cut off the supplies the Israelites desperately needed in a time of famine. This would then further weaken the people, making them easy to conquer. With the nation's fall, the assassination of the royal house would follow. And God's promise to David of a continuing dynasty would be impossible to fulfill.

Initially, David may have been too preoccupied with fighting battles on all fronts to pay much attention to the famine. He probably felt that the drought was a natural, seasonal phenomenon.[6] Only after three years (roughly the length of time he spent fighting Israel's enemies) did he seek God's face and inquire the reason (21:1*b*. cf. Deuteronomy 11:11-17; 28:12,14-15,24).

What is important to us is the fact that while David and the men of Israel were fighting foreign wars, their problems were multiplying. All was not well at home. Their families were experiencing difficulties. And slowly but surely the effects of the famine impacted everyone.

All of this corrects a common but mistaken emphasis in the church today, that if we walk with the Lord we will enjoy lives of freedom from care, prosper in whatever we do, and be endlessly happy. Any deviation from this rule, any absence of the evidence of God's blessings on one's life, is assumed to be a sign of hidden, unconfessed sin. The experiences of David refute such heterodoxy!

With these thoughts in mind, let us take a look at the activities of the Philistines, Moabites, Syrians, and Edomites.

OUTLINE

With 8:1 we come to another major division of the book.[7] Joyce Baldwin states that the words "After this it came to pass that..." do not indicate a strict chronology.[8] We agree that exceptions can be found to support her position, but in our opinion the use of this phrase marks the next major step in the development of the Biblical writer's theme. Furthermore, as we compare chapter 7 with chapter 8, it is hard to escape the cause-and-effect relationship between the two, and the fact that the author is deliberately setting forth the next significant event in David's life. In addition, as was shown in the Introduction, observance of these divisions reveals the unique theme of the writer (verified by Psalm 89:19-29).

In the present division, therefore, we have

GOD'S SOVEREIGNTY IN EXPANDING THE KINGDOM (8:1–12:31).

A brief outline will place all of the events in perspective.

- External Threats to the Nation (8:1-14).
    War With the Philistines (8:1)
    War With the Moabites (8:2)
    War With the Syrians (8:3-6*a*)
        Summary (8:6b)
    Digression: Giving Honor to God (8:7-12)
        Spoils of War (8:7-8)
        Submission of Hamath (8:9-10)
        Summary (8:11-12)
    War With Edom (8:13-14*a*)
        Summary (8:14*b*)

- Internal Administration of the Nation (8:15-18)
    Digression: A Reminder of a Friendship (9:1-13)

- Further Threats to the Nation (10:1–12:31)
    War with Ammon (10:1-19)
    Digression: Adultery and Its Aftermath (11:1–12:25)
    Victory Over Ammon (12:26-31)

We will treat only 2 Samuel 8 at this time.

EXTERNAL THREATS TO THE NATION (8:1-14)

The transitions of the Bible, like those in life, are often abrupt (and perhaps unexpected). In chapter 7 we read that the Lord had given David and the people of Israel rest from all their enemies (7:1*b*). Now, however, the peace Israel had enjoyed is shattered. Through no fault of their own, they are ushered into a series of wars that come annually one upon another. In the end, some of Israel's enemies join together in a coalition.

Bible critics claim that an editor (or a series of editors) who compiled various accounts of David's wars lumped into a single sequence all of his victories to build up David in the minds of his readers.[9] Others see the events of 8:1-14 as preceding the fulfillment in David's lifetime of God's words in 7:11.[10] But they fail to take into account David's later battles against the Philistines (21:15-22), and perhaps other nations as well.

We can take the opening statement in the same way we have past references (cf. 1:1; 2:1; 7:1; etc.), as indicating continuity (though allowing for a lapse in time between events), and find no warrant for the belief that here we have a potpourri of wars that extend over the remainder of David's life.

War With the Philistines (8:1)

We are not surprised to read that the first nation to rise against Israel is Philistia in the west. The Philistines had always been the inveterate enemies of God's people. The account of the battle is very brief. We read only that David's forces defeat (lit. "smite") the *metheg ha-ammah*. Some translators have taken these words as a proper noun. Quite literally they mean "bridle of the mother city." A quick reference to 1 Chronicles 8:1 provides an explanation. David captured Gath (the "mother city") and her towns (referred to in Hebrew as her "daughters") out of the hands of the Philistines.[11]

Gath was the most powerful of the Philistine pentapolis, and being also the most southerly, controlled all trade from Egypt along the route called "The Way of the Sea."

War With the Moabites (8:2)

The next to attack are the Moabites,[12] who live east-southeast of Jerusalem and east of the Dead Sea.[13] What causes David's former friends to attack Israel is not told us. Dr. A. F. Kirkpatrick[14] points to an old Jewish tradition that claimed the king of Moab betrayed David's trust and murdered his parents (cf. 1 Samuel 22:3-4). This is unlikely, for upon becoming king (either in Hebron or Jerusalem) David would most assuredly have brought his parents (if they still lived) to live with him.

In all probability the attack of the Moabites is to be seen as some special act of treachery. When the devil prompts people to participate in some evil act they may act on false information by which they rationalize their deeds.

From 2 Samuel 23:20 we conclude that it was sometime during this campaign that Benaiah distinguished himself by killing the two *'ariēls*. But who were these *'ariēls*?

The closest etymology is *'ari*, "lion." When this is linked with *-ēl*, "god," it would appear as if these two *'ariēls* were two brothers known for their bravery who fought in the name of one of Moab's gods (cf. Isaiah 29:1-2,7). As with Hercules, they may have worn lion's skins as mantles. The apostle Paul asserted that demons are behind the worship of the different gods (1 Corinthians 10:19-21). In all probability, these men went into battle in the name of a particular deity, and he empowered them so that they could accomplish remarkable feats. If this is so, then it makes Benaiah's defeat of them all the more remarkable!

The Moabites field a formidable force against Israel. After a bitter fight, David's army is victorious. The breach of faith on the part of the Moabites is of such a nature that David has two-thirds of the army executed.[15] This ensures that, for at least a generation, the Moabites can not again attack Israel. The country is then placed under tribute.

War with the Syrians (8:3-6a)

The next nation to flex its muscles against David is Syria (or Aram) to the north.[16] Those who do battle with Israel are from two sectors: Zobah, the initial aggressors, aided later on by reinforcements from Damascus.

Damascus lay to the east of Zobah and, at this period of history, was of lesser significance. Zobah was situated between the Lebanon and Anti-Lebanon mountain ranges. It was a powerful kingdom with numerous city-states subject to it. Its king was Hadadezer.

With the mention of this king's name we are faced with a slight textual problem. In 10:16-19 and in 1 Chronicles 18:3ff., he is called "Hadarezer" (corrected in the NASB to "Hadadezer"). How is this difference to be explained? Are there errors in the Bible? And if so, how does this affect the doctrine of inerrancy?

The solution is simple. The letters *d* (ד) and *r* (ר) in Hebrew are easily confused. Most likely, an early copyist made an initial error, and this was perpetuated as copies of his manuscript were made. Allowing for human error in the transmission of the text to us (covering a period of three and a half millennia!) does not assail the trustworthiness of the Bible. Inerrancy applies only to the original "autographs" or documents. As the human element entered into the propagation of the texts, errors occurred. But none of them are significant enough to affect any doctrine. And most of the supposed errors can be corrected easily and without elaborate explanation.

Hadad was the name of a Syrian god. The name Hadadezer meant "Hadad is [my] help(er)." The name of this pagan deity was also used by certain kings of Syria, e.g., Ben-hadad, "son of Hadad" (1 Kings 15:18).

Hadadezer, realizing that the Philistines and Moabites had failed militarily, and that much depended upon him, goes to "the River" (i.e., the Euphrates) to establish his supremacy there. Had he been successful, he could have cut off all trade to Israel from the East. And with Israel already suffering the effects of famine, such an act would have had a disastrous effect on their economy.

David, as a wise leader, takes the initiative and intercepts him. Hadadezer had not expected such strong opposition and sends to Damascus for aid.[17] The people of Damascus respond quickly, but after the dust of the conflict has settled, Israel has sent a combined total of twenty-two thousand men from this alliance to their deaths (8:5b).

David also captures Hadadezer's chariots and horses. Most of the former are burned while the latter are hamstrung[18] and released. In this way David ensures that Hadadezer will not quickly rise up against him again.

The battle had probably ended in or near Damascus and away from Zobah. David shrewdly places garrisons[19] throughout the area formerly controlled by Damascus. He also requires of them an annual tax or levy.

From David's point of view, the battle with the Syrians in the north is made all the more complicated because the Edomites (according to the superscription of Psalm 60), chose this precise time to attack Israel's southern border. David then has to divide his forces and he sends Joab and Abishai to repulse the invaders.

Summary (8:6b)

The Biblical writer then adds, "And Yahweh helped David wherever (lit. 'in all places' where) he went." This sentence seems to have been included in the narrative to assure us that, no matter what strategy the enemy used—whether chariots or cavalry, disciplined troops or difficult terrain—the Lord always prospered His anointed. And while each style of fighting called for a different strategy, and none of the victories came easily, the Lord always gave David success.

All of this finds a parallel in our lives. At times we, too, feel so harassed and overwhelmed that we are tempted to ask, "Where is

God in all of this?" David sets us an example of perseverance against seemingly insuperable odds. He did not know of the evil minions that were spurring on his enemies, but he placed his trust firmly in God. He called upon the Lord in his despair, and He heard him. In the end he could write:

> Through God we shall do great things;
>   For He shall tread on our foes (Psalm 60:12).

At no time, however, could David and his men slacken their efforts and become complacent. Every physical effort had to be exerted to gain the victory. From this we have reinforced in our minds the fact that God never does for us what we can do for ourselves.

Digression: Giving Honor to God (8:7-12)

Spoils of War (8:7-8). David dutifully devotes the spoils of war, which were rightfully his, to the Lord. These represent a vast wealth. Among the spoils are shields[20] of gold that had been the proud possession of Syrian generals (i.e., high-ranking "servants" of Hadadezer). As the firstfruits from his victories, these are set aside so that one day they can be smelted down and used in the embellishment of the Temple that his son will build.

In addition, there is an innumerable supply of gold, silver, and bronze from Betah[21] and Berothai (two regions, the latter near Baalbek, that apparently acknowledge David's suzerainty, switching their allegiance from Hadadezer to him). They willingly pay him a large tribute.

Satan's strategy in stirring up these kings against David has so far failed. What is illustrated for us in the text is the way in which the Lord makes even the wrath of these kingdoms to turn to His praise (see Psalm 76:10).

Submission of Hamath (8:9-10). When To'i (also referred to as To'u in 1 Chronicles 18:9), king of Hamath on the Orentes River,[22] over one hundred miles north of Damascus, hears of David's victory over Hadadezer, he sends his son, Joram, to David's court.

Joram's name had formerly been "Hadoram," a shortened form of Hadadoram, meaning "Hadad is exalted." To show subservience to David and acceptance of his suzerainty, To'i also chooses to honor David's God. He changes the name of his son to "Joram," meaning "Yahweh is exalted."

Some indication of the esteem in which David is now held by other monarchs may be gleaned from the fact that he is twice referred to as "*King* David" in these verses.

Joram's mission is to establish an alliance between Israel and Hamath. The people of Hamath voluntarily become Israel's vassals and commit themselves to paying an annual tribute. The wealth of gold, silver, and bronze that Joram brings with him is "sanctified to Yahweh" and reserved for later use in the adorning of the Temple.

Summary (8:11-12). Between the precious things that are offered to King David and the spoil that he takes from captured kingdoms, he brings to Jerusalem an untold wealth.

In the enumeration of his victories and of the spoils that he dedicates to the Temple, mention is also made of victories over Philistia, Amalek, and the sons of Ammon. Three Philistine wars have been fought, and David's share of these conquests must have been great, for Philistia was a wealthy nation. It is probable that in the case of the Amalekites the reference is to previous victory (cf. 1 Samuel 30:1-29). If this is so, then David must have anticipated the possibility of one day building a Temple to the Lord and begun early to make provision for its embellishment. But there is another possibility. One Ammonite war is still future (see ch. 10). If this is the one intended by the Biblical writer, then it is probably mentioned here for the sake of completeness.

In listing these details, the author is apparently showing that it was David's policy to devote the riches secured from each campaign to the Lord. He honored Yahweh in all he did, and it is not surprising that God exalted him.

War with Edom (8:13-14a)

The war with the Edomites[23] south of the Dead Sea is conducted during the war against the Syrians of Zobah and Damascus. Apparently, there was some collusion between these (and perhaps other) powers. Hadadezer attempted to cut off supplies to Canaan from the north, and the king of Edom quite possibly attempted to do the same from the south.

No reasons are given for this new outbreak of aggression, and all the writer of 2 Samuel states is that David put garrisons "throughout Edom" and that the Edomites become his servants bringing tribute. These garrisons serve a dual purpose: (1) They ensure that no further insurrection takes place, and (2) they keep open the supply route from the Gulf of Aqaba.

Some Bible scholars have discerned what appears to them to be a contradiction between Psalm 60 (which states that twelve thousand Edomites were killed in the Valley of Salt[24]) and 2 Samuel 8:13 (where we read that David killed eighteen thousand Syrians in this same valley). They have conjectured that inasmuch as the words for Syria (אֲרָם) and Edom (אֱדֹם) are very similar in Hebrew, perhaps a scribe inadvertently made a mistake while copying the original manuscript. If so, then the different totals would indeed indicate a discrepancy.[25]

It seems likely that after defeating Hadadezer, David hastily went south to help Joab and Abishai. Hadadezer, perhaps to erase the shame of his loss, hastily raised a small army from the cities and towns under his control and sent it south to aid the Edomites. (If we look ahead in the Biblical narrative to 10:6-16, we will see that Hadadezer will also send Syrian mercenaries to support the Ammonites in their war against Israel. This raises an important question: Why then should those Bible scholars who dispute the text think it out of character for him to reinforce the ranks of the Edomites? It is a question negative Bible critics have been loath to answer). Both Syrians and Edomites sustained heavy losses, the former losing eighteen thousand men and the latter twelve thousand.

But more important than the reconciling of different figures in the Scriptures is the evidence that there must have been collusion on the part of Israel's enemies. Only as a result of God's help was Israel able to emerge from this period of severe trial intact. This is of encouragement to us, for on those occasions when we, too, face the onslaught of forces that threaten to overwhelm us, David's God is the one on whom we can rely, for "He is our refuge and strength, a very present help in [time of] trouble" (Psalm 46:1).

Summary (8:14b)

It is one of the great lessons of the Bible that those who honor the Lord are honored by Him. David, we read, was helped by God in all that he did.

INTERNAL ADMINISTRATION OF THE NATION (8:15-18)

Having considered the external threats to both Israel's autonomy and the divine promise of an enduring dynasty, we come now to take a look at the way in which David administered the country.[26] If the record of his warlike activities was given to us briefly, the functions and the duties of his advisors is even more abbreviated.

First, we read that David serves in the capacity of a *shāpat*, "judge."[27] A *shāpat* was one who stood in the tradition of those appointed by

Moses to decide matters of dispute (see Exodus 18:17-26; Deuteronomy 1:13-18). David, however, was the supreme judge of his people and his duties approximated those duties borne by Moses, the great lawgiver. Each tribe had its own judges, and only matters of great consequence or irreconcilable differences were then referred to the king.

David's activities show us his desire for righteousness and justice to characterize his administration. He was not so taken up with spiritual matters (cf. 8:11) or the things that contributed to his popularity (cf. 8:13*a*) that he neglected the poor and the helpless, the widow and the orphan.

Some of David's psalms (e.g., Psalm 72 [that many believe was written *for* Solomon—note the conclusion]; and Psalm 101) show how concerned he was to be a righteous king.

Twice in 8:15 we have the word *all.* David reigns over *all* Israel, and administers justice and righteousness for *all* the people. He is impartial. He does not favor special interest groups. Judah does not fare better than Zebulun, Issachar or Naphtali. Nor does he favor the wealthy of Ephraim or the numerous descendants of Manasseh. Scripture presents him as an ideal king (Isaiah 9:7; Jeremiah 22:2-4; 23:5) and a true precursor of the Messiah Himself (see Psalm 89:3-4).

As a wise king, David also delegates authority to capable subordinates. Joab is the general over the army and directly responsible to the king. He had won this honor when Jebus was captured (1 Chronicles 11:6). David knows Joab's nature and does not altogether trust him. That is why he also divides his "Mighty Men" into groups (23:8-23; 1 Chronicles 11:10-25). "The Three" are a part of his tribunal whenever there is a war to wage.

Jehoshaphat is the *mazkîr,* "recorder." The Hebrew is derived from the word "to remember." We are not given an intimation of Jehoshaphat's duties, but it seems likely that he was the official historian, the keeper of all state records (much like our Librarian of Congress), and the one who took responsibility for keeping the king informed about important matters, as well as the names and accomplishments of visiting dignitaries. Some writers believe that he was the "royal herald."[28] It is probable that he also communicated the commands of the king to those who were to carry them out.

The religious leaders are Zadok and Ahimelech.[29] Zadok (who is mentioned here for the first time) is the son of Ahitub and has been given oversight of the Ark (15:24-29). He is a descendent of Aaron through Eleazar (1 Chronicles 6:12). Ahimelech, the son of Abiathar, is likewise a descendant of Aaron, but through Ithamar and Eli.

The priests had successively established centers of worship in

Gibeon, Shiloh, and Nob. Gibeon had been vacated as the tribes moved into Canaan and began taking possession of the land. Shiloh had been destroyed by the Philistines. And Saul had slaughtered the priests of Nob. Only Abiathar had escaped.

The priests who serve during the time of David are divided into twenty-four courses, and each course serves for a limited period (i.e., two weeks).[30] This system was still in operation in New Testament times (cf. Luke 1:5,8).

A systematic arrangement is likewise made for the Levites. Some are assigned to serve in the central sanctuary, others are porters, then there are those who are singers, and a certain number serve at times as teachers and judges of the people.

Nothing is said here of Samuel's "Schools of the Prophets." That these schools continued is evident, for we read of them much later on in the days of Elijah and Elisha. It is highly probable that Nathan and Gad had been trained by Samuel and that they now teach in these schools as occasion requires.

Seraiah is David's "secretary," or in the opinion of some historians of this period, his "secretary of state."[31]

And Benaiah is captain of David's bodyguard (23:23). The Cherethites and Pelethites may have been Cretans or (as certain Bible scholars believe) people from Gath. Whatever their origin, they are probably descendants of the "Peoples of the Sea" who had settled in southern Canaan. They are more reliable and less open to court intrigue than Hebrews who may have been inclined to place tribal loyalty above their devotion to their king.

Finally, we are told that David's sons were *kōhănîm*, "priests."[32] Most readers of the sacred text stumble over this term because priests were designated by God to come only from the tribe of Levi and the family of Aaron, not from David's line or the tribe of Judah.

The eminent Bible scholar Dr. H. H. Rowley believed that at this period of history the priesthood was not yet regarded as hereditary or as limited to the tribe of Levi.[33] However, what is more likely is that at this early period of Israel's history the word *kōhēn* (the singular of *kōhănîm*), meaning "priest," had more than one meaning. David evidently gave his sons government positions. They probably served in much the same capacity as modern "cabinet ministers" in a monarchial system (cf. 1 Chronicles 18:17).

What is important is the fact that David did not allow his children to be reared in luxury or idle indifference to the needs of the people. He assigned them responsibilities in keeping with their growing abilities. In these positions they gained hands-on experience of life, benefitted from the wisdom of those about them, and learned how to govern effectively.

THE STRENGTH OF HIS MIGHT

In this chapter we have seen David beset on all sides by enemies. He did not know why, all of a sudden, everything seemed to be going wrong. That he was able to maintain his mental, emotional, and spiritual equilibrium is most praiseworthy. How he did this is of importance to each one of us, for his experiences find a parallel in our own lives.

We may not be at war in the same sense David was, but we must not forget that the apostle Paul admonished us to be on our guard against the devil (cf. Ephesians 6:10-17). Furthermore, threats to our well-being via economic pressures, hostile opposition, and relational flare-ups may not be of Satanic origin, but they do make their presence felt (cf. Psalm 119:121, 122*b*, 134, 139, 153, 157, 161, 170).

We need to be reminded of the spiritual warfare being waged continually in different realms. Satan is not limited in any of his schemes. He prefers, however, to work behind the scenes. Much of his work, therefore, is indirect. But it is nonetheless real.

How, then, are we to understand the Devil's wiles?

Some people will not enter a room or attend a meeting unless they first "bind Satan." Others see in any form of dissent the activity of the Adversary. A friend of mine gave me some material from a church she'd been invited to attend by a co-worker. This particular church had gone to the extremes of identifying the different areas of Satanic activity (e.g., there was "a spirit of heaviness," "a spirit of slumber," "a spirit of infirmity," "a spirit of jealousy," "a spirit of haughtiness," and at least a dozen more). Each was supposed to be a manifestation of some form of demonic activity.

In this regard, Dr. Ray C. Stedman's words are especially apropos:

> The New Testament gives absolutely no warrant for this type of approach. The apostles very seldom mention the direct attack of Satan against human beings. There are a few instances of it, but after our Lord physically left the world there seems to be a diminution of the evidences of demonic activity. These dark powers were stirred up by his presence on earth...[and] in the Epistles we do not find the same concern for demonic activity as we do in the Gospels. There is much about Satan in the letters of Paul but there is little of the direct attack of satanic forces.[34]

As we have pointed out, the majority of the attacks of the devil against Christians are indirect. Depression, tiredness, ill health (cf. 3 John 1:2), carnality (i.e., any manifestation of the flesh, including jealousy), pride, et cetera, are a part of our fallen nature. And the Bible provides adequate counsel to correct these manifestations of Adam's image in us without having to resort to exorcisms and the like.

To be sure, Satan uses our weaknesses and attacks us where we are most vulnerable. That is why it is imperative for us to walk in the Spirit so that we do not fulfill the lusts of the flesh. Because we seldom know when he will launch his attacks we are exhorted to put on the "whole armor of God." Note Paul's encouraging words:

> Finally, be strong in the Lord, and in the strength of His might. Put on the whole armor of God, that you may be able to stand firm against the wiles (or schemes) of the devil. For our struggle is not against flesh and blood, but against the rulers, against the powers, against the world forces of darkness, against the spiritual forces of wickedness in the heavenly places (Ephesians 6:10-12).

Paul did not counsel all kinds of bizarre rituals.

Martin Luther was convinced of the reality of the warfare in which the Christian is engaged. In his well-known hymn "A Mighty Fortress Is Our God," he wrote:

> For still our ancient foe
>   Doth seek to work us woe;
> His craft and power are great,
>   And, armed with cruel hate,
> On earth is not his equal.

What then are we to do? When we fear we may have failed or experienced some crushing defeat, where can we go for help? Or when we have done what we believed to be right and others turn against us, what should we do? Where do we find the courage to carry on? And in times of great weakness, when we are very much aware of our vulnerability, what provisions have been made that will enable us to "stand firm"?

In Times of Confusion, Prayer Is Essential

David knew of these experiences. His psalms reveal how often he felt discouraged and on the verge of despair. Note, for example, the superscript of Psalm 60. Next, in the opening stanza, he admits to feeling rejected by God. He acknowledges the effect of continued harassment upon him. He feels "broken"—emotionally crushed by the weight of adverse circumstances. In his extremity, however, he prayed to the Lord. His requests were simple, yet sincere. He asked the Lord to restore him (and his people) to His favor.

David next acknowledged that the enemy had broken through his defenses and made inroads into his life (and the lives of his people). His prayer was that the Lord would heal these breaches. At no time did he try to minimize the hardships he and his people were experiencing nor tone down his bewilderment over the adverse events that seemed to lack a suitable cause. He then reminded the Lord that those who revere (i.e., walk in reverential awe of) Him have the right to call upon Him:

> That Your beloved may be delivered.
> Save with Your right hand, and answer us!
> (Psalm 60:5).

In short, in times of confusion, we must pray!

In Times of Despair, Remember God's Purpose

David kept his equilibrium because, in the midst of difficulties too numerous to mention, he was kept on course by remembering God's eternal purpose for His people. The "I will" statements of Psalm 60 remind us that God is invincible. He is sovereign over the nations. They serve His purpose. David may have had to contend with proud Moab (cf. Isaiah 16:6), haughty Edom (cf. Obadiah 1:3), and recalcitrant Philistia (Psalms 60:8; 108:9; Isaiah 14:29, 31), but all of them would know God's displeasure.

Inasmuch as the Lord is sovereign over all things and will bring His purposes to pass, we know that He has a bright destiny for us. In times of despair, then, we should remember that His overall plan and purpose includes us.

In Times of Opportunity, Remember Faith is the Key

Finally, in David's experience his faith was restored as he thought of the Lord. By faith he saw himself entering the capital of Edom. Psalm 60, verse 10, contains two rhetorical questions. They sum up David's former lack of confidence. Then he asks for God's help (Psalm 60:11). He knows that reliance on human resources or alliances is insufficient. Powerful forces are arraigned against him, and so he places his confidence is in the Lord.

> Through God we shall do valiantly,
> And it is He who [working through us]
>   will tread down our adversaries (Psalm 60:12).

As David's groans of bewilderment and frustration gave way in God's presence to confidence and determination, so the Lord can transform us from tired and despondent victims of the world's injustices into happy and grateful victors. Let us remember, therefore, that in times of opposition, faith is the key!

REMINDER OF A FRIEND

2 Samuel 9:1-13

What is *kindness*?

The *Random House Dictionary* defines the word as

> 1. the state or quality of being kind: *kindness to animals.* 2. a kind act: *his many kindnesses to me.* 3. kind behavior: *I will never forget his kindness.* 4. friendly feeling; liking.[1]

This really doesn't clarify for us the intrinsic quality of kindness, but focuses more on the extrinsic actions (i.e., what a kind person does). If we may borrow a statement from Scripture, that most often "the lesser [person] is blessed of the greater" (Hebrews 7:7), then what we see in life is poor or unfortunate or downcast people helped in some way by a kind individual who is in a position to be their benefactor.

It was once common to hear people speak of "the milk of human kindness." This phrase described someone whose attitude and actions were marked by generosity, graciousness, and goodness. Historically, it was first used by Lady Macbeth to describe her husband. In her opinion he was too compassionate to kill Duncan so that he might ascend the throne of Scotland.[2]

Conversely, as we look at acts of *kindness* from a different perspective, we know that it is possible for feigned benevolence to mask ulterior motives. Alexander Pope warned us of the danger which lies behind a false front.

> Not always actions show the man: we find
> Who does a kindness is not therefore kind.[3]

But kindness need not be a cloak to hide the hideous defects of human nature. Nor should it be a salve to ease the pain caused by greed, self-gratification, or guilt. It can be the spontaneous response of a generous disposition.

I well remember a kindness shown me and my family when we lived in Dallas, Texas. I was enrolled in seminary. My wife and I had sold everything we owned to make the trip to the United States. We missed not having a car and felt as if we were in a kind of prison. Our movements were restricted to the distance separating our apartment from the seminary four blocks away, and with young children needing room in which to discharge their abundant energy, we missed not being able to go to a park where our sons could play on the swings or hit a ball.

On one particular Sunday afternoon, a friend, Bob Williams, knocked on the door of our apartment. When I opened the door, it was to see him dangling his car keys in front of him. He and his wife Marjorie had thought that we might like to go out for a drive. Out of the kindness of their hearts, they allowed us to use their car. More than three and a half decades have passed since that day, yet their kindness to us is as fresh in my mind as if it had happened yesterday.

All of this serves to reinforce the fact that it is easier to focus our attention on kindly acts than to define kindness itself. To properly understand *kindness*, we must go to the Bible. In the Old Testament kindness is usually a translation of the word *hesed.* This word is used to describe the heart of someone who is good. The root idea is "faithfulness" to a relationship, or "loyalty" to a friend, one's country, or a cause. But there are times when *hesed* is used to "to demonstrate lovingkindness."[4]

In the New Testament, kindness is represented by the words *chrestos* and *'agathos* and their cognates.

The former conveys the idea of moral goodness that enables a person to be friendly and kind toward others without obscure, hidden motives. The pattern or example given us is God's unlimited benevolence, even toward those who are His enemies (Romans 2:4; 11:22; Ephesians 2:7; Titus 3:4). His kindness is a reflection of His moral uprightness, wholesomeness, and dependability (cf. Matthew 7:11, 17ff.; John 7:12; 12:35; Acts 9:36; 2 Thessalonians 2:16).

The latter word (*'agathos*) looks at goodness that is seen in perfection (Mark 10:17-18; John 7:12), kindness (Matthew 20:15), benevolence (1 Peter 2:18), dependability (1 Thessalonians 3:6), and purity of heart as well as life (Matthew 12:35; 1 Peter 3:16).

As we focus our thoughts on 2 Samuel 9, we cannot help but notice the repeated use of the word "kindness" by David. And in his actions we are given a graphic example of one person's kindness to another.

THE HISTORIC SETTING

The passage begins with the words,

> Then David said, "Is there anyone left of the house of Saul, that I may show him kindness for Jonathan's sake?"[5]

The word *then* introduces the result of some action or circumstance. It presumes an understanding of the cause.

Those living at the time this history of God's people was written would have known of the facts behind David's inquiry. We, however, are compelled to look for a suitable explanation, and the wars recorded in chapter 8 do not provide a proper setting.[6] With the cessation of hostilities, David's first thought as a "shepherd" would have been the welfare of his people. We are at a loss, therefore, to explain his sudden desire to show the kindness of God to a survivor of Saul's family.

Most scholars agree that the events of 2 Samuel 21:1-9 took place during the three-year period when the men of Israel were fighting for their nation's survival. If this is so, then the problems of the Israelites during the years of warfare were aggravated by a famine that gained in severity with each passing year.

What we read in 2 Samuel 8 corrects our impression of the kind of trials people of Bible times endured. We tend to think of the difficulties they faced as singular, not complex, and then we wonder how their example can in any way serve as a model for us (cf. 1 Corinthians 10:11). If Israel was not only surrounded by enemies but also facing problems at home caused by a famine, then we can better understand the relevance to us of that which God has chosen to be recorded for our instruction (cf. Romans 15:4).

As with Israel of old, our problems are often multifaceted. We know what it is like to face both external and internal pressures. Frequently, when we are contending with problems at our place of work, difficulties of a different nature arise from another source. A child becomes ill or is sent home because he was fighting in school, elderly parents reach a point where they can no longer care for themselves and need to move in with us, a close relative or friend sickens and perhaps dies, or a wife finds that she can no longer cope and threatens to leave. It is comforting for us to know that the complexities of David's trials approximate our own.

At first, the famine was probably just an annoyance or a minor source of anxiety. The people most likely thought that it was "just a bad year" and comforted themselves with the thought that "next year the rains will come on time and everything will return to normal." But when the famine continued, David eventually had to make time to inquire of the Lord the reason (21:1*a*).

In responding to his earnest inquiry, the Lord told him that the nation was being punished because Saul had broken the covenant Joshua had made with the Gibeonites (21:2; cf. Joshua 9:3,15-20). Without provocation, Saul had attempted to exterminate an entire group of people. This sin had never been confessed, and the wrongs he had done had never been righted. Because of Saul's having ignored God's Word, his descendants are now to be punished.

Since the Gibeonites were the ones sinned against, David asks them what justice they will accept so that the famine can be lifted from the land. Believing that the sins of the father are visited upon the children,[7] the Gibeonites ask that a token number of Saul's household be hanged so as to exonerate them in the eyes of the people (21:3-6).

It is after these descendants of Saul have been executed that David was moved with compassion and asked, "Is there anyone left of the house of Saul...?"

OUTLINE

In treating the events of this chapter, the Biblical writer digresses from the wars David has been waging to provide us with a brief glimpse of an act of selfless altruism. The recurring theme is to be found in the word *ḥesed*, "kindness":

"...show *kindness* for Jonathan's sake" (9:1);
"...show the *kindness* of God" (9:3); and
"I will surely show *kindness* to you..." (9:7).

In the New American Standard Bible the divisions of the chapter are marked by the word "then" (vv. 1, 5, and 9). This translation of the Hebrew word *waw* (meaning "now," "and," or "then," and, depending on the context, "but") makes the divisions of the chapter easy to identify.

We have, therefore...

- The Inquiry of the King (9:1-4)
- The Summons of the King (9:5-8)
- The Instructions of the King (9:9-13)

Dr. William G. Blaikie is anxious to portray David's character in the best light. He contrasts this passage with the wars of chapter 8:

> It is a proof that the bloody wars in which [David] had been engaged had not destroyed the tenderness of his heart, that the very chapter which follows the account of his battles opens with a yearning of affection—a longing for an outlet to feelings of kindness.[8]

Instructive, too, is the fact that David's kindness toward Jonathan's son grows out of, and is an evidence of, his supreme regard for the honor of God.

THE INQUIRY OF THE KING (9:1-4)

After all David had suffered at the hands of Saul, we would understand if he had let the deaths of Saul's sons go unmourned. He might also be forgiven had he thought of the retribution of the Gibeonites as poetic justice. David's magnanimity, however, shines through this account and reveals a side of his nature that might easily be overlooked.

No sooner does he verbalize his thoughts (9:1) than he sends messengers to ascertain the true state of affairs.

We may be sure that the task of these messengers was a difficult one. With the hanging of seven of the late king's household still fresh in the minds of the people of Benjamin, we can safely presume that those having the needed information would not readily reveal the whereabouts of Saul's heirs. David would most certainly have been blamed for the execution of these men, and the real reason for this action was most likely not widely known. Even among those who knew the truth, we may be sure that there were bound to be some who would not believe what they had been told.

There is a tendency in the human heart to believe the worst about people. Dissidents, therefore, who were still loyal to Saul, would think David's enquiry a ruse to eliminate anyone else who might be regarded as a threat to his well-being.

After much searching, David's messengers locate a former high-ranking "servant" named Ziba. He had served in Saul's palace at Gibeah, and is now living in Transjordan with his family. He is evidently a prosperous man, for he has twenty servants (9:10*b*).

When Ziba appears before David, the atmosphere may have been strained.

"Are you Ziba?" asks the king.

"I [am] your servant," is the cautious reply (9:2).

"Is there not yet anyone of the house of Saul to whom I may show the kindness of God?" (9:2-3a).

The words "not yet," which seem to us to invite a negative answer are, in reality, a Hebraism expecting a positive reply.

Also, in speaking with Ziba, David uses the general name for God, 'Ĕlōhîm, not the covenant name, *Yahweh*. This probably indicates that he did not sense in Ziba one who was motivated by spiritual principles. Ziba responds: "There is still a son of Jonathan who is crippled in both his feet" (9:3b).

Ziba evidently wishes to protect Jonathan's son, so he makes him as insignificant and anonymous as possible. This is evident from the fact that he does not mention his name but stresses instead his condition. It is as if he is saying to David, "He's worthless to you. Leave him where he is."

But David's motives are altogether different.

"Where is he?" he asks.

And Ziba is compelled to answer, "He is in the house of Machir, the son of Ammiel, in Lo-debar" (9:4).

This last bit of information served in David's time the same purpose as a street address today. David hastily sends a palladium and an armed escort to Lo-debar to bring Mephibosheth to court.[9]

Lo-debar[10] was situated east of the River Jordan on the border of Gad (Joshua 13:26). It has been identified by some scholars with Debir. The meaning of the name "Lo-debar" is uncertain. It is generally believed that the village was on the fringe of civilization, facing eastward and overlooking miles of barren, trackless desert. It was apparently so insignificant that in Amos 6:13 the name Lo-debar is used as a synonym for something without value (i.e., nothing).

THE SUMMONS OF THE KING (9:5-8)

In spite of the close relationship that had existed between Jonathan and David, it is unlikely that Mephibosheth[11] had heard anything good about Israel's new king. He had been only five years old when his father had been killed. And now, as he is being brought to the palace, he most likely experiences both fear and resentment at the summons. (The recent execution of his relatives would be sufficient to cause him to feel fear, and being compelled to do something against his will would have engendered in him a sense of resentment.)

As Mephibosheth is shown into David's presence, the contrast between the warrior-king and the crippled grandson of Saul is impossible to exaggerate. The one is confident in the goodness of God to him; the other, though a prince from birth, has known only the bitterness of life's misfortunes.

Mephibosheth shuffles toward David's throne. When he has covered about half the distance he stops, lets his crutches fall to the floor, and prostrates himself before the king. And David, looking at the young man, asks: "Mephibosheth?"

"Here is your servant!" is the response that comes from the crippled heap on the floor.

Sensing the young man's fear, David quickly reassures him.

> "Do not fear, for I will surely show kindness to you for the sake of your father Jonathan, and will restore to you all the land of your grandfather Saul; and you shall eat at my table continually" (9:7).

Mephibosheth's reply shows the extent to which his sufferings have affected his sense of personal esteem. He again prostrates himself before David. "What is your servant, that you should regard a dead dog like me?" (9:8).

Dr. William Blaikie paints a vivid pen-portrait of what Mephibosheth's life had been like up to this point.

> Naturally of a timid nature, and weakened in nerve by the accident of his infancy, he must have grown up under great disadvantages. His lameness excluded him from sharing in any youthful game or manly exercise, and therefore threw him in company of the women who, like him, tarried at home. What he had heard of David had not come through a friendly channel [but from] partisans of Saul, and was not likely to be very favourable. He was too young to remember the generous conduct of David in reference to his father and grandfather; and those who were about him probably did not care to say much about it....
>
> He had a profound sense of the greatness which David had achieved and the honour implied in his countenance and fellowship (i.e., being the king's friend). But there was no need for his humbling himself so low. There was no need for his calling himself a dead dog—the most humiliating image it was possible to find....
>
> This shattered condition of both mind and body commended him all the more to the friendly regard of David. Finding him modest and respectful, David had no difficulty in the case. The

kindness which he showed him was twofold. In the first place,
he restored to him all the land that had belonged to his
grandfather; and in the second place, he made him an inmate of
his own house, with a place at his table, the same as if he had
been one of his own sons. And that he might not be embarrassed
with having the land to care for, he committed the charge of it
to Ziba, who was to bring to Mephibosheth the produce or its
value.

Every arrangement was thus made that could contribute to
Mephibosheth's comfort. His being a cripple did not deprive
him of a place at the royal table, for David bestowed his favours
not on the principle of trying to reflect lustre on himself or his
house, but on the principle of doing good to those who had a
claim on his consideration.

It might be thought by some that such an incident as this
was hardly worthy of a place in the sacred record; but the truth
is, that David seldom showed more of the true spirit of God
than he did on this occasion.[12]

One word of clarification is needed. In David's plan, Mephibosheth
is to bring his entire household to Jerusalem. The food from Saul's
lands is for their sustenance, not his own.

THE INSTRUCTIONS OF THE KING (9:9-13)

Dr. Blaikie has already made mention of David's instructions to
Ziba. The lands held by Saul had reverted to the crown when Saul's
dynasty came to an end. They had remained nominally Ish-bosheth's
during his lifetime, but when David was anointed king over all Israel,
they became his. Now he freely restores them to Mephibosheth. His
words to Saul's servant are explicit:

> "All that belonged to Saul and to all his house I have given to
> your master's grandson.[13] And you and your sons and your
> servants shall cultivate the land for him, and you shall bring in
> [the produce] so that your master's grandson may have food
> [for his household]; nevertheless Mephibosheth your master's
> grandson shall eat at my table regularly" (9:9-10).

To this royal command Ziba responds: "According to all that my
lord the king commands his servant, so your servant shall do" (9:11).
Some indication of the passage of time is alluded to in verse 12.

Mephibosheth had been five years old when his father and grandfather had been killed in battle. He is now old enough to have a son. It is true that people in the ancient Near East married soon after puberty, but we believe that the period from David's reign in Hebron and his wars with the various nations would add about fifteen years to Mephibosheth's age. He would therefore be at least twenty, and perhaps slightly older depending upon the age of Micah.[14]

The chapter concludes by showing that David is as good as his word. Mephibosheth eats at his table as one of his own sons. His lameness and inability to return David's favors do not obstruct David's benevolence to him.

REFLECTING ON THE GRACE OF GOD

True kindness is an attitude of the heart. It is an evidence of the grace of God remaking our natural disposition so that we begin to show His nature to those about us. Kindness is seen in our deeds, but it must not be confused with the things we do. It can be observed in a look or felt in a touch. It is a language which the deaf can hear and the blind can see.

Kindness Is Freely Expressed

David's kindness toward Mephibosheth was freely expressed. The young man did not merit it and could not earn it.

In the history of the Christian church, the kindness of Selina, Countess of Huntingdon, stands out like a beacon on a dark night. She had come to faith during a time of illness. Her husband was upset by her conversion and Methodist leanings, and called in an Anglican bishop "to restore her to a saner mind." But her resolve to follow the Lord only grew stronger, and she did not hesitate to share her beliefs with her aristocratic friends. In time she became the friend and supporter of George Whitefield and of John and Charles Wesley.

When her husband died, Selina sold her jewels and with the proceeds built chapels for the poor. She also relinquished her expensive residences and liveried servants to purchase theaters and halls in London, Bristol, and Dublin that were converted into churches. These she supplied with distinguished clergymen. In time, she also established a preacher's college to train young men for the ministry.

Through her many acts of kindness, she aided the reformation movement in England, Wales, and Ireland. And when doctrinal differences threatened to separate Whitefield and the Wesleys, she intervened and was able to bring about a reconciliation between them. Selina freely expressed what was in her heart by her generosity and acts of Christian love.[15]

Kindness Is Graciously Shown

David elevated Mephibosheth to a position on par with his sons. He did not expect any reciprocation. His kindness was graciously bestowed.

Some years ago, I was sent to the United Kingdom on a book-buying trip for a university with satellite schools in different countries. While passing through Yorkshire, I visited Haworth, the home of the famous Brontë sisters.

Charlotte Brontë only lived to the age of thirty-nine. The strict rules implemented by her father could have turned her into a cruel and vindictive person. The only happiness she knew was when he allowed her to marry at age thirty-six. Then, for a brief spell, she knew what it was like to be loved unconditionally.

When Charlotte died, she was buried in the churchyard where her father was the aging pastor. A young blind girl was present. She had begged neighbors to take her over the wet, snowy roads so she might weep at the grave side of the one who had been kind to her and through whom she had been given hope and encouragement.

After the mourners had gone away, a lonely woman came and stood by the grave. This solitary soul had been ostracized by the people of Haworth. She had been seduced by a man who promised her more than he was prepared to deliver. When she conceived, he left her. Long before her baby was born, she was cast out and spurned by the people of the village. A stigma was placed upon her and she was excluded from the company of Christians. Charlotte had reached out in love and compassion to this woman.[16] And for her many kindnesses she is remembered to this day.

In my youth I was deeply impressed by Spencer Tracy's portrayal of Henry M. Stanley in *Stanley and Livingstone*. As the years have gone by, I have acquired most of the books written by both Henry Stanley and David Livingstone. I knew nothing of Stanley's early life, however, until I read his autobiography.[17] His story is sufficient to move even the hardest of hearts.

Stanley never knew his father and was disowned by his mother. From his earliest years he was forced to live in a workhouse for orphans, where he was surrounded by misery and cruelty. Love was denied him and he yearned for someone to show him kindness and understanding.

As the years passed he became hardened and cynical.

One day he ran away. In time he signed on as a cabin boy and went to sea. The ship docked in New Orleans. Tired of the floggings and harsh treatment, Stanley jumped ship and walked into the city to make a new life for himself. He stopped by the door of a store, where a gentleman was reading the morning's newspaper, and asked for work.

This man took him into his home, adopted him, and gave him his own name, Henry Morton Stanley. He washed him and fed him and treated him with the tender affection of a father. And tears, which no amount of cruelty could induce, began to pour down the young lad's face.

No one knew what this young boy would one day accomplish. It was kindness graciously shown that gave him a new beginning.

Kindness Has Its Unexpected Reward

Kindness sometimes brings an unexpected reward. When we first learned of Mephibosheth, he was staying in the home of Machir, of the tribe of Manasseh, in Lo-debar. Machir was faithful to the house of Saul and unlikely to change his political loyalties.

The kindness David showed Mephibosheth must have impressed Machir so that in time his resentment toward David gave way before the goodness that was in David's heart. Years later, when David fled from Absalom, Machir was one of those who voluntarily supported and sustained the king and his court (17:27-29). In this act of generosity David's kindness to Mephibosheth received an unexpected reward.

Henry Burton wrote:

> Have you had a kindness shown?
>   Pass it on;
> 'Twas not given for thee alone,
>   Pass it on;
> Let it travel down the years,
> Let it wipe another's tears,
> 'Till in Heaven the deed appears.[18]

A WAR THAT COULD HAVE BEEN AVOIDED

2 Samuel 10:1-19

A few years ago, the television program *60 Minutes* featured the story of a successful plastic surgeon. When he retired, he decided to use his skills to help those in a poor part of the city where he lived who could not afford his services. According to the CBS report, he worked as hard in his retirement as he had done while in regular practice.

After reconstructing the face of one woman, he was sued by her because she thought that he could have made her more beautiful. The "before and after" pictures shown by the CBS news team indicated a remarkable improvement. Unfortunately for this surgeon, his kindness was repaid by ingratitude.

Alexander Mackay was a missionary to Central Africa. He had studied literature, mathematics and engineering at Edinburgh University, Scotland, and later entered the University of Berlin, where he specialized in draftsmanship and surveying. Upon graduation he declined a lucrative position in the United Kingdom so that he might go instead to Uganda as a missionary.

When Mackay set out for Lake Victoria, he had to construct a two hundred and thirty mile stretch of road to get there. He then began teaching the Africans how to read and write. The chief of the district, King Mtesa, was very pleased with what Alexander Mackay was doing and gave him protection.

Later, when Mwanga succeeded Mtesa, persecution broke out. Mackay was repeatedly flogged with a whip made of hippopotamus hide. The third time this happened he was presumed dead and thrown into the bushes for the wild animals to eat. His kindness and sacrifice were treated with calloused indifference by those who were his beneficiaries.

I am frequently approached by mothers (and occasionally fathers) who weep with grief on account of their adolescent children. Often they tell of being either bereaved or left by their spouse, and through trials too numerous to mention, they have struggled to keep the family together. They have also reared their children to the best of their ability. Their endurance, and the many sacrifices they have made have received short shrift from their sons and daughters, and bitter criticisms have been leveled against them.

Statements prefaced by, "You don't understand me" or "You never allow me to—" or "Why can't we have—?" or "I want—" cause struggling parents untold pain. Their kindness, it seems, has gone unrewarded, and they feel as if their children have turned to "bite the hand that fed them."

All of us at one time or another have sought to befriend someone or show kindness to an individual, only to have our motives misunderstood. The gossip wires begin to hum, and we find out later that the very ones we tried to help maligned us behind our backs. The question facing us is, How should we conduct ourselves in such circumstances?

An incident from the life of David speaks directly to these issues. It concerns his kindness to the son of the king of Ammon.

OUTLINE

The opening scene of 2 Samuel 10 continues the theme of *ḥesed*, "lovingkindness," begun in chapter 9. What is recorded proves beyond doubt that David was *not* interested in extending the borders of his empire. He was at heart a man of peace and would much rather live in harmony with his neighbors.

Chapter 10 must be interpreted within the larger context of 8:1–12:31 which treats *God's Sovereignty in Expanding the Kingdom (8:1–12:31)*. Within this section we have observed thus far

- External Threats to the Nation (8:1-14)

- Internal Administration of the Nation (8:15-18)
   Digression: Reminder of a Friendship (9:1-13)

We come now to note

- Further Threats to the Nation (10:1–12:31)[1]
   War With Ammon (10:1-9)
   Shameful Treatment of Israel's Ambassadors (10:1-5)
      Purposeful Reinforcement by Ammon's King (10:6-8)

A War That Could Have Been Avoided

Resourceful Division of Israel's Forces (10:9-14)
Wilful Opposition to Israel's King (10:15-19)

As we shall see, the insults Hanun heaped on David and the men of Israel plunged his nation into a war that could have been avoided.

FURTHER THREATS TO THE NATION (10:1–12:31)

War With Ammon (10:1-19)

Shameful Treatment of Israel's Ambassadors (10:1-5). The text is clear and unadorned. Hanun's father, Nahash, has died. Nahash had been the enemy of King Saul (1 Samuel 11). He may have been very young at the time he planned to bring the tribes of Israel on the east bank of the River Jordan under his authority. And perhaps he mellowed with age. Whatever changes had taken place following his defeat by King Saul, when the rift between Saul and David occurred, Nahash felt kindly disposed toward David.

Just when Nahash showed kindness to David is not recorded. What is significant is that David remembers that Nahash had "treated him loyally" (*'āśâ...'immādî ḥesed*), that is "showed him kindness (*ḥesed*)." His immediate response on hearing of Nahash's death is to send an embassage to comfort his son. "I will show kindness (*ḥesed*) to Hanun...just as his father showed kindness to me" (10:2).

Dr. William G. Blaikie has correctly observed:

> Powerful though David had proved himself in every direction in the art of war, his heart was inclined to peace. A king who had been victorious over so many foes had no occasion to be afraid of a people like the Ammonites. It could not have been from fear therefore, that when Nahash the king of the Ammonites died, David resolved to send a friendly message to his son.[2]

Joyce Baldwin has shown, however, that David's well-intentioned message to the new king of Ammon initiated a whole train of events that were to his disadvantage and must have raised the question whether it is prudent to "show kindness" to anyone.[3]

David's envoy probably caused a stir among the leaders of the people in the capital of Rabbah (modern Amman), for it is certain that they knew of Israel's recent victories over the Philistines, Moabites (Ammon's southern neighbors), Syrians (Ammon's northern neighbors), and Edomites. While these wars may well have occasioned caution on the part of the Ammonites, an embassage conveying condolences was the custom then as it is now.[4] Diplomacy, therefore, was called for, not actions based on suspicion and fear.

In addition, Hanun's advisors should have been better informed concerning the commencement of hostilities. At no time did Israel provoke an attack on the part of the Philistines, Moabites, Syrians, or Edomites. These nations had all been the aggressors. The counsel these high-ranking officials gave Hanun, therefore, was distorted by their own fears (10:3*a*).[5]

All of this highlights the fact that certain people are incapable of perceiving good in others. As a result, they attribute the worst of motives to those who wish to do them good. Their immaturity and/or insecurity place them in an invidious position, and it is nearly impossible for them to trust anyone.

This is illustrated for us in Hanun's reaction to the negative opinions of his advisors. He disregards all protocol (which was a well-established part of an Oriental court) and reverses the policy of his father by subjecting David's men to the greatest humiliation possible. Half of their beards are shaved off and their long cloaks are cut off at the waist. The men are then sent back to David.

For us to understand the full significance of what Hanun did, we need to realize that in eastern countries a man's beard[6] was a sign of his manhood. It was a symbol of his virility. To tamper with it was considered an insult, and to cut it off was to invite dire retribution.

Likewise, the deliberate cutting off of one's garments with the intent of exposing the genitals was to inflict the utmost indignity upon the person scorned. It was the kind of act that only the strong could do with impunity (cf. Isaiah 20:4). It violated the individual's sense of honor, caused him to experience extreme shame, and was tantamount to saying that he was impotent (for otherwise he would have prevented what had happened).

David's ambassadors were noble men. Hanun's actions caused them to feel demeaned and dishonored. And inasmuch as they were in Ammon representing their king, what was done to them was looked upon as being done to David as well.

It is approximately fifty miles by road from Jerusalem to Rabbah, and so it is a long walk home. Word precedes David's ambassadors and, as soon as David learns what has happened, he sends a runner to intercept them in Jericho (*Tell-es-Sultan*). They are told to remain there until their beards have grown again.

The fact that David does not send clothing as well may indicate that his ambassadors had either bought garments en route to Jericho, or perhaps Shobi, Hanun's brother, had supplied them with clothing as soon as it was safe for him to do so. If this is true, then it was the first time he would show kindness to David (cf. 17:27). And the fact that he was not killed when Rabbah finally fell to the Israelites might indicate that his life was spared on account of his kindness to David's men.

Purposeful Reinforcement of Ammon's Army (10:6-8). The Ammonites realize that what they have done is tantamount to a declaration of war. They know that they have made themselves odious to David, and to all intents and purposes, diplomatic relations have been severed (cf. Genesis 34:30; 2 Samuel 16:21).

It is important to notice that David does not retaliate. In this respect he acts as a most worthy example of Christ, who, when He was reviled, did not respond in kind but committed Himself to Him who judges faithfully (1 Peter 2:23).

The Ammonites, accustomed to dealing with people of their own ilk, hastily augment their forces with Syrian mercenaries from Beth-rehob[7] (on the northern border of Israel) and Zobah. They also prevail on the kings of Maacah[8] and Tob[9] to join forces with them.

For the people of Zobah, this seems to be a good opportunity to get even with David.

Only when David hears that the Ammonites are preparing for war does he send Joab and his regular army to Rabbah. By themselves the Ammonites do not constitute much of a threat, so David does not accompany the troops into battle.[10]

All of this raises the question, Did David know of the Syrian reinforcements or only of Ammon's preparations?

Joab seems to have been unaware of the presence of Syrian mercenaries (10:9), for he marched his men to Rabbah and into a trap. Later on, when David learns that Syrians have gathered to attack him (10:17ff.), he personally leads his men into battle. It seems likely, therefore, that when David first heard of the Ammonite build-up, he did not know that they had secured the help of Syria.

Resourceful Division of Israel's Forces (10:9-14). It would seem as if Joab and the army of Israel march to Rabbah by the most direct route (via Jericho and Heshbon). If Joab had known of the presence of Syrian reinforcements, he would most certainly have taken a less direct route.[11]

As soon as the Israelites prepare to attack the Ammonites who have drawn up in battle array in front of the city gates (10:8), Joab is made aware of the approach of the Syrians from the rear.[12] Acting quickly and decisively, he separates "the Mighty Men" and those under them from the militia.[13] Then he says to his brother, Abishai,

"If Aram (i.e., Syria) is stronger than me, then you shall come and help me (lit. be for me), but if the sons of Ammon are stronger than you, then I will come to help you. Be strong, and let us be strong for our people and for the cities of our God; and may Yahweh do [what is] good in His eyes" (10:11-12).

His use of the words, "Be strong, and let us show ourselves courageous for the sake of our people and the cities of our God"[14] may have been picked up as a battle cry. Dr. J. P. Fokkelman believes that Joab's concluding statement, "and may Yahweh do what is good in His sight," shows Joab to be a true believer.[15]

It seems more likely, however, that, being unsure of the outcome, Joab fatalistically leaves the matter in God's hands. Such is most often the attitude of those of Joab's background and temperament.

It should be noted that Joab took on the most difficult task himself. And, being a man of action, he was proactive. He took the initiative and attacked the Syrians. His frontal assault took them by surprise and they fled before the might of David's elite corps.

As soon as the Ammonites learn of what has happened, they retreat into the city (10:14a). But for reasons not explained in the text, Joab does not press his advantage (10:14b). Perhaps it is already late in the season, and he knows that he and his men do not have sufficient supplies to last through the winter. We may be sure that the Ammonites would have brought into the city of Rabbah everything edible. The men of Israel would not have gained much by sending out raiding parties to bring in supplies from the villages (cf. 1 Samuel 13:17-18).

It is also possible that Joab may have felt he had carried out his commission and so returned to Jerusalem to report to David.

Another explanation for his withdrawal may be deduced from verses 15-19. Joab may have been given an early intelligence report of the build-up of Syrian forces at Helam (10:16). His return to Jerusalem may have been to coordinate his forces with "all Israel" and to march with David to attack these regiments before they could attack Israel.

Wilful Opposition to Israel's King (10:15-19). We are not surprised, therefore, when the scene shifts from Rabbah to Helam (probably modern *'Alma*), approximately thirty-five miles east of the Sea of Galilee.[16] The Syrians are smarting as a result of their recent defeat and decide to regroup and consider their next move. Hadadezer believes that a larger force will succeed where his previous coalition failed. Acting upon his instincts, he sends messengers northward and calls for all the help he can muster. A vast force rallies around his banner. And to ensure he is not "out-generaled" again, he commissions his veteran commander, a man named Shobach, to lead the army.

David must have had his own method for gathering intelligence, for he is aware of Hadadezer's movements. He decides to act swiftly and decisively. Quickly gathering all the fighting men of Israel together, he leads them across the Jordan. The Syrians also have their spies watching for such movements and so are aware of his approach. When the Israelites arrive at Helam, the Syrians are ready. A terrific battle ensues. The armies are evenly matched. In the end, the Syrians are forced to flee. They leave behind on the battlefield charioteers, cavalrymen, infantrymen...and Shobach. All are dead (10:18).

With verse 19 we once again take note that what Israel's enemies intended for evil God turned around and used for the good of His people. He extended Israel's border, for when those kings who were formerly the vassals of Hadadezer understood the extent of their defeat, they willingly pledged allegiance to David and became his servants.[17]

The Syrian-Ammonite alliance was also broken, and from this time onwards the Syrians feared to help the Ammonites (10:19).

Psalm 124 may have been composed following this victory, for David looks back over several battles "when *men* rose up against us" (e.g., Philistines, Moabites, Syrians, Edomites), and then he praises the Lord for delivering His people from those who hated them (Psalm 124:2-8).

IMPORTANT ISSUES

Throughout this section we have seen the Lord working on David's behalf. He has sovereignly extended the borders of Israel and increased the wealth of His people by having surrounding nations pay tribute to them. All of this prefigures what will happen in the Millennium, when "great David's greater Son," the Lord Jesus Christ, will rule over the nations of the world (cf. Isaiah 60:5,11).

In this chapter, we are also shown an all-too-prevalent side of human nature in the suspicion, doubt, and apprehension with which David's delegation to Hanun was received. The attitude of Hanun's advisors was a reflection of their religious beliefs. The gods of Ammon were fearsome and suspicious, cruel and sadistic, and it is not surprising that the Ammonites became like them (see Psalm 135:15-18, noting v. 18).

All of this reinforces the teaching of Scripture that as a person thinks in his heart, so is he (Proverbs 23:7; Matthew 15:18-20*a*). In those places where the fear of the Lord is not to be found (see Genesis 20:11) and the rule is "might is right," there flourishes all that is worst in human nature (e.g., scorn and disrespect for the rights of others, pride and oppression, craftiness and greed, wilfulness and cruelty).

Unrestrained Conduct

David's kindness to Hanun was rejected, his motives were ridiculed, and his ambassadors were humiliated.

Kindness is a precious trait. To trample it underfoot is evidence of a calloused disregard for one of the finest qualities of human nature. In committee meetings and planning sessions, unscrupulous people often have a great advantage over those who are gracious and forbearing. Their penchant for arrogance and the ease with which they find fault may cause them to be heard above the rest, but it does not mean that their plans or ideas are the ones that should be followed.

Those who are disdainful of others are also skilled in pointed repartee. Their put-downs and belittling comments inflict great hurt on those who are sensitive and considerate. Even though their dictatorial manner tends to be convincing, their views are not necessarily right. In actual fact, as is illustrated in this chapter, the counsel they give may be totally wrong!

Dr. William Blaikie's words are weighty and worthy of our consideration:

> They [i.e., those who are overbearing] have little sense of the sin of [their words], and they toss them about without scruple. Such poisoned arrows inflict great pain, not because the charges are just, but because it is horrible to refined natures even to hear them. There are two things that make some men very sensitive—the refinement of grace, and the refinement of the spirit of courtesy. The refinement of grace makes all sin odious, and makes a charge of gross sin very serious. The refinement of courtesy creates great regard to the feelings of others, and a strong desire not to wound them unnecessarily.[18]

The Bible exhorts us not to answer a fool according to his folly (Proverbs 26:4). The foolish person is not lacking in mental powers; rather he misuses them. He has cast off "the fear of the Lord" (Proverbs 1:7) and consequently thinks and acts according to the standards of the times (Proverbs 14:1, 9; Jeremiah 17:11). As a result, he or she is easily led and in the course of time, becomes rash, senseless, and unreasonable.

David answered Hanun appropriately. He was bigger than the insults thrown at him. He chose to ignore the empty folly of a man who was unworthy of the office he held. Only when Hanun began preparing for war did David take appropriate action (cf., Proverbs 12:23).[19]

Political Move

The leaders of Ammon did not wait for a formal declaration of war. Arrogant and brash, they believed they could succeed where Philistia, Moab, Syria, and Edom had failed. Being intelligent (though unwise) people, they developed a plan to catch the Israelites in a pincer movement. At great cost to themselves, therefore, they hired Syrians to help them.

The Ammonites also planned that the Syrians would be the ones taking the risk. They would be in an open field, approximately twenty miles from the nearest fortified city. By contrast, the Ammonites, if hard-pressed, could retreat within the protective walls of their capital.

So it is among the godless. Their first thought is for themselves. In times of difficulty those who have been manipulated into helping them are left vulnerable and defenseless.

Careful Plot

All the vaunted wisdom of the Ammonite leaders, coupled with the flawless execution of their plan, was insufficient to gain the victory. They were ignorant of history, otherwise they would have known that "Yahweh is not restrained to save by many or by few" (1 Samuel 14:6b). Their hearts had become hardened. They were senseless, a nation of evildoers. Their spiritual condition, to borrow the words of Isaiah, was incorrigibly sinful. The whole head was sick, and the heart was faint. In looking upon their spiritual condition, God saw that from the sole of the foot to the top of the head there was no soundness. Everywhere there were bruises and welts and open sores (see Isaiah 1:5-6).

Sometimes these traits are manifest in the home, in a marriage partner or a child, and sometimes they are found in an office. Out of sheer necessity, those caught up in such a situation are compelled to take appropriate action. It is then that their reliance must be on the Lord. As they divide up their resources, they need the kind of wisdom that comes down from above that is first pure, then peaceable, gentle, willing to yield to the sovereignty of God, unwavering in its commitment to the truth, and without hypocrisy (see James 3:17).

Only as they are armed with spiritual resources can they persevere in doing what is right. And in His own good time the Lord will give them the victory.

Stubborn Intransigence

Even though we may be able to handle those who are predisposed to violence, what should be our response to those whose stubborn intransigence will not yield? Are we supposed to allow ourselves to be intimidated when they add to their ranks a "top gun" or a "heavy hitter" such as Shobach?

As we know from the story, Hadadezer sent across the Euphrates for reinforcements. He also prevailed on neighboring Arab tribes to join forces with him in an effort to crush the power of Israel.

That a very large number of Mesopotamian Syrians responded to the invitation of Hadadezer is apparent from the number of those killed (v.18). The strength of the opposition was so serious that David was now constrained to take the field.

> The Syrian troops were commanded by Shobach.... The resulting battle must have been a death-struggle between Syria and Israel. But again the victory went to the Israelites. And among the slain was...Shobach, captain of the Syrian host. It must have been a most decisive victory, for after it took place all the states that had been tributary to Hadadezer transferred their allegiance to David. Syrian power was completely broken. All help was withdrawn from the Ammonites who were now left to bear the brunt of the hostilities they had begun.[20]

David's imprecatory psalms give us a clear picture of how we can face such relentless opposition. David was completely identified with the Lord and His plans for His people. God's enemies were his enemies. That is why he could utter words of imprecation.[21]

Many look with disdain on the imprecatory psalms. They criticize the psalmist for his harsh feelings toward his enemies. Then they adopt a "holier than thou" attitude and say that David (and others who prayed similar prayers) knew nothing of the enlightenment of grace. But this same sentiment is found in the New Testament usage of the word 'anathema (see Galatians 1:9). Was the apostle Paul also a stranger to grace when he pronounced his curses on those who preached a false gospel?

Thirty-plus years ago, when I had the privilege of studying under the late Merrill F. Unger, the question of the abiding relevance of the imprecatory psalms was raised in class. I do not remember all that Dr. Unger said as he replied to the question, but I do recall that he prefaced his remarks by saying, "You have to be a very spiritual person to pray that kind of prayer."

David was so identified with the Lord that he wanted for his people only what God wanted for them. This made it easy for him, when Israel was unjustly threatened, to pray for the overthrow of their enemies. We, too, should be encouraged to bring before the Lord our concerns. And to the degree that we are identified with Him and His will, we can confidently look forward to the answer to our prayers (cf. Psalm 55:22-23; 1 Peter 5:8).

A MOMENT OF WEAKNESS

2 Samuel 11: 1-27

One of southern California's lesser known attractions is the La Brea
Tar Pits. Situated on the edge of downtown Los Angeles, this primeval site is mainly visited by school children on field trips.

On an overcast Saturday morning, my wife and I decided to visit
the Los Angeles Museum of Art. When we had finished looking at the
exhibits, we walked the short distance from the museum to these
famous tar pits.

The entrance led immediately toward an open section where centuries ago tar had collected and replaced the sand. A layer of water
covered the oily mass. Gas bubbles escaped at irregular intervals,
releasing a sulphurous odor. Across from the fence that circled the
tar pit were huge cement mastodons. One had become caught in the
ooze and was slowly sinking into the mire while its mate and calf
stood helplessly by trumpeting their concern.

Adjacent to the first of the tar pits is a museum. Inside we saw
fossil remains that had been dredged from the bottom of the different pits. Some of these had been pieced together by staff paleontolo-
gists. The result of their efforts gives modern viewers a picture of
primeval life in this part of the world. Saber-toothed tigers, with huge
incisors, show how fearsome these creatures must have been. The
skeletal remains of a small mastodon have been reassembled and
covered with look-alike skin and shaggy hair. And then there are the
remains of a variety of antelope, birds, and rodents that all sank to
their death in these pits.

But how were these animals drawn toward these traps? And what
possible relevance might this have for us today?

Well, rain is scarce in southern California. It falls mainly between
the middle of December and the end of February. The rest of the

year is dry and (from late spring through early fall) hot. Naturally, for most of the year, water is hard to find.

Rain falling on the tar would not sink into the earth but would offer what appeared to be a refreshing pool of water. Animals could come to the brink and drink freely. As evaporation caused the water to recede from the edge of the tar-filled pit, animals would have to step onto the soft surface in order to reach the water. Their feet would begin to sink into the ooze in much the same way they would into soft mud–except that it would be much, much harder to extract their feet from the tar. Provided the tar was not too deep and the animals could feel firm ground underneath them, they could struggle free. However, the further they had to advance to get to the water, the less likely they could regain the safety of the bank. If they were unable to extricate themselves from the soft, clinging tar, then they would slowly sink into the pit with nothing to stop them.

These animals had been lured with the promise of a thirst-quenching drink of water. But many of them found instead a slow, agonizing death. In their case, the temptation to slake their thirst proved fatal.

All of this has a bearing upon the culture of our times and the principles found in this portion of God's Word.

OUTLINE

With 2 Samuel 11 we come upon a digression. The Biblical writer has used this literary device before. The section from 11:2–12:25 is a good example of his departure from the history of events to discuss something of importance for his readers.

The theme of this division (covering 8:1–12:31) is *the sovereignty of God in expanding the kingdom.* In an earlier chapter, we saw how the Lord turned the tables on Philistia, Moab, Syria, and Edom to extend Israel's borders and give His people control of vital trade routes. In other words, what began as a series of unprovoked attacks and unwanted wars ended with Israel in command of territory from the Tigris/Euphrates valley in the north to the Gulf of Aqaba in the south. Now the wealth of these nations poured in to Israel.

David, after showing *ḥesed,* "kindness," to Mephibosheth (ch. 9) and graciously attempting to console Hanun following his father's death (10:1-2), found himself embroiled in a war with Ammon (10:6-14). As we put chapter 11 into the context of these events, let us refresh our memories on the scope of this entire division. It includes

- External Threats to the Nation (8:1-14)
- Internal Administration of the Nation (8:15-18)

Digression: Reminder of a Friendship (9:1-13)
- Further Threats to the Nation (10:1–12:31)
  War With Ammon (10:1-19)
    Digression: Adultery and Its Aftermath (11:1–12:25)
  Victory over Ammon (12:26-31).

At this time we will look only at the contents of 2 Samuel 11. Sufficient for us to note is the fact that the events took place *during* the Ammonite war. Here is an outline of this chapter:

The Setting (11:1)
  The Unexpected Temptation (11:2-5)
  The Successful Cover-up (11:6-27*a*)
  The Divine Perspective (11:27*b*)

The exposure of David's sin (12:1-25) and the victory over Ammon (12:26-31) will be the subject of the next chapter.

Dr. J. P. Fokkleman[1] has pointed out that the story of David's adultery is very short. Everything is told in twelve lines (in a Hebrew Bible). David's attempts to extricate himself from the consequences of his sin, like those of an animal caught in a tar pit, show that he had become trapped in a predicament of his own making. He was now incapable of showing *ḥesed* ("loving-kindness"). The events of this chapter, therefore, stand in stark contrast to the tender regard he showed Mephibosheth and the comfort he wanted to extend to Hanun.

Digression: Adultery and Its Aftermath (11:1-27)

The Historic Setting (11:1). David has suffered greatly at the hands of would-be exponents of the Word. We are told with much emphasis that he should have gone to the battlefront with his men; that he had grown soft and become lethargic as a result of a life of self-indulgence; and that he only fell into temptation because he remained in Jerusalem.

Actually, there are many important lessons to be learned from this chapter. But only as we build our understanding of what took place upon a sound interpretation of the data will we be able to apply the text accurately and reliably. The first matter to be cleared up, therefore, is whether the accusations of David's critics have any validity. And let us remember that God's Word is strangely silent when it comes to these charges. David's critics are the ones who need to advance Biblical support for their views.

Kings normally began their campaigns of conquest with the beginning of the dry season (e.g., spring).[2] It seems likely that Joab had been forced to break off his attack on Ammon the previous year because the Syrian build-up in the north had required the entire army move to a new location. The siege of Rabbah, therefore, had to be put on hold. This gave the Ammonites time to prepare for the coming Israeli invasion.

Hanun, of course, knew of his nation's weaknesses and enlisted the aid of all his vassals.[3] They became his first line of defense. He also laid up a significant amount of food, for the people of Rabbah are able to withstand a protracted siege.

When hostilities are resumed, Joab and the fighting men of Israel quickly defeat those under an obligation to help Hanun (11:1). They then march on Rabbah. Their intent is to surround the capital of Ammon, cut off their food and water supplies, and eventually force the inhabitants to either surrender or come out of their citadel and engage Israel in one last desperate attempt to stave off defeat.

Early visitors to this Transjordanian town (before it was thrust into the twentieth century and modernized) described Rabbah as situated at the end of a narrow gorge. The royal city sat on top of a

> turfed plain, completely shut in by low hills on every side,.... This [walled] city Joab took [12:26]. But there still remained... the citadel, perched in front of Rabbah on a round, steep, flat-topped mamelon, past which the stream flowed rapidly through a valley contracted at once to a width of five hundred paces. As if to complete the natural defenses, on its other side were valleys, gullies, and ravines, which almost isolated the citadel.[4]

From incidental references in the text, it appears as if the siege of Rabbah lasted for at least a year, and perhaps longer. While we may be sure that David would much rather have been with his men, affairs of state (cf. 8:15) demanded that he remain in Jerusalem. The claim of many Bible teachers that David had become indulgent and that the sinews of his will had become soft is without foundation. Dr. A. F. Kirkpatrick writes:

> The statement [David tarried at Jerusalem] prepares the way for the narrative that follows, *but does not necessarily imply that David was to blame for remaining in Jerusalem*. Joab was a capable and trustworthy commander; the siege of Rabbah was likely to be tedious; and the judicial and administrative duties of the king would make a long absence from the capital

undesirable. David did not go to the first Ammonite war (10:7), though in the more formidable attack of the Syrians he took the command in person (10:17f.).[5]

While we have advanced the belief that the siege lasted for about a year, the late Merrill F. Unger was inclined to the belief that it took two years.[6] Whatever the period of time, David could ill afford to be away from his administrative duties for such an extended period. His critics have erred in their assertion that he had become weak, irresolute, and self-indulgent.

An Unexpected Temptation (11:2-5). One object of Scripture is to paint sin in its true colors. No friendly flattery or false modesty draws a veil over this dark episode in David's life. The events are recorded as a warning, showing that even good men may yield to temptation and fall into sin; that one sin almost inevitably leads to others; and that sin, even when repented of, brings punishment in its wake.[7]

On hot, sultry afternoons in the Middle East, work stops and people look for whatever shade may be found.[8] This siesta time continues until the sun begins to set. Then a refreshing breeze springs up.

As with the other inhabitants of Jerusalem, David seeks relief from the oppressive heat in a special structure, perhaps a tent pitched on the flat roof of his palace (cf. 4:5-6; 16:22. See also Judges 3:20, 24-25). On this particular afternoon, as the sun begins to set, he rises and begins pacing back and forth. The verb used indicates that he is preoccupied with some matter and so walks to and fro on the roof.[9]

From this vantage point he is able to look out over the city. Spread before him are the homes (many of them consisting of only one room) of his people. Here and there men are taking up again their trade that had been laid aside while everything beneath the cloudless sky baked in the sun's merciless rays. The women too are beginning to make their way to the Gihon Spring to fill their waterpots. David can hear their happy laughter as they talk with one another.

Quite unexpectedly his attention is drawn to a courtyard a short distance from his palace. There he sees a woman bathing. The writer of the story describes her as "*very* beautiful."

Bathing in a courtyard may at first strike us as immodest. However, had we lived in such a hot climate, with no air-conditioning in our home and with the water kept in a large jar in the courtyard, we might have found that bathing in an enclosed courtyard was an accepted (though probably not a common) practice. No one could see into the courtyard from the street, so this made the woman's actions less risque than might at first be imagined.[10]

David could not help the first glance, but once he had seen her *he could have averted his eyes* (cf. Job 31:1) and refused to indulge his senses. In all probability, he found the sight a pleasant diversion from the matters that had been weighing on him. So he continued to watch her.

Exactly how sin was conceived in his heart we do not know. It is difficult for us to think of David allowing lustful thoughts to occupy his mind, and we do not want to be guilty of imputing to him anything more than is stated by the inspired chronicler. James, our Lord's brother, warned us that we are tempted when we are carried away and enticed by our own lust. And lust, when it has been conceived, brings forth sin (James 1:14-15).[11]

Dietrich Bonhoeffer, in his book *Creation and Fall and Temptation*, has the following astute observation:

> In our members there is a slumbering inclination towards desire which is both sudden and fierce. With irresistible power, desire seizes mastery over the flesh. All at once a secret, smoldering fire is kindled. The flesh burns and is in flames.... At this moment God is quite unreal to us, he loses all reality, and only desire for the creature is real.... Satan does not here fill us with hatred of God, but with forgetfulness of God. The lust thus aroused envelops the mind and will of man in deepest darkness. [And] the powers of clear discrimination and of decision are taken from us.[12]

Probably, as David continues to gaze down on the woman and take in her every movement, his passions become inflamed. He wants her. Although he is not aware of it, his feet have begun to sink into the miry tar of his lust.

At first, he may have thought that this beautiful woman was unmarried. If so, he could take her into his harem. But who is she? He has to find out. And so he sends one of his servants to inquire about her.

When word is brought back to him, he learns that she is Bathsheba, the daughter of Eliam,[13] the wife of Uriah the Hittite. *This information should have checked his passionate impulse at once!* Not only is she the daughter and granddaughter, respectively, of two of his dearest friends, Eliam, his faithful associate, and Ahithophel, his wise counselor—she is also married to Uriah, one of his loyal soldiers (23:39).

As king, David is obliged to uphold the Law (cf. Exodus 20:14; Leviticus 18:20; 20:10; Deuteronomy 5:21).[14] He also has the responsibility to protect and maintain the rights of his subjects. William J. Deane comments on David's ignoring of these responsibilities:

All such considerations [as friendship and responsibility] are feeble barriers against the gratification of an overmastering passion. Lust conceived and cherished brings forth sin. David makes no endeavor to avoid the strong temptation; he sends for the woman; he overcomes her scruples; he uses his position to influence her to yield to his wishes.[15]

If this had been a Hollywood script, it would have dwelt at length on the events of that night. God passes over the scene in David's bedroom with a single statement: "he lay with her" (11:4).

Some subtle allusions in the text prepare us for what is to follow. Bathsheba's "bathing" was evidently in fulfillment of the teaching of Leviticus 15:19ff.[16] During her menstrual period, she had become ceremonially "defiled." Her bathing was a part of the rite of purification.

According to the Jewish *Talmud* and other ancient sources, a woman was believed to be most fertile immediately following her menstrual cycle. David, however, disregarded the obvious implication of the ceremonial washing he had observed. As with the animals that were caught in the La Brea Tar Pits, he now desperately wants to drink of the waters of sensual delights. To do so he throws caution to the winds. And he, not Bathsheba, is held accountable for what took place that evening (cf. Psalm 51). David's passions mastered him. Bathsheba could do little to oppose his will.

It is true that in a case of rape a woman was expected to cry out and struggle to free herself (cf. Deuteronomy 22:24ff.). Bathsheba may have tried to reason with David or plead the fact that she was already married. But she does not appear to have offered much resistance. She quite probably felt herself unable to withstand the advances of her king. To call for help would bring the palace guards, but that would result in humiliation for herself as well as David. And how could she possibly explain her presence in the palace to Uriah?

After rising from David's couch, Bathsheba "purifies herself from her uncleanness" (see Leviticus 15:18).[17] The fact that she performs this ceremonial washing indicates that she is at heart a pious woman. While she had broken God's moral law, she still adheres to the rituals of the ceremonial law. She then returns to her house (11:4c).

We have no means of knowing how Bathsheba felt as she walked the short distance to her home. Did she feel dishonored and guilty as a result of what had happened?

We do know that a few weeks later she realizes she is pregnant. She knows that her condition cannot be hidden for too long and that adultery is punishable by death (Leviticus 20:10).[18] Something must be done...and soon. Fortunately, she does not panic. Whereas others might have become fearful to the point of desperation, she retains her presence of mind. Her actions are limited to a letter she sends to David. It is simple, yet eloquent:

"I am with child."

Bathsheba does not attempt to fix any blame nor does she engage in any threats. And she does not tell David what to do. Instead, she provides him with the facts and leaves him to take whatever course of action he deems best. Then she waits.

A Successful Cover-up (11:6-27a). On receiving Bathsheba's letter, David commissions one of his fastest runners to go to Joab, fifty miles away. He is to take the most direct route, and deliver a note to Joab. Uriah the Hittite is to be sent to him at once (11:6). The pretext is to know how the battle is progressing. David's ulterior motive, however, is to have Uriah spend a few days at home. He presumes that having been away from his wife for a while (perhaps months), Uriah will in all probability make love to her. Then, when the child is born, Uriah will think it is his.

We have not heard of Uriah before this, and a few facts about him will help us understand him better. His name (*'Ûrîyâ*, "Yahweh is my light") indicates that his parents were God-fearing people. The Hittites were an Anatolian race who had established themselves in Syria in the second millennium B.C. After the collapse of the empire around 1200 B.C. (i.e., two hundred years before the time of our story) their civilization dispersed among smaller states in northern Syria and, in the course of time, became predominantly Semitic. It is probable that Uriah's family came from one of these settlements.

Uriah must have wondered why David had specifically summoned him to return to Jerusalem. Being well disciplined, however, he obediently hurries to the palace.

When he is ushered into David's presence, the king asks him about the progress of the war and the morale of the troops. Uriah's reply is not recorded. Is this because David was not listening? We know that his real desire was to have this loyal soldier spend time with Bathsheba.

When Uriah has finished his report, David says, in effect:

"Go down to your house. Wash the dust off your feet.[19] You've come a long way. Take a few days off. You've earned some rest" (cf. 11:8).

As a sign of special favor, David also sends a present (most likely of food) after Uriah so that he and his wife can suitably celebrate his brief respite from the rigors of war.

Uriah, however, is a man of honor. He spends the rest of the day and the evening with the king's servants. He even sleeps on the floor at the door of the palace. The next morning, when David instructs a messenger to summon Uriah so that he can send him back to the front, he is told that he is still there. This necessitates a change of plans. David calls for Uriah, and asks: "Uriah, haven't you come from a journey? Why didn't you go down to your house?"

To the king's inquiry Uriah responds:

> "The Ark and Israel are staying in temporary shelters (i.e., booths), and my lord Joab and the servants of my lord [the king] are camping in the open field. Shall I go down to my house to eat and to drink and to lie with my wife? By your life and the life of your soul, *I* will not do this thing" (11:11).

His emphasis is obvious. He is committed to doing his duty. Right now he is a soldier and under an obligation to maintain himself in mental and emotional readiness. And his oath ("By your life...")– added for emphasis–is unique. The exact wording occurs only here in Scripture, though similarities to each part of it are found elsewhere. Furthermore, his *"I"* is emphatic. The point is that Uriah is a man of integrity.[20] His high sense of duty compels him to exercise self-restraint.

The contrast between Uriah and David at this juncture could not be more pronounced. On the one hand we have the king unscrupulously trying to obscure his sensuality and self-gratification; and on the other, the noble sense of responsibility, singleness of purpose, and self-control of his subordinate.

David responds to Uriah's attestation of loyalty with some degree of ambiguity: "Stay here today also, and tomorrow I will let you go" (11:12).

In saying this, David may have had in mind the thought that Uriah, knowing he will not be sent back to the front lines until tomorrow, and with nothing else to do, will go and visit his wife. But David delays his departure by two days (11:12b). And still Uriah holds fast to his integrity.

At the end of the third day it is evident to David that his plan is not going to work. With rising misgivings, he invites Uriah to dine with him. They eat and drink, and David deliberately tries to make him drunk. He hopes that the effects of the wine will weaken his officer's resolve. But Uriah drunk is more noble than David sober. And so, once again, he lies down to sleep with David's servants.

David cannot sleep. He feels himself sinking...sinking.... He must devise a plan; one that will work! But what can he do? How can he extricate himself from the consequences of his actions?

It may have been in the early hours of the morning that he decided to have the Ammonites do his dirty work for him. To be successful, however, he will need Joab's help.

So the next morning David gives Uriah a letter to take to Joab. It is brief and to the point:

> "Set Uriah in the forefront of the hottest battle, and retire from him, that he may be struck down and die" (11:15).[21]

As with Lady Macbeth in the killing of Duncan, David feels that he has gone too far to turn back.[22] His plan is a desperate one. But it is the only one he can think of to extricate himself from the quagmire that threatens to engulf him. The bottom line is: Uriah must be terminated. His death, however, must look natural. He must become a casualty of war.[23] And so, as with Bellerophon in Homer's *Iliad*, righteous Uriah carries his own death warrant to Joab.[24]

As we have noted before, Joab is a corrupt man. He had not hesitated to murder Abner (3:23-32), and he had smarted under David's rebuke and distrust ever since. Now, David wants him to collaborate in a dishonest act, and he is happy to comply. As William Deane has pointed out,

> The king was thus putting himself in [Joab's] power; he could no longer reproach his nephew with the treacherous murder of Abner, now that he was equally guilty. By making Joab his accomplice in the crime he deprived himself of the right of objection to any of the latter's violent proceedings, and afforded ground for grave doubts as to the sincerity of his religion, and a growing suspicion that he was at heart as lawless and unscrupulous as Joab himself.[25]

While Bathsheba waits, not knowing what David is doing (or if he will do anything), David also waits. Everything now depends on Joab.

Joab is as shrewd as he is unprincipled. He carefully assesses the situation and takes note of where Ammon's forces appear strongest. A plan takes shape in his mind. It involves putting Uriah at the head of a party that is to attack the city's main gate. This is where Rabbah's elite corps has been stationed. David had planned for only Uriah to be murdered; Joab's plan results in the loss of many lives.

As Uriah and his men approach the gate (possibly with the intention of setting fire to it), Ammon's valiant men come out and hand-to-hand fighting ensues. From verse 17*b* it appears as if Uriah was killed by these defenders. Verse 24 intimates that he and his men were successful in pressing their attack but fell before the archers who shot at them from the wall of the city.

Mr. L. Oliphant personally visited Rabbah and reflected on Uriah's death.

> [I] looked sheer down about three hundred feet into the wady, and four hundred feet into the other, I did not wonder at its having occurred to King David that the leader of a forlorn hope against these ramparts would meet with certain death, and consequently assigning this position to Uriah. The only possible point from which that officer could have advanced was at the apex, where the low neck connects the citadel with the high plateau beyond; but even here he would have had to charge an almost hopeless escarpment.... Portions of the colossal gateway and the massive wall flanking it, at the point where the low neck joins the apex of the triangle, still remain to attest the truth of this narrative, and to identify the spot where Uriah met his fate.[26]

Uriah bravely carried out his orders, never questioning his superior officer. And in his death, David lost one of his finest officers as well as a trusting friend.

After the fighting, a messenger is sent to David with a report of the battle. It is evident from 11:18-21 that David had always been solicitous of the safety of his men and did not hazard their lives unnecessarily. Joab expected David to react in anger at the large number of casualties. The Septuagint embellishes the Biblical text and reads:

> And Joab's messenger went to the king to Jerusalem, and came and told David all that Joab had told him, even all the things concerning the war. And David was angry with Joab, and said to the messenger, "Wherefore did you approach up to the city to fight? Who killed Abimelech the son of Jerubbabel? Didn't a woman throw upon him a piece of a millstone from the wall, so that he died at Thebez? Why then did you approach the wall [of the city]?"

But this is not the impression we get from reading the original text

(11:22-24), for David's reply is mild. As soon as he learns that Uriah has died in the fighting, he says:

> "This is what you shall say to Joab: 'Do not let this thing displease you (lit. be evil in your eyes), for the sword devours one as well as another. Make your battle against the city stronger and overthrow it.' And so encourage him" (11:25).

We may be sure that Bathsheba knew nothing of David's plans or of the apparent success of the cover-up. When she receives word of her husband's death, she spends the customary period (probably seven days[27]) in mourning. How sincere her grief is is not known. Being at heart a righteous woman, we may assume that she genuinely grieved her loss. Uriah had been a good husband, even though his inflexible commitment to duty may have made it hard to live with him.

Even in her grief, though, there may well have been feelings of guilt, for his death gave her a ray of hope. She could always say that Uriah was the father of her child, and he would not be there to deny it.

David, however, had been greatly impressed with Bathsheba for, to complete the cover-up, he determines to take her as his wife (not as a concubine). In light of this, his next move may have taken Bathsheba by surprise. He sends for her as he had done before, only this time she enters his house to become his bride. As far as palace gossip is concerned, the official report may well have been that he had promised Uriah, if anything should happen to him, to care for Bathsheba.

And so, to all intents and purposes, the cover-up is complete. After their marriage, the glare of publicity dims and the criticism that often follow those in public office abates. In the safety and relative seclusion of the palace, Bathsheba spends the remaining months of her confinement. As far as appearances are concerned, everything is fine. The guilty pair keep to themselves their clandestine activity.

The Divine Perspective (11:27b). If David was pleased with himself for having succeeded in getting out of the mess he was in and regaining solid ground, God was not. We read, "But the thing that David had done was evil in the sight of Yahweh." He had sinned against the Lord (cf. Genesis 20:6; Psalm 51:4). His desire to be a man of integrity, lead his people righteously, and walk before the Lord with a pure heart, had received a severe setback.

When we sin against the Lord, we lose the joy of His presence (see Psalm 32:3-4). We then become depressed. Our consciences accuse us. Our spirits are in turmoil. We feel anxious and life loses its zest.

David repressed his feelings of guilt. He did not acknowledge before the Lord what he had done. In grace God gave him time to repent.

THE FALL OF A GOOD MAN

It seems scarcely possible that David, the "sweet singer of Israel," the composer of a hundred psalms, and the man who more than any other character in the Old Testament prefigured the Messiah could become guilty of adultery and murder. How did this happen? What led up to his fall? Why did he act the way he did? And what safeguards may we employ so as to avoid becoming trapped in the tar pit of our own particular temptations?

David's fall illustrates for us the origin and growth of temptation. Many preachers and writers have discoursed at length on David's sins,[28] and because this field has been examined so thoroughly, we will concentrate instead on *the dynamics of temptation*. The value of this approach is that we will be better prepared to recognize Satan's strategies in all areas of life.

First, however, we shall need working definitions of *immorality* and *temptation*.

While *immorality* is commonly limited to sexual impropriety and has been defined as "conduct contrary to the established principles of morality,"[29] this is too limiting and doesn't teach us very much. In practical terms, *we are guilty of immorality each time we treat a person as a "thing" and invest things with the value that properly belongs to people*. People (not things) have been made in the image of God (Genesis 1:26-27). To use people to serve our own ends is immoral, and this applies as much to an employer who exploits his employees as it does to someone who engages in pornography. In short, when our needs, desires, or wants are elevated above what is best for others, then we become self-serving and are guilty of immorality.

Temptation has been described as *the enticement of a person to commit sin by offering "some" seeming advantage*. There are three basic ways in which we may be tempted to sin. We read of them in 1 John 2:15-17.

Do not love the world[30] nor the things in the world. If anyone loves the world, the love of the Father is not in him; because all that is in the world, *the lust of the flesh* [what I want to do], and *the lust of the eyes* [what I want to have], and *the vainglory of life* [what I want to be], is not of the Father, but [is] of the world. And the world is passing away and its lusts; but the [one] who does the will of God remains unto the ages (i.e., forever) (emphasis added).

The "world" is the present system, organized under Satan in opposition to God (John 12:31; 14:30; 16:11). We, as believers, have been called out of this system; and while we are still in the world, we are not to be of it (1 Peter 2:9. cf. 1 Corinthians 5:10; 2 Corinthians 1:12).

Omni magazine recently carried an article entitled "Too Tempting to Resist," by Anthony Liversidge.[31] The writer cites research by Daniel Wegner, a psychologist at the University of Virginia, in which Dr. Wegner believes that certain notable evangelists whose TV ministries reached millions of people and whose sex scandals have shocked the nation may not have been guilty of hypocrisy as was first imagined. To prove his point he asked several groups of people *not* to think of white bears (or pink elephants). The harder they tried not to think of white bears (or pink elephants), the more they found themselves thinking about them.

He then applied this principle to temptation. The more preachers rail against sexual immorality (and they have to think about it to describe it and preach against it), the more they repress their own urges and create enticing images in the minds of their hearers. In other words, the more one may try to resist thinking about something desirable (in David's case, a beautiful, naked woman), the more the desire intrudes into the thought processes. And the more one tries to suppress the desire, the stronger it grows.

According to Dr. Wegner, the sex scandals that have rocked the church in recent years were inevitable. When certain thoughts became allied with a corresponding desire, pressure mounted until these desires could no longer be contained. After this it was just a matter of time before the thoughts were acted out to release the tension that had built up inside.

What I Want To Do

Some indication of the extent to which "the lust of the flesh" predominates in our culture is to be found in television commercials. The slogans are constantly changing, but their message remains the same: "Have it your way," "Do something good for yourself," "You've earned the right to ——," or "You owe it to yourself."

This temptation is one to which we all fall prey at one time or another. The basic thrust of it is hedonistic. It is aimed at satisfying our wants. And virtually anything is acceptable "provided no one gets hurt."[32]

As the apostle Paul pointed out, however, the real outlet for "the lust of the flesh" is to be found in fornication, uncleanness, lewdness, idolatry (or covetousness; cf. Colossians 3:5), sorcery (i.e., all forms of spiritism), enmities, strife, jealousy, acts of rage, rivalries, divisions, sects, envyings, drunkenness, revelings, and things like these (Galatians 5:19-21). And when these occur, someone certainly does get hurt.

David had reached a stage in life when he was particularly susceptible to "the lust of the flesh." He felt secure. Most of his hard-fought battles were behind him. He could now enjoy some of the rewards of his labors. But what made him so vulnerable?

He was nearing fifty, and in all probability his virility had been waning for several years.[33] When he saw a beautiful woman bathing, he welcomed the sight as an agreeable distraction from the pressures of administration. The sight of her aroused in him intense desires that he had not experienced for years. And with complete disregard for her or the law he was honor bound to uphold, he sent for her. He may have rationalized to himself that he only wanted to talk to her, but he ended up seducing her. Then, he used the power of his position to overcome any scruples she may have had.

In other words, *he acted immorally*. Let us note well that "the lust of the flesh"–the desire for satisfaction that arises from within–causes us to disregard the rights of others in order to do what we want.

What I Want To Have

If "the lust of the flesh" has its roots in the abuse of power, "the lust of the eyes" has to do with the way we go about obtaining the things we want or believe we deserve.

Many legitimate desires are not in and of themselves sinful. Elderly people on a fixed income that continually slips toward the poverty level may wish that their Social Security could be increased so that their declining years might be free from anxiety. A mature young woman may desire to have a husband, the satisfaction of knowing she is loved, and the security of a home. And those who have been married for some time may long to rekindle their early romance. These are legitimate desires. And, of course, we could each compile a list that could go on and on.

"The lust of the eyes," however, brings into focus our inordinate desires. The essence of this temptation is to have more–for the satisfaction we believe it will bring us or the way it will enhance our image in the eyes of our colleagues or neighbors. This desire for things has to do with externals, with objects we believe will enhance our well-being and improve our standing in the community.

The basis of this temptation lies in our propensity to be attracted by outward appearances–fine clothes, an expensive car, a lavishly furnished home–and having seen something, to want it. In time, this form of temptation gains such a mastery over us that we seek to meet our innate needs for significance by adding to our possessions. Often, we exploit others in order to feed this insatiable craving.[34]

In David's case, he wanted to have Bathsheba because of the feelings she aroused in him, and he used his position to gratify these desires. He followed the dictum: "If you want it, take it." And so we read,

He sent messengers [for Bathsheba] and took her, and...lay with her (11:4).

She was some*thing* he wanted.

What I Want to Be

If "the lust of the flesh" finds its fulfillment through the abuse of power, and "the lust of the eyes" in the use of our position in order to acquire the things we think will make us happy, "the boastful pride of life" comes to fruition in the aggrandizement of self. For example, we may daydream of winning a Nobel Prize, writing the "great American novel," or being promoted to the executive suite with paneled walls, plush carpet, handsome desk, and matching accessories. Involved in this kind of fanciful revery is "the boastful pride of life."

Many of our wishes may be relatively harmless. But they center in self, and so we need to beware. Our thoughts reveal what is in our hearts–the desire to be looked up to and admired, praised and fawned over, quoted and respected, receive accolades from our company or the college we attended, and be invited out to the best restaurants where we meet only the most influential people.

The boastful pride of life is the spirit that sets as its goal rank, wealth, power, education, talent, cleverness, or any other gift so as to be the source of envy or admiration of one's peers. And it despises those who do not possess what we believe to be important.[35]

Inherent in each one of us is (1) a need to love someone, (2) a need to be loved by someone, and (3) the need for competence. These desires are legitimate. Ironically, their illegitimate use parallels the three forms of temptation the apostle John wrote about. When these ordinate needs are not met through legitimate courses of action, we experience the temptation to meet them in inordinate ways.

Temptation, regardless of the form(s) it takes, is centered in ourselves. It is egocentric and manifests itself in a self-centered lifestyle.

But are we locked into the kind of situation described by Dr. Daniel Wegner? Is succumbing to temptation inevitable? Are we doomed to have our thoughts gain eventual mastery over us?

In Romans 6, the apostle Paul described the resources of the believer, which are found in *a vital union with Christ in His death and resurrection* (Romans 6:4-7). Because we are united to Christ, His victory over temptation and sin and death becomes ours. In and of ourselves we are doomed to fail because we are weak (Romans 7:7-25). However, as we consciously see ourselves *in Him* we come to realize that when He died for sin we were positionally "in Him." We are therefore dead to sin. And when He rose from the dead, we rose in Him (Romans 6:8-10). A new lifestyle is possible as we appropriate the benefits of His resurrection life.

When we are tempted, we should reckon (i.e., count it as true) that we are dead to sin (Romans 6:11). The Holy Spirit can then make real in our experience what is described by Paul in this portion of Romans (Romans 6:12; cf. 8:2-4). He is the One who empowers us so that we no longer yield our bodies to sin (Romans 6:13).

David enjoyed the presence of the Holy Spirit in much the same way we do (cf. 1 Samuel 16:13). He could have recognized sin as it reared its ugly head, and he could have availed himself of the power of God to overcome the temptation that was presented to him. Instead, he entertained the thought which eventually became the deed.

God has given us all we need for this life and godliness (2 Peter 1:3). It is our responsibility to avail ourselves of the resources He has provided for us and so avoid sinking into the quagmire of our lusts.

GRACE UPON GRACE

2 Samuel 12:1-31

Imagine you are playing a word association game with some grade school children in Sunday school. You give them a name, and they supply another one that goes with it. When you say, "Adam and—," they supply "Eve".

When you ask, "Abraham and—?," they will most likely give you "Sarah" or "Isaac".

And to "Jacob and—?," they will probably respond with "Esau".

To the question "David and—?," they will in all likelihood say "Goliath."

But from junior high school onwards a change takes place. To the question "David and—?," the response is invariably "Bathsheba."

Even non-Christians know of David's sin with Bathsheba. And many are unwilling to let us forget that one of the greatest men of God of all time was both an adulterer and a murderer. All of this serves to reinforce the words of the Lord God through Nathan, that by his deed David gave the enemies of the Lord occasion to blaspheme.

While non-Christians frequently use this story to excuse their own failings, Christians often misuse or distort it. Let me illustrate this point with two examples that represent many who suffer under a heavy load of guilt.

Darci and Dick had been married for twelve years when Darci began an affair with a man who worked in her office. After several clandestine meetings, Darci found that she was so chronically unhappy and afraid that she broke off the relationship.

Some friends noticed that she was deeply depressed. The light had gone out of her eyes, and she often seemed to be moody. She would also begin crying for no apparent reason. Her friends suggested that she contact me. At our first meeting, she opened the conversation by saying: "Dr. Barber, you cannot help me, and I'm just wasting your time and mine by being here."

As we talked, I found out that her feelings of guilt were compounded by fear. She was afraid that her husband would find out and divorce her. She was also afraid that her children (and grandchildren if she ever had any) would grow up under the cloud of her sin. When I asked her why she believed this, she was quick to remind me that "God visits the iniquities of parents on their children to the third and fourth generation."

I continued to ask Darci about her belief system and where she got some of her ideas. She said this is what her church taught. Then she went on to refer me to the incident of David's sin with Bathsheba (even though she was not sure if it was in the Old or the New Testament). She again reminded me of the teaching of Scripture concerning David, "And the sword (i.e., trouble) will never depart from your house." From this she had concluded that she was doomed to a life of unhappiness, and what she had done would be an unending source of trouble for her family.

When Darci's parents were suddenly killed in a car accident, she was convinced that it was her fault. It was one of God's many punishments He was visiting on her for her sin. When I questioned her about her views, she quickly pointed to David and asked rhetorically, "After all, didn't He take away David's sons?"

As her depression deepened, she continued to see herself as worthless, unlovely, and unlovable; and doomed to a life of perpetual unhappiness on account of her brief affair.

It was plain that Darci knew nothing of grace, and in approaching the problem she was locked into what psychologists call a "self-fulfilling prophecy."[1] Her belief system was such that, apart from the death of her parents, she was subconsciously acting in a way that brought about what she feared most (see Job 3:25). These "fulfillments" of her fears convinced her that other forms of punishment were sure to happen.

Over many months and with numerous retrogressions into her former pattern of thinking, Darci came to a place where she could confess her sin to the Lord and receive forgiveness from Him. Our primary focus during these sessions was Psalms 32 and 51. Then she had to struggle with the need to forgive herself. As the truth of Scripture transformed her thought processes, she came to rejoice in God's free, unmerited remission of her sins.

When we left Illinois to come to California, Darci was happier in her relationship with Dick than she had ever been before.

The situation of Mark and Monica is also of interest to us. They were new Christians and had recently joined the church to which my wife and I belonged. One day Monica phoned me. She was weeping hysterically. She was seven months pregnant with their first child, and instead of this being a joyous time for them, it had become one of the most painful experiences of their lives. I agreed to meet with her and Mark for lunch so that we could discuss what had happened.

At a home Bible study they were attending, they had innocently let drop the fact that they had engaged in premarital sexual relations and had only married when Monica found that she was pregnant. When the group broke up for coffee and refreshments, the hostess took the two of them aside. So forcefully had she spoken to them that her words were etched into their minds. They could repeat them verbatim:

> "Your child is cursed of God. If he survives infancy he will grow up reprobate. The two of you will experience nothing but grief in your marriage, for God cannot and will not bless the union of those who disobey His word. Adultery is *the* most heinous of all sins. God's wrath now abides on you!"

When Mark and Monica stammered out their bewilderment, this woman opened her Bible to passages of Scripture where certain verses were underlined in red. The first was Hebrews 13:4. She made them read it aloud. They felt humiliated. The next was 2 Samuel 12:9-12. Then she told them that, as with David, they had "despised the word of the Lord" (even though, unsaved at the time, they were ignorant of it). As the import of the verses they had read burned their way into their hearts, their fear was that "the Lord would raise up evil against them, and trouble would never depart from their house" (12:11*a*).

No wonder Mark and Monica were distraught! The joy of their salvation was gone. They felt condemned. In one night, all hope of happiness had been swept away. And what was worse, the group of believers who had welcomed them a few weeks before now shunned them.

Because these are not isolated incidents, a careful consideration of 2 Samuel 12, is essential. To accurately understand what is taught, we will need to be careful not to read into the text more than is there. At the same time, we must be loyal to what God has revealed, see sin for what it is, and not minimize the seriousness of David's offense.

OUTLINE

As we observed earlier, the division of 2 Samuel that extends from 8:1–12:31 shows us God sovereignly extending the kingdom. A review of the scope of God's dealings with Israel will place these events in their proper context:

- External Threats to the Nation (8:1-14)
- Internal Administration of the Nation (8:15-18)
  Digression: Reminder of a Friendship (9:1-13)
- Further Threats to the Nation (10:1–12:31)
  War with Ammon (10:1-19)
     Digression: Adultery and Its Aftermath (11:1–12:25)
  Victory over Ammon (12:26-31)

Second Samuel 12 is part of the author's digression that takes place during the Ammonite war. David's failure to confess his sin is connected with 11:27*b* by a transitional period in which we see God's patience in giving His servant time to repent. The contents shows us (1) God's stern rebuke of His servant (12:1-15*a*); (2) His solemn judgment of His servant (12:15*b*-23); and (3) His grace in blessing His servant (12:24-25). God's grace is further seen in the victory He gives David over the Ammonites (12:26-31).

Digression: Adultery and Its Aftermath (12:1-25)

Part one (11:1-27) of this digression was treated in our last chapter. Part two (12:1-25) has to do with God's restoration of His erring servant. *The message of the Bible is redemptive, not judgmental, and this passage highlights God's grace in forgiving David his sins and bringing him back to a place of blessing.* That is why David could later write:

> How blessed is he whose transgression is forgiven,
> Whose sin is covered!
> How blessed is the man to whom Yahweh does not impute
>   iniquity,
> And in whose spirit there is no deceit (Psalm 32:1-2).

God's Patience in Giving His Servant Time to Repent. The Lord graciously gave David about a year in which to repent of his sins and seek forgiveness.[2] The fact that David did not do so indicates that he was repressing all feelings of guilt (cf. Psalm 32:3-4). Had he expressed his contrition over what he had done, there would have been no need for Nathan to be sent to the palace to reprove him.

Throughout his life, David's heart had been tender and sensitive to conviction. His psalms speak eloquently of his desire to walk blamelessly before the Lord (Psalm 101:2. cf. Psalms. 18:30, 32; 19:7). He is called a man after God's own heart (Acts 13:22 AV) because he lived continuously in reverential awe of the Lord. He was open to the truth. There was nothing in his life that he felt compelled to hide.

When he committed adultery with Bathsheba, however, and later had Uriah murdered, he was confronted on the one hand with the enormity of his sin and on the other with the need of self-preservation. Stoning was the penalty for these sins. He, therefore, sought to cover up what he had done and would not allow conviction to operate at a conscious level.

Such denial causes "dissonance." The mind and the emotions can no longer operate in harmony. This, in turn, brings inner conflict. In David's case, when he consciously denied what he had done, he experienced additional tension. He was still tender and desirous of enjoying fellowship with the Lord, but these sentiments were at enmity with his refusal to acknowledge the enormity of his sins.

People in this state frequently experience sleeplessness, bad dreams or even nightmares, irritable spells that become more and more frequent and of longer duration, restlessness, muscle tensions, and, in short, are not pleasant to be around. They may try to project an "I'm okay" attitude, but their body and their emotions are under stress because the mind refuses to deal with the truth.

During the year in which David covered his sin, he must also have experienced feelings of depression, for loss of any kind–and particularly loss of fellowship with the Lord–will cause anyone to feel depressed.[3] And when depression is aggravated by an awareness of *guilt* or *fear* or *anger* toward oneself or another, then that person is caught up in a cycle of emotions that stifles the work of the Holy Spirit in his/her heart. Eventually, this leads to despair.

After about twelve months, during which time God has given David every opportunity to turn to Him in repentance, the Lord takes the initiative and steps in to break the cycle of repression of sin. He sends Nathan the prophet to the king. David, though the supreme leader in the land, was not above the Law of the Lord (cf. Deuteronomy 17:15, 18-20). He could not sin with impunity. The task of the prophet was to encourage him in hard times and to rebuke him in God's name if he disobeyed His Word or failed to honor Him (cf. 1 Samuel 13:13; 15:13-30).

God's Stern Rebuke of His Servant (12:1-15a). As Nathan walks through the streets of Jerusalem toward the palace, his heart is heavy. He and David have been friends for many years. It grieves him that he is now charged with such a solemn duty.

The segment of Scripture that describes his reproof of David is bounded by the words "*he came* to the palace [and]...*he went* to his house" (12:1*a*, 15*a*).

In keeping with the principles of good communication, Nathan tells David a story–a *masal* or juridical parable[4]–that he hopes will not only arouse the king's interest but also bring his mind and emotions into harmony with one another. The story involves what appears to be a real-life situation.[5] It concerns two men, the one rich and the other poor. And David, who knows firsthand the pain of life's inequities, is sensitive to any oppression of the poor and helpless by the affluent and influential (Psalm 72:4. cf. Proverbs 13:23; 28:16; Ecclesiastes 4:1; Jeremiah 21:11-12; 22:3).

A revision of the Greek Bible made by Lucian of Antioch (c. A.D. 300) adds an explanatory comment to the text. It states that Nathan also asked David to "Pass judgment on this case for me." But such a view does Nathan a gross disservice. He knew the Law and was fully aware of the fact that a fourfold penalty was to be extracted from the guilty man (Exodus 22:1). There is nothing in 12:1ff., to suggest that he invited David to render a verdict.

Nathan's parable is a surprisingly simple one. We read:

> "There were [two] men in one city, [the] one rich, and [the] other poor. The rich [man] had very many flocks and herds; but the poor [man] had nothing, except one little ewe lamb which he bought and had kept alive; and it grew up with him and with his sons; it ate of his morsel (i.e., food), and drank from his cup, and it lay in his bosom, and it was to him like a daughter. And a traveler[6] came to the rich man; and he spared to take of his own flock, and from his herd, to prepare for the traveler who had come to him; instead he took the ewe lamb of the poor man, and prepared [food] for the man who had come to him" (12:1-4).

Lovers of animals will have no difficulty empathizing with the poor man. Nor will they find it strange that this man would raise the lamb as one of his family. The lamb became like an only daughter that cheered him when he came home tired and worn from a hard day's work.

But as the story progresses, an ominous chord is struck. A visitor comes to see the rich man. Instead of taking a lamb or a calf from his own abundant flocks and herds, this rich man steals the poor man's solitary pet.[7]

David, who has listened intently to Nathan, is overcome with anger. He can stand no more. In hot indignation he says:

> "[As] Yahweh lives, surely the man who did this [is] a 'son of death';[[8]] and he shall repay fourfold[[9]] because of the ewe lamb, because he has done this thing *and because he had no pity*" (12:5-6, emphasis added).

He is indignant that anyone should be so uncaring and insensitive to the rights and feelings of others.

Nathan's parable has had the desired effect. David's mind and emotions are once again working in harmony. The breakdown of inner communication between these parts of the self has been corrected. The dissonance has disappeared, and congruence has returned. With the inner functioning of his mind and emotions restored, David has placed his finger on the source of the problem: *The man had shown no mercy!*[10]

A lack of mercy—of feeling compassion for other people—is the foundation of crime. Rape, murder, theft, slander, pornography, and all of the works of the flesh stem from a heart that is merciless. No thought is given to the victim. And based on David's statement, "he had no pity," Nathan is able to say to him, *"You are the man!"* (12:7a).

In seeking to cover his own sin, David had shown no compassion. He had overcome any of Bathsheba's possible resistance without giving thought to her feelings or to the emotional pain and suffering their intercourse might inflict upon her. And when his actions were threatened with exposure, he had coldly and deliberately ordered the death of Uriah. Now, all of a sudden, in response to Nathan's accusation, he senses his sinfulness.

With 12:7b we pass from God's challenge through Nathan to consider His chastisement of David (12:7b-15a). Nathan now addresses David in the first person. He is God's mouthpiece. As a theocratic leader of the people, he speaks and acts on God's behalf.

The Lord begins with a reminder of His sovereign election and preservation of David and the way in which He had blessed him.

> "Thus says Yahweh, the God of Israel, 'I anointed you as king over Israel; and I delivered you from Saul's hand; and I gave to you the house of your master, and the wives of your master I gave into your bosom (i.e., into your embrace);[[11]] and I gave you the house of Israel and Judah (to rule over); and if [these

had been] too little, I would have added to you like those and like those (i.e., more power, pleasures, and possessions like the ones just mentioned). Why have you despised the word of Yahweh, to do evil in His eyes?'" (12:7b-8).

David had lacked nothing. And if he had wanted more lands or wives or properties, the Lord would have given them to him.

David now feels the full weight of his sin. He had flagrantly disregarded all God's goodness to him. He was honor bound to uphold the Law. In clear violation of all that he knew to be right, he had (1) committed adultery with Bathsheba, (2) plotted the death of Uriah, who had done him no wrong, and then, to cover his sin, (3) taken Uriah's wife. He was guilty of both sexual impurity and murder. And he deserved to die.

Having exposed David's crimes, the Lord now sovereignly details his punishment. Retribution will be in kind. David is told:

"'And now [the] sword shall not ever turn aside from your house, because you have despised Me, and have taken the wife of Uriah the Hittite to be to you a wife.' Thus says Yahweh, 'Behold I [am] raising up against you evil from your own house, and shall take your wives before your eyes and give [them] to your neighbor, and he shall lie with your wives in the sight of this sun. For you acted in secret; but I will do this thing before all Israel.'" (12:10-12).

Some people believe that from this time onwards David never slept well at night; was always anxious, wondering what new calamity would come upon him; and went to his grave weighed down by guilt, fear, and remorse. But even if we take David's future trials as God's "punishment" for his sins, and exclude God's grace of forgiveness, what He said through Nathan does not mean that David would experience judgment daily or weekly or even monthly, or that he and his family would be at war with their enemies or at enmity among themselves all the time. As we shall see in the following chapters, difficulties did arise, but sometimes they were confined to a specific day or to a period of time that was limited in its scope. And it is true that, spread out over the next twenty years there would be the deaths of Amnon (13:23-29), Absalom (18:15), and Adonijah (1 Kings 2:25).[12] But how can one prove that these deaths were in fulfillment of 12:10-12?

The same preachers who pronounce such a heavy woe on David also have a lot to say about "his wives being raped in the sight of the sun," claiming that this was fulfilled when David fled from Jerusalem.

As we shall see, Absalom will appropriate his father's harem (16:21-22), but this act cannot be in fulfillment of 12:11 for they were not taken from David as he looked on (i.e., "in David's sight [i.e., before his eyes"]). Plainly, some other explanation is needed.

The waters are muddied even more by these exponents of the Biblical text, for they make strong assertions about God's righteousness and the need for purity of life (with which we are in hearty agreement!) but exclude all thought of God's grace being shown to David following his repentance.

But let us return to the story.

On hearing God's indictment of him through Nathan, David's immediate response is to admit his guilt. "I have sinned against Yahweh," he says (12:13).[13]

And Nathan's immediate response is:

> "Yahweh has also put away your sin; you shall not die. Only because by this thing (i.e., by your actions) you have caused Yahweh's enemies to scorn His name, also the son who is born to you shall die" (12:13b-14).

Then Nathan leaves David's presence and returns to his home (12:15a).

As we consider the events of the last few minutes, one thing is impressed upon us: It is God's grace in forgiving David's sins. *No sacrifices had been included in the Levitical system for adultery and murder. Forgiveness, therefore, had to be solely on the basis of God's free, unmerited favor.* And this grace was in spite of the fact that by his crimes David had given occasion to the enemies of the Lord to blaspheme Him.

But this still leaves unexplained the words "Yahweh *has taken away* your sins" (12:13). The verb *he'ebir*, "has taken away, has put away," raises the question, How? Sin cannot simply be swept under the rug or written off like a bad debt. It must be atoned for. And so the questions remain, "By what means will God remit or 'take away' David's sins?" and "By whom?"

Most modern exponents of this passage believe that since David himself was not to die, the sin was transferred to the child who, though innocent of all wrongdoing, was made to bear the sin of his parents (cf. Leviticus 16:7-34).[14] The fine evangelical Bible scholar, Dr. William Blaikie, explained it this way:

> The Lord, in the exercise of His clemency, had been pleased to remit [David's sins]. But a palpable proof of His displeasure was

to be given in another way–the child of Bathsheba was to die. It was to become, as it were, the scapegoat for its father.[15]

This explanation is hard for us to accept. We are Occidentals and do not think in terms of Oriental relationships. Whatever our difficulties, it is the best solution offered thus far.

God's Judgment of His Servant (12:15b-23). It seems like only a short time after Nathan's departure from the palace that the son of David and Bathsheba becomes ill. While Bathsheba cares for him with true maternal devotion, David prostrates himself on the floor and refuses both food and water.

There is something remarkable about the intensity of his grief and anxiety. As with fathers before and since, he hurt deeply to see his son languishing. Knowing that he was the cause of this misfortune, he set about praying for him, hoping that God would be gracious and relent and let his son live. And so, as the hours lengthen into days, David maintained a lonely vigil.

God is indeed gracious, but because His enemies have been given occasion to scorn His name, He shows His sovereign displeasure by punishing David in the person of his son.

Such was David's prayer and fasting that his trusted counselors become concerned for his health. They tried to induce him to eat, but he refused. Then, when the child died, they were afraid to tell him, fearing that he may take his own life. David, however, heard them whispering among themselves and deduced that his son was dead. When he asked after his son, they confirmed his suspicions.

To their amazement, David arose from the floor, washed himself, anointed himself with oil, changed his clothing, and went into the house of the Lord where he worshiped Him. His servants had expected David to mourn after the child died, not before; and now, when others are mourning, he acts as though nothing is wrong.

To their request for an explanation of his conduct, David replies:

> "While the boy [was] alive I fasted and wept, for I said, 'Who knows, Yahweh may pity me and [keep] the boy alive.' And now he has died; why [should] I fast? Am I able to bring him back again? I shall go to him, but he shall not return to me" (12:22-23).[16]

There was a rational explanation for his seemingly incongruous conduct. David's answer has been of encouragement to many troubled parents whose young offspring have died before coming to know Christ personally. His words *"I shall go to him"* speak eloquently

of reunion beyond the grave. David had a strong belief in the after-
life, and he was sure that he and his son would see each other again.
And this same belief has sustained grief-stricken fathers and mothers
through the ages. Their lost child has passed into the Lord's presence without any unhappy recollections of sins committed or opportunities for service lost.

Before leaving this story, there is something else to which William
Blaikie has drawn attention.

> One other fact we must notice ere passing from the record of
> David's confession and chastisement–the moral courage he
> showed in delivering the fifty-first psalm to the chief musician,
> and thus helping to keep alive in his own generation and for all
> time coming the memory of his trespass. Most men would have
> thought how the ugly transaction might most effectually be
> buried, and would have tried to put their best face on it before
> their people. Not so David. He was willing that his people and
> all posterity should see him the atrocious sinner he was.... With
> a wonderful effort of magnanimity, he resolved to place himself
> in the pillory of public shame, [and] to expose his memory to
> all the foul treatment which the scoffers and libertines of every
> age might think fit to heap on it. It is unjust to David, when
> unbelievers rail against him for his sin in the matter of Uriah, to
> overlook the fact that the first public record of the transaction
> came from his own pen, and was delivered to the chief musician,
> for public use.[17]

David was truly a great man whose Godward relationship took
precedence over everything else. Of encouragement to each one of
us are his words:

> Out of the depths I have called to You, O Yahweh.
> Lord, hear my voice;
> Let Your ears be attentive to the voice of my prayers.
> If You, Lord, will keep (an account of) iniquities,
> O Lord, who could stand?
> But with You there [is] forgiveness,
> That You may be feared (i.e., reverenced) (Psalm 130:1-4).

And now, from the evidence of the Lord's gracious forgiveness
of David, we pass to consider His restoration of him to a place of
favor.

God's Sovereign Grace in Blessing His Servant (12:24-25). After the events described in 12:20-23, David goes to console Bathsheba. Unable to bear children while married to Uriah, her grief at the loss of the son she never thought she would have must have been very great.

Bathsheba could have turned on David in anger and blamed him for the pain and misfortune that had come upon her. Instead, she finds comfort in his love and words of reassurance. This indicates that, at some time in the past, she had genuinely forgiven him the wrongs he had done to her. And with forgiveness, there was no remembrance of past offenses. This made possible the growth of true love and mutual devotion.

We are not told what David said to Bathsheba, but Scripture does tell us that, growing out of their affectionate commitment to each other, they ended the evening by enjoying sexual intimacy. And Bathsheba conceives. The writer then carries forward this part of the story. Another son is born. To him, David[18] gives the name "Solomon,"[19] from *salom*, "peace," in accordance with the word of the Lord to him (see 1 Chronicles 22:9).[20]

In this we see once again God's grace in operation. He has forgiven David his sin and is now blessing both him and Bathsheba by giving them another son. *The cycle of the sins of the father being visited upon the children to the third and fourth generation has been broken by David's repentance.* As a result, God is now free to bless them. He not only gives David the name of this child before he is born (a name signifying the *peace* that now fills their hearts), but He also adds grace to grace by telling Nathan to go to the palace with an additional word of reassurance: The child is to have a second name, *given to him by the Lord Himself*: Jedidiah, "Loved of Yahweh."

All of this serves a twofold purpose: It highlights the grace of God on the one hand, and on the other it corrects the erroneous views that have grown out of a misuse of this chapter. The Lord had not only forgiven David his sins (when there was no prescribed ritual to atone for such offenses); He had also restored both David and Bathsheba to fellowship and a position of blessing.

In the opinion of some historians of the period, God's naming of Jedidiah conferred on him "royal legitimation."[21]

We discredit the character of God, however, if we fail to see His grace throughout this chapter. And what He did for David and Bathsheba He is prepared to do for all who are caught up in the maelstrom of their own sensuality. If they will repent and turn to Him confessing their sins, He is faithful and righteous to forgive them their sins and cleanse them from all unrighteousness (1 John 1:9). And with forgiveness and cleansing comes restoration to His favor!

Victory over Ammon (12:26-31)

The lengthy digression (11:2–12:25) over, the Biblical writer now returns to the war with Ammon. Joab and the men of Israel have been laying siege to the city for approximately a year. Victory is near. Joab sends a message to David:

> "I have fought against Rabbah, also I have captured the city of waters. And now, gather the rest of the people, and encamp against the city, and seize it; lest I seize the city and it be called by my name" (12:27-28).

Joab's use of direct speech invests the narrative with a vivid quality. We can almost see him attacking the fort that has guarded the people's access to the Jabbok River.[22] Now, with this in his hands, the Ammonites will soon be forced to either surrender or come out of the citadel for one last desperate attempt to drive the invaders from their land. And Joab realizes that the honor of defeating Hanun rightly belongs to David, for he was the one insulted when his ambassadors were humiliated.

The king gathers all the fighting men of Israel together and goes to Rabbah. No record is given of the battle itself. The Biblical text states only that he fought against it and captured it (12:29).

The people who had treated his ambassadors with contempt are now taught the folly of their leader's pride. And the crown formerly worn (presumably) by Hanun is placed on the head of David. Because of its weight scholars have postulated that it may have been suspended over Hanun's throne as the emblem of his right to rule the people. Others have assumed that the crown was worn by Milcom, god of Ammon. Joyce Baldwin writes:

> The transfer of the crown from the head of the Ammonite king (whose name is not mentioned now, despite its repetition in 2 Sa. 10:1-5) to the head of David symbolized the transfer of power over Ammon to the Israelite king. The weight of the gold (the *talent* was about 30 kg., or 66 lbs)[23] and the crown jewel were indicative of the splendour of Ammon's throne.[24]

The people are then subjected to forced labor. They are made to cut wood, sharpen iron implements, and work in the brickyards.[25] Dr. G. C. O'Ceallaigh believes the Ammonites were forced to raze their own city with iron picks and mattocks.[26] If this was so, then they never completed the task.

Once again the Lord has honored and blessed His servant. Those who affirm that, from chapter 11 onwards, we have only a description of David's misfortunes are shown to be in error. The Lord has blessed David both in his house and on the field of battle.

WHERE SIN ABOUNDED

When writing the believers in Rome, the apostle Paul stated, that "where sin abounded, grace did much more abound" (Romans 5:20 AV).[27] All sin is seen as an offense against God (Psalm 51:4). And while the Lord will by no means clear the guilty (Numbers 14:18), He does provide a way whereby repentant sinners may be justified before Him.[28]

Because we, too, are sinners, it is instructive to see how God's grace operates.

God's Grace Seen In His Patience

We must not overlook the fact that God has given to each one of us freedom of choice. He is honored when we choose to do what is right in His sight. David's actions displeased the Lord (11:27*b*). In grace, He gave David about twelve months in which to repent of his sin. David, however, did not act responsibly during the time of Bathsheba's pregnancy. He felt that, as king, he could pull down the shades on their affair and, in time, the gossip would become muted and people would forget. But God did not forget. Instead, He waited patiently for His servant to turn to Him confessing his sin.

Throughout history, we are given examples of God's patience and longsuffering (cf. Romans 3:25; 9:22; 1 Peter 3:20). But we should not test the Lord to see how much we can get away with, for then we may find that He has to discipline us as He did those who, on a former occasion, rebelled against Him (cf. Hebrews 3:12, 15-19). His patience shows us His love, for He does not want to chasten us but rather gives us time to act responsibly and repent of that which has separated us from Him.

God's Grace Evident in His Use of Means

The Lord did not have to send Nathan to David. He chose to do so with the specific intent of restoring David to a position of usefulness and blessing. Notice too that Nathan, as God's envoy, dealt kindly yet firmly with David. The parable he told brought into harmony David's rational thought processes and poorly aligned emotions so that *he* was ready to acknowledge his sinfulness. At no time did David feel coerced into making confession.

A pastor whom I met several years ago is proud of the number of times he has confronted people in his church (or even fellow pastors) with the rumored reports of their wrongdoing. He believes that he has some God-given ability to be a "Nathan" to safeguard the purity of the church. He confronts all whom he believes may have deviated from the path of righteousness. His direct line of questioning (e.g., "When was the last time you saw—?" "Is there anything about your relationship with—that I should know about?" and "Have you had sex with him/her?") is *not* Biblical. The Bible does not permit the kind of cross-examination that results in self-incrimination.

Nathan used the right approach. He knew that it was against Biblical law to try to get a person to witness against himself. Only if a couple has been found *in coitu*, "in the very act," can such an approach be used, and even then Christ showed us a better way (see John 8:1-11). Otherwise charges must be confirmed in the mouth of two or three witnesses (see Numbers 35:30; Deuteronomy 17:6-7; 19:15).[29]

And to this day the Lord uses means–the right means–to bring us to repentance. At no time, however, does He coerce us or force us to do what we do not want to do.

God's Grace Manifest in His Forgiveness

When David confessed, "I have sinned," he was immediately forgiven. There was no conditional approval or lengthy probation. He was immediately restored to favor with the Lord so that he could enjoy the blessings of his God (cf. Psalm 89:27-29).

One of the most tragic stories of a life wrecked by sin concerns Oscar Wilde. He had a brilliant mind and earned the highest academic honors at Oxford University; he was a scintillating writer, and won the highest rewards in literature; and he had all the charm that gracious manners could bestow upon a person. But he fell into temptation and sin and was sent to prison. While in jail he wrote a lengthy letter to Alfred Douglas, the judge who had condemned him. It was later published in an abridged form under the title *De Profundis*, "Out of the depths..." (after the opening words of the Latin edition of Psalm 130). Part of what he wrote reads:

> The gods had given me almost everything. But I let myself be lured into long spells of senseless and sensual ease...Tired of being on the heights I deliberately went into the depths in search

of new sensation.... I grew careless of the lives of others. I took pleasure where it pleased me.... I forgot that every little action of the common day makes or unmakes character, and that therefore what one has done in the secret chamber, one has some day to cry aloud from the house-top.... [And] I have ended in horrible disgrace.[30]

Oscar Wilde confessed his wrongdoing and showed in his letter how much prison had changed him. But his judge could not forgive him and restore him to his former prominence. Later on, in another work titled *The Ballad of Reading Gaol* (i.e. Jail), published several years after he was released from prison, Wilde again wrote of his experiences:

Ah! Happy they whose hearts can break
And peace from pardon win!
How else may man make straight his plan
And cleanse his soul from Sin?
How else but through a broken Heart
May Lord Christ enter in?[31]

If Oscar Wilde wrote this of himself and from his heart, then we may be sure that Christ forgave him. And the same Lord is willing to forgive each one of us our sins if we will confess them to Him.

God's Grace Revealed in His Blessing

Once forgiven of his sins, David was immediately restored to favor with God. His blessing upon him was twofold: He blessed both David and Bathsheba by enabling Bathsheba to conceive again, and He blessed David by giving him victory over Ammon.

Bathsheba's pain at the loss of her firstborn must have been very great. However, the Lord graciously and magnanimously gave her another son in the place of the one she had lost. Then He did something unprecedented. *He* named the baby *Jedidiah, "Loved of Yahweh."*

In the interim, while Bathsheba was carrying the child of promise, God gave David the victory over the sons of Ammon. God did not have to do this. He could have punished him by letting Ammon beat Israel. This would have forced David to return to Jerusalem in disgrace. But with David's confession, his sins were blotted out, and the Lord remembered them no more (cf. Psalm 103:12; Isaiah 38:17c; 43:25; 44:22; Micah 7:19). The full severity of what the Lord had planned to do to David and his house was lifted. David had been restored to God's favor.

A story is told of a tragic accident that illustrates on a human level the power of forgiveness.

A mechanic for JAARS (Jungle Aviation and Radio Service, a division of the Wycliffe Bible Translators) had been momentarily distracted from his task and failed to tighten sufficiently a B-nut on the plane he was servicing. Sometime after the Piper Aztec was airborne, it exploded and seven people were killed in a fiery crash. Among them were Doug Hunt, the chief pilot for JAARS, and Darlene Bee, a recent Ph.D. graduate from Indiana University who was a brilliant linguist.

An inspection of the wreckage showed that the midair explosion had occurred when a fine jet of fuel spray escaped from the B-nut on the fuel line. The mechanic was haunted by his guilt. He later confessed that the funeral was a terrible ordeal; the sight of the caskets lined up in the little open-sided church hit him like a blow in the stomach. He felt sick and wished he could die. "How could I face my friends? How could I face myself? I was overwhelmed with guilt. I was a failure."

God's grace, however, was at work in that small outpost, and the surviving family members and co-workers readily forgave him. "I felt forgiveness from everyone around me—my co-workers, and most importantly, the pilots who continued to trust themselves to my skill and workmanship. I knew their total, loving acceptance."

It took time for this mechanic to realize that God too loves and forgives and accepts us.[32] But He does. And whether it is the story of someone in the jungles of New Guinea or a king of a small country in the Middle East, God's ability to forgive and restore us to a position of favor with Him is designed to encourage us, particularly when we feel we have "blown it" and would rather go off into some corner in guilt-ridden despair.

THE IMPORTANCE OF OUR CHOICES

2 Samuel 13:1-39

In the early days of sailing vessels, the goal of many European entrepreneurs was to find a way to India and the Orient. Overland caravans were subject to plunder along often dangerous routes. As the thoughts of these enterprising businessmen turned to the sea, they began sending out intrepid mariners to find a way around Cape Point— the place where the Indian and Atlantic Oceans meet. Their aim was to send ships down the west coast of Africa, around the southern tip, and on to Asia, where they would trade goods for the gold and precious stones, silks and other fabrics, spices and perfumes.

Bartholomew Diaz was the first modern explorer to venture around the tip of Africa (it was then known as the "Cape of Storms," but its name was later changed to the "Cape of Good Hope"). On nearing Madagascar, however, Diaz' crew rebelled and threatened to mutiny if he did not turn back. He reluctantly did so. Before they had made much progress, the ship was beset by a terrific storm, and was tossed about like a cork in the white water of a swiftly flowing river. Diaz looked for a bay he had seen on the outward journey, believing that if he could find shelter on the leeward side of this inlet he and his men could ride out the storm.

Amid the gusting winds and the driving rain a bay was sighted, and Diaz sailed into it. He did not know that he had entered a bay, southeast of Cape Point, where there was no safe anchorage. No wonder he named it "False Bay." His choice was a costly one. With the gale still blowing at full force, he now had to tack back and forth to regain the open sea. Only then could he sail around Cape Point, turn north, and eventually reach the safety and seclusion of Table Bay.

Diaz' choice to enter False Bay nearly cost him and his crew their lives. His decision reminds us of something someone once said, "We

make our choices, and then our choices turn around and make us."
We may make our decisions with the best of intentions, only to find
that events do not turn out as we had hoped.

Noah Webster defined *choice* as follows:

> The act of choosing; the voluntary act of selecting or separating
> from two or more things that which is preferred; or the
> determination of mind in preferring one thing to another;
> selection.[1]

This is true of the teenager choosing a college as well as the young
adult deciding on a career. It is a part of the commitment of an individual trying out for a track team or a place in the band. It faces those
who choose to marry, as well as homeowners who set out to buy the
home of their dreams. It is part of the commitment of parents to each
newborn child, and it plays a vital role in the parenting process. Eventually, it finds fulfillment in one's plans for retirement. We all make
choices. In time, however, our choices determine the quality of our
lives and the kind of relationships we will enjoy.

In 2 Samuel 13 we see this process in operation in the household
of King David. We naturally expect the sons of such a great and godly
man to turn out like their father. Our anticipation is that they will
grow to adulthood to be wise and good stewards of the freedom God
has given them. And we are disappointed when we find that the older
two do not.

I have counseled many parents of wayward children and can vouch
for the fact that they, like David, have tried their best to rear their
children in the fear (i.e., reverential awe) of the Lord. When their
children turn their backs on the truth, they face both disappointment and disillusionment and question where they went wrong. But
let them take heart. Great men and women in Bible times faced similar situations. Abraham's grandsons, Jacob and Esau, were a disgrace;
Jacob's sons were unfit for the position of honor to which the Lord
had elected them; Eli's sons perverted and prostituted the priesthood; and Amnon and Absalom brought David pain and sadness.

Neo-Victorian writers place the blame for the choices Amnon and
Absalom made on the evils that were rife in the harems of the ancient Near East. They claim that, in these quarters, each mother com-
peted with the others for the advancement of her children. But was
this true of David and his wives? The Biblical text is silent and does
not even once hint that David's house was plagued by the bickering
and rancor common in the households of sheiks and emirs. From

the record, it appears as if each wife had her own quarters (perhaps her own residence close to the palace). And as each son grew up, he was given a house of his own (cf. 13:7-8, 20). It seems, therefore, as if David deliberately tried to avoid the kind of problems that plagued the families of other rulers.

Other writers have interpreted 2 Samuel 13-20 as the beginning of David's sorrows—the just punishment (they believe) for his adulterous relationship with Bathsheba and his plot to murder Uriah. This is a popular though mistaken view. Chapters 13 through 20 span between eighteen to twenty years, and the events recorded in them do not fit the description of the punishments God said He would visit upon David. It is preferable to conclude that, when David repented of his sins, the Lord forgave him and relented of the evil He had said would come upon David (cf. 24:16. cf. Psalm 106:45; Jeremiah 18:8; 42:10; Joel 2:14; Jonah 3:9-10).

Our understanding of this chapter will be greatly enhanced if we see in it an account of the *choices* made by David's sons. Each acts independently and with a view to securing what he wants. In the decisions he makes, he unwittingly shows how unfit he is to succeed his father on the throne.

In the eyes of the people of Israel, Amnon is the crown prince and heir apparent. Chileab, the son of Abigail, is not mentioned, and we are left to presume that he has died. Absalom stands second in line to succeed his father. But as we shall see, there is enmity between Amnon and Absalom that goes beyond sibling rivalry. Solomon is but a babe, a year old, and it is doubtful if anyone pays much attention to him. As with Mary in Luke's record of the birth of Christ (see Luke 2:51*b*), Bathsheba probably treasures in her heart the events surrounding his birth and God's singular choice of him.

Amnon, as the oldest of David's sons, feels himself secure and sure to succeed his father. But Absalom, the handsome son of two royal lines, looks upon Amnon as a competitor.

OUTLINE

Chapters 13–20 of 2 Samuel deal with *God sovereignly sustaining the kingdom of His anointed*. Chapters 13 and 14 form a prologue and provide an indispensable backdrop to the remaining section of 2 Samuel which records attempts to either disrupt or destroy the kingdom. Chapters 15–19 record Absalom's attempt to steal the hearts of the people (15:2-6) prior to usurping the throne (15:10ff.); and finally, in chapter 20, Sheba attempts to lead a rebellion that is a direct consequence of the seeds of dissension that Absalom had sown (19:8*b*-10; 20:1ff.).

This section may be outlined as follows:

- Prologue: Strife over the Right of Succession (13:1—14:33)
    - The Shameful Rape of a King's Daughter (13:1-22)
    - The Vengeful Assassination of a King's Son (13:23-39)
    - The Deceitful Plan of the King's Servant (14:1-33)
- An Attempt to Seize the Throne (15:1—19:39)
- An Attempt to Divide the Nation (19:40—20:26)

We are left to presume that, apart from these activities (and some events from the Appendix which conclude this book), David spent the last two decades of his life in relative freedom from the trials that had been so much a part of his early life. David is now in his early fifties. His battles are behind him, and he appears intent upon maintaining the peace both within his home as well as in the empire.

PEOPLE IN THE STORY

Because we will be reading about some new individuals, a few details about them will help us understand their relationship to one another.

Absalom is the powerful and imperious son of David and Maacah, daughter of the king of Geshur (3:3*b*). He is both a king's son and a king's grandson.

Tamar is the very beautiful sister of Absalom who, with her brother, is the descendant of two royal families.

Amnon is David's oldest son and heir apparent to the throne.

Jonadab is David's nephew and a friend of Amnon. He is a shrewd and unscrupulous man.

Servants belonging to Amnon or Absalom.

Talmai, king of Geshur, David's father-in-law and Absalom's grandfather.

Watchman, court officials, and a *messenger.*

THE NEED FOR CAUTION

We have noted in earlier chapters some of the difficulties that face translators of the Biblical text. In this section we will encounter some additional problems. What is disturbing is the frequency with which some of our most popular versions of the Bible reflect information from the Septuagint (LXX), the Dead Sea Scrolls, or the Lucianic or Latin manuscripts.

The translation used in this chapter (as in each chapter of this book) is based upon the Masoretic (Hebrew) Text. The difficulties have not been ignored. I have attempted, however, to be faithful to the original text and to offer a paraphrase where a literal translation is either too tedious or too difficult.

PROLOGUE: STRIFE OVER THE RIGHT OF SUCCESSION (13:1–14:33)

The Shameful Rape of a King's Daughter (13:1-22)

Unfulfilled Longing (13:1-2). Although the first part of this chapter has to do with Amnon, the opening statement introduces us to Absalom. He is now eighteen or nineteen years of age, handsome, and ambitious.

The fact that he is mentioned first, and that Tamar is described as his sister (not David's daughter), gives some indication of his familial pride and assertion of power. From verse 20 we glean the fact that he is very protective of Tamar. He also has an uncanny knowledge of his elder brother, Crown Prince Amnon.

Amnon stands in Absalom's way of ascending the throne, and although David is only in his early fifties, this has not stopped Absalom from casting a lustful eye on the crown. Amnon is like Esau in that he is swayed by his fleshly passions. He is unlike Esau, however, in that he lacks independent thought and action. He also stands in Absalom's shadow, for his mother had no social standing prior to her marriage to David during his "outlaw" years, whereas Absalom's mother was a princess.

Amnon fancies himself in love with his half-sister Tamar. However, the laws of consanguinity do not permit him to marry her (see Leviticus 18:9,11; 20:17; Deuteronomy 27:22), and this causes him considerable frustration.[2] Tamar is a virgin[3] and on this account may have been confined to special quarters. Any form of sequestering would have made it difficult for Amnon to talk with her. So great is his desire for her that he becomes fretful.

Secret Counsel (13:3-7). These verses begin with an ominous "but."

> *But* Amnon had a friend, and his name [was] Jonadab, the son of Shimeah, David's brother; and Jonadab [was] a very wise (shrewd, crafty) man. And he said to him, "Why [are] you, the king's son, so weak morning by morning? Will you not tell me?" And Amnon said to him, "I love Tamar, the sister of my brother Absalom." And Jonadab said to him, "Lie down on your bed and pretend to be ill, and your father will come and see you; and you shall say to him, 'Please let Tamar my sister come in and give me food to eat; and let her make the food before my eyes, so that I may see and may eat of her hand'" (13:3-5).

Jonadab, David's nephew, has sometimes been confused with Jonathan (21:21), but it is most likely the two were brothers. Jonadab is described as *ḥākām*, "subtle, crafty, shrewd, clever."[4] What follows reveals his knowledge of human nature as well as the unscrupulous bent of his personality. His character is flawed. His counsel is according to what people want to hear, not what is right as taught in God's Word.

While Jonadab had no way of knowing what Amnon would do when he and Tamar were alone in his house, we may be quite sure that he had anticipated that Amnon would try to seduce her. And he was perfectly willing to be a party to such depravity. In counseling Amnon, therefore, Jonadab was, in effect, laying a trap for Tamar.

As expected, when David hears that Amnon is ill, he lays aside affairs of state so that he may visit his son. When he inquires how Amnon feels and what might reverse his languor, Amnon replies:

> "Please let Tamar my sister come and she shall make 'dumplings' before my eyes, and I shall eat from her hand"[5] (13:6b).

This was such a childish petition that Joyce Baldwin felt it necessary to point out that "most mothers would have had no patience with such a request."[6] David, however, after his many years of war, prefers peace. He probably feels it is a weak and indulgent request for a grown man, but rather than enter into an argument with his sick son, he relents. And so Tamar is sent to Amnon's house.

Willing Service (13:8-10). On entering her brother's home, Tamar immediately begins making the "heart-shaped dumplings"[7] her brother has requested.

It is possible that in Amnon's twisted thinking, his request for such food to be made[8] "in his sight" would signal to Tamar that he wanted more from her than a meal. The fact that she did not pick up on his subtle suggestion may be explained on the grounds that he was supposed to be very ill—too sick to even rise when the king came to visit him.

Amnon's picayune attitude is seen in his ingratitude. When Tamar pours out the "dumplings" from the pan, he refuses to eat them. Instead, he issues a stern command for everyone (including the maid who had most certainly accompanied Tamar to his house) to leave the room. His words are harsh:

"*Hôṣî'û kol-'îš mē'ālay,*" (i.e. "Get everyone away from me!"). And he and Tamar are then left alone. Amnon now begins to move in on his prey. He says: "Bring the food into the inner room, and I shall eat from your hand" (13:10).

Although Tamar may have had some misgivings, she remembers that it was her father who had sent her to Amnon. In accord with her brother's wishes, therefore, she obeys.

Courageous Resistance (13:11-13). When Tamar attempts to feed her brother, he grabs hold of her. She suddenly realizes that he is not ill. He phrases his desire in the form of a request: "Come lie with me, my sister" (11:11*b*).

But Tamar is filled with fear. She struggles to get free. He is too strong for her, however, and so she tries to reason with him. She points out that he will incur public disapproval.

> "No, my brother, do not humble me, for [such a thing] is not done in Israel. Do not do this foolishness!" (13:12).

The men and women of Israel—the people whom Amnon presumes he shall one day rule—will not take kindly to having an incestuous king govern them. Furthermore, they will look upon him as a foolish person. Tamar's usage of the word *nĕbālâ*,[9] "folly, foolishness" (see Isaiah 9:17; 32:6) properly describes a serious disorderly and unruly action resulting in the breaking of an existing relationship.... It indicates the end of an existing order consequent upon breach of rules which maintain that order (cf. Deuteronomy 22:21; Judges 19:23; 20:6, 10; Jeremiah 29:23).[10] It is the same root word from which the name Nabal is derived (see 1 Samuel 25:25).

When this fails to stop Amnon, and while still struggling with her brother, she tries a different approach. Assuming that, in trying to overcome her reluctance, he has told her of his love, she asks:

"And I, where could I cause my disgrace to go?" (13:13*a*).

If he really loves her, he will not expose her to shame and humiliation and forever deprive her of the opportunity of marriage. And if his words of love are in truth empty, then he should consider his own future (13:13b). He will be an outcast, one from whom decent people withdraw.

Finally, in desperation, she suggests that Amnon ask their father to give her to him in marriage (13:13c). They can then be married and he can make love to her as often as he desires. The Law forbade such a union (cf. Ezekiel 22:11), but perhaps on account of Abraham's marriage to Sarah (Genesis 20:12), David might be prepared to allow it.[11] At any rate, this would enable her to escape from her present predicament.

Humiliating Violation (13:14). But Amnon will not listen. Since she will not yield to his wishes, he forces her. The Biblical text reads: "But he was not willing to listen to her voice, and [as] he was stronger than [Tamar], he humbled her and lay with her" (13:14).

Rape is a heinous crime! It is an act of coercion involving violence, the acting out of anger[12] mingled with the sadistic gratification of one's sexual desires. As such it is a complex crime involving a wide range of emotions. And the victim feels violated and somehow unclean, as if she has become contaminated by the perpetrator's depravity. After the incident she is often left in physical pain, and for a time may feel emotionally numb. When this wears off the horrors of the actual event continue to recur as the "video" of what happened is replayed over and over in her mind. Her emotions will most likely alternate between rage and despair, and she may wonder if there was anything she could have done to prevent what happened to her.

If appropriate psychological help is not forthcoming, the person who has been raped is left to cope with life as best she can. Depression sets in, for she senses inwardly that she has lost something of intrinsic worth to her (e.g., her purity, dignity, sense of worth). All of this hinders her ability to establish or maintain a meaningful relationship with a husband or even relate well with other males within her family and men outside her home. Thoughts and feelings that are repressed may surface years later in nightmares, and these reminders of the past will hinder her full recovery.

Intervention should be prompt and compassionate. In our day, it is very important for the victim to have a medical examination to determine the possibility of any transmissible disease. Then the family should be notified. The period of outward adjustment and the development of coping mechanisms must be worked through tenderly and in an environment of unconditional love and acceptance.

There is hope of recovery, however, and some information from another instance of rape may aid our understanding of the offense as well as the possibility of restoration. When Dinah, Jacob's daughter, was raped by Shechem (Genesis 34:2), Moses used the word *'ana*, "to humble, to defile," to describe what happened to her. It is the same word used by Ezekiel to describe the desecration of the Temple (Ezekiel 23:38).[13] And in this connection there lies an important thought. In Ezekiel's time, an unholy act had occurred. It was not the fault of the Temple of the Lord that it had become defiled. Appropriate action needed to be taken to cleanse it and restore it to full usefulness.

The same is true of rape. The victim needs to realize that what happened was not her fault. Feelings of guilt, therefore, and an attitude of self-blame will only hinder her recovery. Family and friends need to assist in the restoration process. Anger toward or blaming of the victim will not help the situation, nor will the attitude that the victim is now somehow "ruined." Of primary importance, therefore, is the victim's self-perception.

Of secondary importance is the way the victim views her attacker. His actions need to be seen in the light of his depravity. She needs to realize that either now or in the future, he will have to bear the full consequences of his sins.

Graceless Rejection (13:15-16). According to Exodus 22:16 and Deuteronomy 22:28-29, if a man seduced a virgin who was not engaged to be married, he was obligated to make her his wife by paying the bridal price. Furthermore, he could not divorce her or send her away (*sallehah*, the word used in divorce documents) as long as he lived.

This is what Amnon was now obliged to do. He chose, however, to send Tamar away, and again we see his failure to obey the Word of the Lord. His passion satisfied, he now hates Tamar with a great hatred; in fact, the hatred with which he now hates her is greater than the love with which he had formerly loved her.[14] And he says to her: "Get up! Go!" (13:15*c*).

His words are heartless and cruel. But Tamar responds:

> "No, for this evil in sending me away [is] greater than the previous one that you have done to me (i.e., in raping me)" (13:16).[15]

Tamar is more knowledgeable of the Law of the Lord than her brother, and she refuses to go.

Heartless Expulsion (13:17-18). But Amnon will not listen. He is unable to control his passions, and he will not receive instruction from others. His heart appears set against doing what is right. Instead of heeding Tamar's wise words, he calls for his servant and says to him:

"Now send this [woman] out from me, and bolt the door after
her" (13:17).

His words are contemptuous. They convey an attitude of calloused
disrespect and indifference to the rights and feelings of his sister. He
is arrogant, and his tone of voice is most likely abrasive. His anger
stands in marked contrast to the supposed "love" that previously
caused him to set Tamar on a pedestal so that he thought it impossible to ever do anything to harm her.

But how are we to explain this sudden reversal of emotion?

On the one hand, Amnon may have hated himself for having forced
Tamar to participate with him in an act that was the exact opposite
of what he thought possible. This would have produced within him a
sense of guilt. In retrospect he did not like what he had done. Guilt
feelings then generated within him a sense of loathing and self-hate.
He now felt angry with himself for having acted as he did. Such sen-
sibilities are very destructive. He could not stand these negative feelings and so projected his anger outward on to Tamar. And not being
able to stand the reproach which he either felt inwardly or saw in
her eyes, he had her thrust out of his presence.

It has also been conjectured that deep down inside of Amnon there
was a hatred of Absalom. Although he may not have been aware of it
at the time, in the irrationality of his emotions, his rape of Tamar
may also have been designed to humiliate or show his mastery over
his brother.

Whatever the reason for Amnon's anger—projection of blame on
to Tamar or a desire to humiliate his pompous brother, or both—he
instructs his servant to throw Tamar out. The Hebrew *me'alay*, "away
from me," further adds insult to the injury Tamar has already suffered. It implies that her presence has become burdensome to him.
And "bolting the door after her" is Amnon's way of trying to distance
himself from the memory of what has taken place. But repressing
the thought of his crime was no way to handle the situation.

Amnon's refusal to receive counsel or submit himself to the Law
of the Lord indicated clearly to the first readers of this story that he
was unfit to succeed his father on the throne.

Misguided Counsel (13:19-21). Joyce Baldwin has observed that,
to Tamar, the sound of the bolts sliding into their sockets in the door
frame of Amnon's house was symbolic of the "door to marriage [be-
ing] bolted against her for good."[16]

Tamar is grief-stricken. Her well-balanced, mature disposition is
evident in her sorrow. She is in touch with her feelings. She does not
try to repress her emotions. She knows that she is not to blame and

therefore should feel no guilt as a consequence of what has happened. But she is a realist and mourns the fact that, in her culture and as a king's daughter, she will never be able to marry. Amnon is the only one to whom her father can give her.

As evidence of her grief, Tamar throws dust or ashes on her face and hair; she tears her long, sleeveless robe; and, laying her hand on her head as if to soothe the pain (cf. Jeremiah 2:37), she walks through the streets toward her house crying bitterly (13:19).

Her full brother, Absalom, is told about her, and he hastens to find her. When he sees her, he asks: "Amnon, your brother, has [he] been with you?" (13:20*a*).

It is apparent that he knows Amnon's personality and is well aware of what he is capable of doing. Then he counsels her:

> "But now, keep silent, my sister; he [is] your brother; do not set your heart on this thing" (13:20*b*).

No counsel could have been worse! Instead of receiving encouragement from her family to share her feelings freely and without fear of her confidence being betrayed, she is told to remain silent. This also involves refraining from asking for any redress in terms of the Law (Deuteronomy 22:28-29). It is obvious that Absalom is thinking only of himself. And he is already plotting his revenge (cf. 13:32, noting the words "from the day that he violated his sister"). Tamar, however, as the victim, is treated as "damaged goods." She remains unmarried and desolate in the house of her brother Absalom.

David has been severely criticized for not taking steps to punish Amnon and do for Tamar what the Law allowed. We are told by his detractors that he was powerless to act because he saw rising before him the specter of his own sin with Bathsheba. But those who make such charges read their own feelings into the passage. A man who would courageously publish his confession of wrongdoing (Psalm 51), and have it sung in worship services in the Tabernacle, would certainly have had the fortitude to confront others and seek to lead them to repentance (cf. Psalm 51:13).

David could take no action against Amnon because no charge had been made. Absalom had specifically said to Tamar to "keep silent" and not ask for any redress according to the law (13:20). Quite naturally, David was outraged. He had been lied to and deceived by his son. And no king likes to be used as a pawn!

David's true feelings have been obscured by certain modern versions that add to verse 21 the words "but he would not hurt Amnon because he was his firstborn." This addition has slender

documentary support. It is not found in the Hebrew text. It is found
in the Septuagint (LXX). However, as is well-known, there are occasions where the Septuagint freely paraphrased the Hebrew
(Masoretic) Text, and there are numerous instances where the translators inserted thoughts of their own. This is one of them, and it is
evident that the translators added these words on their own authority.

The first readers of this story would know that David could not do
anything to right the wrongs done to Tamar because she had not
approached him to act on her behalf!

Intense Hatred (13:22). In all of these events, Absalom behaves
shrewdly. He gives Amnon no cause for concern but waits patiently
for the time to act.

And so two years pass uneventfully.

The Vengeful Assassination of a King's Son (13:23-39)

The boundaries of this part of the narrative are marked by two
references to time: "*after two years*" (13:23) and "Absalom fled and
remained in Geshur *for three years*" (13:38).

The opening statement, *lišnātayim yāmîm,* "in two years [of] days
(i.e., full years. cf. Genesis 41:1; Jeremiah 28:3, 11), shows the span of
time during which Absalom's anger neither diminishes nor abates. If
others had forgotten the wrong done to Tamar, he had not.

But for one so young to harbor resentment for so long a period
alarms us. It also tells us a great deal about Absalom. He is vindictive
and lacking in that Godward grace that should lead a sinner to forgive another on the same basis he, himself, hopes to be forgiven his
sins by an omniscient and omnipotent God (cf. Matthew 6:14-15; Luke
6:37c).

An Invitation to a Feast (13:23-27). Absalom plans his next move
carefully. When fear of reprisal has waned, and as the shearing season draws near, he invites the king and his entire retinue, together
with the princes, to a *mišteh,* "feast." It is to be held at Baal-hazor
near Ephraim.[17]

The end of sheepshearing was usually a joyous occasion called
a *yôm ṭôb,* "a good day"—a Hebraism to describe the feasting and
merriment that actually lasted for several days (cf. Genesis 38:12-13;
1 Samuel 25:26,36).

Absalom is sure that his father will decline the invitation, but he
must secure Amnon's presence, and the easiest way for him to do
this is for Amnon, as the heir apparent, to represent his father. So
with his plans carefully laid, he comes to the king and says:

"Behold, your servant [even] now has shearers; please let the king and his servants go with your servant (to celebrate the end of the sheepshearing season)" (13:24).

As expected, his father replies: "No, my son, let us not all go, and shall we not be too heavy [a burden] for you" (13:25).

David's words are a polite way of saying, "We are too many, and our very numbers will place a great strain upon you."

To ensure that his father understands the sincerity of his invitation, Absalom continues to urge him to come. Finally, he says in effect, "Well, if you will not come, at least let Amnon represent you" (13:26a).[18]

At first David is hesitant. He responds: "Why should he go with you?"

Absalom does not reply to this question but continues to urge upon David his desire for all the king's sons to attend. So David finally relents. Amnon and the king's sons (excluding Solomon, who is only three years of age and scarcely significant enough to be reckoned among David's sons) then receive an invitation to go to Baalhazor to celebrate the end of the sheepshearing.

An Assassination at the Feast (13:28-39). Whether Absalom hired assassins to help with the serving or entrusted the dastardly deed to his own retainers is not known (13:28). Either way they would be referred to as "his servants."

He begins by setting before his guests a sumptuous feast. When Amnon is "merry with wine," Absalom gives the signal. From that moment on, everything happens very quickly—so quickly that the king's other sons are taken completely by surprise. There are knife thrusts, screams from Amnon, and perhaps a table or two overturned. Then Amnon's blood-soaked body rolls from his bench to the ground, where it lies in the dust.

Afraid that they will be next, each prince jumps on his mule and heads south as fast as he can. And Absalom, with Tamar's rape avenged (cf. Genesis 34:25-26), rides northward to Geshur,[19] his grandfather's kingdom. And there he remains for three years (13:37-38).

Absalom's treachery clearly indicates that he is unfit to succeed his father.

Meanwhile, in Jerusalem, all is not well. A report precedes the arrival of the king's sons. It is inaccurate and misleading. A messenger relates: "Absalom has struck all the sons of the king, and not one of them is left" (13:30).

The words "not one of them is left" reinforces the erroneous first part of the evil tidings. No wonder the king and his courtiers are overwhelmed with grief. Each tears his clothes to show that he shares David's sorrow (cf. 1:11-12; 3:31-35), and David prostrates himself on the floor (cf. 12:16-17).

It is to the king and these grieving noblemen that Jonadab offers his "consolation:"

> "Do not let my lord say (i.e., suppose) [that] all of the young men, the sons of the king, have been killed; for Amnon alone is dead. For by the mouth of Absalom it has been appointed *from the day* of his defiling of Tamar, his sister" (13:32, emphasis added).[20]

Why did Jonadab keep the knowledge of Amnon's danger to himself? Knowing that Absalom was planning revenge, the very least he should have done was warn his friend!

Almost simultaneously, a watchman, standing on duty in a tower, sees many people coming in haste along the road north of Jerusalem. Modern writers have given this road the name "Horonaim," for it links Jerusalem with the "two Horons," modern *Beit 'Ur el-Foqa* and *Beit 'Ur el-Tahta*, lying a couple of miles apart (about ten and twelve miles, respectively) northwest of Jerusalem.[21] In returning to Jerusalem, the king's sons probably take the road that runs past Bethel and joins the Horonaim road near Gibeon.

Jonadab immediately seizes upon this as confirmation of the truth of his report to the king (13:35). Everyone else at court mourns the death of the crown prince, but not he.[22]

The text of 13:39 is difficult to translate.[23] The verb is feminine, and this necessitates a feminine noun as the subject. In the original text, however, David is the subject. Furthermore, the word order for "David the king" is unusual. This has led certain translators to emend the text from the Septuagint. They have changed "David" (דָּוִד) to "spirit" (רוּחַ).

The meaning, however, seems to be that David wanted to go out ('al) "against" Absalom, but he did not do so for this would necessitate going to war against his father-in-law. And he mourned for Amnon for many days because he was dead.[24]

Absalom spends the time of his exile in Geshur, just north of the border of Israel.[25] There he acquires a taste for pageantry that contributes to the choices he will make in the future. Luxuriating in the splendor of his grandfather's court, he has the leisure time to plan his next move.

THE IMPORTANCE OF OUR CHOICES

We have noted in this chapter the choices of the two main charac-ters, Amnon and Absalom. Both were young men. Each selected a course of action—the one involving his sexual passions and the other murder—and these *choices* then determined their future.

Some well-known lines in James Russell Lowell's poem "The Present Crisis" underscore the importance of our choices.

> Once to every man and nation
>   comes the moment to decide,
> In the strife of Truth with Falsehood,
>   for the good or evil side;
> Some great cause, God's new Messiah,
>   offering each the bloom or blight,
> Parts the goats upon the left hand,
>   and the sheep upon the right,
> And the choice goes by forever,
>   'twixt that darkness and that light.[26]

When Joshua sensed that the Israelites were turning back from their commitment to the Lord their God, he challenged them with the words,

> "But to Yahweh your God you shall cling...for Yahweh your God [is] He who is fighting for you.... But if you turn away at all...know certainly that Yahweh your God shall not continue to expel these nations from before you.... Now, then, fear Yahweh, and serve Him in sincerity and truth, and turn away from the gods which your fathers served...*Choose for yourselves today whom you will serve...but as for me and my house, we will serve Yahweh*" (23:8*a*, 9-13*a*; 24:14-15, emphasis added).

Some years later, after Israel apostatized from the Lord and suf-fered the withdrawal of His blessing, Samuel confronted the people with the need to reaffirm their allegiance to the Lord. He spoke to all the house of Israel, saying:

> "If you [are] returning to Yahweh, put aside the gods of the stranger from your midst, and the Ashteroth; and prepare your heart for (lit., to) Yahweh, and serve Him only, then He will deliver you from the hand of the Philistines" (1 Samuel 7:3).

But Israel failed to remain constant. They continuously departed from the Lord and were eventually taken into captivity. After seventy years in the province of Babylon, Cyrus, king of Persia, gave the exiles a choice of either returning to Judah themselves or else remaining in Persia and supporting those who wanted to go back to their homeland.

> "Who [is] [there] among you of all His people? His God is with him, and let him go up to Jerusalem which [is] in Judah, and rebuild the house of Yahweh the God of Israel—He [is] God— which [is] in Jerusalem. And all who remain in any of the places where he sojourns there, let the men of that place assist him" (Ezra 1:3-4).

Scripture informs us that the number of those who returned totaled 42,360 (Ezra 2:2-64).

But choices do not face only God's people. Years later, when Xerxes ascended the throne of Persia, he sought to extend his empire into Europe. He was opposed by the Greeks. They determined to remain a free people. The final battle was fought on the plain of Marathon. The Greeks won, and their victory set the course of European history for the next several hundred years.[27]

After the decline of the Persian and Greek empires, when Rome "ruled the [then known] world," Pompey became emperor. The people languished under his misguided rule. Fearing interference from Julius Caesar, Pompey forbade him to cross the Rubicon.[28] Julius deliberately chose to cross this river and by doing so challenged Pompey's right to rule the empire. He defeated Pompey in a series of battles, and after further victories, he was welcomed into Rome as the liberator of his people.

At a later time, when the Roman empire was virtually in ruins and the Turks were threatening to dominate Europe, Charles ("the Hammer") Martel chose to stand against the invading Muslims. He defeated them in the Battle of Tours, France. His decision to stop their advance turned the tide of history.

When the British people grew tired of the oppressive rule and unjust practices of King John, they decided to band together and demand of him certain freedoms. The meeting took place on the plain of Runnymede. King John came there intent upon destroying the coalition. Such was the commitment of the leaders that he was compelled to sign the *Magna Carta*[29]—and this became the charter of the people's liberty.

And let us not forget the work of our own Continental Congress. Made up of individuals who were not afraid to make hard decisions, they took a stand for liberty and opened the way for the drafting and ratification of our Constitution.[30]

Our choices and decisions may not be as momentous and far-reaching as the ones just mentioned, but the ingredients are the same. We are aided in making the right choices by our willingness to live our lives under the authority of the Word of God.

ACTIONS OF AN HONEST MAN

2 Samuel 14:1-33

Diogenes, the Greek philosopher, is said to have lit a lamp and walked through the streets of Athens in broad daylight shining the light into the faces of the citizens whom he passed. When asked what he was doing, he replied that he was looking for an honest man.

Thomas Jefferson believed that "honesty is the first chapter of the book of wisdom," and that "every honest man will suppose honest acts to flow from honest principles."[1]

Honesty, however, is becoming an increasingly rare trait. We seldom see "honest acts flowing from honest principles" except in the character of people like Eric Liddell, about whose early life the film *Chariots of Fire* was made. He risked becoming a national disgrace at the Paris Olympic Games when he refused to run on a Sunday.

By disqualifying himself from the finals, Britain's hope of a gold medal vanished overnight. Thinly veiled criticism in the press called in question the practicality of his religious beliefs. At the instigation of some of his friends, Liddell was allowed to run in the finals of the 400 meters—a race for which he had not trained. He not only won the race but finished five strides ahead of his nearest competitor. Then, in keeping with his plans before the Olympiad, he turned his back on the celebrity status that had suddenly become his and went to China as a missionary.[2]

If we were to become modern lamp-toting children of Diogenes, we would find that men and women of fidelity, virtue, and equity are relatively few in number. And what is even more alarming is the fact that our social milieu has come to resemble the world of Isaiah (cf. Isaiah 1:4-6) and Habakkuk (cf. Habakkuk 1:3-4) and the other Old Testament prophets. Injustice abounds, and the righteous are oppressed on account of their beliefs.

All of this makes the teaching of 2 Samuel 14 a most vital one, for

in it we see David acting in his integrity. But lest we entertain the
fantasy that his life was different from our own, let us remind ourselves that he was surrounded by men and women whose cunning,
connivance, intrigue, and insidious corruption made it hard for him
to live out his beliefs. In this chapter, foremost among those who did
not share his commitments was Joab.

BACK ROOM POLITICS

Second Samuel 13:37b-39 forms a transition that covers the three
years of Absalom's exile. We read:

> And [David] mourned for his son [Amnon] all the days (i.e., for
> many days). And Absalom had fled and gone to Geshur, and
> [he] was there three years. And David determined to go out
> against Absalom, for he had been comforted concerning Amnon,
> for he was dead.

These verses comprise a necessary prelude to the attempt on the
part of Joab to have Prince Absalom brought back to Israel. But
whereas Absalom had not repented of his crime during the years of
his exile, David's integrity has stood the test of time. His attitude
toward Absalom had not changed.

David's integrity is demonstrated in three ways in 13:37–14:33:

- The consistency of his attitude toward Absalom, even when
  an increasing number of people in the realm wanted his return;

- His willingness to fulfill his vow to the woman of Tekoa even
  though it had been extracted from him under false pretenses;

- The genuineness of his forgiveness of Absalom when the latter
  appeared to be repentant and sought reconciliation with the
  king.

But why were the people of Israel *so* interested in Absalom? What
had he done to earn their favor?

There are always those who are perpetual worriers. They have an
eye to the future. They are concerned about what will happen *if* such-
and-such takes place. In a monarchy, their concern is with succession and who will be king after So-and-so. With David in his mid-fif-
ties, there were those in Israel who speculated that he might not
have much longer to live. If so, which of his sons would follow him

on the throne? And so an "Absalom party" came into being. One of the prime leaders was Joab.

Others, however, favored change for different reasons. Now that the nation had been established and the wealth of the surrounding countries was beginning to pour into Israel, the affluence and higher standard of living caused many to favor an easing of religious restrictions. David's critics could not understand why he set aside so much silver and gold for the Temple (which had not yet been built). If allowed to circulate, this wealth could further boost the economy.

In Jerusalem, there seemed to be an unexpressed attitude that implied, "We don't need to rely on religious fervor as much now as formerly. The worst is over. We're now a nation that must be respected by the other nations. We've come a long way on our own, and religious leaders are no longer needed to the same extent as in the past."

All of this may have grown out of the fact that God could not be seen. So Joab and Absalom and others may have thought that the teaching of the theocracy was outmoded—at best a device developed by the priests to give them some leverage in affairs of state.

But God is the One to whom we are all ultimately accountable. Those living in Israel at the time of our story, who were concerned over David's successor, overlooked the fact that when one of God's representatives passes from this earthly scene, *He* appoints his replacement. They, however, acted in such a way as to imply that God had taken a vacation and left them in charge. They believed that Absalom was the kind of forward-looking man upon whom to build for the future. He had none of his father's religious scruples that so many felt were hindering the development of international policies.

THE PROBLEM OF SUCCESSION

In the last chapter, we noted that as some of David's sons grew to manhood they cast lustful eyes on their father's throne. Amnon, as the oldest, felt that the crown should be his. The law of primogeniture had not been established in Israel, but this did not stop him from coveting the position held by his father. Absalom also wanted to be king. After murdering Amnon, he was forced into exile. His plans, therefore, had to be put on hold. Joab, as we have noted in an earlier chapter, was an irreligious man. His Godward relationship was left for emergencies when his wisdom and ingenuity seemed inadequate for the crisis he or the nation faced. In his assessment of the situation, Absalom, with his fine physique and handsome appearance, would make an ideal king. And so he was in the vanguard of those wanting change.

OUTLINE

As we noted in our last chapter, the theme of 2 Samuel 13 to 20 reveals the *sovereignty of God in sustaining the kingdom of His anointed.* This was done at a time when others wanted to wrest it from him. Chapters 13 and 14, form a prologue to chapters 15–20.

In chapter 14, we continue our study of the introductory section that describes "Strife over the Right of Succession." We had earlier outlined the parts of this section as follows:

- The Shameful Rape of the King's Daughter (13:1-22)
- The Vengeful Assassination of the King's Son (13:23-39)
- The Deceitful Plan of the King's Servant (14:1-33)

The events in this chapter focus on Joab's deception of the king by means of the wiles of a wise woman from Tekoa.[3] Then, in chapters 15–19, there will be an attempt on the part of Absalom to wrest the kingdom from his father; and finally, in chapter 20, Sheba will try to drive a wedge between the northern tribes and those in the south.

The remainder of the book is comprised of an appendix.

STRIFE OVER THE RIGHT OF SUCCESSION
(13:1–14:33, Continued)

The Deceitful Plan of the King's Servant (14:1-33)

The Plan (14:1-3). Most of our translations imply that David pined for Absalom and longed to go to him. They infer that he could not and did not do so because as king, he had to maintain the law. But as a father, he loved Absalom and blamed himself for his son's failings. They then enlarge upon the inner struggle he felt between the love of a father for his erring son and the duty of the king who had to punish the offender.[4]

This view is difficult to harmonize with 14:24, where we read: "And the king said, 'Let him (Absalom) turn to his house, and my face he shall not see.'"

A careful reading of those verses that form the transition between these chapters (i.e., 13:37b-39 and 14:1-3) reveals that David's anger was still directed (*'al*) "against" Absalom.[5] Joyce Baldwin explains, "David longed intensely to march out against Absalom, for he was grieved about Amnon, that he was dead."[6]

David, however, could not take up arms against Absalom and bring him to trial because this would necessitate going to war against his father-in-law. Also, to demand that Talmai send his daughter's son back to Israel for sentencing and execution would be to place the old man in an invidious position. David, therefore, allowed Absalom to remain in exile. But he did not for a moment compromise his beliefs. He was caught in a difficult situation, and he is to be praised for not making it worse.

At the time of the events of 2 Samuel 14, Absalom is in his early to mid-twenties. He has the outward bearing of a king, and the only obstacle to the fulfillment of his or Joab's plans is to overcome the reluctance of David and have him recalled (14:1).

The dilemma Joab faces is how to "change the face of the matter" (14:20). He, therefore, enlists the help of a wise woman. He sends to Tekoa and brings from there one who is known for her ability to tell stories. He says to her:

> "Pretend now to be a mourner and please put on garments of mourning, and do not anoint yourself with oil; and you shall be as a woman who [has been] mourning for the dead [for] many days. And you shall go to the king and speak with him, according to this word."

And Joab put words into her mouth.

He knows that David's plans for the future of the kingdom differ from his own, so he devises a way whereby Absalom may be recalled. To do this, however, he must make David's greatest strength (i.e., his Godward relationship) into a weakness. He, therefore, enlists the aid of this articulate and shrewd woman from Tekoa[7] (modern *Khirbet Tequ'*)—a town ten miles south of Jerusalem. He coerces her[8] into collaborating with him in an act of deception[9] (cf. 14:16,19).

This woman is, in all probability, a widow who has an only son (so a part of her story may well have been true). Her circumstances may approximate the story she is to tell the king; and, to add realism to Joab's plot, she is to pretend to be a mourner, put on old clothing, refrain from using any oil to protect her skin from the effects of the hot, dry wind off the desert, and appear as if she has been grieving the loss of loved ones for many years.

The Presentation (14:4-7). It is evident from this passage that David was in the habit of determining judicial matters inside the palace. This will become important as we consider Absalom's strategy in 2 Samuel 15. When the woman from Tekoa is given audience with the king, she prostrates herself before him. From all that she has heard of David, she knows that he is the champion of the poor and the desolate. Her opening words, "Help (*Hosi'a*, 'Save'), O king" (14:4), are respectful and immediately get his full attention. Then she waits for him to respond.

"What shall be (i.e., What shall I do for) you?" he asks.

Then she answers:

> "Truly I [am] a widow woman, and my husband [has] died, and your servant had two sons; and the two of them fought in the field, and there was none to deliver (i.e., part) them; and the one struck the other, and killed him. And behold, the whole family has risen against your servant, and [they have] said: 'Give up him who smote his brother, and we shall kill him for the life of his brother whom he has slain, and we shall destroy also the heir.' And they shall quench my coal which is left, so as not to set (i.e., leave) my husband a name and remnant on the face of the earth" (14:5b-7).

The parallel between this widow's situation and David's own tragic circumstances is not perceived by the king. He is too intent upon her case to think of himself. The essence of her situation involves "the avenger of blood" (see Numbers 35:15-21). Her plight is eloquently embodied in the phrase, "so they will extinguish my coal which is left." Her son was her sole support—a "solitary coal" in a dying fire—and since there was no such thing as Social Security in those days, nor any form of welfare, her situation would be desperate if he were taken from her.

Those Bible scholars who have studied the sociology of the times have shown that a widow's predicament was indeed pitiful.[10] Hiring herself out to clean the houses of the wealthy for a "mite" a day was her only real option.

David is faced with a difficult decision. How shall he rule on this matter? His integrity is to be seen in the fact that he does not allow himself to be influenced by the pathos of the widow's story or any extenuating circumstances. It is true that this woman's son is her sole support. It is also true that should he be killed, her husband's name will perish.[11] There is, in addition, a hint in her words of the greed of the people of her tribe: "and destroy the heir also." Apparently, the family was more interested in his estate than they were in justice.

As a godly judge, David steels himself against the emotional impact of her story and carefully weighs the evidence. First, the information is all hearsay. The explanation given is that "the two struggled together in the field, and *there was no one* (lit. no deliverer between) to part them." This also implies that there were no eye-witnesses (cf. Deuteronomy 17:6). The surviving son may be innocent or guilty, but there is no way to prove either one.

Second, the members of the extended family have not accompanied the woman to press their claim (as was expected in cases of this nature), so it must be presumed that they realize their case is weak. As far as David knows, the son who died might have been the one to instigate the fight. If so, then the surviving son would have acted in self-defense. In the absence of evidence to the contrary, the young man must be assumed innocent until proven guilty. Finally, at worst, the woman's son is guilty of manslaughter, for there is no evidence of premeditation on his part.

The Promise (14:8-11). Basing his decision on the known facts, David moves to dismiss the case. He will send his ruling to the elders of the city via a royal courier. "Go to your house. I will give orders concerning you" (14:8), he says.

To his surprise, the woman continues with her plea.

> "On me, my lord O King, let the iniquity [be] and on the house of my father, and the king and his throne [shall be] guiltless" (14:9).

Most women in Scripture kept their communication short and to the point (cf. Judges 4:6-7,14; 13:6-7,10,23; Ruth 2:10,13; 3:9; Esther 5:4; 7:3-4,6). This woman's continuance in pressing her case strikes us as a departure from the norm. Her words also appear unnecessary in light of the king's judgment.

Initially, David may have felt that this woman was prepared to bear the consequences of his decision should later events show that there had been a miscarriage of justice.[12] In reality, 14:9 is a most clever and ambiguous transition that makes possible the introduction of Joab's "hidden agenda." David, however, is unaware of this and continues to act in his integrity. He assumes that the woman is being gracious and again tries to dismiss her. His words are kind and intended to be reassuring:

> "Whoever speaks to you, you shall bring him to me, then he shall not touch (i.e., trouble) you any more" (14:10).

The woman from Tekoa appears loath to leave until David takes an oath to safeguard herself and her son.

> "Please let the king remember Yahweh [his] (lit., your) God, that the avenger of blood not destroy anymore, and that they may not destroy my son" (14:11).

Her words are carefully chosen. The trap has been set, and David is about to walk into it. Her goal is to have him irrevocably commit himself to a course of action by entering into an oath. And David, always willing to encourage those who need support, says: "[As] Yahweh lives, not one hair of your son shall fall to the earth" (14:11).

The trap has been sprung, and the woman is now in a position to pressure David into fulfilling the real intent of her visit.

The Appeal (14:12-17). Before introducing her "hidden agenda," she courteously asks, "Please let your servant speak a word to my lord the king" (14:12*a*).

David may have been irritated by her persistence when he had thrice given his verdict (14:8, 10, 11*b*), and he responds: "Speak."

The woman's manner now changes. She assumes the role of an accuser. Her words are blunt—so blunt that we are shocked by them and the accusing tone with which they must have been uttered.

> "And why have you planned thus against the people of God? Yes, in speaking this way the king is one [who is] guilty, in that the king has not brought back his outcast one. For surely we do die, and [are] as water that is spilled on the ground that cannot be gathered up; and [yet] God does not take a life, but has planned (i.e., devised) plans so that the outcast is not cast out from Him" (14:13-15).

Her charge, "Why have you planned this thing *against the people of God*?" indicates that the real issue in the minds of many in Israel is a successor to the throne. David, she states, cannot expect to live forever, and there's talk among the people about bringing Absalom (though she never mentions his name) out of exile. So far the king has made no move to restore his banished son. And yet, she asserts, this is what God does. He devises means so that His banished will not perish away from His presence.

From her words it is possible to conclude that a formal decree of banishment had been issued following Absalom's flight. If so, then all Israel would have known of the king's displeasure. Now, however, David finds himself indicted by the Tekoaite for failure to act in a God-like manner. Yahweh, the woman has assured him, seeks for ways of reconciliation. But he, instead of conducting himself as the Lord would have done, has done nothing. By implication, he has himself become guilty of not placing the interests of the nation above his desires for justice.

David might have objected to the woman's story and also her entrapment. The case he had passed judgment on bore little resemblance to his own son's premeditated murder of his brother.[13] Absalom had killed Amnon in cold blood before many witnesses (cf. Deuteronomy 19:15); he was not David's sole remaining heir; and being even now in exile, he was not in any immediate danger of the "avenger of blood." Furthermore, his decision in favor of the widow's son could not lawfully be used to establish a precedent, because she had presented him with a fictitious set of circumstances.

David, however, had been deceived into invoking the name of the Lord, and he feels himself obligated to act in the spirit of his oath. He is in the same kind of position the Lord Jesus Christ will be in on the night of His betrayal when Caiaphas will charge Him in the name of the Lord to witness against Himself: "I adjure You by the living God, that You tell us if You are indeed the Christ, the Son of God" (Matthew 26:63).

The Lord Jesus will be under no obligation to witness against Himself. Out of respect for the name of the Father, and setting the honor of God above His own welfare, He will comply. "I am" (Mark 14:62).

David has listened without interruption to the woman's application of her situation to his own. While he has been carefully processing her words, one question has remained unanswered. "Who put her up to this?" The only reasonable answer is Joab.

The woman from Tekoa knows human nature well. She senses intuitively what is going on in the king's mind. Before he can ask his question, she answers it.

> "And now that I have come to speak this word to my lord the king, [it was] because *the people* (the reference is vague) made me afraid; and your servant said, 'Let me speak now to the king; perhaps the king shall do the word of his servant; for the king has listened *to deliver his servant out of the hand of the man* [seeking] *to destroy me and my son* together out of the inheritance of God.' And your servant said, 'Please let the word of my lord the king be for rest (i.e., comforting); for as a messenger of God, so [is] my lord the king, to understand good and evil; and Yahweh your God shall be with you'" (14:15-17, emphasis added).

Whereas before she had addressed the king in a bold, accusing manner, now she is once again deferential. She refers to herself as David's "maidservant,"[14] and sees him as her deliverer. She also flatters him for his ability to discern between good and evil.[15]

The Inquiry (14:18-20). Kings do not like to be used as pawns,

and David is no exception. He senses that Joab is behind this cha-
rade. He had probably known for some time that his general was a
strong force behind the "Absalom Party." Not that Joab had ever been
disloyal to David, but in thinking ahead, he had determined that
Absalom—handsome in appearance and controllable—would make
a "good" king.[16]

David's question is direct:

> "Please do not hide from me the thing that I am asking you. Is
> the hand of Joab with you in all this?" (14:18- 19*a*).

To which the woman replies:

> "[As] your soul lives, my lord, O king, none [shall turn] to the
> right or to the left from all that my lord the king has spoken; for
> your servant Joab, he commanded me, and he put in the mouth
> of your servant all these words; in order to change the face of
> the matter, Joab your servant has done this thing. But my lord
> [is] wise, according to the wisdom of an angel of God, to know
> all that is in the land" (14:19*b*-20).

The Tekoaite is quick to point out that Joab had wanted to "change
the course of affairs." And then, with a flattering reference to the
wisdom of the king, she hints at the need for him not to let Joab
know that she had confessed to his coercion. This said, she respectfully leaves his presence.

The Return (14:21-24). Joab is summoned to appear before the
king. When he does so, David gives no hint of the woman's confession. He does not want to give Joab an excuse to make good on his
promised threat (14:16,19*b*). Instead, he lets Joab know that he has
seen through his deceptive scheme, and then says: "Go, bring back
the young man Absalom" (14:21).

There is in David's reference to Absalom as a *nā'ār*, "young man,"
a note of affection.[17] However, inasmuch as his son has not taken the
initiative and asked for forgiveness, on his return to Jerusalem he is
not to see the king's face. Instead, he is to go to his own house, where
he will remain under virtual house arrest.

We might have hoped that, after killing Amnon, Absalom would
have changed. Certainly, we would have liked to see him return to
his homeland different than before. But such is a forlorn wish.
Absalom remains unchanged except for the fact that his heart is now
more implacable than before.

Psalm 109:18 gives a stern warning to those who persist in evil. David, in describing a certain adversary, said:

> And he put on (i.e., clothed himself with) cursing as his robe, and it came into his body like water, and as oil into his bones.

Habitual sinning makes a permanent impression upon us!

Several years ago, while on a vacation in Colorado, Utah and Wyoming, my wife, sons, and I visited the Dinosaur National Monument in northern Utah. There we saw huge fossilized bones of dinosaurs long extinct. Under normal circumstances, these bones would have crumbled into dust centuries ago. However, mineral-rich water, under considerable pressure, became fused with these bones so that they now have acquired a metallic content. And this has made them impervious to decay.

It is this kind of process that the psalmist describes. A person may become so possessed by his or her anger, greed, hatred, bitterness, critical attitude, or sordid lifestyle that their depravity permanently distorts their personality. Over time, their character undergoes a change. Evil becomes a part of their personality (cf. Psalm 109:17-18).

This is apparently what had happened to Absalom.

Parenthesis: His Appearance (14:25-27). The Biblical writer now digresses to give us some additional information about Absalom. He seemingly has everything. His physical attractiveness and popularity prepare us for what will follow. He can "turn on the charm" when he wishes to do so (15:6). But he is also vain. When his hair is cut once a year, he has it weighed. And year by year it is found to be the equivalent of two hundred shekels, *'eben hammelek,*[18] by "the king's weight" or according to the "royal standard."

The shekel was the basic unit for weighing grain and other commodities. Archaeologists have dug up weights used on scales, and from these they have been able to determine that the weight of a shekel varied over time and in different locations, being between .39 and .46 ounces. "The king's weight" is presumed to have been .457 ounces, making the weight of Absalom's hair around 5.5 pounds. For this to be preserved for us by the Biblical historian shows that Absalom placed weighty significance on something of inconsequential value.

Absalom's three sons and one daughter had either been born to him while he was in exile or else come to bless his home during the two years of his house arrest. None of his wives are named, but his only daughter is called Tamar, after her father's sister.[19] We may be sure that the children's aunt derived great pleasure from them, perhaps looking on them as compensation for the children she would never bear.

Even grandchildren, however, fail to bridge the gulf between David and Absalom. The king may have been tricked into bringing Absalom out of exile, but this does not mean that the past has been erased. There has been no confession of sin on Absalom's part or any request for forgiveness.

The populace may have welcomed the young prince's return, but the king does not. The justice the Law demands has not been carried out. And apart from repentance, there can be no mercy. Even Joab realizes that he has labored in vain, and loses interest in Absalom.

The Reconciliation (14:28-33). The fact that Absalom "did not see the king's face" for a full two years indicates the strength of David's convictions.[20] Eventually Absalom begins to chafe under the imposed restraint. Joab had been the one to secure his return from exile, so Absalom believes that Joab should now gain for him an audience with the king.

Accordingly, he sends a messenger to Joab, summoning him to his house. But Joab refuses to come. Again Absalom summons him, and again he declines. Exasperated, Absalom decides to send a "message" Joab will not be able to ignore. Just before the barley harvest, he has his servants set fire to Joab's crop. This act is to be done openly so that Joab will know who gave the order.

Now Joab is incensed. In a rage, he storms into Absalom's house and demands an explanation: "Why have your servants set my allotment (i.e., my portion of the field) on fire?" (14:31).

To this Absalom replies:

"Behold, I sent to you, saying, 'Come here, and I will send you to the king, saying, "Let me see the king's face; and if there is in me guilt, then you shall kill me"'" (14:32).

Joab is now convinced of the need to do as Absalom has commanded. He does not wait for a reminder. He quickly goes before David and requests an audience for Absalom.

Absalom is confident he can win the king over. When Joab brings him into David's throne (or council) room, Absalom prostrates himself on the floor, implying his total submission to the king and his loyalty to the crown. David understands this sign of penance and in grace raises Absalom to his feet. He then gives him a kiss of reconciliation. His forgiveness of Absalom is real, and Absalom is forthwith restored to his favor.[21]

THE ISSUE OF INTEGRITY

In this story we have seen David conduct himself with integrity. Though surrounded by unscrupulous people, he still conducts his affairs honestly and in accordance with the teaching of Scripture.

Three cameos in this chapter each reveal his honesty: (1) He was not prepared to compromise the Law of the Lord for the sake of public approval; (2) he fulfilled his promise to the woman lest any failure detract from the honor of His God; and (3) when he forgave Absalom, he meant it.

Honesty in Adhering to What Is Right

Granville Sharp, one of the forgotten heroes of Christendom, was a man who adhered unalterably to the truth, regardless of public opinion. He believed that slavery was wrong, even though nearly all of his friends owned slaves.

On one occasion, he befriended a slave who had been severely beaten by his master and then turned loose to die. He nursed the man back to health and then found a job for him so that he could be self-supporting. Two years later, the slave's former owner saw him in the streets and sued Sharp for "unlawfully detaining the property of another."

Sharp sought and obtained legal representation, but as soon as his counsel found out who the judge would be, he withdrew from the case. After going from one lawyer to another, Sharp was compelled to defend himself. He did so...and lost.

All of this did not diminish his commitment to seek justice for those who were oppressed. One legal battle followed another, until one day he again faced his nemesis—the judge who had ruled against him at the beginning.

So weighty were Sharp's arguments, and so thorough was his knowledge of the issues, that this honored judge reversed his previous decision and ruled in Granville Sharp's favor. One biographer wrote:

> The character of Granville Sharp is of the highest order; but it is also the most plain and easy to be understood, as it was always shown without artifice or disguise. It is that of a man who, gifted with rare endowments, and led by the disposing hand of Providence to do good, found his heart irresistibly directed to

the relief of unmerited sufferings.... To the advancement of these sublime purposes he moved forward by a clew (i.e., clue) that admitted of no mistake, and that could not be broken. Intimately convinced of the divine origin of the Scriptures, and of their containing the only certain grounds of our temporal and eternal welfare, he resolutely applied the whole faculties of his understanding, and bent the whole vigor of his mind, to search with accuracy their strict and unquestioned meaning. [Though a layman] the languages in which [the Scriptures] were delivered to us, were made the objects of his profound inquiry, that he became one of the ablest interpreters of them, that has appeared to the present day.[22]

As with David, Granville Sharp was a man of integrity. He adhered unalterably to the truth regardless of what his friends said or thought of him. And such was his commitment to doing right that neither adverse public opinion or opposition could turn him from the course that he chose to follow.

Honesty in Keeping His Promise

Second, David placed the honor of God above his personal welfare. He fulfilled his promise, even though he could have shown that he was not obligated by law to do so.

The pressure of this world's system of values is such that it is becoming more and more difficult for Christians to be men and women of integrity. Whenever I think of integrity "in the marketplace," I am reminded of Marie Loizeaux, who for many years was the editor of Loizeaux Brothers. I had labored long and hard over a manuscript on the book of Nehemiah. In due course I submitted it to Loizeaux Brothers and waited to see if it would be accepted.

In time, Marie wrote me and told me that Loizeaux Brothers would be happy to publish my book. I waited (im)patiently for a couple of months for a contract. When it did not arrive, I wrote a cautious letter to Marie inquiring if perhaps it had been sent and become lost in the mail.

Marie replied, confirming that Loizeaux Brothers would publish my book. Then she added a few words that I have never forgotten: "We don't issue contracts. What we say is what we do."[23]

Marie, and the company for which she worked, shared something in common with David: Honorable intentions that were matched by honest deeds.

Honesty in Forgiving an Offender

Finally, often in interpersonal relationships, forgiveness is conditional. We want to wait and see if the person who has offended us has changed and whether he or she will hurt us again. When Absalom led David to believe that he was truly repentant, David forgave him and restored him to his favor. His forgiveness was real.

A most remarkable example of forgiveness is Corrie ten Boom's pardon of the German soldier whose cruelty was torturous for her and her sister when they were imprisoned in a concentration camp.

Corrie ten Boom and her family suffered a great deal when Holland was overrun by the Nazis during World War II. She and her sister were arrested and later placed under sentence of death. In the concentration camp, there was a guard who was one of the most savage and heartless men she had ever met. He delighted in humiliating and degrading her and her sister. He had jeered and virtually raped them as they stood in the de-lousing shower.

After the war, when Corrie was ministering in Germany, she suddenly met this guard face-to-face. He told of his conversion to Christ and, stretching out his hand, asked: "Will you forgive me?"

Corrie admits that she stood there speechless. A coldness clutched at her heart. She knew that it was her duty to forgive him, but how could she, after all he had done? She prayed silently, "Jesus, help me!"

Then, woodenly and mechanically, she thrust out her hand to take the one offered to her. As she did so a strange sensation overcame her. She felt a current extending down her arms and she ended clasping his hand with both of hers. A warm sense of reconciliation flooded her entire being. "I forgive you, brother!" she cried. And she meant it. In writing of the incident she says, "For a long moment we grasped each other's hands." Later she admitted, "I have never known the love of God so intensely as I did in that moment!"

Corrie learned that to forgive is to set a prisoner free—and to discover that the prisoner was you.[24] But how is someone able to forgive so completely? How was David able to forgive Absalom...and mean it? His forgiveness was not conditioned on Absalom's worthiness. It was gracious, and it gave Absalom a new start.

The answer lies in David's Godward relationship. As we study his psalms (as well as those written about him), we find that his closeness to the Lord gave him a sense of *security* (Psalms 4:3; 9:9-10; 17:8; 18:2*a*,3,6; etc.), *significance* (Psalms 6:9; 8:3-8; 9:12*b*; 18:16-19; etc.), and *satisfaction* (Psalms 9:1-2; 13:5-6; 17:15; 18:20-24; etc.). He did not need to prove himself to the Lord. He was happy in God's *acceptance* of him (Psalms 5:11; 11:7; 20:1-4; etc.), His *affirmation* of his worth (Psalms 9:4; 18:34-36; etc.), and His *approval* of his service as well as his deeds (Psalms 15:5*b*,7; 16:10-11; 18:37-39; etc.). A careful reading of his psalms will bring these thoughts into clearer focus.

Also prominent in his psalms is his desire to be a person of integrity (Psalms 7:8; 25:8-10,21; 26:1,11; 41:12; 78:70-72; 101:2). Because his confidence in the Almighty was mingled with his walk before the Lord in the light of His Word, congruency was established between his thoughts and his actions. This chapter gives us three vignettes to illustrate the point.

David was a man of like passions with us. What he achieved is possible for us as well, as we place ourselves under the authority of the Scriptures and make its teaching the rule for our lives.

AN ATTEMPT TO RESHAPE THE WILL
OF GOD

2 Samuel 15:1–16:14

How do you define ambition? What do you believe motivates a person to strive to achieve his or her best? When does an ambitious person face the dangers that can be detrimental to himself or herself and those whom he or she professes to love? To look at matters from a different point of view, what does the Bible teach about handling the inequities of life caused by those who are inordinately ambitious?

As might be expected, our word *ambition* comes from the Latin *ambire*, "to go about." It was first used of those in Rome who desired to have people vote for them and/or their cause. They would "go about" canvassing for votes.

In our day, and in a positive sense, the word *ambition* describes the desire to attain some special objective or goal. Psychologically, the term is used to delineate the purposefulness that normally occurs in healthy personalities. For one's goals to be reached, planning, dedication, effort, and persistence are all necessary.

Yet caution is also needed. Noah Webster warned that ambition has a negative side to it. This is seen in "an eager or inordinate desire for preference, honor, superiority, power, or attainment."[1] As we shall find in this segment of 2 Samuel, Absalom planned well. He was dedicated to the task he had set for himself. He exerted effort. And he was persistent. Yet he failed because his inordinate desire for the throne caused him to act independently of the Lord. He disregarded the theocracy.

As we study the lives of men who were regarded by their contemporaries as "ambitious," we find that their desire for superiority, love of glory, or eagerness for distinction was often fostered against a background of high idealism. For example, consider the quest for excellence in the athletic metaphors used by the apostle Paul.[2] His writings express the ideas of dedication in training as well as in the actual contest (cf. 1 Corinthians 9:24-27). When we apply these allusions to the spiritual life, they affirm the legitimacy of living to please God (2 Corinthians 5:9) and desiring to lead a quiet life (1 Thessalonians 4:11).

However, there is a flip side. Scripture warns against selfish ambition (Philippians 1:17; James 3:14, 16), and to our surprise we learn that even those who spread the Gospel may do so from unworthy motives.

The realized ambitions of some people have been of distinct benefit to mankind. But where ambition is governed by greed, self-interest, or pride, it becomes sinful. When this happens, a person's achievements can be injurious to themself as well as those associated with them.

For the Christian, therefore, the central focus of life should be Christ. Such an orientation helps to keep one's inordinate desires from becoming distorted by the quest for self-satisfaction that results in an inflated opinion of oneself. Those caught up in an earthy mind-set or lifestyle often overlook the fact that pride goes before destruction, and a haughty spirit before a fall (cf. Proverbs 16:18 AV).

As our story unfolds, we cannot help but note that Absalom, David's son, wants his father's throne. He is arrogant, willful, and feels that the crown would look much better on his head. How he lays the groundwork for his coup is the subject of this chapter.

OUTLINE

As we have noted, the section from 2 Samuel 13:1–20:26 has as its theme the sovereignty of God in preserving the kingdom of His anointed. We have also observed that chapters 13–14 provide the necessary background to explain Amnon's death. Now nothing but the will of God stands in Absalom's way as he pursues his goal of seizing the throne.

The two remaining divisions of this section treat:

- An Attempt to Seize the Throne (15:1–19:39)
- An Attempt to Divide the Nation (19:40–20:26)

Several scholars have described the symmetry of these chapters.[3] Their views are worth noting. The outline we have used is thematic and adheres to the kingdom motif of the book. As we shall see, the Lord will sustain His anointed in the face of powerful opposition.

AN ATTEMPT TO SEIZE THE THRONE (15:1–19:39)

Removal of a God-Anointed King from the Throne (15:1–16:14)

Seduction of the People (15:1-12). No sooner has Absalom been reinstated in the king's favor than he begins to build himself up in the eyes of the people.

> And it was after this that Absalom prepared for himself a chariot and horses, and fifty men running before him (15:1).

Professor Arnold A. Anderson, of the University of Manchester, England, has stated that it is not impossible that during his (Absalom's) exile it was *Adonijah* who had become or came to be regarded as the heir apparent.[4]

If this is so, then it would explain why Absalom found it necessary to project the image of being the one who would succeed his father.

Jerusalem's topography is unsuitable for chariots and horses. The Mosaic Law restricted the use of horses lest a king or his people become puffed up with pride (see Deuteronomy 17:16). Absalom's chariot would not have been able to move through the streets with any speed; and this may have aided his purpose, for it would have given the people more time to look with adoring eyes upon the grandeur of his person and the splendor of his train.

Absalom not only has a team of horses, but he also employs[5] fifty men to run before him. While the Biblical text is silent as to their function, in other countries such individuals were used to clear the way before the dignitary who was coming down the narrow street. If this was the function of Absalom's retainers, then they would have cried out, "Clear the way for Prince Absalom," and this would have further drawn attention to him.

William J. Deane has observed that if Absalom was

> handsome in person, he was no less winning in manner, courteous, affable, and of honeyed speech, and was regarded by general acclamation as one in every way fitted for sovereignty....He imitated the heathen monarchs by setting up a grand equipage and...David's unpretending style of living was quite eclipsed by the pageantry of his brilliant son.[6]

With all of the appurtenances in place, the stage is now set for the second phase of Absalom's plan, namely, winning the confidence of the people.

During his years in exile, as well as in the period of time when he was under virtual house arrest, Absalom must have planned how he was going to take over the kingdom. He now begins to implement his strategy. Each morning he rises early and takes up a position at the gate (the place where, in the towns and villages of Israel, judicial matters are settled). When an Israelite would come to see the king, Absalom would call to him and ask, "Of what city [are] you?"

If the man answered, "Your servant [is] from one of the tribes of Israel,"[7] then Absalom would say in a confidential manner, "See, your matters [are] good and right; and [yet] there is no listener [appointed] by the king [to hear your complaint]" (15:3).

This was not entirely true. David, as we know, was accustomed to settling judicial disputes in the palace. It was probably more convenient and most likely served his purposes better. He had a recorder present to make a note of his decisions, and his assistants could ensure that before a case came to him for trial all parties to the dispute had been notified.[8]

In light of this, we are forced to ask if David knew of Absalom's activities? When his "caseload" diminished and his courtiers saw Absalom sitting in the gate, word must have been brought back to him of the young prince's activities. Why, then, didn't he stop his son from adjudicating matters when this task was rightfully his?

Because of Absalom's cunning, the true intent of his actions was kept from all David's friends, advisors, and staff. The king and his confidants saw only the conduct of one who, having been forgiven his offense, was now trying to do something for the benefit of the people. Furthermore, from evidence in Psalms 38, 39, and 41,[9] we conclude that during this time David probably suffered from a prolonged illness. While he persevered with his duties, he was quite possibly grateful for Absalom's services and inclined to overlook the prince's grandiosity.

William Deane explains Absalom's plan:

> The king's duties were very arduous, and involved great personal attention and labour. He was the supreme judge of his subjects; he had to sit and try every cause that might be brought to him; and as the kingdom was now wide in extent, and accordingly the cases which came for decision became yearly more numerous and important, it often happened that suitors were unable to get a hearing, or suffered long delays, or departed

dissatisfied with the royal verdict. Absalom took advantage of this state of things in order to spread abroad a feeling of discontent, and a vague desire for change.[10]

The most diabolical part of the young prince's presentation came when he intimated his own dissatisfaction with all that the king was doing and hinted at the possibility that he was better suited for the role of judge than his aging father.

> "Who shall make me a judge in the land? Then (lit., And) every man who has a dispute shall come to me, and then [with] justice I will declare him right" (15:4).

His words are a subtle invitation for the people to secure for him this judicial appointment. But he wants more than the position of "attorney general." He wants the throne. He tells people what they want to hear, with the result that, had he been a judge, justice would have been perverted. He is not interested in doing what is right but only in using the office to further his own ambitions.

Absalom's vanity is also fed whenever a litigant recognizes him and pays him typical Oriental homage. On these occasions he rises to his feet, embraces the individual, and kisses him. And so, over a period of four years,[11] he steals the hearts of the people from the king.

At the end of this time, Absalom (who is now about twenty-eight or twenty-nine, with David fast approaching sixty), believes that the time has come for him to stage a *coup*. To do so, however, he needs permission from the king to go to Hebron, the place of his birth, and offer sacrifices there. He believes that, with a suitable number of slaughtered calves and sheep, God will be persuaded to prosper his cause. And if not, then he will succeed without the help of the Almighty.

With pretended piety, he asks the king for a leave of absence:

> "Please let me go to Hebron and I shall pay my vow that I vowed to Yahweh; for your servant vowed a vow when I lived in Geshur, in Aram (i.e., Syria), saying, 'If Yahweh shall surely bring me back to Jerusalem, then I shall serve Yahweh'" (15:7-8).

We may validly ask why it took Absalom so long to remember his vow. Perhaps he could offer, by way of explanation, the fact that David's health was only just beginning to improve and so this was the first opportunity he had had to fulfill his promise to the Lord.

Unwilling to hinder any Godward aspirations on the part of his children, David assents. "Go in peace" (15:9), he says.

These are the last words David will ever speak to his son. As Matthew Henry has so wisely remarked, "He who aims at the crown, aims at the head that wears it."[12] Absalom may well go in peace, but he will return in war.

David, on account of his long illness, may have been unaware of his fading popularity. Any drop-off might easily be attributed to his poor health, which had prevented him from moving about among his people. But he had also reigned for about thirty years, twenty-two of them in Jerusalem; and with the years of peace, the people have lacked an external threat to bind them together. All of this has made Absalom's task much easier.

When we add to this the general disenchantment of the people with David's administration, their criticism of him for devoting so much of the riches to the Temple, then we can see why they were vulnerable to Absalom's schemes. He had an easy time manipulating them into wanting a change.

But Absalom had not won the hearts of the people by deeds of valor. He had shown no courage or devotion to them. Even now he knew nothing of the difficulties his father had faced when he had united the tribes. Nor can he be credited with extending Israel's borders and securing the crossroads that have brought the wealth of caravan merchants into Israel. He knows only that a new generation has grown up to whom the earlier prowess of his father is mere hearsay.

So, taking two hundred men from Jerusalem (who know nothing of his nefarious plans, but whose presence will imply that he has the sanction of the king), Absalom sets out for Hebron. This had been the place of his birth and the site of the capital of Judah. While he is journeying south, his messengers scatter throughout the tribes. They have instructions that, as soon as they hear the sounding of the ram's horn (or *šofar*), they are to proclaim "Absalom reigns in Hebron" in each marketplace and city gate.

In addition, Ahithophel, David's longtime friend and former counselor, is summoned from his home in Giloh.[13] Apparently, he had withdrawn from court following David's affair with his granddaughter, Bathsheba (cf. 11:3 and 23:34*b*). Now all of his skills are at the disposal of the usurper.

At the height of the festivities, when Absalom believes that God has been sufficiently placated with offerings to prosper his plans, he gives instructions for the ram's horn to be blown. And others throughout the land carry the signal to the tribes and villages. Everywhere the cry goes up, "Absalom reigns in Hebron!"

So carefully have Absalom's plans been made that the people are taken by surprise. Those favorable to change respond positively, and any who are ambivalent either remain silent or are won over by the excitement of those whose hearts Absalom has stolen.

Evacuation of the City (15:13–16:14). It is interesting to note the Biblical writer's emphasis on *the king* in this section. While he does refer to David by name, he does not want his readers to lose sight of the fact that David is the rightful occupant of the throne (cf. 15:15ff.).

With the trumpets having been blown and the announcement made, a loyal messenger runs to the palace. He is given immediate audience with the king and hastily recounts the facts as he understands them. "The hearts of the men of Israel have gone after Absalom" (15:13).

Once again, the message the king receives is exaggerated (cf. 13:30). King David, however, has no time to verify it. Speed is of the essence. He accepts the communique as accurate and immediately orders the evacuation of the palace. He must have been crushed by the calloused hypocrisy and heartless cruelty of his son, but he does not allow his personal grief to render him ineffective. Rejection lies latent in the words, "the hearts of the men of Israel are one with Absalom." But even the realization that he has been deprived of what was most precious to him (namely, the love of his people) does not diminish his ability as a leader.[14]

Flight from the city seems to be the only logical course of action. Though Jerusalem has stout walls and could withstand a seige, the king has no means of knowing who in the city is loyal to him. He is also reluctant to expose it, and those in it, to the exigencies of war. Further, he knows that if he can forestall a confrontation with Absalom now, his own forces may be augmented by loyal supporters who will leave their homes to join him.

Feeling confident that no harm will come to innocent members of his house, he leaves ten concubines to look after the palace. Then he makes his way to the outskirts of the city. There he stops by the side of the "last house"—presumably some well-identified landmark—just before the descent into the Kidron Valley. His servants pass on before him, together with the Cherethites and Pelethites.[15] We have noted earlier that these were foreigners who formed his bodyguard and were under the capable leadership of Benaiah.

Six hundred Gittites are also among those leaving the city. Their number indicates that they probably constitute a regular regiment.[16] They have probably been with David for the past thirty or more years (cf. 15:18. cf. 1 Samuel 23:13; 25:13; 27:2; 30:9). It is likely that they make up David's private army.

Ittai of Gath[17] is the leader of these men. As he is about to take the path leading down into the Kidron Valley, the king stops him.

> "Why do you go, even you, with us? Turn back and remain with the [new] king, for you [are] a stranger, and also you [are] an exile; [go] to your place (i.e., your home). You came in [only] yesterday, and should I today make you to roam (i.e., to go up and down) with us, while I go where I go? Turn back, and take your brethren with you [in] kindness[18] and truth (i.e., may God's lovingkindness and truth) go with you" (15:19-20).

David's words "you came [only] yesterday" are intended to make it easy for Ittai to turn back. In actual fact, Ittai had probably been with David for many years. During this time their friendship had grown. Though at one time he had been an idolater, Ittai has been won to faith in Yahweh as the only true God by what he has seen in David's life. His reply is one of the most significant testimonies in all the Bible.

> "[As] Yahweh lives, and as my lord the king lives, surely in the place where my lord the king is, there your servant shall be, whether for death or life" (15:21).

Ittai's confession of faith in the Lord and his loyalty to the crown touch David deeply. His love and devotion stand in marked contrast to the ingratitude and perfidy of Absalom. Being heartened by Ittai's words, David says: "Go and pass on" (15:22).

So Ittai and his household, together with his men and their wives and "all their little ones," cross the Kidron and begin the slow ascent of the Mount of Olives.

Those within the city who are loyal to the king and have heard of what is happening leave their homes and places of business and come down to the valley separating Jerusalem from the surrounding area. The sight of the aged king, white hair crowning his head, leaving the city where he has reigned with such honor is too much for them. They give expression to their grief in loud weeping (15:23a).

As David begins the ascent of the Mount of Olives he sees Zadok[19] and all the Levites coming to meet him. In their midst is the Ark of the Covenant—the symbol of God's presence. Having the Ark with him would certainly give David an advantage, for those going into exile would sense that God was with them. David, however, does not need such assurance. With genuine gratitude for this token of loyalty, he says to Zadok:

> "Take the Ark of God back to the city; if I find grace in the eyes of Yahweh, then He will bring me back, and show me it and His dwelling place. And if He says this, 'I have no delight in you'; [then] I [am] here, He shall do to me as [seems] good in His eyes" (15:25-26).

While many contemporary writers are convinced that David was being punished by God for his adultery with Bathsheba, the cause of the chastening was definitely not as obvious to David as it is to his critics. The text is silent; and where God's Word gives no intimation of the divine will, we would do well to refrain from idle speculation. Ten years had passed since David's moral lapse, and God could have punished him long before now.

It is fairer to David, and to the views he expressed in Psalms 3 and 4, to realize that he did not know why this calamity had befallen him *and those with him* (for they had to endure the chastening along with their king). His trust in the Lord, however, is absolute, and he bows before God's will.

We, too, are often ignorant of the reasons why adversity enters our lives. We may examine our consciences to try and find the cause. When there is none, it is helpful for us to do as David did and meekly submit ourselves to the One who has permitted the trial to enter our life (cf. Psalm 34:15-22).

Having spoken to Zadok, David now sees Abiathar, the priest at Nob, joining the exiles at the base of the Mount of Olives. Abiathar does not announce his presence to David but merely begins to wend his way to the summit.

As we try to reconstruct the events, it appears likely that as soon as Abiathar heard of Absalom's actions, he quickly journeyed to Jerusalem to join the king. Some Bible scholars, however, believe that he offered sacrifices on the king's behalf.[20] If he did, then it would have had to be a hurried sacrifice, for Absalom was even then nearing the city. What may be meant by "and Abiathar went up" is that he had already begun the ascent of Olivet when the king saw him.

David immediately sees in these faithful friends the means of obtaining firsthand information of Absalom's activities. Also, their position as priests will give them a certain guarantee of immunity. Absalom may distrust them, but he can hardly do away with these appointees of the Lord. Such an act would immediately alienate devout people from him. So even if he is suspicious of them, their role as priests will give them a measure of protection.

David turns to Zadok (as the officiating priest in Jerusalem), and says:

> "Return to the city in peace, and Ahimaaz, your son, and Jonathan the son of Abiathar, your two sons with you. See, I will wait by the fords of the wilderness until word comes from you to declare to me (i.e., until I receive word from you)" (15:27-28).

So Zadok and Abiathar return to Jerusalem. As they do so, David takes the path that leads to the summit of the Mount of Olives. He walks barefoot and has his head covered—signs of humility and contrition—and weeps as he climbs to the top of the hill. He feels acutely the actions of his son, and he fears for the safety of his people.

David is perhaps halfway up the hill when a person overtakes him with the news that Ahithophel[21] is among the conspirators with Absalom. This is tragic news, for Ahithophel's counsel in those days was as sound and reliable as if someone had inquired of the Lord Himself. (The vileness of his defection is preserved for us in Psalm 55:12-14.)

David immediately turns to the Lord, and asks: "I pray you, O Yahweh, make foolish the counsel of Ahithophel" (15:31).

The emphasis of his prayer in the word order of the Hebrew text is to be found in the first and last words: "Make foolish...O Yahweh." The first is a request growing out of the devastating news he has just received. His concluding thought is of the covenant-keeping God of Israel. He then leaves the matter in His hands.

As the king reaches the brow of the hill, he pauses for one last look at the city. There he kneels in meek acceptance of God's will, before beginning the descent toward Bahurim in the territory of Benjamin. No sooner has he disappeared from view than Absalom and his followers come in sight of the city. A few minutes earlier and they would have seen the king and the people approaching the summit. They could then have pursued, overtaken, and killed them.

As David begins the descent, he encounters another friend coming to meet him. It is Hushai the Archite.[22] Although David is unaware of it, the Lord has heard his prayer (cf. Isaiah 65:24; Jeremiah 33:3) and has sent Hushai as the answer. Hushai's appearance reveals his grief. His coat is torn and he has earth upon his head. As soon as David sees him, he says:

"If you pass on with me, then you shall be on me a burden; but if you return to the city, and say to Absalom, 'I, O king, am your servant. I also [was] [the] servant of your father before now, and now I [will] also [be] your servant'—you shall thwart (or frustrate) the counsel of Ahithophel. And [are] not there with you [in Jerusalem] Zadok and Abiathar the priests. And it shall be, every thing that you hear from the house of the [new] king, you shall report to Zadok and Abiathar the priests. See, there [are] with them their two sons, Ahimaaz to Zadok, and Jonathan to Abiathar; and you shall send by their hand to me everything that you hear" (15:33-36).

So Hushai, David's friend,[23] does so.

But David and those who are with him have other needs as well. Fighting men need food and water to keep up their strength, and the women and children need not only food and water but also shelter if they are to survive for any length of time. During the day there is the merciless heat of the sun, and at night the extreme cold. What are they to do?

David has only just begun the descent toward Bahurim[24] when he is met by Ziba with sufficient food to see them through the first day. Ziba had laden two donkeys with a variety of provisions (16:1). And what the donkeys were unable to carry his servants bring to the king. On seeing Ziba, David asks: "What [are] these to you (i.e., what are these things that you have brought)?"

And Ziba answers:

"These asses [are] for the household of the king to ride on, and the bread and the summer fruit [is] for the young men to eat, and the wine for the weary to drink in the wilderness" (16:2).

David's next question has to do with Mephibosheth. "And where [is] the son of your lord?"

To which Ziba replies:

"Behold, [he] [is] staying in Jerusalem, for he said, 'Today the house of Israel shall give back to me the kingdom of my father'" (16:3; cf. 19:24-30).

The validity of Ziba's words may be challenged. It is doubtful if there had been any communication between the two of them or if Mephibosheth even knew of the large gift that Ziba had prepared for David. Ziba most likely lived in or near Gibeah, in the territory of

Benjamin, whereas Mephibosheth had his home on the outskirts of the royal city. Gibeah was several miles from Jerusalem. What is most likely is that as Ziba was en route to Jerusalem, he saw the king and those with him climbing the Mount of Olives. He, therefore, took a path that would enable him to intercept the king.

We will discuss Ziba again when we treat the events of 2 Samuel 19:24-30. For now, we shall note only the contrast between this former servant of King Saul and the friends of the king whom David had met on this eventful day. They had all wanted to go into exile with David, Ziba did *not* volunteer to do so!

David is so grateful for the food that he accepts Ziba's slander of Mephibosheth at face value. His response is indicative of his trust in people. "Behold, to you [is] all that [belonged] to Mephibosheth!" (16:4).

And then the procession that had halted while David and Ziba spoke with each other moves on again. The Lord had supplied the need for food and refreshment even before David had asked for it.

Eventually they reach Bahurim. At this little town, where David may have proposed to halt for a while to give the women and children time to rest, the exiles are met by Shimei, son of Gerar, a descendant of the house of Saul. Although separated from the exiles by a ravine, Shimei advances toward David, and curses[25] him as he does so. He also throws dust and stones at him. He believes that his malicious invectives are justified because of David's treatment of the family of Saul.

We know that David had treated the house of Saul well, but Shimei was not aware of this. He knew only the scuttlebutt that had circulated about and had never attempted to verify any of the information he had come to believe. He may have felt that David was responsible for the execution of Saul's descendants (cf. 21:1-9), or he may have believed that David and his men were with the Philistines at Aphek when Philistia fought against Israel and Saul and his sons were killed. Whatever his beliefs, David is the object of his scorn and the target of the stones he throws.

While the king bears Shimei's insolence well, Abishai feels differently. He is convinced that Shimei has reviled the Lord's anointed and deserves to die.[26] He asks David for permission to go and separate this scoundrel's head from the rest of his body (16:9). David, however, restrains his impatient nephew.

> "Let him curse, because Yahweh has said to him, 'Curse David'; and who shall say [to Him], 'Why have You done so?'...Behold, my son who came out of my loins is seeking my life, and also

surely now the Benjamite [wishes me dead]; leave him alone, and let him curse, for Yahweh has spoken to him. Perhaps Yahweh will look upon my affliction, and Yahweh will return good to me for his cursing this day" (16:10-12).

It is unlikely that the Lord had spoken to Shimei and told him to curse David, for Shimei's choice of words were not the kind the Lord would have sanctioned. It is more likely that David, realizing that everything comes from either God's direct or permissive will, believed that God was allowing it as a part of His chastening. So he meekly accepts what is being meted out to him.

After a weary journey of about fifteen miles, David and those with him arrive at the plain that stretches eastward to meet the River Jordan. They are tired and sleep on the ground. And David, who earlier that day had felt the weight of adversity resting heavily on his shoulders, now senses inwardly the assurance of God's blessing. He has helped him weather the storm. The battle to regain the throne is not over, but the outcome is certain. He knows that with God's aid he will be successful. Before he goes to sleep he pours out his soul in a psalm of confidence.

"Answer me, when I call, O God of my righteousness;
You gave room to me in [my] distress.
Have mercy on me and hear my prayer.

"O Sons of men, until when (i.e., how long)
[will you turn] My glory into shame?
Will you seek [after] a lie? Selah.

"But know that Yahweh has set apart the one who
is godly for Himself;
Yahweh hears when I call to Him.

"Tremble and do not sin;
Speak within your own heart on your bed,
and be still. Selah.

"Offer the sacrifices of righteousness
and put your trust in Yahweh.
Many are saying, 'Who will show us [any] good?'
O Yahweh, lift up on us the light of Your face.

"You have given (i.e., put) gladness in my heart.
more than [in the] time their grain and their wine multiplied.

In peace together I will lie down and sleep;
For You, O Yahweh, [You] alone make me dwell in safety
(Psalm 4:1-8).[27]

And so David goes to sleep.

HOW TO HANDLE THE INEQUITIES OF LIFE

How are we to handle the inequities of life? The key is to be found
in David's prayer (Psalm 4). David was mindful of God's omnipres-
ence and lovingkindness. He had suffered one of the cruelest blows
known to mankind. His son, to whom he had shown the grace of
God, had turned against him. William Shakespeare has King Lear reflect upon such betrayal. He says:

> "How sharper than a serpent's tooth it is
> to have a thankless child."[28]

Absalom had shown himself to be thankless. But he was heartless
and cruel as well. His eyes were on the throne, and he was fully prepared to kill his father to get it!

All of us have experienced rejection in one form or another. Our
circumstances may not have been as dramatic as David's, but we
have all felt the deep pain of being treated as a thing rather than as a
person of worth. How are we to cope with such feelings?

David, as we have seen in an earlier study, was secure in his relationship with the Lord. In the crisis that had been so suddenly pre-
cipitated upon him, he had turned to the Lord, and God had "enlarged" (Psalm 4:1 AV) his capacity to handle adversity.

There is doubt among expositors over who is speaking in Psalm
4:2. If it is the Lord (and this is probable), then the words may be
addressed to Absalom and his co-conspirators. He is saying in effect
that they should think of what they have done. They have reduced
the theocracy to nought and treated God's right to rule over His
people as if He were nonexistent. During the night, however, when
their thought processes are active, the Lord gives them the opportunity to repent of their actions. *Selah* at the end of the stanza may be
His way of causing them to pause and reflect on Israel's past and the
glories of having the Lord of Hosts as their Suzerain.

If David is speaking of himself, then he is grounding his prayer in
his integrity. He has also assessed what Absalom and his followers
have done, and he has seen through their self-seeking (vanity) and
empty profession of concern for the people. Rebellion against the

Lord and the teaching of His Word cannot succeed for long. In the end, it is doomed to fail.

David's confidence lies in the fact that God has set apart the godly for Himself. He has a special relationship with those who seek after righteousness. And He hears when they call on Him for help.

Psalm 4:4 is another verse which, in David's poem, may represent the Lord addressing those who have erred from the way. Or it may be David's words of encouragement to those who "suffer the slings and arrows of outrageous fortune" and are now ready "to take up arms against a sea of troubles."[29]

Regardless of the people addressed, the words of this psalm constitute a call to remember the greatness and glory of God. We are to stand before Him in reverential awe. Rebellion against Him is doomed to fail. Any act of wilfulness cannot be hidden from Him.

Conscience, which may go unheeded during a busy day, becomes active at night. We can, and indeed should, engage in introspection when we go to bed and confess our sins to the Lord. This done, we can enjoy a night of untroubled sleep.

Even in times of severe trial, men and women of integrity should thank God for His many kindnesses to them. Such praise is regarded as a "sacrifice" of righteousness. And because times of adversity do not disappear overnight, people should put their trust in the Lord.

David, as a good leader, is also in touch with the needs of his people. He has picked up on conversations around the fires and even discussions between people who perhaps did not know that their softly spoken words were being heard by anyone else. He knows that they are saying among themselves, "*Who will show us any good?*" All he has to do is reflect on the events of the day and he can see the number of times the Lord has demonstrated His goodness to them.

There was the faithfulness of Ittai of Gath that had encouraged him so much; the loyalty of the priests Zadok and Abiathar, who were prepared (with all the Levites) to go into exile with him; and the unexpected appearance of Hushai. In all of these things he saw God's encouragement in his affliction. And then there was Ziba, who had brought some much-needed food. These men had "showed them good," but the spiritual sight of the people was not conditioned to see in such events the hand of God. They suffered from myopia and needed one such as David to keep their thoughts turned heavenward.

As David reflected upon what had happened, he could say with sincerity that the Lord had put more gladness in his heart than was evident among the farming communities scattered throughout the land following a bumper harvest. It was characteristic to celebrate the end of the harvest with feasting and dancing. It was a time of merriment. David, however, knew more joy in adversity than they did in prosperity.

So, with his confidence in the Lord's mercies reinforced by recollections of God's past blessings to him, he wrapped his mantle about him, lay down on the ground, and went to sleep.

THE PEOPLE'S CHOICE

2 Samuel 16:15–17:23

For many years I have met weekly with my good friend Dr. Gary Strauss of Biola University, La Mirada, California. Out of our discussions have come two books and numerous insights into the counseling process. Our goal has been to determine how the Bible may be applied to the needs of hurting men and women.

One of the tragic circumstances we frequently encounter is the pain godly parents bear when their children go astray. All too often, society, the church, and their own parents (if they are still living) blame them for not having done better. But none of this is as deleterious as the condemnation they heap on themselves. Now, the happiness they once experienced when their children were little, is a far cry from the agony of heart they endure as they have to cope with a wayward son or daughter.

Some of the questions they invariably ask are, "Where did I (we) fail? We did all we could to rear our children in the nurture and admonition of the Lord. We gave them love and invested our lives in them. What more could we have done that would have prevented—?"

As we have probed each situation, we have found that often one or more of their children's teachers, and then later on their children's peers, have turned them against the beliefs, values, and goals of the home in which they were being reared. The result is a lack of suitable principles to guide them followed by waywardness that is difficult to correct.[1]

It is important to realize that even people living in Bible times had children or grandchildren who grew up to be rebellious. Abraham, for example, had two grandsons who were as unlike and ungodly as he was gracious and God-fearing (Genesis 18:19). The older, Esau, was a sensual, immoral man (Hebrews 12:16); and the younger, Jacob, was a habitual liar and swindler (Genesis 27:36).

Ten of Jacob's sons were factious and willful. They were filled with jealousy and hatred for their younger brother, Joseph. Such was their resentment and animosity toward him that they even planned to kill him (Genesis 37:18-20). But there would be no profit in his death, so they chose instead to sell him into slavery (Genesis 18:25-28).

By contrast, the sons of Joseph, who were born in Egypt, grew up to become godly men (Genesis 48:5,13-20). And so did the sons and daughter of Amram and Jochebed (Exodus 3:1–4:17; 6:20; 15:20-21). The daughter of the outcast Jephthah was a spiritually-minded young girl (Judges 11:34-40), and so was Samuel, the firstborn son of Elkanah and Hannah (1 Samuel 1:28; 2:18ff.; 3:1ff.).

David, we know, diligently taught his sons the "fear of the Lord" (cf. Psalm 34:11-22), and he prepared them as best he could for lives of beneficial service (see 2 Samuel 8:18 where they served as "cabinet ministers"). The two oldest, Amnon and Absalom, early showed their lack of fitness for leadership. We assume, however, that David's other sons served commendably in the positions to which they were appointed.

How, then, are we to explain why some children from good homes aspire to godliness, while others rebel against the instruction of their parents?

In tackling this problem, Gary shared with me an important illustration. He explained that the process, as well as the outcome, of each person's life is determined by the choices he or she makes. He went on to describe life as a chain-link fence. A wire in the middle of the fence, equidistant from the top and the bottom, has been stretched along the entire length to give it stability. It serves the same kind of purpose as norms and standards do in real life. Each place where one link interlocks with another represents a decision. The ones above the central divide represent good decisions. Conversely, those below the central line represent negative (or sinful) decisions.

Over a period of time, a pattern emerges. Parents may early detect the predisposition of their child toward negative thinking and, consequently, unhealthy and unwholesome conduct. They may try to influence their child in positive ways, but by the time of adolescence, their influence diminishes considerably. And each decision their child then makes has more of an impact on the direction of his or her life than before.

It was thus with Absalom. He had early entertained thoughts of one day becoming king. All obstacles—filial, familial, and spiritual—had to be removed. Amnon was the first to go. John Dryden has described the situation in his imaginative poem, "Absalom and Achitophel."

...Amnon's murder, by a specious name,
Was called a just revenge for injured fame.
Thus praised and loved the noble youth remained,
While David undisturbed in Sion reigned.
But life can never be sincerely blessed:
Heaven punishes the bad, and proves the best.[2]

Of course, Dryden was not entirely accurate. It is difficult for a poet to be precise when the flow of the meter influences his choice of words. David was very angry over Amnon's murder. Absalom disregarded all thought of consequences and, even in exile, was contriving ways of removing his father from the throne. Also we must not overlook the fact that Absalom, in seeking to secure the throne for himself, first minimized and later disregarded all thought of the theocracy.

OUTLINE

Because each chapter or section of the Bible must be interpreted in light of the context, we need to remind ourselves of the Biblical writer's purpose. The theme of the Book of Samuel is God's sovereign rule over His people through a representative whom He appoints. David had been chosen by God (Psalm 78:70ff.) and accepted by the people (cf. 2 Samuel 2:4; 5:1-3). Absalom had neither been chosen by God nor elected by the people. He secured the throne for himself by graft and corruption, and only belatedly was he anointed king (19:10).

Throughout the division running from 2 Samuel 15:1 through 20:26 we see God sovereignly sustaining the kingdom. The two sections that make up the bulk of the material are preceded by a prologue that describes how Absalom and not Amnon came to the throne of Israel (13:1–14:33). The remaining portion may be divided as follows:

- An Attempt to Seize the Throne (15:1–19:39)
- An Attempt to Divide the Nation (19:40–20:26)

AN ATTEMPT TO SEIZE THE THRONE (15:1–19:39)

In our last chapter, we focused attention on "The Removal of a God-Anointed King from the Throne" (15:1–16:14). Now we will consider "The Mistakes of a Self-Appointed King on the Throne" (16:15–17:23).

The Mistakes of a Self-Appointed King on the Throne (16:15–17:23)

A Triumphal Entry (16:15). David and his followers have no sooner disappeared down the eastern side of the Mount of Olives than Absalom rides into Jerusalem with Ahithophel at his side. The usurper receives from the fickle populace every intimation of delight. The people line the streets to the palace and cheer approvingly as he passes by. All of this may have caused him to feel inwardly exonerated for his deception of his father. And the people, judging solely on the basis of externals, get exactly what they want.

Absalom enters the throne room and takes his seat where his father had so often sat. We may be sure that, following his return from exile, he had often thought of the changes he would make to that hall, and indeed, throughout the palace. Perhaps his mind had been filled with ideas based upon the things he had seen and heard in Geshur. He may have determined that, while David had the walls paneled with cedar, he would embellish them with linen hangings from the Orient. He would have only the most lavish carpets on the floor. And he most likely determined that his regal munificence would be such that his fame would be spread throughout the Near Eastern world.

A Test of Loyalty (16:16-19). Absalom is about to hold court when Hushai the Archite enters the room. He has removed the dust from his hair and put on fresh clothing. His opening greeting is spoken with great sincerity: "May the king live!"[3]

For many years Hushai has held the honored position of "the king's friend"[4] (16:16; 1 Chronicles 27:33*b*). It seems out of character for him to now be pledging allegiance to Absalom. Absalom, however, fails to realize that there are two ways of taking Hushai's greeting. In reality, the Archite is saying that he is loyal to the true king (i.e., David), but he is also interested in doing what is best for the usurper, the son of his friend.

Absalom is unsure of Hushai's motives but does not reject him out of hand. His thinking seems to be, "If Hushai is genuinely interested in serving me, then he can be useful. But he will need to be tested." Absalom begins the testing process by asking:

"[Is] this your kindness (*hesed*) to your friend (i.e., to David)? Why have you not gone with your friend?" (16:17).

To which Hushai responds:

"No, for he whom Yahweh has chosen, and this people [have appointed], even all the men of Israel, for him I shall be, and with him I shall remain.... Whom should I serve? Should I not [be] before (i.e., in the presence of) his son? As I served in the presence of your father, so shall I be in your presence" (16:18-19).

Hushai's response to Absalom's questions is masterful. There is first a strong denial of any disloyalty. This is followed by an avowal of his intent to serve Absalom and, wherever possible, seek his highest good. But his first duty is to the Lord and to the one whom He has set over His people (namely, David).

In Hushai's words there is also an emphasis on the father-son relationship. It is evident that he is already trying to reach out to Absalom in hope of turning him from the wrongful course he has chosen to follow. Joyce Baldwin describes the implication of Absalom's inquiry as well as Hushai's answer:

> Absalom's double question reveals his misgivings, but he does not notice that there are two ways of taking the answer of Hushai, who again avoids mentioning names. Hushai is indeed remaining loyal to his master, David, chosen by the Lord and the people.... By asserting that he will serve his master's son, Hushai lays stress on the very relationship which Absalom has severed.[5]

Absalom, still intoxicated with the adulation of the crowd, is blinded by his own imagined importance. He hears only what he wants to hear. As John Dryden has pointed out,

> What cannot praise effect in mighty minds,
> When flattery soothes, and when ambition blinds.
> Desire of power, on earth a vicious weed,
> Yet, sprung from high, is of celestial seed:
> In God 'tis glory: and when men aspire,
> 'Tis but a spark too much of heavenly fire.
> Th' ambitious youth, too covetous of fame,
> Too full of angel's mettle in his frame,
> Unwarily was led from virtue's ways,
> Made drunk with honor, and debauched with praise.[6]

In all probability, Absalom decides to wait and see if Hushai's counsel is reliable. He will do so by pitting him against Ahithophel. For the present he treats his father's friend with disdain and Hushai of necessity has to withdraw.

A Terminal Rift (16:20-22). In holding court, Absalom turns first to Ahithophel.

> False Achitophel...
> A name to all succeeding ages cursed.
> For close designs and crooked counsels fit;
> Sagacious, bold, and turbulent of wit:
> Restless, unfixed in principles and place,
> In power unpleased, impatient of disgrace.[7]

He says to him: "Give your counsel, what shall we do?" (16:20).

Ahithophel knows the concern of the men now under Absalom's command. They fear that if David is successful in turning the tide of battle, Absalom may sue for peace and, as the king's son, be pardoned or sent into exile. But they could not expect the same leniency. The first prerequisite, therefore, is to make the breach with David impossible to mend. And so Ahithophel answers:

> "Go in to the concubines of your father, whom he left to keep the house, and all Israel shall hear [that] you have become odious to (lit. with) your father; and the hands of all who [are] with you shall be strong" (16:21).

Whereas Hushai had spoken of the father-son relationship, as if trying to appeal to whatever nobility might still reside in Absalom's heart, Ahithophel counsels the very opposite. His words are designed to destroy the last vestige of hope for reconciliation between father and son. His counsel, therefore, is clear. He encourages Absalom to act decisively. His recommended plan of action is diabolical. While it was customary in the ancient Near East for a new king to acquire the harem of the deceased or deposed monarch, incestuous relationships between a son and the wives of his father was abhorred![8] Seen in this light, Ahithophel's counsel goes against the explicit teaching of Scripture (see Leviticus 18:7-8, 20; Deuteronomy 22:30; 27:20)!

God's words to David through Nathan (12:11) had never been carried out. All associated with the palace, Ahithophel included, knew of them. As we have observed in earlier chapters, God had apparently turned from His intended punishment of His servant. Ahithophel, however, determines to "fulfill" this prophecy. It will serve to humiliate David in the eyes of the people[9] and at the same time strengthen Absalom's hand. And if any of the people complain of the young king's actions, it can always be claimed that he was fulfilling what had been decreed by the Lord a decade earlier.

Most people would be inclined to accept such reasoning. Only on closer examination of what the Lord actually said are we reminded of the fact that, for this prophecy to be fulfilled, David's wives would have to be violated *in his presence* (i.e., "in his sight").

But why bother with technicalities when the plan appears to be so perfect? A gullible people will most assuredly exonerate Absalom from the charge of incest, for those in positions of authority will argue that he was fulfilling the Lord's predetermined will.

In Absalom's acquiescence to Ahithophel's recommendation, we see the lengths to which his ambition has carried him. A tent is soon pitched on the roof of the palace. David's concubines (whom David thought, according to the customs of his people, would be safe from all harm) are brought to Absalom. Absalom gives no thought to their feelings or possible humiliation. They are treated as things to be used to further his selfish plans.

In appropriating his father's concubines, Absalom is symbolically announcing to the nation that his father cannot protect that which is nearest to him. David is powerless to stop him. Absalom can now do whatever he pleases. And the confidence of the men in the army is strengthened, for they now know that nothing can restore Absalom to his father's favor. The rift between them is complete.

The Biblical writer then comments on the wisdom of Ahithophel (16:23). From a human point of view, and apart from Biblical norms, his wisdom was remarkable. In a single move he could achieve a multifaceted purpose. Whereas other strategies might have been time-consuming or required careful planning, his recommendation accomplished his intent with ruthless efficiency.

A Tactical Blunder (17:1-4). We have been given an example of Ahithophel's wisdom, and we now know the kind of man whom Hushai must defeat. Ahithophel, however, is not finished. He realizes that the success of Absalom's rebellion depends on the strategy he adopts in the first few hours of his reign. And as a wise man he is anxious to capitalize on the gains that have been made thus far. He accordingly approaches the young monarch with a recommendation:

> "Please let me choose twelve thousand men, and I shall pursue after David tonight, and shall come upon him, and he shall be weary and feeble-handed, and I shall cause him to tremble, and all the people who [are] with him shall flee; and I shall smite the *king* by myself, and shall bring back all the people to you, and all shall return, [except] the man whom you are seeking; all the people shall be in peace" (17:1-3, emphasis added).

Once again Ahithophel's counsel is wise. He knows what is needed to ensure the success of the conspiracy. He proposes that he be allowed to pursue David without delay. All he needs is a small army of twelve thousand select men. He will overtake David while he is weary and in a vulnerable position. He promises that he will win an easy and bloodless victory. The people with David will be unable to resist the sudden onslaught of his superior force. They will flee without striking a blow, and he will have no difficulty seizing and killing the old king. With his death, all opposition will collapse, and the entire nation will submit itself to Absalom's rule.

Joyce Baldwin has drawn attention to Ahithophel's "slip of the tongue" when he mentioned "the *king* only."[10] So far there has been a studied attempt on the part of Absalom and Ahithophel to avoid all mention of David by name or to refer to his rank or relationship with Absalom. This slip indicates that in his heart Ahithophel knew who really belonged on the throne.

> And the thing was pleasing (i.e., right) in the eyes of Absalom, and in the eyes of all the elders of Israel (17:4).

This is the first time we have had a reference to the "elders" of the nation. Their inclusion in Absalom's court shows how far-reaching was the defection from David.

Several statements in this section that are found in some English translations (e.g., "as a bride comes home to her husband," 17:3, and "a sow snared in the wild," 17:8) are not based upon the Hebrew text. They have been included from the Septuagint. Their inclusion in certain modern versions is regrettable.

For some reason not explained by the Biblical writer, Absalom decides to test Hushai's counsel. Perhaps it is the unanimous approval of all the elders that causes him to think this will be a good time to assess Hushai's commitments. Therefore, he commands some of his attendants to bring Hushai before him.

> "Please call [in] Hushai the Archite, and we shall hear what [is] in his mouth, even [what] he [has to say]" (17:5).

Hushai is ignorant of what has transpired, and it is necessary for him to be informed of Ahithophel's counsel before he can render an opinion. He is in a difficult position. So prudent and feasible is the recommendation of Ahithophel that it seems impossible for his counsel to be defeated by another plan.

Hushai, however, knows that if Ahithophel's plan is carried out, David will be caught on the open plain before he can cross the River Jordan. He will be virtually defenseless, and all that Ahithophel has said he will do will be accomplished with relative ease.

Absalom's incestuous actions have shown him to be reprobate. Hushai cannot now appeal to the father-son relationship as he had done before. To prevent the adoption of Ahithophel's plan, he must try to sway the emotions of those present. But he is in the invidious position of not having time to think through a plan of action or prepare a logical rebuttal. He must think on his feet. His emphases, as well as his fumbling for words and repetitious statements, are represented in the following literal translation.

> "Not good [is] the counsel that Ahithophel has counseled at this time. You have known your father and his men, that they [are] mighty men, and they [are] bitter of soul like a [she]-bear bereaved of her cubs in the field; and your father [is] a man of war, and shall not lodge with the people. Behold, now, he is hidden in one of the pits, or in one of the places (possibly caves); and it shall be, at the falling (of any of your men) among them at the beginning, that whoever shall hear [whatever he hears] shall say, 'There has been a slaughter among the people who follow Absalom.' And he [among your troops], he also the son of valor, whose heart [is] as the heart of a lion, shall utterly melt, for all Israel knows that your father [is] a mighty man, and those who [are] with him sons of valor. So this (lit. that) I counsel: Let all Israel be diligently gathered to you, from Dan (in the north) to Beersheba (in the south), as the sand that [is] by the sea for multitude; and you yourself shall go to battle [at the head of your army]. And *we* shall come in to him in one of the places where he shall be found, and we shall fall on him as the dew falls on the ground; and of all the men who [are] with him not even one shall be left to him. And if he is taken in a city, then all Israel shall bear ropes to that city, and we shall draw it into the valley torrent until there shall not be even a pebble found there" (17:7-13, emphasis added).

Hushai's careful use of the word *we* has the effect of disarming the young monarch. He also states that this is not only the wrong time to go out after David, but that if Ahithophel went after him he would most likely not be able to find him. If he did, Absalom could count on significant losses. This might result in "all Israel" hearing an exaggerated report about the number of deaths. Then, as a consequence of the false rumor, the fighting men would lose heart.

Instead, "all Israel"—all the fighting men—from Dan to Beersheba should be gathered together. Then, with Absalom riding at the head of a huge army, they will find David and descend upon him in such numbers that he will not be able to escape.

Hushai's real counsel is for delay. This will give David time to recover from his fatigue and the despondency of flight, as well as gain the security of some well-fortified city. The pause will also give the people time to reflect on what they have done. Once the events of the revolt are seen in their true perspective, Absalom will begin to lose the momentum that has carried him to the throne.

Hushai's counsel pleases the deluded prince and the men of Israel. They all begin to mutter,

"The counsel of Hushai [is] better than the counsel of Ahithophel" (17:14*a*).

With her usual aplomb, Joyce Baldwin sums up Hushai's strategy:

> At this point [17:14*b*] the narrator permits himself a comment in which he reveals his judgment that from Absalom's standpoint Ahithophel had given *good counsel*. The fact that Absalom disregarded it for the advice of Hushai, which was designed to protect David, he saw an example of the Lord's intervention in order to overthrow Absalom, for by following Hushai's advice Absalom went to battle and lost his life. He had been persuaded by a speech that pulled the wool over his eyes, one full of vague references: *"some other place"* (v. 9), *some place where he is to be found* (v. 12), *a city* (unnamed v. 13), at least one ambiguity (whose people fall), and an obvious contradiction between the picture of David as a mighty man at the beginning (v. 8) and his overthrow at the end, trapped by superior numbers. When had David ever been worried by the sheer size of the forces against him? Nevertheless, Hushai's rhetoric won over the war cabinet; Absalom saw himself at the head of a huge, victorious army, and the delay necessitated by further recruitment of reinforcements gave David the opportunity to shape his troops, recover strength, and decide on the terrain advantageous to him in the coming battle. But first he needed news of Absalom's intentions.[11]

Having accepted Hushai's counsel, Absalom probably instructs Amasa to raise an army (17:25).

The Transmission of Information (17:15-22). But Hushai's work is not over. He must communicate quickly with David. With orders being given about where and when the combined forces of Israel and Judah are to meet and what the plan of attack will be, Hushai leaves the palace. He goes to the Tabernacle, ostensibly to worship. There he confers with Zadok and Abiathar. He relates to them exactly what has taken place. Then he says:

> "And now, send quickly and tell David, saying, 'Do not stay in the fords of the wilderness tonight; and also, be sure to pass over [the River Jordan], lest there be a swallowing up (i.e., destruction) of the king and of all the people who [are] with him'" (17:16).

Hushai has no means of knowing if Absalom will change his mind or how speedily the army will be assembled. From 17:16 ("lest the king...be destroyed") and 17:21 ("Rise up, and cross the waters quickly, for thus has Ahithophel counseled against you"), it appears as if Hushai feared Ahithophel might gain Absalom's ear after he had withdrawn from the throne room. If so, then Absalom might reverse his decision. Hushai, therefore, is concerned that he might not have gained for David as much time as he had hoped.

Zadok and Abiathar cannot leave the precincts of the Tabernacle for fear of arousing suspicion. They, therefore, send a loyal and trustworthy maid to fetch water from the spring of En-rogel[12] (modern *Bir Ayyub*) outside the city where, in anticipation of taking information to David, they have their sons, Jonathan and Ahimaaz, in hiding.

As soon as the lads receive the message, they try to slip away unnoticed.[13] A young and impressionable youth, possibly awed by Absalom's regal manner, sees them and reports the matter. It is possible that, at his insistence, he is shown into Absalom's presence. There he has the opportunity to converse one-on-one with the man he so much admires. Such is often the influence of public figures upon the young.

Jonathan and Ahimaaz probably see the soldiers or servants of Absalom trying to close in on them, so they take refuge in the home of a man in Bahurim who is known to be loyal to David. While Shimei is also from this Benjamite town, it is evident that not everyone continued to adhere to the dynasty of Saul or was in sympathy with Absalom.

While the man whose house the boys enter probably stays by the door to stall those sent to apprehend the sons of Zadok and Abiathar, his wife takes Jonathan and Ahimaaz and conceals them in a well.

She then places a covering over the mouth of the well and scatters some *haripot*, "grits" or "sand" on it.

It is possible that the house-to-house search takes longer than expected, for when Absalom's servants do arrive, the woman's husband is no longer there. We assume, therefore, that he had to go out on business. So the two young men, kept incommunicado, must exercise patience, for they do not know what is going on.

When the searchers knock on the door and demand to know the whereabouts of Ahimaaz and Jonathan, the woman says: "They are passed over the brook of water" (17:20b).

Just where this "brook of water" or "watercourse" was, we do not know. We do know that Absalom's men searched for the lads in vain.

As soon as it is safe, the woman opens up the well and the lads climb out. Though they have been delayed in carrying out their errand, they run through the night to bring the message to David. Once they are in David's presence, they pass on Hushai's message:

"Rise up, and quickly pass over the waters, for Ahithophel has counseled this against you" (17:21b).

David and his men arouse their wives and children. Then in an orderly manner they cross the ford of the Jordan River, and by dawn all have placed the river between themselves and Absalom.

A Tragic End (17:23). The Biblical writer now takes us back to the palace...and Ahithophel. It is still the day of Absalom's triumphal entry into the city. With the success of Hushai's plan, Ahithophel knows that Absalom faces certain defeat. He realizes that the young king has thrown away the advantage of his coup. It will now be only a matter of time before David regains the throne.

Ahithophel leaves the palace. The sun is beginning to set in more ways than one as he traverses the cheerless miles between Jerusalem and Giloh. On arriving at his home, he "sets his house in order" (i.e., pays any debts and distributes his estate among his heirs), then he hangs himself. It is a tragic end for such a gifted man.

A STUDY IN CONTRASTS

It is difficult to escape the way in which the primary characters in this section are played off against one another. Absalom sets himself in opposition to David, and Ahithophel is opposed by Hushai. Both Ahithophel and Absalom are seen to be in defiance of the theocracy; whereas by their attitudes and conduct, Hushai and David are found to be submissive to the Lord and eager to see His will done in Israel.

The Downhill Slide

Ahithophel had been David's counselor (15:12; 1 Chronicles 27:33*a*). Though he was probably older than his sovereign, the two men had been good friends ("equals," see Psalm 55:13. cf. Psalm 41:9). They had enjoyed "sweet fellowship" together, and had accompanied each other to the house of God.

As we have noted, the rift in their relationship was probably caused by David's adultery with Bathsheba. But whereas God had forgiven David, Ahithophel had not. Even David's open declaration of his wrong (see Psalm 51) did nothing to cool Ahithophel's anger. As such Ahithophel illustrates for us the dangers of unabated anger (cf. Ephesians 4:26, 31) compounded by a lack of forgiveness.

His attitude and actions remind me of a couple whom I know well. Their lives are etched in tragedy. At one time, Cedric and Sandy were in a Sunday school class I taught. They had a "perfect" marriage, with two "perfect" children—a boy, Brian, and a girl, Nancy. Their home was complete. They were faithful in their church attendance; and if anything needed to be done, you could be sure that one of them would volunteer to do it.

As their children progressed through the teen years, their son, Brian, got his girlfriend pregnant. Cedric and Sandy were first stunned, then angry, and finally humiliated. The frequently asked question was, "What will happen if any of our friends find out?"

To keep everything hush-hush, they arranged with the girl's parents to have her sent away for the period of her pregnancy. They paid all of her expenses. They even arranged for the baby to be adopted by a Christian couple.

But the young girl was not the only one to be sent away. Brian was too. Cedric and Sandy felt shamed by his actions. They feared what their friends might say if any of them ever found out. So Brian was given a large sum of money and "sent to an uncle in Texas to complete his schooling." But what was made abundantly clear was the fact that they were disinheriting him and never wanted to see or hear from him again.

It was possibly much the same for Ahithophel. A lack of forgiveness caused the heart of this wise and gifted man to become so hardened that even the arrival of grandchildren (born to David and Bathsheba) failed to soften him. And when God gave evidence of His favor toward Solomon by renaming him Jedediah, Ahithophel remained unmoved.

The root of Ahithophel's problem was pride. He felt humiliated when it became known that a member of his family had been seduced into an act of adultery. He felt outraged—but not for Bathsheba's honor. He sensed that he lost the esteem of his friends as well as Israel's intelligentsia. And his anger burned. He wanted nothing more than to humiliate David and make him suffer. So intransigent did he become that he was even ready to thrust his own sword through his former friend's body (17:2).

Pride may be defined as a love of oneself or self-absorption with one's status, behavior, reputation, or skills. Solomon, Ahithophel's grandson, would later warn people that pride precedes destruction (Proverbs 16:18). It places the haughty person in an undesirable relationship with God (Proverbs 29:23. cf. James 4:6; 1 Peter 5:5). And when pride hardens a person's heart so that he or she becomes stubborn and resistant to the will of God, then that individual may suddenly be destroyed (Proverbs 29:1).

Joyce Baldwin favors us with a discerning analysis of Ahithophel's last hours.

> Calmly [Ahithophel] accepted [Absalom's decision to raise an army] and resolved what he would do. The steps he took all contribute to the picture of a very calculating statesman, totally aware of all that is at stake, who follows to its bitter conclusion the path of logic and reason. [In the end] this man of iron coolly took the time to go to Giloh, make sure all his affairs were in order, and only after that committed suicide by hanging himself. It was a tragic end for an undoubtedly able man, who...had turned traitor.[14]

By contrast, Hushai, whose counsel Absalom chose to follow, was eager to preserve justice and practice righteousness (cf. Isaiah 56:1*a*).

The Upward Climb

Hushai was both humble and loyal. His commitment was to the truth. To gain the ends he sought—which were best for all concerned—he allowed the youthful monarch to believe what he thought he heard. But in his opening remarks to Absalom, there were subtle reminders of his father and of his familial duty. Hushai lived in reverential awe of God. He had a servant's heart and went to Jerusalem to do his utmost for his king, the king's son, and the nation. This singleness of purpose enabled him to see the issues clearly.

We do not find in Hushai a false modesty, nor was he desirous of praise. He had an accurate understanding of his own strengths and weaknesses as well as the strengths and weaknesses of the young

king. The situation into which he was thrust was an extremely difficult one. He had to attempt to nullify Ahithophel's counsel while playing on Absalom's naivete and vanity. And he did it without attracting
attention to himself.

To properly understand Hushai, we must also take note of his fidelity. Throughout the brief time he was in Absalom's court, even
though surrounded by the faithless "elders of Israel," he never abandoned the things he believed in. When compared to the elders of the
nation and the multitudes in Jerusalem who had welcomed Absalom
into the city, he was like Abdiel in John Milton's *Paradise Lost*,

> Among the faithless, faithful only he,
> Among innumerable false, unmoved,
> Unshaken, unseduced, unterrified,
> His loyalty he kept, his love, his zeal.[15]

He was unwavering in his commitment to the Lord, and to the one
whom He had placed on the throne of His people.

The Path of Destruction

From a consideration of the character of Ahithophel and the contribution of Hushai, we turn to reflect upon the polar goals and ob-
jectives of Absalom and David. As we seek to assess the nature of
Absalom, we find that the years from his birth in Hebron to the assassination of Amnon have been passed over in silence. How did he
develop such passion, violence, and self-will? His parents had named
him "Father of peace." David's "outlaw" years were over, and he was
looking forward to settling down to a more natural and predictable
lifestyle. How was it that Absalom failed to fulfill the expectations of
his parents?

The path Absalom chose for himself may well have begun with his
mother. She had *not* been reared under a theocracy. While she probably embraced the worship of Yahweh when she married David, her
culture adhered to the laws of primogeniture, in which the eldest
son of a king succeeded his father on the throne. As the son of two
royal lines, and therefore more of "royal blood" than Amnon, Absalom
stood third in line. When (as we assume) Chileab died, Absalom
thought that only Amnon blocked his ascent to the throne. And by
the time he is introduced to us in chapter 13, the enmity between
him and Amnon is well-established.

The influence of Absalom's mother, therefore, may have played a strategic role in the development of his character, even offsetting the influence David had on his children.

In the story there are also indications of Absalom's affluence and abuse of power. The feasts he hosted were lavish, and the entourage he provided for himself exceeded anything King David may have had. And such was his arrogance that he did not hesitate to burn Joab's barley fields when it suited his purpose. Yet with all that, he had the ability to mask his feelings so that few knew what was going on in his heart.

A somber note is struck when Absalom's actions are seen in light of the theocracy. God's will was viewed as an impediment to his plans. In time he must have rationalized how this, too, could be set aside. For instance, when he went to Hebron to proclaim himself king, he took none of the priests with him. They were regarded as hindrances to his rise to power.

The direction of Absalom's decisions, aided by Ahithophel, led inexorably downward. He did not hesitate to take his father's concubines as his own and defile himself with them (while also violating them). It could only be a matter of time, therefore, before his life of defiance of God and His laws led to his demise (see Hosea 8:7; Galatians 6:7-8).

The Path of Submission

As we turn to David, and in particular the psalms[16] he wrote during this time of adversity, we see that he made the right decisions.

Perhaps he was still weak from his protracted illness when word was brought to him of Absalom's revolt. Hebron is only about nineteen miles from Jerusalem, and he realized the imminent danger he and those with him faced. His old warrior instincts revived. He gave immediate instructions to vacate the palace and leave the city. As the late E. M. Blaiklock, for many years professor of classics, University of Auckland, New Zealand, has pointed out,

> The wilderness was always a symbol of security in Hebrew thought. David had proved its reality over the long years. The city was a trap. In the desert was hope. With bitter clarity David saw that Jerusalem was a snare…. The choices, at that critical moment, were plain. It was obviously a matter of retreat in one of three directions. First, there was the coastal plain where the old Philistine foe offered small security. Second, there was the way north, where tribal disaffection lay. Since Absalom [was to the

south], the only way left was down to the Jordan valley, and across to Mahanaim. This involved a tactical maneuver of great peril, a retreat across the front of the enemy. It reveals David's renewed vigor of mind that he saw...that this is what he had to do.[17]

And so David left the city and made his way eastward. He bore with submissive fortitude the chastening he did not understand and yielded his will completely to the will of God (cf. 15:25-26). Then, in dependence upon God's unfailing faithfulness, he made the kind of decisions that were necessary. His prayer at the close of the day was one of thankfulness. He and his people had made good their escape.

THE GREATNESS OF GOD

One matter remains. Though unseen, God was definitely active in all that transpired. He orchestrated events so that David and those who were with him disappeared from view moments before Absalom came in sight of the city. He made provision for information to be taken to David and provided food for the exiles. And He prompted Hushai to go to meet David, arranging for their paths to intersect after the king had heard of Ahithophel's defection.

In His sovereign wisdom, He is never startled by what people may do. He is never caught off guard as we are, when we are surprised by someone's treachery or trickery. Throughout Absalom's scheming, He remained unmoved. And when Absalom and Ahithophel turned their backs on Him and His administration of the nation, treating the theocracy as a faded tapestry that was now of little worth, He let them play out their hand.

But when the inspired penman permits us to peer ever so briefly behind the curtain that separates this world from the next, we find that Yahweh had ordained to thwart the good counsel of Ahithophel, in order that He (lit. Yahweh) might bring calamity upon Absalom (17:14b). And He did so in answer to David's fleeting prayer, "Make foolish, O Yahweh, the counsel of Ahithophel" (15:31).

In addition, what happened in Absalom's court was not accidental. The young king did not know that his fate had been sealed and that he was merely acting out the final scenes of a drama that he had choreographed with God's acquiescence. The ending, however, would surprise him. And later, the quelling of the revolt and the restoration of David to the throne of Israel would be little more than the reflex of God's sovereign will.[18]

ABSALOM'S NEMESIS

2 Samuel 17:24–19:8b

Ambition. The word evokes different images in the minds of different people. To some it is the necessary ingredient that enables them to escape the shackles of mediocrity and pursue a course of action that leads to success. To others, however, it brings to mind painful experiences of the past—experiences of being trampled underfoot or shafted by aspiring, uncaring individuals who did not mind how many people they trod on as long as they got what they wanted.

Wise men of the past have had the opportunity to observe ambitious people, and from their cogitations has come the consensus that "ambition destroys its possessor."[1] Even Noah Webster, whose noteworthy insights have been noted in an earlier chapter, defined ambition as "the eager and sometimes inordinate desire for something, as preferment, honor, superiority, power, fame, wealth, etc.; or the desire to distinguish oneself in some way."[2]

The pages of history brim with examples of people whose ambitious plans led ultimately to their downfall. Julius Caesar, for example, attained to greater prominence in the Roman Empire than any of his predecessors. Yet he desired a position above that which he had been given. He wanted to be king. On one occasion he was repeatedly offered a diadem, but he half-heartedly rejected it when the crowd showed their disfavor.

In the end, leading politicians began to conspire against him. Some of his friends were included in their number. One day on a fateful visit to the Senate in Rome, he was stabbed repeatedly by the conspirators and fell dead beneath Pompey's statue. At his funeral, his longtime friend Mark Antony gave the oration.

> I come to bury Caesar, not to praise him.
> The evil that men do, lives after them;

The good is oft interred with their bones;
So let it be with Caesar. The noble Brutus
Hath told you, Caesar was ambitious;
If it were so, it was a grievous fault;
And grievously hath Caesar answer'd it.[3]

Men, however, are not the only ones to succumb to ambition. Women are also susceptible. The name Catherine de Medici has become synonymous with the quest for power. She was born in Florence, Italy. Her father was Lorenzo de Medici, who called himself "The Magnificent," and ruled Florence as if he were a king.

Lorenzo married his daughter to Henry, the son of the king of France, and in time she became queen. Four sons and two daughters were born to them. Even while her husband was alive Catherine did all she could to advance her fortunes through her children. And when Henry died, she continued to acquire authority and influence by using her family as a means to that end.

During her lifetime, three of her sons sat on the throne of France. Her two daughters, Elizabeth and Margaret, were married to the king of Spain and the king of Navarre, respectively. Her unbounded ambition led her to sacrifice both France and her children in the vain hope of satisfying her pathological desire for power.

To further gain the ends she sought, Catherine played Catholics against the Huguenots, and vice versa. At times, she favored one group and then, changing sides, favored the other. Later, when it suited her political goals, she orchestrated (through her son) the massacre of the Huguenots on St. Batholomew's Day.

When her son Charles IX died, his younger brother became Henry III. During his reign, Catherine continued to manipulate both political and religious matters. By now, the leading parties in both spheres had become aware of her evil and selfish schemes, and they exposed her machinations. Henry was assassinated, and she spent the rest of her life friendless and alone. None mourned her death, and her only enduring legacy is that she is remembered as an unscrupulous, dictatorial, and cruel woman.[4]

The inordinate desire for power, wealth, or influence knows no boundaries. It even invades the ministry.

Thomas Wolsey wanted to become England's first pope. He pursued his goal with ruthless efficiency. In time he became one of the most wealthy men in all England—even more wealthy than the king, Henry VIII. The whole country, however, groaned under his tyranny.

Dr. J. R. Green, in his *History of the English People* has described the way in which Providence appeared to tolerate Wolsey's career of unbridled oppression, unrivaled wickedness, and uncontrolled ambition. Ultimately, his desire for self-advancement betrayed him into an act of treason. This is how Dr. Green described what happened:

> The hour of reckoning at length arrived. Slowly the hand had crawled along the dial-plate, slowly as if the event would never come; and wrong was heaped on wrong, and oppression cried, and it seemed as if no ear had heard its voice, till the measure of the wickedness was at length fulfilled. The finger touched the hour; and as the strokes of the great hammer rang out above the nation, in an instant the whole fabric of iniquity was shivered to ruins.[5]

Of course, the list of ambitious people whose obsession brought disaster upon themselves and those nearest to them could be multiplied *ad infinitum*. And numbered among these gifted (but misguided) men and women is Absalom!

We are reasonably comfortable reading about ambitious people of the past. We can put a convenient distance between us and them so that the truth of our fallen nature is not made too threatening. What does become disturbing, though, is an understanding of what drives such people and the extent to which we may possess similar traits. The heart of the matter lies in one's *preoccupation* with self or chronic self-centeredness. It is manifested outwardly in a triad of vices: vanity, exhibitionism (or grandiosity), and arrogant ingratitude.

Often the ambitious person is also found to be intensely individualistic, hedonistic (i.e., a seeker after pleasure), engaged in a quest for peak experiences, and skilled in the art of manipulation.

When all of this is applied to Absalom, we find that he was vain (i.e., individualistic [see 14:26; 18:18]), given to grandiosity (15:1), and haughtily ungrateful (cf. 14:33 with 15:10). He was also manipulative (13:24-26; 14:29-32; 15:7-8), and intent on getting what he wanted.

The more we study his life, the more parallels we find between him and people we know or read about...and perhaps even ourselves. He used his good looks to draw people to him. But after they had served his purpose, they were cast aside. As a result, he led an emotionally isolated life.

We are also given cause to question Absalom's understanding of the difference between good and evil, in himself and in others. This facet of his life was either fatally flawed or had never really developed through the usual process of socialization. In fact, it may be questioned if he could distinguish good from evil outside of what he wanted for himself.

Psychologists who have attempted to treat self-absorbed people such as Absalom find that their attitudes and actions are destructive of their marriages and interpersonal relationships. In addition, as parents, they tend to dominate and sometimes destroy their children's sense of well-being. The usual warm, sensitive, caring context of nondirective counseling is wasted on ambitious people. Instead of proving helpful, it often arouses within them feelings of intense anger, guilt, and despair. In the end, the counselor has the feeling that he or she is talking into the wind or writing on the sand. His or her words are either swept away without really being heard or else an incoming wave removes their effect, leaving no trace of anything that has been said.[6]

The contents of this portion of God's Word (17:24–19:8*b*) further enlarges our understanding of ambition.

OUTLINE

As we have noted in earlier chapters, the theme of 2 Samuel 13:1–20:26 is *the sovereignty of God in preserving the kingdom of His anointed.* He had promised David that He would establish him on the throne. Even though Absalom and others might try to thwart His purpose, we will find that the Lord will keep His word. The prologue (13:1–14:33) dealt with the character and conduct of David's two older sons, Amnon and Absalom. Then, a closer examination of 15:1–20:26 showed that it consisted of two sections of uneven length:

- An Attempt to Seize the Throne (15:1–19:39)
- An Attempt to Divide the Nation (19:40–20:26)

The central person in the "attempt to seize the throne" is Absalom. He has already been shown to be unfit to lead God's people, and yet these chapters record his rise to power, seemingly unhindered by the Lord (whose suzerainty he was defying) or by the people of God who should have remained loyal to their God-appointed king. The fact that Absalom succeeded in his plans is a sad commentary on the spiritual state of the people.

AN ATTEMPT TO SEIZE THE THRONE (15:1–19:39)

The contents of this section has included (so far) a discussion of the "Removal of a God-Anointed King from the Throne" (15:1–16:14), and the "Mistakes of a Self-Appointed King on the Throne"

(16:15–17:23). We now have the "Battle of the Two Kings for the Throne" (17:24–19:8*b*).

The Battle of the Two Kings for the Throne (17:24–19:8b)

Preparation for the Battle (17:24-29). Once across the River Jordan, David makes for Mahanaim. From a human point of view his position is precarious. He does not know how soon Absalom might come after him. The new king will have the advantage of speed, while David's own pace will be slow on account of the women and children with him. And they need food and shelter.

Absalom's deceitful ways (15:1-6) have apparently made little impact on those living east of the Jordan River. Also, as we saw when we were introduced to Mephibosheth, many in Gilead still remained loyal to Saul. Absalom's most dangerous threat, therefore, might come from this quarter.

It is surprising that David decides to make Mahanaim the center of his operations. This had been the capital of Saul's son, Ish-bosheth. Our concern is that God's rightful king might not find many loyal subjects in this part of his realm. However, instead of being overcome by anxiety or fear, David composes a song and sings it to himself as he and those who are with him make their way toward the city. We cannot reproduce in English the rhythm of the Hebrew, but we can read his words and learn of David's confidence.

> O Yahweh, how my foes have multiplied!
> Many [are] [the ones who] rise up against me.
> Many [are] saying of (lit. to) my soul,
> "There is no help (or deliverance) for him in God." Selah.
>
> But You, O Yahweh, [are] a shield around me;
> My glory and He who lifts up my head.
> [With] my voice I cried to Yahweh,
> And He answered me out of (lit. from) His holy mountain. Selah.
>
> I lay down, and slept;
> I awoke, for Yahweh kept (i.e., sustained) me.
> I do not fear myriads of people
> Who have been set against me all around.
>
> Arise, O Yahweh! Save me, O my God!
> For You have struck all my enemies on the jaw;

You have broken the teeth of the wicked.
To Yahweh [belongs] salvation (or deliverance);
Your blessing [is] on Your people. Selah.
                    (Psalm 3:1-8. cf. Psalm 31:7-8, 19-22).

The Biblical writer, having dealt ever so briefly with David, moves now to tell us about Absalom (17:24*b*). We do not know how long a time elapses before he crosses the Jordan and prepares for battle, but it must have been fairly soon, for the period from his inauguration in Hebron to his death in the Forest of Ephraim could not have exceeded six weeks.

We do know that Absalom has been very active. His army has been raised, and his spies have informed him of David's whereabouts. His general is Amasa, Joab's cousin (see 1 Chronicles 2:16-17).[7]

As soon as his plans are in place Absalom crosses the Jordan, and he and his men camp in Gilead. Their force is a large one, and they do not fear any reprisals from the local inhabitants. But neither do they receive their help.

While Absalom has to contend with a long supply line, David receives assistance from three unexpected sources. Shobi, the son of Nahash (10:1-4), Machir who had cared for Mephibosheth (9:4), and Barzillai who has lived in Gilead all his life (see 19:31-40), become his benefactors.[8]

Dr. William G. Blaikie comments on the generosity of these gracious men:

> Dark though David's trials had been, and seemingly desperate his position, he had not been left alone...the devotion of strangers, as well as the fidelity of a few friends, had cheered him, and had the worst disaster befallen him, had his troops been routed and his cause ruined, there were warm and bold hearts that would not have deserted him.[9]

So once again, the Lord shows David that His lovingkindness has not been withdrawn from him. Belonging to Him does not make us immune from the trials of life, but He does help us through them (see Psalm 34:19-21).

The Young King's Defeat (18:1-8). The delay brought about by Hushai's counsel (17:5-13) has given David enough time to organize his forces and choose the site of the battle. Instead of waiting for Absalom to attack him in the city, he takes the initiative and divides his force into three groups, placing Joab, Abishai, and Ittai over these divisions. David most likely keeps the Cherithites and Pelethites with him, planning to go into battle at the head of his men. But the fighting men of Israel are opposed to such an idea.

"You shall not go out [with us], for if we flee they shall not set [their] heart on us; and if half of us die, they shall not set [their] heart on us, for now [you are] like ten thousand [of] us; and now [it is] better that you be a helper for us from the city" (18:3).

They rightly believe that if in the coming battle David were seen, all forces would concentrate on capturing and killing him. They know that they are facing a very large army, and David is too valuable a person to be sacrificed so easily. Furthermore, if the tide of events goes against them, he can always send reinforcements (i.e., his bodyguard) from the city.

So David reluctantly remains in Mahanaim. In acquiescing to the wishes of his men, he says: "I shall do that which is good in your eyes" (18:4).

He then charges Joab and Abishai and Ittai to "deal gently" (*lĕ'aṭ*, "protect, treat kindly") with Absalom.[10] He is confident of success, and knowing that he will be restored to the throne, he wants to show kindness to the usurper.[11] This charge is also made in the hearing of his men (18:5b, 12b).

The battle is described very briefly (18:6-8). The location is the Forest of Ephraim (indicating that Gilead must have been well forested at this time). It may have been given its name when settlers from Ephraim, west of the Jordan, settled there (see 1 Samuel 13:7; 31:7).[12] The terrain favors small groups of fighting men and is a decided disadvantage to a large force.

The Biblical writer proceeds to give us the results of the battle before treating the events that lead up to Absalom's demise. While no mention is made of any losses among David's forces,[13] Absalom's losses are considerable.[14] In the forest, his men quickly lose all sense of direction with the result that more men from his army perish through becoming lost than as a consequence of the battle. David's army is most likely augmented with Gileadites, and they probably serve as guides as well as warriors. Consequently, David's losses (if any) are negligible.

In the bewilderment of not knowing where his militia is fighting, Absalom comes suddenly upon a group of David's men. He is astride his father's mule. He believes that he can easily outdistance these infantrymen. He turns to flee. And, indeed, he makes good his escape, for he leaves David's soldiers far behind him. Urging his mule on as fast as possible and weaving in and out of the stands of trees,

he makes a sudden turn. Immediately in front of him is a large tere-
binth or oak (afterward known as *hā'ēlâ haggĕdôlâ*, "*the* large tree")
with spreading, "entwining"[15] branches. Before he can duck or swerve
out of the way, his head becomes wedged in a fork among the
branches. And his mule canters off leaving him suspended between
heaven and earth.

The tradition that Absalom's hair became caught in the tree may
be traced back to the Talmud[16] and Josephus. In his *Antiquities of the
Jews*, Josephus writes:

> But all David's men ran violently upon Absalom, for he was easily
> known by his beauty and tallness. He was himself also afraid
> lest his enemies should seize him, so he got upon the king's
> mule and fled; but as he was carried with violence, and noise,
> and a great motion, as being himself light, he entangled his hair
> in the large boughs of a knotty tree, that spread a great way,
> and there he hung after a surprising manner; and as for the beast,
> it went on further...but he hanging in the air upon the bough,
> was taken by his enemies.[17]

As interesting as these details are, they embellish the Biblical
record with information that is not necessarily accurate. The truth
of the matter is that one of Joab's men happened to come across the
hapless prince and ran to Joab to report the news. "Behold, I saw
Absalom hanging in the oak [tree]" (18:10).

Joab's response is sarcastic and unnecessarily cruel. He mocks
the man and his report.

> "And behold, have you seen [Absalom]; then why did you not
> strike him there to the earth, and [call] on me to give you ten
> pieces of silver and one girdle?" (18:11).

The ten pieces of silver imply a large reward, and the "belt" or
"girdle" most likely refers to promotion (e.g., similar to being given
an extra stripe in the army today).

But the man is unmoved. While others may fear Joab, he does not.
He is intent upon obeying the king's command. His reply shows his
courage as well as his resolve:

> "Yea, though I weighed in (lit. on) my hand a thousand pieces of
> silver, I would not put forth my hand to [strike] the son of the
> king; for in our ears the king commanded you and Abishai and
> Ittai, saying: 'Be careful, [you] who [go] against the youth,

against Absalom.' Or I would have dealt falsely against my soul, for any matter is not hidden from the king, and you would have set your hand against [me]" (18:12-13).

At this Joab loses patience with the soldier. "I will not wait thus before you" (18:14), is his abrasive reply.

He must also have demanded to be taken to the place where Absalom had last been seen, for the man leads him there. Absalom has not been able to free himself, though we may be sure he had tried.

Many scholars believe that verses 14-15 contain two separate and conflicting accounts of Absalom's death: the one by the hand of Joab, and the other as a result of the sword thrusts of Joab's armor bearers.[18] Dr. G. R. Driver, however, offers a different explanation. He believes that Joab took three *šĕbāṭîm*, "stout sticks," which he struck against Absalom's *lēb*, "chest," in order to pry him loose.[19] Absalom was then killed by Joab's personal retainers.

Dr. H. W. Hertzberg offers a slightly different interpretation. He believes that Joab threw three darts into Absalom's (*lēb*) chest. This started the flow of blood and marked him for death while he was still alive in the tree. Then, when the young prince had been cut down, Joab's armor bearers finished him off. The rationale for this act was to make Absalom's death a corporate killing. Then no one could know for certain who inflicted the final wound before he died.[20]

These explanations show that it is not necessary to postulate separate manuscript traditions or internal inconsistencies in the Biblical text. Logical explanations are readily available.

One point, however, is almost universally overlooked. It is the wisdom of the soldier's remark that nothing could be kept secret from the king. Joab should have listened to him, for he spoke the truth. Nothing could be held back from David, and David's later words to Zadok and Abiathar (19:13) seem to imply that he had learned of Joab's culpability in the death of his son.

Dr. William G. Blaikie sums up for us the nature of Absalom's death and the mode of his burial.

> [He was] so slashed and mutilated under the swords of Joab's ten men, that no one could have told that it was Absalom that lay there. This was God's judgment on the young man's vanity.
>   The mode of his burial is particularly specified. They threw him into a great pit in the wood, and laid a great heap of stones upon him. "And all Israel (i.e., Absalom's entire army) fled every one to his tent." The [symbolism] of Absalom's burial seems to

have been to show that he was deemed worthy of the punishment of a rebellious son [cf. Deuteronomy 21:18-21], as appointed by Moses; and a more significant expression of opinion could not have been given. The punishment of a son who remained incorrigibly rebellious was to be taken beyond the walls of the city, and stoned to death.[21]

Dr. Blaikie then goes on to show how serious a matter it is to disown the authority of one's parents or to neglect their counsel. The Biblical narrative concludes this section on Absalom with a statement to the effect that during his lifetime he had built a tomb for himself at the confluence of the Kidron Valley and the Valley of Hinnom. His body was never exhumed and placed in it. Later Jewish writers preserve a tradition to the effect that as people would pass by Absalom's tomb outside Jerusalem they would throw a stone into it and say:

> Cursed be the memory of rebellious Absalom; and cursed for ever be all wicked children that rise up in rebellion against their parents.[22]

God's judgment upon Absalom seemed long delayed. But when the day of reckoning came, nothing could thwart it. In this connection some words spoken by Anne of Austria to Jules Mazarin are most apropos: "God does not pay at the end of every week; but in the end He pays."

A Veteran General's Report (8:19-33). At the sound of the blowing of the ram's horn, Joab's men gather together to receive a report of the battle. On learning of the victory, Ahimaaz, the son of Zadok, asks for permission to run to Mahanaim to tell the king.

Apparently, good men were chosen to carry good news, and Joab knows that David will not receive well the report of Absalom's death (18:20). He, therefore, chooses someone unknown to the king to carry the message to Mahanaim. His choice is a Cushite,[23] from the region south of Egypt, the land which we today refer to as the Sudan.

To insure that the matter of Absalom's death is played down, Joab says to him, "Go, tell the king that which you have seen" (18:21).

And so the Cushite, who had not seen Absalom killed, bows to Joab and then begins his run. The route he takes is direct as a crow flies, but it leads up steep ravines and across difficult terrain.

Ahimaaz continues to plead with Joab and asks for permission to run after the Cushite. Joab cannot understand his eagerness, for what reward would there be to come in second? Finally, he relents: "Run" (18:23), is all he says.

And that is all Ahimaaz needs to hear. The young warrior-priest takes a different, longer route. He goes by way of the plain. An observer able to see both men would note at what point Ahimaaz overtook the Cushite even though neither runner could see the other.

Meanwhile, in Mahanaim David is sitting between the pillars of the gateway leading into the city. Watchmen patrol the walls, and one is stationed above the gate. As the day wears on, he sees a runner and calls down to the king. The aged monarch replies: "If [he is running] by himself, [the] tidings in his mouth [are good]" (18:25).

The implication is that if there had been a rout of the army, there would have been more than one runner trying to gain the security of the city.

Then the watchman sees another runner and again calls down to the king. David, who is confident of victory, believes that he, too, bears good news (18:26).

The watchman, who has been observing the runners closely, calls once more to the king:

> "I see the running of the first [man] as the running of Ahimaaz, the son of Zadok" (18:27a).

This reinforces David's earlier belief that the runners bring good news. "He (lit. This) is a good man, and he comes with good news" (18:27b).

The word *ṭôb*, "good," is emphatic in David's statement of belief.

When Ahimaaz comes within calling distance of the city gates, the first word he utters is "*Shalom*," ("Peace"). Most translators paraphrase the sentiments he wished to convey as "All is well" or "Good news" or something similar.

Then, as Ahimaaz comes up to the king, he prostrates himself before David with his face to the ground. Perspiration runs in rivulets down his neck, his hair is wet, and his body is soaked with sweat. He says:

> "Blessed [be] Yahweh your God who has (lit. was) shut up the men who lifted up their hand against my lord the king" (18:28b).

David's primary concern is for Absalom. His inquiry is simple and direct: "Peace...[is there peace] to the young man, to Absalom?" (18:29a).

Perhaps Ahimaaz immediately recalls Joab's words (18:20) and so pretends he does not know. His words are difficult to translate, for it is evident that, in addition to being out of breath, he has been caught off guard and is stammering out his reply:

> "I saw the great tumult, when [I was] sent [by] the king's servant, [who sent] even [me] your servant, but I do not know what [it signified]" (18:29b).

David is comforted by the realization that the watchman had seen a second runner. He tells Ahimaaz to stand aside and then waits for the Cushite to reach the city. His words are reassuring:

> "Receive [good] news, my lord O king! For Yahweh has vindicated you today out of the hand of all those rising up against you" (18:31).

But when David asks, "[Is it] peace to the young man, to Absalom" (18:32a), the Cushite responds:

> "Let the enemies of my lord the king, and all who have risen up against you for evil, be as the young man [is]" (18:32b).

The meaning is clear. Absalom is dead!

The Aged King's Lament (19:1-8b). David's grief is great. The emphasis of his lament[24] is obvious, for Absalom's name is mentioned three times in these verses and the word "son" is mentioned five times. Various explanations have been offered for David's great sorrow. We believe that William Blaikie comes closest to explaining the real reason:

> The worst fears of his heart were realized—Absalom was dead. Gone from earth for ever, beyond reach of the yearnings of his heart; gone to answer for crimes that were revolting in the sight of God and man....
>
> Grief for the dead is always sacred; and however unworthy we may regard the object of it, we cannot but respect it in King David. Viewed simply as an expression of his unquenched affection for his son...it showed a marvelously tender and forgiving heart.
>
> Yet Absalom had died in rebellion, without expressing one word of regret [to either God or his father], without one request for forgiveness, without one act or word that would be pleasant

to recall in time to come…. In this rebellious condition he had passed to the judgment of God. Was not the great pit of the wood into which his unhonored carcass had been flung, a type of another receptacle of his soul? What agony [to David's heart] to think of the misery [of his dear son] who had died impenitent and unpardoned?[25]

In David's grief over Absalom's lost state, however, he neglects those who have loyally supported him (19:2-3). Dr. A. F. Kirkpatrick explains the scene as the men returned from the front lines:

> The news of David's outburst of grief for Absalom was at once reported to Joab, while he was still on the field of battle, and it became generally known throughout the army. So deeply affected were they by the king's sorrow, that all thought of rejoicing was at an end. Instead of returning to Mahanaim in military order with shouts of triumph, they stole back silently in small parties as men would do who had disgraced themselves by flight in battle. The behavior of the people was a striking testimony to their regard for David.[26]

In defense of David's grief over Absalom, all I can say is that when I have had occasion to counsel someone whose loved one has died without accepting Christ as his or her Savior, the awful realization of their eternal destiny sometimes produces the kind of reaction we see in David. They become oblivious to all other considerations and seem to endure in measure the fearful torment of the one who has so recently passed from this earthly scene. In time they need to be shaken free from this maudlin preoccupation, and in David's case the words of Joab serve that purpose.

Toward evening Joab loses patience with the king. He forcefully reminds him of his duty. His scathing rebuke is unduly harsh, and he exaggerates certain issues. Furthermore, the cruelty of his words seem to be a means of directing David's attention away from his own culpability.

As we eavesdrop on the room above the gate, Joab is speaking:

> "You have today shamed the faces of all your servants—those who delivered your life today, and the life of your sons and your daughters, and the life of your wives, and the life of your concubines—by loving (lit. to love) those who hate you and to hate those who love you. For you have declared today that you have (lit. that there is [to you]) neither officers nor servants.

For I know today that if Absalom [were] alive, and all of us today [were] dead, that then [it would be] right in your eyes. And now, rise up; go out and speak to the heart of your servants, for by Yahweh I have sworn, that [if] you do not go out, not a man shall stay with you tonight; and this [would be] worse for you than all the evil that has come upon you from your youth until now" (19:5-7).

The king takes the rebuke well. He does not try to defend himself or argue with Joab about the people's feelings and their reactions. He rises and goes down to the gate of the city. There he speaks personally to all who come to see him. And when "all the people" are gathered before him he most likely addresses them with words of commendation and appreciation.

And so phase one of the rebellion started by Absalom, comes to an end.

SOME THINGS WORTH NOTING

Several months ago my wife and I visited the famous Huntington Library in Monrovia, California. While the Library is known for its rare books, it is equally well-known for its luxuriant gardens and numerous paintings that adorn the palatial rooms and wide passageways of the Huntington estate. We walked through one sequestered garden after another, noticing where each variety of exotic plant came from, and then we went indoors to escape the heat.

I was eager to show my wife the famous Gutenberg Bible—one of very few copies of the first printing still extant. After scanning carefully the type, neatly set in columns, we proceeded to look at the paintings that hung on the walls of this large ballroom. I noticed some works of art by Joshua Reynolds, and this immediately brought to mind something I had read many years earlier. Later, when we came across a painting by George Romney hanging next to one by Reynolds, I told my wife the story.

Romney was ambitious. He aspired to become a great painter. When he heard Joshua Reynolds say that marriage spoiled an artist, he deserted his wife and two children and went to London to pursue fame and fortune. The years passed, and he scarcely saw his wife again until he was dying. Then, destitute of funds and without friends, he made his way home.

It is to his wife's eternal credit that she took him in and nursed him until he died. Alfred Tennyson has preserved the pathos of Romney's situation in a poem titled "Romney's Remorse." In this poem he describes an imaginary conversation between Romney and someone who has come to visit him in his final hours. To his friend's words of encouragement, "Take comfort, you have won the Painter's fame." Romney replies:

> "The best in me that sees the worst in me,
> And groans to see it, finds no comfort there."[27]

George Romney's ambition won him worldly honors, but in the hour of his death these were of no comfort to him. He confessed that his life had been wasted.

Life's true values are to be found in relationships, not riches or fame or influence. Romney had spent his life on a lost cause.

It is the Lord who rewards those who are faithful to Him. In this connection, Dr. Henry C. Morrison tells of an incident that took place when he and his devoted wife returned to the United States after spending many years overseas. They had traveled much in the service of Christ and had grown old together. Unknown to them (for they traveled tourist class) Teddy Roosevelt was on the same boat. He had been in Africa on a hunting expedition.

Literally thousands of people swarmed the docks to greet Mr. Roosevelt, but no one was there to meet the Morrisons. At this the devil planted a thought in Dr. Morrison's heart: "Aha, see how they greet the men of the world, and you—one of God's preachers—without a single soul to greet you."

Henry Morrison shared this thought with his wife. He also expressed to her how hurt he was because of the neglect of God's people. But Mrs. Morrison, always the support of her husband, whispered sweetly to him: "Yes, but Henry, you are not home yet."[28]

Who can tell what kind of welcome awaits us when we enter heaven? There we will be greeted as heirs of Christ's kingdom (Romans 8:17; Galatians 4:7; Titus 3:7), and the Lord Himself will wipe away all tears from our eyes (Revelation 7:17; 21:4). With the apostle Paul, therefore, let us make it our ambition to be well-pleasing to God.

HEALING THE WOUNDS
OF WRONGDOING

2 Samuel 19:8c-39

In the Louvre Museum in Paris, at the head of a flight of stairs, stands "The Winged Victory." The lighting in this part of the museum has been so arranged that the attention of visitors is immediately drawn to this statue. It depicts the goddess Nike, with wings unfurled, bringing victory to the Greeks.

When a team of French archaeologists began excavations on the Aegean island of Samothrace, they found only the pieces of this beautifully carved statue. Not knowing what they had found, they carefully packaged the remains and transported them to Paris. Reassembly, however, was found to be impossible, because no one knew how the pieces fitted together. So the project was laid aside.

Years passed. One day a curator noticed similarities between certain facets of the sculpture and an image on an old Greek coin. Once the museum staff knew what the statue looked like the task of restoration became relatively simple. Now this work of art awes hundreds of thousands of visitors each year.

In many respects, David faced a similar situation in Israel following his victory over Absalom. The task of reconstruction was made difficult for him because the men of Israel, now without a leader, had fled to their own homes (18:17b).

And there were other problems as well:

- David had no godly precedent to follow. Those in other countries, who had been faced with a similar situation, had zealously put to death all who had risen against them.

- David did not know who among the tribes was loyal to him. The elders (i.e., leaders) of the people had sided with Absalom.

- David also knew that any reunification of the nation would have to make allowance for human nature and a wide range of human emotions.

- In spite of David's godly leadership, the people had grown spiritually apathetic. He could not appeal to their Godward aspirations, for they had turned their backs on the Lord and His right to rule over them when they had followed after Absalom.

- David realized that reconciliation would have to be based upon some common principle or desire that the people deemed important.

The process of restoration David followed—while using the best choices open to him—was not without its difficulties. The pressures he faced were far from ideal.

All of this being true, what are we supposed to derive from the story before us?

We tend to idealize those who lived in Bible times and to believe that the problems they faced were easily resolved. Such was not the case. They were often in a worse position because they had no clear precedent to follow and Biblical revelation was not complete. As in the case before us, they had to grapple with complex difficult situations and were compelled to make the best decisions they could based upon their circumstances and the pressures they faced.

OUTLINE

In assessing the way David sought to bring the tribes together, we would do well to keep clearly in mind the flow of events. Absalom's attempt to seize the throne had failed. He was now dead. The nation lay shattered in innumerable pieces. A positive, purposeful plan of reconstruction was needed. But even as David undertook this task, the seeds of dissension sown by his son continued to bear their evil fruit.

As we have observed already, this overall section of 2 Samuel falls into two primary divisions:

• An Attempt to Seize the Throne (15:1–19:39)
• An Attempt to Divide the Nation (19:40–20:26)

This chapter brings us to the end of the first division.

AN ATTEMPT TO SEIZE THE THRONE (15:1–19:39)

So far in our study of this section, we have considered the removal of a God-anointed king from the throne (15:1–16:14), the mistakes of a self-appointed king on the throne (16:15–17:23), and the battle of the two kings for the throne (17:24–19:8b). We come now to look at the events that culminate in the restoration of the God-anointed king to the throne (19:8c–39).

Restoration of the God-Anointed King to the Throne (19:8c-39)

Like books between a set of bookends, so David's return to Jerusalem is made memorable by his meeting with certain friends and the grace he shows toward those who have opposed him. Dr. P. Kyle McCarter of Johns Hopkins University has written:

> The account of David's return journey to Jerusalem has two aspects, which coexist with some tension. This is, on the one hand, the record of a series of meetings reminiscent of the outward journey. The meetings on David's flight raised questions and concerns, inviting the audience to look ahead with some anxiety to the events to come. The meetings on David's return offer reassurance, representing the resolution of many of the earlier concerns, such as the defection of Meribaal (viz., Mephibosheth) and the threats of Shimei. In one sense, then, the present section contains a spirit of resolution. At the same time, however, there is a spirit of renewed conflict here. The circumstances and events of the return of the king precipitate an outbreak of sectional hostility that will have to be resolved before the kingdom can finally be regarded as secure.[1]

A Retrospective Glance (18:17b; 19:8c). With the execution of Absalom, all of his followers had fled. Their champion had been slain. Their cause was lost. Their hearts were now filled with fear for they had acted treacherously toward the Lord's anointed. The epithet *traitor* could now justly be applied to each one of them—from the elders (i.e., leaders) of the different tribes down to the youngest member of Absalom's army whose beard had hardly begun to grow.

The people now waited anxiously for David to take some form of action. Two courses lay open before him: (1) Becoming a dictator and speedily punishing all who had opposed him; or (2) resuming the role of God's theocratic representative to the nation. Dr. William G. Blaikie has shown, David could

> either march to Jerusalem at the head of his victorious army, and take military possession of the capital, or wait till the people should invite him back to the throne from which they had driven him. We are not surprised that he preferred the later alternative. It is more agreeable to any man to be offered what is justly due to him by the affectionate wishes of his people, than to have to claim it as his right.[2]

As we pick up the story, we find that King David gives no intimation of haste. He is content to wait for the right time. In this respect we have much to learn from his example. When a problem arises in our homes or extended family, church or place of employment, some people will always wish to take immediate action to correct it. Of course, there are times when such action is necessary. But when it concerns the reconciliation of opposing parties and the reconstruction of shattered loyalties, patience is often preferable to compulsive action.

Also, from David's experience, we realize that the better part of wisdom is not to impose external conformity but rather to wait for others to experience an internal motivation which makes lasting change possible.

The Question of Rulership (19:9-10). As David waits in Mahanaim, the people become anxious. One topic dominates everyone's conversation: "When will the elders get together and invite the king to return to Jerusalem?"[3] The leaders, however, are loath to take action because they do not know what will happen to them when David resumes power. So "quarrels"[4] become common. The issue is basically between the self-interest of the leaders and militia versus what is best for the people.

The dissension impacts the homes as well as the marketplace; it is prevalent among the wealthy as well as the shepherds in the field. And perhaps the quarrels are accentuated by criticisms of those who had clamored loudest for change and had plunged the nation into a civil war.

Whatever the cause of these angry disputes, certain people are honest enough to admit their mistake. Earlier they may have found their voices drowned by those who had spoken so passionately in favor of Absalom. Now, having cast in their lot with those who had rallied around the usurper, they do not try to deny their responsibility. Instead, they remind everyone of David's exploits and all that he had done for the nation.

> "The king delivered us out of the hand of our enemies; yes, he delivered us out of the hand of the Philistines; and now he has fled out of the land because of Absalom. And Absalom, whom we anointed over us [is] dead, [killed] in battle; and now, why are you silent [as] to bringing back the king?" (19:9-10).

With such an open, honest admission of the part they played in their nation's misdeeds, these people bring a balance to all the arguments circulating wherever people gather. All the while, the *process* through which the people are passing is slowly bringing them (and some respond more slowly than others) to a place where they know what they want and why they want it.

The Invitation to Return (19:11-15). David has loyal individuals who serve as his eyes and ears among the people. They readily relay information to him. As he evaluates the reports, there is a surprising omission. Data from the tribe of Judah is conspicuous by its absence. He believes he knows the reason. Judah, his own tribe, most likely feels acutely the embarrassment of having betrayed him. And they may fear his wrath more than the others.

To try to end the impasse, David sends a message to his faithful allies, Zadok and Abiathar:

> "Speak to the elders of Judah, saying, 'Why are you the last to [do anything to] bring back the king to his house? For the word of all Israel has come to the king, to his house. You [are] my brothers, you [are] my bone and my flesh; and why are you the last to [do anything to] bring back the king?' And say to Amasa, '[Are] you not my bone and my flesh? Thus shall God do to me, and more also if you are not [made] commander [of the army] before me all the days [of your life] instead of Joab'" (19:11-13).

His appeal to the people of Judah is based on kinship.[5] It is the only common ground he can find. Yet there is a hint of personal disappointment in his opening remarks. Judah should have been the first to invite his return, whereas in reality they are the last.

David's choice of Amasa[6] as general of his army is a stroke of genius. It shows the people that there will be no punishment of the guilty. With their fears thus allayed, the men of Judah single-heartedly turn to David as one man (19:14). His choice of Amasa also tacitly reveals that somehow the truth of what took place in the Forest of Ephraim had been relayed to him. The demotion of Joab is just. He has shown himself to be untrustworthy. And so he is replaced by his cousin.

The sudden change that comes over the people of Judah highlights the importance of the emotions in the reconciliation process. Fear can cause a blockage between the mind and the emotions that hinders the will from operating as it should. In like manner, envy or jealousy, pride or deceit, can mar or nullify even the best attempts to bring two people or two parties together. David went to the heart of the matter and laid the fears of the people to rest. He was also wise enough to know that he needed loyal people behind him before he could again ascend the throne. He hopes that his act of clemency will give him that backing.

The people of Judah respond, but not with the enthusiasm the king had hoped for. They send word to him: "Return, you and your servants" (19:14*b*).

There is no expression of remorse on the part of his kinsmen, no pledge of loyalty, and only an implied promise of assistance. The people seem unaware of the heinous nature of their sin, and of the magnitude of David's forgiveness. The message to the king implies the idea of "business as usual." And David, who has suffered such undeserved rejection, and whose confidence needs the reassurance of loving subjects, must proceed without any reinforcement of his worth or confession of his people's need of him.

David understands that the reconciliation of the people, like the reconstruction of loyalties or values or morale, must proceed by logical steps. Sometimes there are delays. Sooner or later, however, a pattern (indicating the course to be taken) begins to emerge. Until then, he presses forward intent on doing the best he can.

On occasion, however, a "piece" in the reconciliation "puzzle" is missing, and it must be located and fitted into place before the work can go forward again. In the present instance the missing "piece" is Israel (specifically the fighting men of the northern tribes). David may have assumed that with Judah taking the lead, the rest of the people would be invited to come and meet him and bring him back to Jerusalem. However, as we shall see, the lack of reassurance of those in the north will cause a delay in bringing the work of reconciliation to completion.

The Submission of the Saulides (19:16-30). As David approaches the River Jordan, the people of Judah and some from the tribes of Israel assemble at Gilgal. Apparently, they are planning a special coronation to reinstate him upon the throne (cf. 19:22c). From there they intend to go to the place where the Jordan can be forded and meet David and his retinue.

Their timing, however, is bad, for when they arrive at the river, they find that Shimei (cf. 16:5-13) and one thousand Benjamites, together with Ziba (cf. 16:1-4), his sons, and his servants, are already there. These people from Benjamin have hastened to cross the river (*wayyṣallĕḥū hayyardēn*, "rush through the Jordan") and have already begun carrying members of the royal household across on their shoulders.

In moving the story forward, the Biblical writer isolates two conversations—the one with Shimei and the other with Mephibosheth—that illustrate the submission of the descendants of Saul to David's authority. The former takes place on the eastern bank of the Jordan, whereas the latter may have taken place outside Jerusalem. They are included together to show the acceptance of David by the house of Saul.

Shimei, of course, has good cause to fear David's wrath. He had cursed him and thrown stones and dust at him when David was on his way into exile. Now he comes pleading for his life. When he sees the king, he falls to the ground before him.

> "Do not let my lord reckon iniquity to me; nor shall you remember that which your servant did perversely in the day that my lord the king went out from Jerusalem, for the king to lay [it] to heart. For your servant knows that I have sinned; and behold, I have come today, the first of all the house of Joseph, to go down to meet my lord the king" (19:19-20).

The term "house of Joseph"[7] is a reference to the northern tribes (cf. Joshua 17:17; 18:5). Shimei's offense was that he had "cursed the Lord's anointed,"[8] and this, according to Exodus 22:28, was a very serious offense. At Shimei's admission of guilt, Abishai wants to make good his previous offer and send him to join his ancestors (19:21). David, however, restrains him.

> "What to me and to you (i.e., what have I to do with you), O sons of Zeruiah, that you are my adversary today?"[9] (19:22a).

David's words are designed to show that the spirit of the occasion does not call for bloodshed. He wishes to secure the goodwill of the "house of Joseph," not further alienate the northern tribes from him. Amnesty is to be given all who acknowledge his right to rule God's people.[10] So he asks,

> "Shall any man be put to death in Israel today? For do I not know that today I [am] king over Israel?" (19:22*b*).

The word *today* stands first in the sentence, indicating its importance. It seems to highlight something more than just the day of his return to Jerusalem. There appears to be a growing consensus among Bible scholars that David had a second coronation.[11] Additionally, it may have been customary then, as it was in later times, for prisoners to be set free and for those who had offended the crown to be pardoned. David's words also seem to suggest that reinstatement to the throne was not an automatic process.[12]

When David turns to Shimei (who is still kneeling before him with his face to the ground) he takes an oath to the effect that he will not execute him.

The second meeting with a Saulide is with Mephibosheth (see 4:4; 9:1-13). Whether Mephibosheth came down to the River Jordan or later met David either in, or as he was approaching, the city of Jerusalem is uncertain. The words *wayhî kî bā' Yĕrûšālaim*, "when he came to Jerusalem," seem to indicate that the meeting took place after the events at Gilgal.

Mephibosheth's appearance is evidence of his mourning.[13] He had neither cared for his feet, trimmed his mustache, or washed his clothes, since the day David went into exile.

David sees these signs of mourning but cannot reconcile them with Ziba's words (see 16:3). Ziba had explicitly told David of Mephibosheth's disloyalty and (supposed) aspirations to be seated on the throne of Saul.[14] So David asks, "Why did you not go with me, Mephibosheth?" (19:25).[15]

Certain emphases in Mephibosheth's reply should not be overlooked. For example, he mentions his submission to David four times (and once more in v. 30).

> "My lord, O king, my young man (i.e., servant) deceived me. For your servant said, 'I will saddle the ass for myself, and ride on it, and go with the king,' for your servant [is] lame. And he slandered your servant to my lord the king, and my lord the king [is] as an angel (messenger?) of God; yet you do what is good in your eyes, for all the house of my father would be nothing except dead men before my lord the king, and you have set your

servant among those who eat at your table. And what right do I
have of any more, even to cry any more to the king?" (19:26-28).

As often happens when one is attempting to settle differences,
David is caught between two people, each with a different story. He
is obviously grateful to Ziba for the provisions he supplied on the
outward journey (16:1, 4). And Ziba has already shown his allegiance
by coming to the Jordan (ahead of David's own kinsmen) and helping the king's household ford the river. Yet these might be the actions of an opportunist, and David has no means of discerning the
thoughts and intents of Ziba's heart.

Now he is confronted with Mephibosheth's avowal of loyalty and
obvious mourning during his absence from Jerusalem. These are such
as to affirm the truthfulness of his words. Yet David responds impa-
tiently to Mephibosheth's words:

"Why do you speak any more [of] your affairs? I have said, 'You
and Ziba shall divide the land'" (19:29).

In any restoration, a leader is disposed to be lenient to offenders;
and it has often been observed in such cases that he seems to do
more, and even to give more, to conciliate enemies than to reward
friends. David's desire to avoid offending Ziba may have made him
less than fair to Mephibosheth.

Mephibosheth, however, responds with the kind of greatness that
reminds us of his father, Jonathan:

"Even the whole, let him take [it all]; [I am content] since my
lord the king has come to his house in peace" (19:30).

He does not insist upon his rights. Nor does he complain that
David's judgment is unjust. Joyce Baldwin sums up the situation
for us.

[David's] decision sounds just, but in fact it unjustly favours
Ziba, who has obtained the property by deception, and it
deprives Mephibosheth, who because of his disability
deserved to be defended against those who would take
advantage of him, of half his estate. The one who comes out
of the incident unscathed is the crippled Mephibosheth, who
rises above financial considerations and takes genuine
pleasure in the return of his lord the king in safety (Hebrew
besalom, i.e. with peace and security restored). It is sad to

see David's grudging response to the genuine warmth of
[Mephibosheth], who has himself suffered, and who
understands what the king has had to endure.[16]

Let us learn from this incident that, in the reconciliation process,
the settling of disputes is always one of the hardest tasks a leader
faces. There are invariably those like Shimei who deserve punishment but, because of a superior's forbearance, are treated with more
latitude than their offense warrants. And then there are those who,
as with Ziba, conceal their true motives behind benevolent acts and
high-sounding phrases. They have the ability to exploit a given situation so that they come out ahead.

Finally, however, there are those like Mephibosheth, who are genuinely altruistic. They are not self-centered. Instead, they are interested in the well-being of others. They seldom get what they so justly
deserve because they do not insist upon their rights. In responding
to David's charge, Mephibosheth was appropriately assertive, but
he left the final decision to David. And when it had been made, he
accepted it without complaint.

The Affirmation of a Friend (19:31-39). The closing scene centers on Barzillai, David's wealthy benefactor. It is significant that the
Biblical writer devotes more space to him than to the other people
whom David encountered on his way back to Jerusalem.

Barzillai has lived his entire life among the mountains of Gilead,
where he has earned a reputation for his intrinsic goodness.[17] This
territory had been settled by the tribes of Reuben, Gad, and half of
the tribe of Manasseh. Under Moses, the Israelites had defeated Og
and Sihon, kings of the Amorites[18] (cf. Numbers 21:21-35; 32:1-33).
Gilead was a fertile region and the flocks and herds of God's people
multiplied rapidly.

When David and his followers had made Mahanaim their temporary home, Barzillai was one of three persons who contributed to
the support of the king and his men, together with their wives and
children (see 17:27-29). He is a venerated octogenarian, who is described as being "very old." Dr. William G. Blaikie writes of his gracious, generous nature:

> He did not ask to see a subscription list, or inquire what other
> people were giving. He did not consider what was the smallest
> amount that he could give without appearing to be shabby. His
> only thought seems to have been, what there was he had to
> give that could be of use to the king. It is this large inborn
> generosity manifested to David that gives one assurance that

he was a kind, generous helper wherever there was a case deserving and needing his aid.[19]

On learning of David's departure from Mahanaim, Barzillai comes down from his home in the highlands of Gilead to say good-bye to his friend. They meet at the River Jordan. The words they exchange are tender and sincere. Neither has the need to impress the other. Each holds his friend in high esteem.

We do not know how or under what circumstances the two first met. There is much about the life of David that is not told us (e.g., how he and Nahash met [see 10:2]; or under what circumstances he and Barzillai became friends). Perhaps Barzillai, as a young man, had journeyed to Naioth to sit for brief periods of time at the feet of Samuel. Or they may have met during an unrecorded visit David made to the area now known as Transjordan. Whenever it was, a strong friendship had developed.

Because Barzillai lived in a sequestered part of the country, there was no compelling reason for him to declare his loyalties and contribute to the support of David. He could have lived out his life unnoticed by Absalom or anyone else on the throne in Jerusalem. But he did side with David at great risk to himself and everyone associated with him. If Absalom had gained the upper hand, he could have punished swiftly and completely those who had aided his father. Barzillai, however, is one of those individuals who is ready to risk all for what he or she believes to be right.

Some people will most assuredly ask, What could have given him such strong feelings of loyalty?

It would appear as if Barzillai was motivated by internal convictions. His Godward orientation led him to believe that David was God's anointed. While others might allow the press of daily events to crowd out spiritual realities, he was of the firm persuasion that Yahweh, though unseen, was the One to whom he was ultimately accountable. He believed that God had called David to the throne and that He had never declared (as He did in the case of Saul) that David had forfeited the right to sit on it. Any attempt, therefore, to drive him from the throne was wrong; and whether Absalom succeeded or failed, he would hold fast to his beliefs. Such men of courage and integrity are few in number today, and it is a sad commentary on our social milieu that hardly any are prepared to take a stand for what they believe to be right.

As David and Barzillai begin to walk together along the bank of the river, David is the first to speak: "You cross over [the river] with me, and I will sustain you with me in Jerusalem" (19:33).

This is a gracious offer, for it includes Barzillai's entire family. Barzillai, however, is not dazzled by the king's magnanimity, even though he realizes that David is paying him a great honor. He feels that the proposal is unsuited to a man of his age. He is already eighty, and each day is adding to the weight of the years. The diminished use of certain of his faculties makes it impossible for him to enjoy the benefits of court life. And besides, he is a home-loving man. His habits have been formed in the context of a quiet, rural town. This is where his roots are, and he is reluctant to try to adjust to a different environment.

Realizing all this, Barzillai graciously declines David's offer:

"How many [are] the days of the years of my life, that I should go up with the king to Jerusalem? I am the son of eighty years today;[20] can I distinguish between good and evil? Can your servant taste that which I am eating, and that which I drink? Can I any more listen to the voice of singing men and women? And why should your servant be any more as a burden to my lord the king? As a little thing, your servant shall cross over the Jordan with the king; and why should the king repay me [with] this reward? Please let your servant return again, and I shall die in my own city, near the burying place of my father and mother.[21] And behold, your servant Chimham! Let him cross over with my lord the king, and you do to him that which [is] good in your eyes" (19:34-37).[22]

Barzillai has no interest in any compensation for his expenses. He and David share something that is far more precious than money—friendship! And that cannot be bought.

Yet, in giving David a reason why he does not wish to go up to Jerusalem, he does not minimize the honor being paid him. His words and attitude reveal a sanctified common sense. He is aware of the possibilities of such a position to a younger man, but realizes that he would only be a burden to the king. His place is in his own home, where he can be cared for without embarrassment when he becomes too frail to care for himself.

Let Barzillai's example be of encouragement to those who are approaching their "golden years." Even in old age there are some compensations. If active pleasures are not to be had, there are passive enjoyments that can fill the waking hours: conversation with old, trusted friends; the reading of good books; the quiet, unhurried meditation upon some portion of God's Word; and listening to good music.

In this connection I am reminded of Dr. Frederick A. Tatford. It was my privilege to know him and to visit with him when he lived in Eastbourne overlooking the English Channel. From this quaint village he traveled to different parts of the world to speak to missionaries and Christian workers. And when not engaged in ministry, he spent time fellowshipping with believers and writing books. This he continued to do well into his eighties. And though he has now passed on to his eternal reward, his published writings continue to bring blessing to all who read them.

As we reflect on Barzillai's words to King David, we note that he was not so taken up with himself that he neglected those who were younger and whose lives stretched on before them. He mentioned to David a young man named Chimham,[23] in all probability his son, and he asked that he be allowed to enter David's service. The king not only welcomed the lad as he would his father, but stated that whatever Barzillai wished for Chimham would be supplied.

The two friends then cross the ford together. Their conversation is the kind that can exist only in the context of mutual trust and admiration. When they part, the king kisses the wrinkled face of his friend. Each one knows that they will never again meet in this world. Then Barzillai returns to his home. Since Barzillai had made no specific request for Chimham, we are left to deduce from later events what God may have been doing for David. In a way that neither David nor anyone else could have imagined at the time, the Lord appears to be *compensating* him for the loss of Absalom.

Did Chimham become "a son" to David? And if so, upon what evidence can such an assumption be based?

Two fragments of information lend support to this belief. The first is found in 1 Kings 2:7. Apparently, Chimham, and later on some of his brothers, ate at David's table. This was a distinct honor and was reserved for the king's sons and those highly favored by him.

The second is even more significant. It is to be found in Jeremiah 41:17 (AV), where mention is made of "the habitation of Chimham" near Bethlehem. From this we can infer several important facts: (1) David treated Chimham as if he were one of his own sons; (2) David gave him an inheritance (i.e. a portion of the land that would be divided between his sons at the time of his death); and (3) Chimham became known for the same godliness as his father (for more than five hundred years later his name was still associated with the portion of ground David had given him). People may preserve the memory of good men and women for a generation, but for Chimham's intrinsic qualities to be remembered for more than half a millennium, he must have been a very good man indeed.

God, it seems, did indeed compensate David for the loss of Absalom. And in doing so, He gave him a much better son than Absalom could ever have been.

David never expected to be compensated for the loss of Absalom. Only as he looked back on the past could he begin to discern, however faintly, the hand of God in his affairs. In God's amazing providence, He gave the grieving father a "son" who fulfilled the aging king's ideal of what a godly posterity should be.

What an example of unexpected grace!

After David and Barzillai have said their farewells, Chimham takes his place next to the king, and they make their way to Gilgal together.

As we see in our imagination David and Chimham making their way to Gilgal, let us not overlook the lingering benefit of David's friendship with Barzillai. Good friends like Barzillai help ease the burden of those who try to bring about a reconciliation between opposing factions. Their thoughts are not of themselves but the good they can do for others. The Lord knew of the new trials awaiting David and used Barzillai to strengthen him for the difficulties that would soon burst upon him.

THE HEALING PROCESS

The impediment that most often prevents reconciliation is pride. Covetousness (or selfishness), lust (of one form or another), dishonesty, envy, graft, anger, jealousy, or vanity all have their roots deeply embedded in pride. It should not surprise us, therefore, to realize that before healing can take place, pride must be rooted out.

Excuses like, "I have been hurt before, and I don't want to be hurt again," are understandable. They are also selfish, for the words indicate that the speaker is more interested in himself or herself than in the family or group to which he or she belongs.

Then there are those who may think of themselves as better than the people with whom they disagree. They will invariably hold themselves aloof from them. Their attitude may be expressed in words like, "I wouldn't stoop that low [to apologize to him or her]," or they will condescendingly say, "I'll apologize to them if they will do so first."

And others may not be prepared to honestly face the facts of their own culpability and so hinder the rebuilding of a marriage, a family, a church, or an organization. Their response is sometimes voiced in words like, "Well, I'm not the only one at fault. There's—. Why don't you go and talk to him/her?"

Defense mechanisms are developed by each one of us so that we may cope with the different situations that arise in the course of our lives. But these mechanisms can also be used in negative ways that block or thwart the work of the Holy Spirit.[24] Only people such as Mephibosheth are truly able to overcome the inequities of life. They do so by not insisting upon their rights. And men and women like Barzillai become the helpers of those who have to endure life's misfortunes.

But let us take a closer look at pride. Both Israel and Judah were guilty of it. Their respective attitudes at Gilgal reveal their arrogance. The tribes of Israel were aware of their size ("we have ten parts of the king"—as if he had somehow been dismembered and portioned out among them), and Judah was cognizant of strong familial ties ("the king is near of kin to us"). The arguments of each group were picayune, yet each contributed to the breakdown of national unity. As passions flared, so did the rhetoric. In the end the only solution (from a human point of view) was separation. But this was neither what God wanted nor was it good for the nation.

Having taken a look at the arrogance and hostility of Israel and Judah, let us also attempt to describe or define pride so that we can understand its operation.

Pride is portrayed in Scripture as an inordinate and unreasonable emphasis on self, manifesting itself in insolence and rude treatment of others. It often attempts to appear in a superior light or endeavors to gain some advantage over others because of some relationship, skill, or belief. It is seen in situations that reveal the proud individual's anxiety to gain applause and distress and rage when slighted. "It is the high opinion that a poor, little, contracted soul entertains of itself."[25]

No person, church, school, organization, city, state, or nation is immune from the evil effects of self-aggrandizement. In the Bible, Israel, Judah, Egypt, Moab, Edom, Assyria, Babylonia, and Philistia were all guilty of pride. And among towns or villages, Sodom, Corinth, and even Jerusalem stand as examples of the effects of this subtle form of evil. Pride was the first sin to tarnish God's universe (see Ezekiel 28:17; 1 Timothy 3:6), it culminated in Pharisaism, and in the opinion of some scholars it will be the last sin to be conquered.

A Biblical study of the Hebrew and Greek words for "pride" indicates that pride deceives the heart (Jeremiah 49:16) and hardens the mind (Daniel 5:20). It brings contention (Proverbs 13:10) and leads people to destruction (Proverbs 16:18). A proud heart stirs up strife (Proverbs 28:25) and is an abomination to the Lord (Proverbs 16:5). God hates a proud look (Proverbs 6:17), and those who engage in vain thoughts or actions eventually stumble and fall (Jeremiah 50:32).

From our study of the rebellion of Absalom through the end of the next chapter (which treats at greater length the division of the tribes that was only concluded with the death of Sheba), we see that pride spawns discontent, ingratitude, presumption, passion (or envy), hatred, wilfulness, and divisiveness.[26]

Plutarch, the Greek moralist and biographer, in his *Apothegms of Kings and Great Men*, preserved for us the closing scene of Scilurus' life. Scilurus gathered about his bed his eighty surviving sons and offered each of them a bundle of short sticks. These he told them to break. When all refused, he took one of the bundles and began drawing from it one stick at a time. Even in his weakened condition he was able to break these sticks with ease. His sons quickly caught the meaning of his object lesson: United they would continue strong, but if they allowed divisions to separate them they would become weak.

The healing of divisiveness can only begin with *honesty*. The people of the northern tribes of Israel were prepared to admit the error of their ways (19:9-10). They made possible the return of David to the throne, and this eventually led to the reunification of the nation. They were also *humble*. There was no hypocrisy in their rehearsal of what they had done. They freely admitted their errors. And they did not try to minimize or downplay David's contribution to the nation because he was from Judah. They set an example for the rest of the nation.

NEW PRESSURES, OLD PROMISES, AND A FEW PRINCIPLES OF LEADERSHIP

2 Samuel 19:40–20:26

Most of us have heard the complaint, "I no sooner take care of one problem when two more arise to take its place." But did you know that the expression arose as a result of the "Labors of Hercules"? In Greek mythology, Hercules was assigned certain seemingly impossible tasks. One was the killing of a gross and freakish animal called the Hydra. This swamp creature terrorized the inhabitants who lived nearby, for it had nine heads.

Undaunted by the rumors, Hercules went to do battle with the monster. As he chopped off one head, two grew up in its place. He soon realized the futility of what he was doing and retired to think the matter over. His nephew, Iolaus, brought him a burning brand and suggested that he sear the neck from which each head was chopped off, thus preventing regrowth. Hercules followed the lad's advice and succeeded in killing the Hydra.

The task facing David as he sought to unify the nation may have appeared to him to be like killing the Hydra. As soon as he thought one problem had been resolved, others arose to take its place. For example, he had no sooner prevailed upon the tribe of Judah to recall him when tribal jealousy caused one of the worst rifts in Israel's history (19:41-43).

David then commissioned Amasa to raise an army and go after the rebels. Amasa failed to do so in the specified period of time, which gave Sheba, the leader of the opposition, time to consolidate his position (20:4-5).

When Amasa, whom David had appointed general of the army,

caught up with Abishai (whom David had turned to when Amasa had failed to return within the three days), Amasa was assassinated by Joab. And Joab then appointed himself head of the army (20:8-10).

As David followed the progress of the militia, it seemed as if the rebel leader was always one step ahead of the men of Judah. Sheba and his followers escaped from one city to the next, and it may have seemed to David as if this "Hydra" would never be laid to rest. He also knew that the longer the division between the tribes lasted, the longer it would take to restore unity to the nation.

With this brief overview of the pressures facing the king, we are in a position to evaluate the contents of this chapter.

OUTLINE

So far in our study of this portion of Scripture (13:1–20:26), we have had occasion to observe *the sovereignty of God in preserving the kingdom* (cf. 7:11b-13).

David's sons, Amnon and Absalom, had scorned the theocracy. Perhaps they felt that it was a useless appendage—a mere tradition— held over from the period of Israel's wandering in the desert. Both these men are now dead.

The introductory chapters devoted to Amnon and Absalom were then followed by two specific attempts to nullify God's explicit selection of David as the one through whom He intended to rule His people. The first section focused on Absalom's *Attempt to Seize the Throne (15:1–19:39).* It included "The Removal of a God-Anointed King from the Throne (15:1–16:14)," "The Mistakes of a Self-Appointed King on the Throne (16:15–17:23)," "The Battle of the Two Kings for the Throne (17:24–19:8b)," and "The Reinstatement of the God-Anointed King on the Throne (19:8c-39)." We come now to Sheba's *Attempt to Divide the Nation (19:40–20:26).* It is divided into three segments of uneven length: (1) "A Confrontation between the Tribes" (19:40–20:2); (2) "The Suppression of the Revolt" (20:4-22); and (3) "The Administration of the Realm" (20:23-26).

In spite of the human attitudes and schemes that have ignored God's suzerainty, He has demonstrated conclusively that, though unseen, He is in control of affairs.

Now, as we consider Sheba's attempt to divide the nation we find that, inserted parenthetically into the narrative, is a painful duty David has to perform (20:3). It has to do with the fate of the unfortunate concubines whom Absalom had taken as his own when he sought to demonstrate his father's powerlessness to oppose him. Having been appropriated by Absalom (against the Law), these women are now regarded as being among Absalom's wives. David cannot take them again lest he and they become defiled (cf. Deuteronomy 24:1-4). But David does not thrust them out as though they are now "damaged goods." He cannot keep them in the palace, for they are no longer his, so he assigns them to special quarters and meets all of their material needs. They remain as Absalom's "widows" until each one dies.[1]

AN ATTEMPT TO DIVIDE THE NATION (19:40–20:26)

A Confrontation Between the Tribes (19:20–20:2)

After leaving Barzillai by the bank of the River Jordan, David and Chimham allow themselves to be escorted to Gilgal. The full potential of their relationship, and what they will come to mean to each other, does not dawn on them all at once. It takes time to grow. Only in retrospect will David see how the Lord has given him a son better than Absalom. These divine compensations are often overlooked by those who are not attuned to the Lord and His ways with His people.

At Gilgal David is reinstated as Israel's king. It is noteworthy that those forming the "inauguration committee" comprise "all the people of Judah and half the people of Israel" (19:40b). Apparently, an attempt had been made to include the northern tribes.

In light of what follows, Dr. G. B. Caird of Oxford University believes the words "and also half the people of Israel" constitute "a foolish interpolation."[2] We know from 19:16-17 that a large contingent of men from the tribe of Benjamin had already come down to the river to meet the king. And Dr. Z. Kallai believes that the tribe of Simeon was included in "Greater Judah."[3]

But how are we to account for the strife of 19:41-43? We may have a partial solution to the problem if we note carefully when the Biblical writer refers to "people" and when he specifically alludes to the "men" of the different tribes. The "people" of Israel are more open to David's return and therefore more likely to respond when they hear by word of mouth what had been planned. The "men" of Israel are still smarting over their gullibility in following Absalom and may have been more inclined to wait for some more substantive assurance of amnesty.

The convocation (which must have occurred in the interval between verses 40 and 41), in which David is again enthroned or reinstated as Israel's king, is passed over in silence. This is strange, for the emphasis of the inspired author is on the kingdom, and it is difficult for us to understand why he omits a matter such as this. A couple of reasons may be offered for his failure to mention what took place at Gilgal.

- David's selection by God and anointing by Samuel were sufficient. And, while in Hebron, he had been accepted by the people as their king with the institution of a covenant. While they had breached this covenant a new enthronement of David could not *add* to what had already been done.

- This division of 2 Samuel looks at threats to the throne. A new danger was in the making. It happened at the height of the festivities. It would be natural, therefore, for this to occupy the mind of God's penman.

Any jubilation at the reinstatement of David as the people's king is muted by the verbal altercation between the "men" of Israel and the "men" of Judah. Initially, the grievance of the men of Israel is lodged with the king:

> "Why have our brothers, the men of Judah, stolen you [from us]? For they brought the king and his household over the Jordan, and all the men of David with him" (19:41*b*).

Any response on the part of the king is drowned out[4] by the words of the men of Judah. Having been disloyal to David, they now over-compensate for their former lapse by trying to show the king how devoted they are. The ensuing argument sounds a lot like sibling rivalry. The writer is careful to preserve the attitude of those involved. The men of Judah answer "*against*" the men of Israel.

In an adversary relationship, interpersonal ties invariably become strained and friction may erupt in open hostility. This is what happened at Gilgal.

The men of Judah: "Because the king [is] near to us. And why [is] this, [that] you are angry about this matter? Have we at all eaten of the king's [bounty]? Or has he given us any gift?" (19:42).

The men of Israel: "Ten hands (i.e. parts) to *me* (i.e. have we) in the king, and also *I* have more [right] in David than you. Why then did you despise

> *me* and was it not *my* word first to *me* (i.e.,
> among ourselves) to bring back *my* king?"
> (19:43, emphasis added).

The translation provided above is a literal one designed to bring out as best we can the emphases of the original text. It will be observed that the singular pronouns "me...I...me...my...me...my..." are used when the northern tribes are referring to themselves. This highlights a certain possessiveness commonly found among the young and the immature. But it also intimates a certain "*unity*" on the part of the "men" of Israel. They know what they want; namely, greater recognition of their role in reinstating the king with the probability that David will favor them in the future. Those in Judah are outraged by such sentiments and fail to take note of the warning signs inherent in the words spoken to them.

As a result, an unfortunate argument breaks out. We read, "And the *word* (the Masoretic [Hebrew] Text uses the singular) of the men of Judah was more forceful than the words of the men of Israel" (19:43*b*). What should have been resolved with kind words and a gracious response now escalates into civil war (cf. Proverbs 16:32. See also Judges 8:1-3; 12:1-7).

William Deane writes:

> The slumbering jealousy between the two sections of the people was roused to fury. The men of Israel complained that the men of Judah had stolen the king away for personal motives; the latter replied that the king was of their kin, and that this was the cause of their action, and not any expectation of special honour and privileges. But the Israelites retorted that they had ten parts in the kingdom for Judah's two; theirs also was the birthright, and they were fully justified in resenting the contemptuous way in which their co-operation had been disregarded. Judah was not inclined to conciliation, and retaliated with fierce and exasperating words.[5]

It seems as if in each crisis, there are those present who exploit the situation to serve their own ends. On this occasion a man named Sheba,[6] a Benjamite, is among the dissidents from the tribes of Israel. Dr. John Bright conjectures that he was a relative of the former king.[7] Sheba is described as a "worthless fellow."[8] He has failed to learn from the Lord's judgment upon Absalom and presumes to be able to rebel against His anointed.

We do not know of Sheba's background and can only presume that he was known to the people of Israel. His words and actions amount to a declaration of war. And not satisfied with verbally exacerbating the situation, he blows the *sofar* (ram's horn) and says,

> "Is not for us a portion in David (i.e., We have no part in David's [kingdom]), and there is no inheritance for us in the son of Jesse; each man to his tent, O Israel" (20:1).

Sheba communicates well. He has the ability to challenge and motivate the people to take action. His protest is based on the old premise that tribal independence is preferable to national unity. And the men of Israel decide to follow him. However, as the late Bernard L. Montgomery pointed out, "Leadership which is evil, while it may succeed temporarily, always carries with it the seeds of its own destruction."[9]

Although David must have been sorry to see the men of Israel withdraw, he does nothing to stop them. His recent reinstatement as king is not the time for open conflict. He also realizes that the new pressures he is experiencing will cease when the head of the "Hydra" is removed. And so, as soon as it is expedient, he makes his way to Jerusalem.

As a sidelight it seems only fair to mention that at Gilgal Mephibosheth had had an ideal opportunity to assert his right to the throne. He could have gotten on his donkey and ridden off after Sheba. Had he done so, the men of Israel would have had a central figure around which to rally. The fact that he did not do so seems strong evidence that he was loyal to David, and that Ziba had indeed maligned him to the king.

The Suppression of the Revolt (20:3-22)

The Instructions of the King (20:3-5). When David enters Jerusalem, we may be sure that those who had wept at his departure now line the streets to welcome his return. But times are tense; speed is of the essence; positive steps must be taken quickly to quell the rebellion, for his intelligence indicates that the resistance to his authority is daily gathering momentum. He knows that it must be stopped at once if he is to avoid disastrous consequences to himself and his people.

As usual, David is proactive. He, too, can issue commands that are easily understood. He summons Amasa (cf. 19:13) and commissions him to gather together Judah's militia. He does not believe that his personal bodyguard (i.e., the Cherithites and Pelethites) together with his mighty men (cf. 23:8-39) will be sufficient to undo the mischief Sheba has done.

David gives Amasa three days to assemble the fighting men of Judah. While some scholars are inclined to think of this as an unrealistic period of time, Amasa could have covered the main cities (e.g., Hebron) himself and delegated to others the conscription in the outlying areas. It is also possible that, as Dr. William G. Blaikie has pointed out, Amasa found the people unwilling to immediately go out to war again. And it is also possible that they were unwilling to accept Amasa as their general.[10] Also some may have actually preferred separation from the tribes to the north.

Whatever the reason, Amasa fails to accomplish the task in the time allowed him by the king.

The Anxiety of the King (20:6-7). The delay worries David. At the end of the seventy-two hours, David calls for Abishai, Joab's brother, to be brought before him. When he is shown into his presence, David institutes Plan B. He says to him:

"Now Sheba the son of Bichri shall do to us more evil than Absalom. You, take the servants of your lord and pursue after him lest he shall find for himself fortified cities and elude you (lit. escape from [our] eye)" (20:6).

Certain commentators believe that David suspected Amasa of turning traitor.[11] This is a remote possibility. It is true that the defection of the people had left the king in doubt about the loyalty of those closest to him. However, it is unlikely that Amasa would turn traitor after having been so freely forgiven his previous offenses.

Abishai musters the mercenaries and they set out after Sheba (20:7). The fact that they are referred to as "Joab's men" immediately sounds an ominous note. All is not well. Joab is no longer their *de jure* leader; his *de facto* acceptance by the men (whom he has led for many years) assures him of their loyalty. Furthermore, it is evident that the men have not accepted Amasa's generalship. Coups are normally staged by the person who can command the army, and the subtle intimation of the Biblical writer is that Joab is powerful enough to topple David from the throne.

The Murder of the King's Appointee (20:8-13). The men under the titular leadership of Abishai head northward. They pause by a "great stone"—possibly a well-known landmark.[12] There they wait, perhaps for information from men sent out as spies. While there, Amasa joins them. He most likely has with him the contingent he has gathered from the cities and towns of Judah.

Joab, Amasa's cousin, steps forward to greet him. But his intentions are far from cordial. With cunning reminiscent of his assassination of Abner (3:27-30), he comes up to Amasa as if to kiss him. "[Is it] well [with] you, my brother?" (20:9).

There is a difference of opinion over exactly what happened next. William Deane describes for us one possibility.

> Joab, who is dressed in his long military cloak, with his girdle outside in which he wore a short sword, advances towards his cousin in friendly fashion. As he hurries forward, his sword apparently by accident falls from the scabbard. Picking it up with his left hand, he goes on, and takes Amasa's beard with his right hand, as the custom was among friends, to kiss him on the cheek. Amasa suspects no treachery, and thrown off his guard, receives a deadly thrust from his unscrupulous relative, who takes the earliest opportunity to rid himself of a dangerous rival.... And the hapless Amasa is left on the roadside wallowing in his own gore.[13]

Others believe that Joab was dressed for travel, and his robe was tucked up so that he could walk about unhindered. When he saw Amasa and began walking toward him, his sword (or long dagger) that was strapped to his side fell into the folds of his tunic. He greeted Amasa cordially, and then lifting the sword from the folds of his cloak with his left hand, he thrust it into Amasa's stomach. The wound was fatal. But instead of putting Amasa out of his misery with a second thrust, he left his victim writhing in agony in the middle of the road. Then he and Abishai called upon the soldiers to join them in pursuing Sheba.

Whatever the precise explanation of what happened, the men (possibly the Judean militia raised by Amasa) are turned off by the gruesome spectacle. Joab's brazen murder of his cousin has stunned them. All of this is compounded by the fact that Amasa has been left to die in agony. It is no wonder that they hesitate to follow Joab.

One of Joab's young men, possibly a junior officer, shows his leadership potential when he sees their hesitancy. He realizes the visual effect of the fallen general upon the men, and drags him into a field. He then throws a cloak over him. With Amasa out of the way, he rallies the men of Judah with the words: "He who delights in Joab, and he who [is] for David, [go] after Joab" (20:11).

It is a clarion call that reminds them of their true mission. And the men of Judah respond. They pass along after Joab, their self-appointed leader.

The Removal of the King's Rival (20:14-22). The pursuit of Sheba is a long one, possibly lasting several weeks and taking the men through the different cities of Israel. And with the knowledge that Joab and his men are following closely behind them, Sheba's forces begin to dwindle. At last Joab and those who are with him corner the rebel and the remnants of his band in Abel of Beth-Maacah.[14] This walled city is approximately twelve miles north of Lake Huleh and a short distance east of the city of Dan.

The people initially give Sheba and his men sanctuary. They neither feel a particular loyalty to David nor pay any heed to the doctrine of the theocracy. They are content to live out their lives in peace, far removed from the conflicts centered in Jerusalem.

The asylum granted Sheba forces Joab and his men to engage in a long and costly seige. They commence building a ramp so they can enter the city over the wall. While this is being constructed, some of the soldiers also set to work undermining the foundation of a portion of the city wall so it will topple over. Either method or both, will enable them to gain access to the city.

As the day of the assault draws nearer, those within the city become increasingly anxious. Their leader is a woman of verbal skill and understanding. The role she plays sheds light on the respect accorded wise women in a society whose business affairs were conducted largely by men.

This woman asks to speak to Joab. Her words have the ring of truth. She does not profess to be loyal to David and apparently uses the name of Yahweh only to lend conviction to her words. She begins by reminding Joab of the history of her people. Then she continues to appeal to him on the grounds of their role within the family of Israel.

> "Often they spoke in days gone by (lit. formerly), saying, 'Surely they will enquire at Abel,' and so they ended [the matter, dispute]. I [am] [of] the peaceful [and] faithful ones of Israel. You [are] seeking to destroy a city, and a mother in Israel. Why will you swallow up the inheritance of Yahweh?" (20:18-19).

The reference to Abel Beth-Maacah being a "mother" in Israel is interesting. Apparently, "daughter" cities had been started in the surrounding area and they were dependant upon their "mother" for their protection and possible livelihood.

Joab is no match for this woman's verbal skills. In making her point, she has gained a decided advantage over her opponent. He wisely does not try to argue with her. His words indicate, however, that he is on the defensive.

> "Far be it! Far be it from me that (lit. if) I should swallow up or if I destroy! Not such [is] the case (i.e., the matter [is] not so)! For a man of the hill-country of Ephraim, Sheba the son of Bichri [is] his name, he has lifted up his hand against the king, against David. Give him [up] by himself, then I shall go from the city" (20:20-21a).

To this the woman replies: "Behold, his head [will be] thrown to you over the wall" (20:21b).

She is decisive, her words carry the tone of assurance. She then tells the people of Joab's terms. They apparently listen to her counsel, cut off the head of Sheba, and throw it to Joab. He blows the trumpet and the people depart (lit. "scatter") from the city. And Joab returns to the king in triumph.

Joyce Baldwin summarizes the situation for us:

> Joab returned to Jerusalem to the king, brazening out the murder of Amasa, and his self-appointment to command the army in the place of Abishai, whom the king had appointed. All this he expected to get away with in light of his success in ending the insurrection against King David. At this point the reactions of David are omitted, but on his death-bed they were made clear to Solomon, who was warned 'do not let [Joab's] grey head go down to Sheol in peace' (1 Ki. 2:6). Though Sheba's rebellion had been quelled, David...was saddled with a general who persisted in killing men whom the king had put in authority.... [He] had killed Abner (2 Sa. 3:27), Absalom (2 Sa. 18:14), and now Amasa (2 Sa. 20:10). David can hardly have welcomed him with open arms, and yet he had saved the kingdom.[15]

Sheba's revolt reminds me of the part Robespierre played in the French Revolution. Although he performed his duties with painstaking efficiency, he was kept out of high office and from the presidency of the National Assembly. He nonetheless laid the groundwork for the revolution by drawing up a constitution based upon the works of the French philosophers of the Enlightenment era.

The monarchy had grown lax, magistrates abused their power, and the people suffered. Religious and racial discrimination were widely practiced, and all of this made it easy for Robespierre to further the goals of insurrection. A deist, he abolished Christianity and sought to institute a "civil religion" with the worship of a "Supreme Being" (but not the God of Biblical revelation).

When the citizens of France stormed the Bastille, Robespierre established a National Convention to indict those not in favor with his policies. He was elected president of the Convention and sought to use his position to further his idea of reform. Initially, it seemed as if everyone was in favor of his policies. However, during his many years as an agitator of insurrection, he had made many enemies. These now conspired to bring about his downfall.

In time, the very people whom he had sought to help turned against him; and the vehicle of execution (namely, the guillotine) that had been used to eliminate those whom he did not favor became the means of his own death. He was beheaded on July 28, 1794.[16]

As with Sheba, Robespierre left God out of his thinking. In the end his talents and labor went for nought.

As we return to King David and the people of Israel, we find that, with the rebellion over, David can now turn to the administration of the realm.

The Administration of the Realm (20:23-26)

With peace restored, David is free to devote his attention to taking care of the internal affairs of the nation. A careful comparison of this section with 8:15-18 shows some changes. These may be accounted for on the grounds that, as the kingdom had expanded, new offices have been added.

The differences in these lists is worth noting.[17]

First, there is the omission of David's name in connection with the administration of the law (cf. 15:3-4). Judicial matters may have been delegated to the leaders of the tribes (who, in turn, had judges in the different cities and villages). David may have instituted this change so as to avoid all possibility of anyone ever again misusing such an office for his own self-aggrandizement. Decentralization was more efficient; and the change from a central judicial administration benefited everybody.

Second, with the expansion of the empire, a need had arisen for someone to supervise the work of those who had been taken captive (cf. Deuteronomy 20:11; 2 Samuel 12:31).[18] Adoram had been given this responsibility. It is also likely that he received the annual tribute from the kingdoms that had submitted to David's suzerainty.

Third, we note that David's sons are no longer said to be "chief ministers." This may indicate David's desire to avoid all semblance of nepotism. However, the use of *wĕgam*, "and also," has caused some Bible scholars to conclude that mention of David's sons was originally included in the text but fell out when a copyist's eye moved from one line to another, leaving out the line referring to them.

One addition to the palace staff is Ira the Jairite.[19] He stands in a special, priestly relationship to David. We are not given any additional information about him and so cannot tell what his duties were.

Other positions remained the same. Joab was over the army. As Dr. William G. Blaikie has pointed out, David was "nominally supreme," but as with other monarchs before and since, he found himself to be the servant of one of his officers.[20] Benaiah was still over David's bodyguard (comprising the Cherithites and Pelethites). Jehoshaphat was the recorder. Sheva was the scribe.[21] Zadok and Abiathar were the priests. And with these men in place, affairs of state ran smoothly for the next ten years.

LEADERSHIP: PRO AND CON

We have considered the nature of David's troubles—how they multiplied and how they were eventually resolved. Now we need to focus our thoughts on why these problems arose and the role played by the different people who exercised leadership among the people.

Of considerable importance is the verbal altercation that took place between the men of Judah and the men of Israel. Long-standing resentments erupted in a heated exchange of words. Passions overflowed, and the anger generated by each group could neither be contained nor channeled in appropriate ways.

The rift between the northern and southern tribes had its origin in the tactless and fractious way in which the men of Judah responded to the criticism of the men of Israel. In this connection, Dr. Leslie B. Flynn recounts an interesting story that illustrates the difficulties that are often experienced when two people or two opposing parties attempt to get along with one another.

Two porcupines lived in the woods of northern Canada. On a cold winter's night, they wanted to huddle together for warmth. As they shuffled closer to each other, their quills got in the way, so they moved apart. A little later on, driven by the cold, they attempted once again to draw warmth from each other. But again their spines needled each other.[22]

And so it was with the tribes of Israel and Judah. The men of Judah could have out-argued the men of Israel (19:42, 43*b*), but this did not resolve the problem. It is obvious that they were more skilled in verbal rejoinders and put-downs, but they did not know how to be conciliatory (cf. Proverbs 16:32). The division they caused did not aid reunion or make David's task of consolidating the nation easier. In fact, it delayed reunification for several months.

But why were the northerners so ready to rebel? Apparently cynicism was widespread. Let me paraphrase the thought of two authorities on human relations and apply their findings to the Biblical text.

> Theirs [i.e., Israel's] was not the best of all possible worlds.... Threat was the operative perception: threat to survival, financial well-being, status, and self-esteem. Self-interest and opportunism marked those who were in touch with the trends within their milieu. Suspicion was on the rise. Trust was on the wane.
>
> It would take time, and leadership, to regain the middle ground between untempered idealism and gothic misanthropy. The people were markedly skeptical combining a tendency to disbelieve coupled with a willingness to be convinced.
>
> At their best they were a nation of *skeptics*: hardnosed but open-minded, realistic in real time but ever mindful of timeless ideals.
>
> By contrast, the *cynics* among them were closed-minded and disillusioned.... They saw selfishness and fakery at the core of human nature...mistrusted politicians and most authority figures, and regarded the average person as false-faced and uncaring....[23]

Sheba was one of the cynics. His words attest to his misanthropy. And it wasn't hard for him to gain a following. The men of Judah had made this easy for him. But leading dissidents from the northern tribes proved harder than he had imagined. In the end, he failed because he could not foster a climate of collaboration.

Bernard Montgomery, who studied the great leaders of history, summarized the essentials of leadership as follows:

> When all is said and done, the true leader must be able to dominate, and finally to master, the events which surround him.... The fundamental elements of leadership will be found in the man, in his sincerity and his self-lessness, and whether he has the right answer. [Two criteria characterize the notable men and women of the past:]
>
> *First.* Their power of concentration.
>
> The capacity to concentrate is essential in a leader; the constant exercise of this ability makes him a disciplined human being. It enables him to simplify the problem, to discover the

essentials on which all action must be based and the details which are unimportant—in fact, to separate the gold from the dross.

Secondly. I note their arrival at a decision.

The capacity for decision is a pre-requisite in a leader.... the most powerful factor is the sincerity of the man, his example, and influence—particularly in respect to Christian virtues.[24]

We know that the fires of discontent had been smoldering for some time, for Absalom had begun fanning the embers of discord during the four years in which he pretended to judge the people. And Sheba, having rejected David's sovereignty, fell heir to this defiance of authority.

But what of David? What kind of leadership did he exercise during this time of crisis?

David was a master in the art of good communication. It did not matter if he was speaking to Amasa or Abishai, his instructions were clear and direct. His words admitted no possibility of ambiguity. He knew what needed to be done and he delegated to others the authority to do it.

Earlier in his discussion on leadership, Bernard Montgomery had pointed out that

> in no case will good results be obtained unless the leader is a man who can be looked up to, whose personal judgment is trusted, and who can inspire and warm the hearts of those he leads—gaining their trust and confidence, and explaining what is needed in language which can be understood.... *the beginning of leadership is a battle for the hearts and minds of men*, and this I firmly believe is the essence of the whole matter.[25]

David possessed this ability; Sheba did not. But David was not the only one who had the ability to rally people to do their duty. The young soldier who challenged the wavering men of Judah with the words, "He who favors Joab, and he who is for David, let him follow Joab" (20:11), likewise knew how to be proactive and motivate the men to take appropriate action. He had the capacity and the will to rally those present to a common purpose, and he had the character which inspired confidence.[26]

And what of Joab? What kind of a leader was he?

Joab was a powerful man. He had many of the traits of a good leader. But he was unscrupulous and opportunistic. He could greet a relative with the words, "Peace, my brother," and stab him in the stomach while the sound of his salutation was still lingering in the air. Montgomery writes perceptively of such people:

> I do not see how anybody can set out to be a leader if his private life is not above reproach. In such cases those he leads will cease to respect him, they will withdraw their confidence, and when that happens his leadership will quickly lose its effectiveness.[27]

This is apparently what happened. Joab's hand in Absalom's murder did not sit well with the men. They continued to follow him, but they had also become watchful of his attitudes and actions. After the assassination of Amasa, loyalty to him began to wane. In 2 Samuel 21 we will read of three wars with the Philistines. They possibly took place during the ten years following the death of Absalom. Joab does not feature prominently in any of them. And when David is dying, he will charge Solomon with these words:

> "And also, you know that which Joab the son of Zeruiah did to me (perhaps referring to the killing of Absalom), [and] that which he did to the two captains of the armies of Israel, to Abner the son of Ner, and to Amasa the son of Jether, that he murdered them; and shed the blood of war in peace...you shall not let his gray hair go down to Sheol [in peace]" (1 Kings 2:5-6).

Joab succeeded for a time, but his influence declined as he allowed selfishness and injustice to rule his passions.

Before we conclude this study, we must also consider the unique qualities of leadership possessed by the wise woman from Abel Beth-Maacah. She proved to be a master in the art of manipulation. Her words led Joab to do exactly what she had determined needed to be done to save her city. She possessed a thorough knowledge of human nature.

Bernard Montgomery again aids our understanding of this important characteristic.

> The leader must also have a genuine interest in, and a real knowledge of, humanity.... He must understand that bottled-up in men are great emotional forces and these must have an outlet in a way which is positive and constructive, and which will warm their hearts and excite their imagination.[28]

She had "a genuine interest in, and a real knowledge of, humanity." She knew the men under Joab had nothing to gain by laying seige to the city. Each one wanted to return to his wife and children and parcel of land upon which their livelihood depended. And she made it easy for them to do so.

While qualities of leadership are alluded to in this chapter, none of us can afford to overlook the power of speech. Our words can challenge, inform, or motivate others. But it is also possible to abuse the use of speech. That is why David prayed,

> Set a guard, O Lord, over my mouth;
> Keep watch over the door of my lips (Psalm 141:3).

And an unknown author could have had this section of God's Word in mind when he or she wrote:

> A careless word may kindle strife;
> A cruel word may wreck a life;
> A bitter word may hate instill;
> A brutal word may smite and kill;
> A gracious word may smooth the way;
> A joyous word may light the day;
> A timely word may lessen stress;
> A loving word may heal and bless.

THE OTHER SIDE OF GREATNESS

2 Samuel 21:1-21

The Books of Judges and Ruth each conclude with an appendix, and the Book of Samuel (comprising 1 and 2 Samuel in our Bibles) does too (see 21:1–24:25). The contents of this appendix contains material that could not be fitted conveniently into the narrative.

It is difficult to identify the periods of time when the incidents that form the appendix took place. Dr. A. F. Kirkpatrick, however, has summarized the material for us.

> This appendix interrupts the course of the history of David's reign, which is resumed in I Kings 1. It is made up of various materials, for which no suitable place could be found elsewhere. The divine government of Israel is illustrated by two national judgments (21:1-14; 24): the genius and character of David by two of his poems (22; 23:1-7); the heroic spirit of the age by the catalogue of David's mighty men, and examples of their exploits (21:15-22; 22:8-39).[1]

Joyce Baldwin, following J. P. Fokkelman, sees a concentric arrangement to these chapters with the poems of King David at the center; on either side are accounts of his mighty men; and at the beginning and end natural disasters which struck the empire during David's reign.[2] The contents are then outlined as follows:

A. Saul's Sin and Its Expiation (21:1-14)
    B. Israel's Heroes and Their Accomplishments (21:15-22)
        C. David's Praise of God (22:1-51)
        C. God's Words to David (23:1-7)
    B. Israel's Mighty Men (23:8-39)
A. David's Sin and Its Expiation (24:1-25)

As convenient as this kind of outline may be, it is unwise to push symmetry too far, for then one may unwittingly overlook or unintentionally ignore the theme of the portion of Scripture under consideration.

OUTLINE

What is revealed in our present chapter is David's vulnerability in the choices he had to make and the wars in which he was engaged. In these chapters, therefore, we see the other side of greatness—examples of the human element in leadership and of the difficult and often unpleasant choices that must be made.

Our story begins with Saul's plan to exterminate the Gibeonites and God's punishment of his sin. This is followed by a touching account of the devotion of Rizpah, Saul's concubine. And the chapter ends with a brief summary of four wars instigated by the Philistines. We have, therefore, a concise description of:

- The Sins of a Father in Israel (21:1-9)
- The Love of a Mother in Israel (21:10-14)
- The Wars of the Sons of Israel (21:15-22)

Central to the discussion are (1) the corporate nature of affairs in the ancient Near East, and (2) the fact that the Lord will by no means clear the guilty unless there is evidence of repentance.

THE SINS OF A FATHER IN ISRAEL (21:1-9)

The Prayer of a King (21:1)

If the famine took place during the events described in 2 Samuel 8, when David and the men of Israel were fighting wars on all sides, then it is easy to see why it was only after three years that the king had the leisure time to inquire of the Lord the reason.[3] William G. Blaikie's comments on David's delay in petitioning the Lord and the prevalent tendency among us to ignore God's "little chastenings" are worth noting.

When the famine extended to a third year, [David] was persuaded that it must have a special cause. Did he not in this just act as we all are disposed to do? A little trial we deem to be nothing; it does not seem to have any significance or to be connected to any lesson. It is only when the little trial swells into one large one, or the brief trouble into a long-continuing affliction, that we begin to inquire why it was sent. If small trials were more regarded, heavy trials would be less needed.[4]

In answer to David's earnest entreaty, the Lord says to him:

"[It is] for Saul and for [his] house of bloodshed, because he put to death the Gibeonites" (21:1*b*).[5]

The reason for the famine was a broken covenant. The background of this story is found in Joshua 9. When Joshua invaded Canaan, he had been taken in by the duplicity of the Gibeonites,[6] who pretended to have come from a distant land. They sought peace with Israel, and a treaty was made with them (Joshua 9:3-15). A short time later, Joshua and the men of Israel learned that they had been tricked. The covenant, however, was binding. It stood firm, and the Gibeonites were punished for their deception by being made "hewers of wood and drawers of water" for the house of the Lord (Joshua 9:22-27).

Saul's breach of the covenant is not recorded in the history of the period, and apart from reference to it here we would not know of it. He had slaughtered a defenseless people, and his sin had so far gone unpunished. Bloodguilt, therefore, rested upon Saul and his house.[7]

In contrast to David, who had confessed his sin and was freely forgiven, Saul had never acknowledged his sin. It had never been forgiven. Saul apparently thought that, with the passing of time, the Lord had forgotten. In this respect, he was like many today who feel that they can sin with impunity. But the Lord does not forget. Only when a person confesses his or her sin does the Lord demonstrate His faithfulness and righteousness and forgive the sin and cleanse the believer from all unrighteousness (see 1 John 1:9).

The Appeal of the Gibeonites (21:2-4)

Upon learning the cause of the famine, David calls the leaders of the Gibeonites together. He tells them what the Lord has told him.

"What shall I do for you? And with what shall I atone *that you may bless* the inheritance of Yahweh?" (21:3, emphasis added).

David, as a wise leader, allows *them* to select an acceptable penalty that will expiate the crime. Two alternatives were generally followed: (1) monetary compensation, and (2) blood-vengeance. As *gērîm*, "resident aliens," protected by oath, they are empowered to make pecuniary claims (e.g., "silver and gold") against Israelites, but they are not protected by blood-feud laws.[8]

The word order of their response is most interesting:

> "Not for us silver nor gold with Saul and his house (i.e., We will have neither silver nor gold from Saul or his house), and [it is] not for us to put a man to death in Israel (i.e., and we have no power to put a man to death in Israel)" (21:4a).

Having declined the former, only the latter is left open. David, however, is puzzled. He replies, "What you say, I will do for you" (21:4b). And they answer,

> "The man who destroyed us, and who schemed against [us] [that] we be wasted from standing in all the border of Israel, let seven men be given to us of his sons, and we shall expose them to Yahweh in Gibeah of Saul" (21:5-6a).

While we may react to this suggestion from the context of our western culture and question how or why seven innocent men should be executed to satisfy the wishes of an aggrieved people, two important truths must be borne in mind: (1) the concept of "corporate personality"—the sins of the father being visited on the children—was firmly established in the laws and customs of people in the Near East; and (2) the Benjamites had benefited from the land left vacant by the Gibeonites and had never repented of Saul's crime nor sought to make any form of redress. Seen in this light, the request of the Gibeonites was most gracious. They could have asked for much more—a life for a life.

Before we inquire into the nature of the judgment upon Saul and consider the problems associated with the selection of the seven, it will help if we digress for a moment to consider a similar situation that illustrates the close connection between the sins of one generation and the next.

When Dr. J. B. Pritchard edited his now famous *Ancient Near Eastern Texts*, he included several of the so-called "plague prayers." One of them, from the land of the Hittites, is particularly apropos. It has to do with a king named Mursilis. During the reign of Mursilis' father, a peace treaty with Egypt was broken. A plague broke out among the prisoners brought back from the raids on Egypt, and it quickly spread to the civilian population.

In hope of averting further loss of life, Mursilis admitted his guilt. His words of confession were sincere. He acknowledged that his father was at fault, and that his father's sin had fallen upon him. He then offered to make restitution and offer appropriate sacrifices.[9]

The Biblical story of the Gibeonites' revenge shares some similarities with this ancient prayer. In each case there was a form of disaster (famine, plague) that threatened the well-being of the people. In each case the reason was a broken treaty, deliberately violated by the central figure—a king, now deceased. And in each case the new king was left to grapple with the problems left over from the previous administration.

The Judgment on Saul (21:5-9)

David accepts the Gibeonites' offer with the words, "I will deliver them" (21:6*b*). But why not insist upon some form of reparation and lay the matter to rest? Dr. Blaikie explains:

> If the nation profited by the unholy transaction, and was thus induced to wink at the violation of the national faith and the massacre of inoffensive people, it shared in Saul's guilt, and became liable to chastisement.... Prince and people therefore were both at fault, and both were suffering for the wrongdoing of the nation. Perhaps Solomon had this case in view when he wrote: "Rob not the poor because he is poor, neither oppress the afflicted in the gate; for the Lord will plead their cause, and spoil the soul of those that spoiled them."
>
> But whatever may have been Saul's motive, it is certain that by his attempt to massacre and banish the Gibeonites a great national sin was committed, and that for this sin the nation had never humbled itself, and never made reparation.[10]

The fact that the Gibeonites declined to receive any monetary compensation and asked only for a token judgment against Saul's house may have come as a surprise to David. Only seven lives were to be forfeited. Seven is regarded as the perfect number in the Near East, and these seven victims will betoken a full and adequate judgment, for they are to be executed before the Lord to expiate His displeasure.

There is doubt among Bible scholars over the exact nature of the execution of these men. The words *wěhōqa 'ănūm* (usually rendered "that we may hang them") are difficult to translate. *Hōqîa* occurs only here and in Numbers 25:4, so we have limited evidence of its meaning derived from its usage. The Rabbis believed that the men were hanged.[11] The Septuagint favors crucifixion in the sun.

But verse 9 indicates that the seven men *wayyippělû*, "fell together."
In Judaism, one form of execution was to hurl the offender over a
cliff. Death came instantly upon impacting the ground. The corpse
was then exposed (i.e., hung in some prominent place) as a warning
to others.[12]

Exactly how the seven were executed is impossible to determine
from the text. It could easily have involved death by being thrown
down some precipice.

But this is not the only difficulty to be resolved. Saul had aimed at
extermination of the Gibeonites. He failed, of course, but this does
not answer the question, "Why did he plan to utterly destroy them?"

Most commentators struggle with the statement "in his zeal for
the children of Israel and Judah." The most plausible explanation is
that this act of misguided "zeal" followed one of Samuel's rebukes of
him for not following the counsel of the Lord. Smarting under what
he believed was undeserved criticism, he sought to show his concern for the purity of God's people by removing these Amorites (21:2)
within Israel from the face of the earth. They were defenseless and
fell as easy prey to his evil scheme.

But were Saul's motives altruistic? William G. Blaikie raises another
important question. Referring back to 1 Samuel 22:7, he asks: "From
whence did Saul obtain the houses and lands that were given to his
court officials?" And the answer: Most likely from the Gibeonites, for
their territory lay within the borders assigned to the tribe of Benjamin.[13] If Dr. Blaikie is correct, then Saul's desire to preserve the
genetic purity of his people was so much window dressing. Like politicians today, they mislead the public into believing one thing, while
planning something entirely different for their friends.

While we may still have reservations about the propriety of ex-
ecuting innocent individuals for the sins of their father, let it be noted
that neither David nor the Benjamites nor those selected for execution raised any objection. They understood the corporate nature of
the family in Israel and believed that the request of the Gibeonites
was fair.[14]

The difficult task of selecting the seven falls to David. He locates
seven of Saul's "sons" and gives them to the Gibeonites. Apparently,
with the handing over of the men also went the (temporary) power
to administer the death penalty.

Those to die for Saul's sins include the two sons of Rizpah, Saul's
concubine, Armoni and Mephibosheth (21:8), and the five sons of
Merab (not Michal, for she died childless[15]), the wife of Adriel from
Meholah (see 1 Samuel 18:19).[16]

Obviously, not everyone knew the reason for David's actions, and his enemies were quick to blame him for trying to exterminate Saul's household and remove from Israel all claimants to the throne. But David had already reigned for many years over the tribes of Israel and Judah, and his victories over the nations surrounding God's people had raised his popularity to an all-time high. So those who sought to discredit him for his actions had other motives for doing so.

Second Samuel 21:7 is an editorial "note" added at the time this history was written to explain the differences between the two Mephibosheth's and the fact that David kept *his* covenant with Jonathan (see 1 Samuel 18:3; 20:17,42; 23:18). The writer wants to present David as faithful to his promise. From the chronology of 2 Samuel, we know that David was unaware of the existence of Jonathan's son at the time these men were executed. Only after these events did he express a desire to show kindness to the house of Saul (see 9:1-13).

The execution of Saul's "sons" takes place at the beginning of the barley harvest (i.e., end of April, in the month called Ziv[17]).

THE LOVE OF A MOTHER IN ISRAEL (21:10-14)

We pass now to consider the reaction of Rizpah to the death of Saul's sons and grandsons. Rizpah,[18] Saul's concubine, knows that her sons have been punished for the sins of her husband, their father. She shows no malice toward David for what has happened. There is no record of any words of denunciation or recrimination coming from her lips. And while her pain must have been great, she evidences no resentment.

Rizpah, of course, is powerless to reverse the sentence, but she does reverse the shame that could have attached to her sons and the grandsons of the late king. The teaching of the Law was clear. A corpse that was exposed to the birds of the air and the beasts of the field was deemed to be dishonored (cf. 1 Samuel 17:44; Psalm 79:2; Jeremiah 16:4).

So Rizpah determines that this will not be their fate. To protect the corpses, she spreads out a piece of sackcloth (a symbol of mourning for the deceased) upon a rock and, in spite of the dangers and the weather, maintains a silent vigil for the next six months. When scavengers that feed on carrion come to eat away at the carcasses, she drives them away.

David is ultimately told about her, and his heart is moved with compassion. But how can he bring to a satisfactory conclusion this unhappy series of events?

He determines to give the bones of Saul and Jonathan and these seven descendants of the late king an honorable burial. He issues orders for the remains of Saul and his sons to be exhumed from their burial place in Jabesh-gilead (1 Samuel 31:8-13) and brought back to the territory of Benjamin. They are then interred in the ancestral burial lot with the corpses of the seven men executed by the Gibeonites.

With respect shown for the dead, the Lord is then moved by prayers of entreaty for the land. From David's words in 21:3, it appears as if the Gibeonites were the ones who prayed for God's favor to again rest upon His people. Then the rains came. The drought was broken; the famine was over.

The lingering lesson from this portion of God's Word is that unconfessed sin is not forgotten. The Lord will chasten us in order to bring us to repentance.

THE WARS OF THE SONS OF ISRAEL (21:15-22)

From "the sins of a father" and "the love of a mother" we pass on to consider "the wars of the sons." These verses are "quite unconnected with the preceding narrative."[19] Joyce Baldwin comments on the place and importance of the wars mentioned in these paragraphs.

Four incidents are recorded here, of which all except the first appear again, with differences in detail, in 1 Chronicles 20:4-8. It seems likely that a roll of honour was kept, in which outstanding acts of bravery, some of which are quoted here, were written and handed down to posterity. The concise style of writing is appropriate for an official honours list.[20]

It is unlikely that the Biblical writer has preserved the sequence of events in which these wars took place, and because there are no indications in 21:18-22 that parallel the wars mentioned earlier in the book, it is more likely that they occurred in the last ten years of David's life.

The war mentioned first is the battle in which the aged King David was nearly killed. But the question arises, Why have these particular battles been inserted into the narrative? And why here? Dr. William G. Blaikie provides us with plausible answers.

In the first place, to give us some idea of the dangers to which [David] was exposed in his military life, dangers manifold and sometimes overwhelming, and all but fatal; and thus to enable us to see how wonderful were the deliverances he experienced, and prepare us for entering into the song of thanksgiving which forms the twenty-second chapter, and of which these deliverances form the burden. In the second place, to enable us to understand the human instrumentality by which he achieved so brilliant a success, the kind of men by whom he was helped, the kind of spirit by which they were animated, and their intense personal devotion to David himself. The former purpose is that which is chiefly in view in the end of the twenty-first chapter, the latter in the twenty-third.[21]

Where the first of the four battles against the Philistines takes place is not mentioned (21:15-17). The confrontation is a long and arduous one, for David grows weary. It is then that Ishbi-benob, one of the descendants of the giant,[22] attempts to kill him.

The description given of Ishbi-benob reminds us of Goliath of Gath. His spear weighs the equivalent of three hundred shekels of bronze (approximately seven and one-half pounds). He also has a new sword, one evidently made especially for him.

Ishbi-benob engages David in combat and appears to be gaining the upper hand. Abishai, one of David's mighty men, sees what is happening and comes to the king's aid. He strikes down the Philistine and kills him.

When the battle is over, David's men take an oath in his presence, saying: "You shall not go out again with us to battle, that the lamp of Israel may not be put out" (21:17*b*).

The metaphor "extinguish the lamp of Israel" (NASB) is very suggestive. It likens the king to the lamp in the sanctuary that was a symbol of illumination.[23] He must not be allowed to die. The loyalty of David's men is noteworthy. He has earned their devotion. He is more than their leader, he is also their trusted friend.

Following this war with the Philistines, in which prominence has been given to David and Abishai and David's relationship with his men, 21:18-22 treats succinctly three other battles against Israel's archenemies to the west.

"Gob" is unknown outside of this passage. The Septuagint has "Gath" and 1 Chronicles 20:4 reads "Gezer." The giants killed in these wars were all from Gath (21:22), and Gob (if there was such a place) may have been a military camp or barracks close by.

In the second battle, the hero is Sibbecai the Hushathite. He is from a place near Bethlehem and is also listed among David's mighty men (see 1 Chronicles 27:11). He strikes down Saph, who was a direct descendant of the giant.

Some Bible scholars, who are anxious to minimize the size of some of Israel's opponents, prefer to read *yĕlîdê hārāpâ'* as the "votaries of Rapha" instead of "who was among the descendants of the Rephaim [giants]." But they fail to deal with the obvious intent of verse 22 and the previous occurrences of these awesome individuals (see Genesis 14:5; Deuteronomy 2:10-11,20; 3:13; Joshua 12:4; 13:12; 17:15).[24]

A third war is waged, and this time Elhanan the Bethlehemite kills Goliath the Gittite. But didn't David kill Goliath (1 Samuel 17:41-51)? Who then is Elhanan?

First Chronicles 20:5 identifies Elhanan as the son of Jair and the slayer of Lahmi, the brother of Goliath the Gittite. It would seem as if, in the centuries of transmission that extend from the era of the Biblical historian to the latest Hebrew documents, an omission occurred when a copyist inadvertently omitted the words "the brother of" from the text.

Rejecting this explanation, some critics have tried to reconcile these two accounts by postulating a family name for David.[25] They conjecture that Elhanan was the family name of Jesse's household and that Jair was the equivalent of Jesse.[26] The most viable solution is to compare the data here with the material in 1 Chronicles and resolve the issue without speculation or conjecture.

The fourth and final war mentioned in this cluster of battles was instigated by the king of Gath. Once again a giant of immense proportions defied the sons of Israel. This time, Jonathan, David's nephew, was the one who killed him.

The Biblical writer then sums up these activities by pointing out that the four Philistine champions were all sons of one man, a giant of Gath. Each one shared a common fate at the hands of David's soldiers, proving that the Lord gives outstanding victories to ordinary men and women. Once the battles are won, the individuals then continue to minister faithfully in their former positions, neither begrudging the loss of celebrity status nor the fact that their positions keep them from enjoying the limelight.

LOOKING BOTH WAYS

In this chapter, we have considered (1) the difficult decision David had to make, followed (2) by Rizpah's devotion, and then (3) the bold deeds of those who were not intimidated by the size of the opposition. Now, as we look back on these events, we do so with the intent of uncovering any principles for ourselves that may prove valuable as we face the future.

Hard Choices

Sin, and particularly punishment for sin, is not a popular topic today. This was not always the case. There was a time in American history when preachers would denounce sin in all of its many forms. During that time it was common to hear gifted orators thunder against sin. Their congregations became accustomed to experiencing feelings of guilt each Sunday. These preachers, however, did not always point the way to the resolution of the guilt they had induced. Now we live at a time of another extreme. Sin makes us feel uncomfortable, so we simply do not talk much about it nor do we hear many clear, authoritative messages on it.

In this chapter, the Biblical writer has discoursed on sin. He has shown us the consequences of unconfessed sin. He has illustrated clearly the fact that we cannot sin and expect to get away with it.

In his perceptive book *Whatever Became of Sin?*, Dr. Karl Menninger traced the decline of an acknowledgment of sin to "the new psychology." He pointed out that our age is prone to speak of certain "wrongness" as error or mistakes or superstition or disillusionment, but not sin. This dismissal of sin from our conscious minds began when wrongful acts were identified with "crime." Some crimes, however, were viewed as symptomatic and therefore treatable. In time crime was described as "illness."

Whereas through the centuries the clergy have been charged with the duty of drawing attention to the sins of society, when sin became equated with crime (and particularly serious crime), their place was taken by the police and judges. Similarly, when crimes became illnesses, the role of the police officer and the judge was assumed by the doctor and the psychiatrist. The worst of sins became nullified of their evil character through the use of psychological jargon, and minor sins were discounted as human weaknesses.

And so it is that sin has virtually disappeared from the vocabulary of the man in the street.[27]

But God's Word does teach about sin and its punishment. And what is more, it does so without confusing the labels. Sin is not the consequence of pathological attitudes like excessive zeal or superpiety, prudishness or Victorian morality, neurotic inhibition or "reaction formation." Sin is a violation of the holiness of God.

In Scripture, "sin" (which includes our thoughts as well as our deeds) is usually portrayed as "missing the mark." The "mark" to which we are to attain is nothing less than "the glory of God" (Romans 3:23)—His impeccable righteousness and purity. Any falling short of this "mark," any wish or action that is contrary to the expressed will of God, is punishable by death (cf. Ezekiel 18:4; James 4:12,17). And those who think they can sin with impunity actually place themselves in God's place as the absolute Lawgiver (cf. 2 Timothy 3:1-2; 2 Thessalonians 2:3-4).

In the passage before us, we have a Biblical example of the consequences of unconfessed sin. The nation suffered. And in the church today, one sinning saint can deprive the assembly to which he or she belongs of the blessing God wishes to give it. And the reason? We are a community of believers and are inseparably united to one another.

In addition, we may have latent in this chapter the reason why some of our prayers go unanswered. It is common for young believers, and even some older ones (when caught in a difficult situation), to make a vow to the Lord. All too often, with the passing of time, these are forgotten. And on this account the Lord may allow some misfortune to enter our lives. If we suspect that this has happened, we should do as David did and ask the Lord the reason why. And when He reveals our sin or sins to us, we should hastily make amends.

When God made known to David the reason for His chastisement, David did not try to enter into a dialogue with God to excuse himself from all culpability and so minimize the penalty (e.g., "It's Saul's fault. I had nothing to do with it."). Nor did he project the blame on to Saul's house, explaining that they could have made restitution at any time during the past ten or more years. He knew that you cannot play with sin and overcome it at the same time. He accepted God's verdict, realized that certain moral and ethical issues were involved, and then took steps to set matters right.

One day someone will write a definitive work on "David the theologian." When this happens, he or she will need to devote space to the issues of sin, forgiveness, and blessing. In the present context, the Gibeonites needed to genuinely forgive the Israelites for plundering and exploiting them, and the evidence of the sincerity of their sentiments was their intercession so that the effects of the drought could be lifted (21:3*b*. cf. Job 42:8-10*a*).

Apparently, this is what happened, for the Lord was "moved by entreaty" for the land. He honored the prayer of those who interceded before Him for the people and once more began to bless them. Let us note that prayer lifts the heart above the inequities of life and moves the hand of God to accomplish that which His people desire of Him.

No Quid Pro Quo

From the importance of owning the reality of sin in our life and the need we have for full and free forgiveness, we turn to consider

Rizpah's noble example of love and devotion. She was caught in a web of conflicting circumstances. First, her husband, Saul, had been killed in battle. Then she had to make her home in Mahanaim, where she became the center of gossip and a pawn in the hands of two men (3:7). And then her sons were taken from her and executed. Her love and devotion earned for her an honored place in God's inspired Word! While few will preach on Rizpah on Mother's Day, God in His infinite wisdom has preserved for us a record of what she did.

Motherhood is precious. When thinking of Rizpah, I am reminded of Cheryl who was a member of a church we attended. After her husband divorced her, she devoted herself to her only child, a son named Chet. The years passed, and Chet grew up to be a strong, able Christian. He was also his mother's pride and joy. Then a dark cloud came over their humble home. Chet was diagnosed as having leukemia. Tests were run, and all sorts of medication and treatment were prescribed. Now the important events were not who won or lost a basketball game, but the number of red and white blood cells coursing through his veins.

Cheryl wisely sought counsel from the church staff, and this helped her greatly. It was hard for her to see Chet go steadily downhill. Somehow her faith sustained her. One night (it happened to be the night Chet died), Cheryl stayed by her son's bedside. He was in a coma. About 10:00 p.m., an accident victim was brought from surgery. The nurse, who had come to know Cheryl well, saw her looking in the direction of the new patient and shook her head as if to answer Cheryl's unspoken question.

The hour hand on her watch slowly marked the passing of time. The only sounds were those of Chet's shallow breathing, the night nurse making her rounds, and groans from the room opposite Chet's where the accident victim lay tossing on his bed. It seemed to Cheryl as if she could occasionally hear words that sounded like "Mother, Mother, where are you?"

Around 2:00 a.m. Chet's breathing changed slightly and soon thereafter stopped. He was gone. At first Cheryl was stunned. She had known that this would happen and had tried to prepare for it. But now that it had happened, she felt a certain indefinable fear and a sense of her personal loss. Then, drawing upon her faith in God's all-wise providence, she got up with the intention of going home. There would be a host of things to do in preparation for the funeral.

As she came out of her son's room, she again heard a groan from the accident victim, and the painful whisper that sounded like, "Mother, Mother, where are you?" She entered the room. The nurse assigned to the patient looked up but said nothing. Cheryl drew up a chair and asked the nurse his name. She didn't know but called the desk to find out. The next time the young man groaned and called out softly for his mother, Cheryl spoke his name and, taking his hand in hers, said: "Here I am."

She then began to talk to him in soft, soothing tones. He complained that he was feeling cold, and she drew some of the blankets around him. When he became restless, she sang softly to him. This quieted him, and he drifted off to sleep. Sometime around 7:30 in the morning, he too died. By now Cheryl was so exhausted she hardly had enough energy to get up and make her way home.

Did it matter that Cheryl was not the man's real mother? No! She was a mother at heart and knew how to reach out beyond her own pain so that she could comfort someone else. Her presence eased a lad's final hours.

Cheryl said nothing to anyone about her lonely vigil. The hospital staff learned from the nurse in his ward what she had done, and one of them told a pastor from her church. When commended by him, she took no credit for her actions. Her only response was that she hoped, if circumstances had been different and it had been Chet who was the accident victim, some other mother would have done the same for him.

Rizpah and Cheryl, each in their own way, exemplify what is best in motherhood. They possessed a quality of selflessness that touches our hearts.

Day of Honor

The remainder of 2 Samuel 21 deals with the victories of David and his men. None of them set out to become heroes. They were ordinary men, devoted to doing their duty, who did not shirk the difficulties that came their way. It would have been easy for each of them, when they saw a man of enormous proportions hacking his way through the Israelites and coming in their direction, to discreetly avoid him. They did not. They tackled each problem as it arose, and the size of the opposition did not intimidate them.

Once their names had been inscribed upon Israel's Honor Roll, they did not think that they had arrived at some enviable plateau where favors would be heaped upon them. They did not try to maintain some coveted "celebrity status" and remain in the public eye. They returned to their duties.

This is the attitude of successful people. They respond positively to a challenge, relish a difficult task, and no matter who is against them, they maintain a positive attitude. David was happy to call these men his friends. His life was fortified and enriched by their company. And they never let him down.

"IN GOD I TRUST"

2 Samuel 22:1-51

When I first met Brad, he was a jumble of conflicting emotions. Fear and feelings of rejection predominated. He also lacked peace, was angry and frustrated, and had more questions than answers. One thing gave him hope, and he carried it with him wherever he went.

As the story unfolded, Brad told me that his wife, Brenda, had left him and taken their two daughters with her. It was several weeks before he found where they were staying.

In one of the ironies of life, the day Brenda had told him she was leaving coincided with a job interview scheduled for 8:00 a.m. Brad felt trapped. He wanted to stay with Brenda and try to talk her out of her decision, and at the same time he could also hear a tape in his mind repeating over and over again her criticism of him for not having a better paying job.

Believing that if he got the job he could talk her into staying, Brad left for the interview. Knowing that Brenda was working the afternoon shift, he promised to call as soon as the interview was over. He also asked her to wait at the house until they had time to talk. She didn't. He called, but there was no reply.

He had made a mess of the interview and was feeling depressed. Knowing that they needed the money, he went to his regular job in the maintenance department of a college near Lake Michigan. He called home at every opportunity, but all that he heard was the telephone echoing through the empty rooms. Then, as the afternoon wore on, he telephoned the place of Brenda's employment. She refused to accept his call.

By quitting time, his feelings of depression had worsened, and he wondered what else could go wrong. Well, it so happened that on his way home he had a flat tire. He checked his spare and found to his chagrin that it, too, was flat. His home was in the country, and he had a good three miles to walk to the nearest gas station. Feeling as if the whole world was against him, he began to walk disconsolately along the side of the road. A couple of cars passed, and he tried to hitch a ride. He knew that they must have passed his car with its obvious flat, but no one stopped to help him.

It began to get cold, and he turned the lapels of his coat inward to cover his chest. One hand held his lapels closed and the other was stuck in his pocket. In addition, the side of the road was uneven, and with the sun beginning to set, he had to watch where he was going. As he picked his way along a particularly rough stretch, he chanced to see a copper cent. His first instinct was step over it. But an inner impulse made him stop, stoop down, and pick it up. It had been badly scuffed by car tires that had ground it against the road. Scratch marks made Lincoln's face unrecognizable, yet somehow the words "IN GOD WE TRUST," close to the rim, were still legible. Feeling somewhat like that coin, Brad put it into his pocket and trudged on along the darkening roadway.

Slowly, the simple message "IN GOD WE TRUST" began to percolate through his thought processes. And hope, at first barely measurable, began to revive. By the time he reached the gas station, he had determined to trust in God no matter how bad his circumstances might become.

At Sunday school the first weekend after Brenda's departure, Brad told the members of his class what had happened and asked for prayer. When they began praying about the different requests, no one prayed for him. He felt terribly let down.

After the session was over, the people in his class stood around drinking coffee before going to the service. But no one came to where he was standing to talk to him. And when he moved close to a circle with a view to being included in their discussion, the men seemed embarrassed by his presence.

Some of the women, however, did not share their mates' reticence. They took the opportunity to unload on him. It was evident that Brenda had shared her grievances with them, for they criticized him for not being an attentive husband, a more able father, and a better provider. He felt humiliated. By the time the women had finished their "loving reproof" he felt so low that a frog in the nearby pond would have had to look down to see him.

Brad decided not to go to the church service but instead to go home and pray. As he reached into his pocket for the keys to his car, he felt the roughened surface of the cent next to the key pouch. And once again, a solitary flame of hope began to flicker ever so faintly.

Reminding himself of his decision to trust the Lord no matter what happened, he repeated to himself the words, "IN GOD I TRUST."

Brad and I met weekly at a coffee shop midway between our respective places of employment. We talked, and as we did so I came to understand more clearly than ever before the deep, deep hurts that pressed down on him. Brenda's constant criticism had robbed him of all sense of worth.

Eleven long months dragged by with no visible improvement in Brenda's disposition toward him. Then, one evening around 9:30, she called and asked if she could come over. He agreed. They spent several hours sharing their feelings, during which time Brenda admitted that the separation was her fault. She had allowed some of the women with whom she worked to talk her into it. She now realized that she had made a tragic mistake. Could she come home?

Brad was only too willing to have her and the girls return to him. That night (really early in the morning) they drove to the apartment where she and the girls had been staying. They packed up a few things, wrapped the girls in blankets, and by morning they were all happily ensconced in their own home.

Brad hopes never again to have to go through such a "gut-wrenching" ordeal. The pain he endured has made him a more compassionate husband and father. But he has learned something far more valuable than lessons in human relations. He has learned what real trust in the Lord is all about. He still has the cent in his pocket. Now, whenever anything disturbs his peace, he reminds himself of the supreme essential of his life: IN GOD I TRUST!

ANOTHER TIME, ANOTHER PLACE

David likewise faced the vicissitudes of life. He knew the sting of malicious gossip, the cruel betrayal of those whom he had trusted and called his friends, the unrelenting persecution of King Saul, the powerful opposition of people within his kingdom as well as those nations who shared common borders with Israel, frequent disappointments in his own family, the debilitating effects of a protracted illness, the death of two of his sons, and the needless harm of a civil war.

His answer, most likely penned toward the end of his life, is contained in the psalm that forms a part of the Appendix with which 2 Samuel comes to a close. Its theme can best be described by the words IN GOD I TRUST!

Certain questions, though, crowd into our minds: Did David write this hymn in his old age? And why did he write it?

Before we formulate any possible answers, we must deal with the negative views of those learned men who deny David's authorship of all or portions of this psalm.

Did David Write this Psalm?

Most scholars believe that David wrote only segments of the psalm. But some deny his authorship altogether. Those who think he may have written portions of it allow for at least two redactors (i.e., special editors who selected, arranged, added to, and embellished the material). Others feel that there were probably several more. They believe these men worked at different times between the ninth and seventh centuries B.C. and ultimately brought this psalm to its present form.

The various views of these scholarly individuals are based on what they have chosen to call the "literary integrity" of the psalm. They have noted the different kinds of literature current during these centuries and claim that these presupposed a rise to prominence of distinct literary genre that only came into use after the time of David. In the opinion of these scholars, the hymn falls into two primary divisions: a "song of thanksgiving" and a "thanksgiving for victory." They are convinced that other material involving descriptions of God's activity (22:8-16) and God's reward of His servant (22:21-28) could not have come from the pen of David. The portions they believe David did not write are supposed to have had their origin in the era of Josiah (c. 640-609 B.C.).

While what has been outlined above forms the general basis from which these scholars approach the text, not all agree on the specifics of what David did or did not write. They have also failed to reach a consensus on what was supposedly added and by whom. Such a lack of agreement is disconcerting. Inasmuch as they have clamored loudly for the need to establish the "literary integrity" of the psalm, we find that their imprecision undermines all confidence in them.

Second Samuel 22:1 states that the psalm came from the pen of David. (It also bears a similarity to Psalm 18,[1] whose superscription clearly states that it, too, was the work of David.) But what are we supposed to make of the "literary genre"?

Not long ago my wife and I spent a delightful Saturday at Laguna Beach, about forty miles from where we live. On our way home, I slipped into the tape deck of the car a cassette of Antonin Dvorak's *New World Symphony*. Dvorak lived in the United States for only a brief period, and while he was here he composed this now famous orchestral work. The movements of his grand masterpiece are diverse. There are quiet pastoral sections as well as stirring marches. In between, there are alternately plaintive and lilting interludes.

If the principles of investigation applied to David's psalm were applied to Dvorak's *Symphony* in an endeavor to ascertain its "musical integrity," then inquirers would have to conclude that Dvorak did not compose the *New World Symphony*. And if begrudging consent was given to the possibility that he did write some of it, there would still be dispute over which parts.

Believing as we do that David wrote this psalm, we still have certain questions to answer: (1) Did he pen these words as a young man when the effects of Saul's persecution of him was still fresh in his mind or in his old age as he looked back over the past? And (2) Why was this psalm written? What purpose does it serve?

When Was the Psalm Written?

The majority of conservative Bible scholars who hold to the unity of this psalm believe that all of it was written by David soon after he ascended the throne of Israel. They claim that the persecution he endured at the hand of King Saul would still be fresh in his mind. They opt for its composition close on the heels of the events of 5:17-25, when the Lord had given him rest from all his enemies (7:1).[2]

An even stronger case, though, can be made for its composition toward the end of David's life. There is evidence in the text itself of his mature reflection upon the consistency of God's goodness to him. Most of the psalm is couched in general terms with his enemies unnamed. This would favor the reminiscences of an old man who wanted to pass on to posterity a testament to the faithfulness and reliability of God. Had he included the exciting events associated with his exploits, his readers might have been sidetracked from his central theme as they entered vicariously into the victories God had given him.

The language of the psalm is vividly pictorial. The word pictures lend themselves to a variety of situations so that all might profit from his insights. An example of this is found in verse 1, where God is described as David's rescuer from his enemies, and not only from the Philistines or King Saul.

But there is also an important psychological reason for the psalm's composition toward the end of the life of the king. When David ascended the throne of his people, remembrance of Saul's persecution of him had already begun to fade under the pressure of many important activities. David had been the vassal of Achish for two years, and the duplicity involved in that relationship, as well as his continual need for watchfulness, would not have been conducive to any form of nostalgic retrospection.

The years in Ziklag gave David some respite from Saul's harassment; and when he became king of Judah for seven and a half years, and only after that king over all Israel, the demands of office and the problems associated with the reuniting of the tribes would have crowded the memories of Saul's tyranny from his mind. Only in the sunset period of his life was there both the leisure and the desire that enabled him to look back over his long life and make a record of the kind of trials and sufferings from which the Lord had delivered him.

Other issues also indicate that David wrote the psalm toward the end of his life. He speaks in general terms of his enemies, but as we look for some identification of them we come to realize that his real enemy had been death (see 22:5-7). Such an awareness would be more natural for an older man, for as David surveyed the past he came to see in a new way that each time he went out to battle, it was as if death was trying to take him captive. Had this happened, God's covenant with him could not have been fulfilled. As it is, he can now praise the Lord, for He had always been there to help him and answer his cry for aid.

Another indication of David's age when he wrote this psalm comes from his experience of forgiveness. A writer penning a psalm "in the spirit" or attitude of David would not have been inclined to include the sentiments mentioned in verses 21-25. Only David could write as he did because he rejoiced in God's mercy toward him. His sins of adultery and murder had been cleansed away, and God no longer remembered them (Psalm 103:12. Cf. Isaiah 38:17c; 43:25; 44:22). And knowing his standing before the Lord, his past sins (now forgiven) were no longer an impediment to him.

Second Samuel 22:26-27 also reflects the kind of wisdom that comes only with age and experience. Then, in verses 28ff., as David moves from his praise of God for His faithfulness to his thankfulness for His help and protection, his words may again be seen as grateful reminiscence after a long life. God's promises had been tested and found to be reliable. The Lord had been his strong fortress (i.e., for defense) and had also trained him for battle (i.e., for offense). His help had made him great!

Second Samuel 22:44-49 looks at events after the wars that arose so unexpectedly in chapters 8 and 10. These wars came *after* 7:1 and the time posited by those who believe that David was a young man when he wrote this psalm.

Finally, the conclusion (22:50-51) intimates that this psalm was written in David's old age when he had earned the right to be heard "among the nations." We believe, therefore, that this psalm should be dated between 996 and 971 B.C.

Why Was the Psalm Written?

As a "senior citizen" in Israel, David wanted to leave to posterity a testimony to the praiseworthiness, dependability, and righteousness of God. This fits in well with the sentiments he expressed in Psalm 51:13. The Lord, who was in a covenant relationship with Israel, had maintained *all* of His "contractual obligations." He had also entered into a special covenant with David, and David's clear note of praise is designed to bear witness to the fact that He had fulfilled all of His promises.

But David's apparent exoneration of himself from all wrongdoing (22:21-25) and boasting of the way in which he had slaughtered his enemies (22:35,38-43) appears to us to be out of character. Also those who misunderstand the culture of the times are quick to point out that these sentiments differ from the humility that has been so evident throughout his life.

In defending the basic meaning of these portions of the psalm, it is necessary to point out that David was not claiming to be sinless. In discharging his duties as king, he had remained loyal to the Lord. He had been obedient to His word, and he had acted in his integrity. He had sought in every way to be so identified with the Lord that, as His theocratic representative on earth, God's enemies became his enemies. Then, on a larger scale, the wars the Israelites fought were God's wars,[3] and the vengeance they exacted from their enemies was looked upon as just retribution for the way in which their opponents had flaunted God's laws.

With these matters setting the stage for what is to follow, we are now in a position to attempt an outline of the psalm.

OUTLINE

Unlike Psalm 18, which has divisions in the Hebrew Bible to mark the stages of its development, this psalm has none. While some writers have superimposed the outline of Psalm 18 upon this portion of 2 Samuel—an approach that is both easy and convenient—we have chosen not to follow their example, lest some important truth be lost.

Without being dogmatic, we would like to offer the following tentative outline, which is based on movements within the psalm itself as well as differences in the literary style and content:

- The Praiseworthiness of God (22:1-4)
- The Dependability of God (22:5-20)
- The Righteousness of God (22:21-51)

Dr. William G. Blaikie reminds us that it was quite like David, at the conclusion of his military enterprises, to cast a grateful eye over what had taken place and acknowledge God's goodness to him.[4] It was also in keeping with his Godward relationship that, at the end of his long and eventful life, he would do the same.

THE PRAISEWORTHINESS OF GOD (22:1-4)

God's Protection of His Servant (22:1-3)

Second Samuel 22:1 is a summary statement covering the entire psalm. We are informed that (like Psalms 3; 7; 18; 34; 51; 52; 54; 56; 57; 59; 60; 63; 142) the contents is based on David's personal experiences. The singular use of *day* does not mean "in one day" but rather refers to the period of adversity (i.e., "at the time...") when these events occurred.

Now the severe trials of David's life are over. His many wars, which had been of relatively short duration (the one against the Ammonites being an exception), were all dwarfed by the duration of the persecution he had endured when he was hounded by Saul. Yet, in spite of all his fears, the Lord had sustained him.

David then bursts forth into fervent praise (22:2-3). He expresses his gratitude to the Lord for His many mercies. Yahweh, the covenant-keeping God of Israel, had been his unfailing Source of protection, deliverance, and success. All that he had achieved was due entirely to the good hand of the Lord upon him.

There is no egoism in David's use of *my* and *me*. Such personal references allow us to see the personal side of his Godward relationship. The sentiments he expressed in these verses could not have been voiced by someone whose relationship with the Most High ([*El*] *Elyon*, "[God] Most High") was founded upon externals (e.g., diverse rituals, fasting, repentance from dead works, instruction about washings, and the elemental points of doctrine).

Faith must be personal if it is to work. Its object must be the Lord Himself, not feelings or any other substitute.

God's Praise From His Servant (22:4)

David also praises God for answering his prayers. The tenses of the verbs show that it was his habitual experience to receive answers to his fervent petitions. They also point to God's continual readiness to meet His servant's needs. Often David had been in dire straits (*sār*, "distress"). In his distress he had called upon the Lord, and He had heard his cry.

It is interesting to note that David expressed himself in the historic present tense. What he was describing had been an ongoing experience all his life. And even now, in his old age, the Lord was there to help him.

Many of us have consciously or unconsciously schooled ourselves to draw the main thought from a sentence or paragraph by omitting secondary and tertiary material. We tend, therefore, to read verse 4 as follows: "I call upon Yahweh, and I am saved from my enemies."

And that gives us the essence of David's gratitude. But he said more than that. He added that the Lord was "worthy to be praised." God was not a harsh, austere, unapproachable deity. He is merciful and gracious, long-suffering and abundant in goodness and truth. Martin Luther wrote:

> This doctrine is in tribulation the most ennobling and truly golden. One cannot imagine what assistance such praise of God is in pressing danger. For as soon as you begin to abate, the comfort of your heart will grow; and then God will be called on with confidence. There are some who cry to the Lord and are not heard. Why is this? Because they do not praise the Lord when they cry to Him, but go to Him with reluctance; they have not represented to themselves how sweet the Lord is, but have looked only on their own bitterness. But no one gets deliverance from evil by looking simply upon his evil and becoming alarmed at it; he can get deliverance only by rising above his evil, hanging it on God, and having respect for His goodness. Oh, hard counsel, doubtless, and a rare thing truly, in the midst of trouble to conceive of God as sweet, and worthy to be praised; and when He has removed Himself from us and is incomprehensible, even then to regard Him more intensely than we regard our misfortune that keeps us from Him! Only let one try it, and make the endeavor to praise God, though in little heart for it he will soon experience an enlightenment.[5]

David felt secure in his relationship with the Lord! He had made Yahweh the Object of his trust. Now in verses 5-20 he explains how he was able to overcome the vicissitudes of life.

THE DEPENDABILITY OF GOD (22:5-20)

In the first few verses, David describes in poetic form his brushes with death and prayer to the Lord (22:5-7). Then, in an extended section, he uses different metaphors and figures of speech to portray God's response (22:8-16). All His creative power had been exerted to save David and maintain His covenantal obligations. David's subjective experience of the support the Lord gave him and His deliverance of him (22:17-19) then culminates in the way in which God had graciously rewarded him (22:20).

God's Answer to His Servant's Prayer (22:5-7)

David's troubles had been life-threatening. Sheol (*šĕ'ōl*, the netherworld, the place of the dead) seemed on more than one occasion to have had him in its grasp. In fear of his life he had called out to the Lord. And He heard him. David's words entered into His temple (*hêkāl*, His heavenly abode), and his cry for help came into His ears. The Almighty was moved to action by His servant's petition.

God's Intervention on His Servant's Behalf (22:8-16)

God's general response to David's intercession (22:7) is made specific in verses 8-16. All the forces of His almighty power were mustered in order to deliver His anointed from death. Every agency of nature was involved in helping him. While the Lord's actions are portrayed in a series of metaphors, we can still see that His haste in coming to the side of His anointed was remarkably swift.

The strength God extended to save David may be seen in the parallel between God's rescue of him from the hand of King Saul and His snatching Israel from Pharaoh (cf. 22:16). There is also a poetic similarity between these verses and the "Song of Moses" after the Exodus (Exodus 15:1-18) as well as the physical manifestations of His presence on Mount Sinai (Exodus 19:9, 16-20).

The truth impressed upon us is of God and nature responding to the prayer of one who is in distress.[6]

God's Involvement in His Servant's Trials (22:17-20)

With the next verses we come to a shift in the psalmist's focus. From the theophany[7] of verses 8-16, David passes on to consider his experience of God's interposition. He portrays the Lord sovereignly drawing him out of the waters that threatened to engulf him (22:17). The Almighty was also the One who delivered him from his enemy who was too strong for him (22:18). When disaster threatened and all seemed lost, the Lord was the One upon whom he could lean for rest and support (22:19). And in the end, in contrast to the "straits" he had known, God brought him into a "broad" (*hammerḥāb*, "the open place [with plenty of room]"[8] (22:20).

Dr. William Blaikie writes:

> No miracles had been wrought on David's behalf; unlike Moses and Joshua before him, and unlike Elijah and Elisha after him, he had not had the laws of nature suspended for his protection; yet he could see the hand of God stretched out for him as clearly as if a miracle had been wrought at every turn. Does this not show that ordinary Christians, if they are but careful to watch, and humble enough to watch in a chastened spirit, may find in their history, however quietly it may have glided by, many a token of the interest and care of their Father in heaven? And what a blessed thing to have accumulated through life a store of such providences.[9]

David had. His trust was firmly fixed in the Lord his God.

THE RIGHTEOUSNESS OF GOD (22:21-51)

The final division of this psalm looks at the reasons for, or the grounds of, David's protection and blessing. Dr. David F. Payne has summarized the sweep of these verses for us:

> The psalm thanks God above all for His faithfulness, to nation and to king alike; but in his meditation on all that God had achieved David was conscious of several other aspects of God's character...
> (a) He never acts without a purpose.
> (b) His actions are fully just, and appropriate.
> (c) His promises can be relied on.
> (d) He gives light and help to His servants as they need them.
> (e) He is the *living* God (verse 47).[10]

God's attributes are set in contrast to the gods of the surrounding nations (cf. Psalm 115:3-8). David's goal was to show that the Lord is absolutely trustworthy.

God's Recompense of His Servant (22:12-25)

These verses are not the expression of a proud, self-righteous man; and those who use them to support their belief that the psalm was written early in David's reign (before his sin with Bathsheba) err in two ways: (1) They misunderstand the nature of forgiveness and the restoration of an erring believer to a place of blessing; and (2) they fail to understand these expressions in light of the king and his relationship to the covenant.

In much the same way that the apostle Paul could say, "I have lived before God in all good conscience to this day" (Acts 23:1*b*. cf. Acts 24:16), and when penning a letter to the believers in Philippi, could write: "as touching the righteousness which is by the law, found blameless" (Philippians 3:6*b*. See also Philippians 2:15), so, when applied to David, all David was saying was that he had maintained God's law to the best of his ability. Joyce Baldwin reminds us that "there is a righteousness according to the law, which does not fall into pride and hypocrisy...and the Lord honours it."[11] Properly understood, all David is implying is that in his capacity as king he had faithfully discharged the duties God had entrusted to him.

God's Relationship with His People (22:26-31)

God has a relationship with all His creatures. This includes those who own His right to govern their lives as well as those who do not. David had observed the ways of the Most High for many years. He had noticed His treatment of the kind and the crude, the pure as well as the devious (22:26-27). And he concluded that God's ways with us are to be trusted.

If God is to help us, then there must be an inner harmony (i.e., congruency) between Him and us. The Lord does not lower His standards, but He does accommodate Himself to our individual personality traits. For example, even with someone such as Jacob, who was "twisted" or "perverted" (see Genesis 27:36; 30:25-43; 31:7), He dealt with him in such a way as to try and turn him from his dishonest practices.

Of particular comfort to an afflicted person is the way in which the Lord sustains and saves His own. In David's recollections of God's past dealings with him, he may have had reference to Saul in 22:28*b* and the Lord's help of him when he fled by night to Samuel (22:29. cf. 1 Samuel 19:11-24). Also included is an oblique reference to his early exploits[12] as an "outlaw" when he and a handful of men had waged a type of "guerilla warfare" against the enemies of His people. He had defeated entire troops of soldiers sent against him (22:30. Cf. 23:9).

Having shown ever so briefly this facet of God's righteous dealings with His people, David concludes this part of his psalm (22:31) with a statement affirming God's integrity and reliability. His confidence was firmly established in the Lord.

God's Right to Be Worshiped (22:32-36)

David's long and eventful life has given him the right to testify to the superiority and reliability of the Lord (*El*, the Mighty One) over all other deities. Others may worship the creation of men's hands (cf. Psalm 135:15-18), even to the point of embracing and elevating these false gods to prominence over people and nations. None of them, however, can compare with Yahweh who provides a secure place of refuge *(sûr,* "rock") for those who trust Him. He alone can be depended on in all types of adversity. His favor is shown to the "blameless," who is then established in his way (22:33).

Dr. A. F. Kirkpatrick's comments on verses 32-35 are particularly noteworthy. He describes

> the unique character of Jehovah, to Whom alone David owes all that he is. Observe how he recognizes that the advantages of physical strength and energy, important qualifications in times when the king was himself the leader of his people in battle, were gifts of God; yet that it was not these which saved him and made him victorious, but Jehovah's care and help.[13]

Such had been the Lord's endowment of him—in giving him agility and strength—that he was given sure footing and success in all the places (i.e., situations) into which the Lord led him. Then, in his old age, as he looked back over the years, he became more and more aware of how much the Lord had helped him. Is it any wonder that he readily acknowledged that God's condescension (in stooping down to assist him) had made him great?

God's Reward of His Servant (22:37-49)

The initial figure of speech, "You have enlarged my steps" (22:37), is unclear. Either David had in mind an experience in which his path seemed to widen so that he could progress unhampered and unhindered by obstacles, or, as in the case of the long-distance runner, God had enlarged his capacity so that he could lengthen his stride.

The former looks at ease of movement, whereas the latter has in mind an increased capacity. Most likely the latter is correct. If this is so, then the difficulties David faced remained. God did not remove them. But He helped him cope with them.

This increased ability also enabled David to pursue, overtake, and destroy his enemies (22:38-39). These opponents had gone into battle trusting in "other gods." They had engaged Israel in hand-to-hand combat in the name of their deity. But Israel's enemies had been routed. The part played by the Lord is now seen to interface with the role David assumed. Verses 40-43 restate how the Lord had helped him, and how David put down all who opposed him.

God's Vindication of His Servant (22:44-46)

In keeping with the blessing of Moses (Deuteronomy 33:29), Israel's enemies had eventually capitulated to God's king. They had also brought tribute and feigned obedience to him. Also such was David's renown that as soon as some of the nations heard that he was coming toward them, they willingly become his vassals.

All of this prefigures the Millennium, when Christ will reign over the kingdoms of the world. The righteous will rejoice and even His enemies will give feigned obedience to Him (Psalm 66:3-4). His worship, however, will be established and those who have willingly submitted themselves to Him will sing His praises.

God Worshiped By His Servant (22:47-51)

Like some great symphony—with its various movements, some soft and some tempestuous, at times worshipful and at other times full of strident movement—that eventually comes to a grand climax causing people to break into applause, so this psalm concludes on a note that establishes God's sovereignty in the mind of the reader. Based upon his knowledge of the Lord and his experiences of the Most High, David could say with confidence "*Yahweh lives.*" He was the Object of his trust (see Psalm 31:6). He had answered his prayers. He had fulfilled all His promises. He had also vindicated His anointed and raised his standard above those who formerly opposed David (Psalm 31:14-15).

As we near the end of this psalm we need to understand who is meant by the statement "You have rescued me from the violent man." Most commentators believe it to be a reference to Saul. But David had not hesitated to mention Saul by name in verse 1, so why should he not do so again? Others, with greater probability, think it may be an indirect reference to Absalom. Because the allusion is veiled, there is good reason to believe that David has reference to his son who had violently torn the kingdom from his hands.

Whereas David may have felt that, during the civil war and his absence from Jerusalem,[14] the nations surrounding Israel might have taken advantage of the situation and attacked Jerusalem, they had not done so for the Lord was preserving the kingdom for His anointed. David, then, could testify to the fact that the Almighty had sovereignly maintained his right to the throne during the crisis caused by Absalom's defiance of the theocracy (cf. Psalm 55:23). He also concludes his psalm with another statement in the historic present tense:

> "[Yahweh is] a tower of salvation (or deliverance) to His king, showing lovingkindness to His anointed, to David and to his seed to the ages (i.e., forever)" (22:51).

God's great promise to David in 7:8-16 had been fulfilled in his lifetime; and based upon His validation of the covenant the Lord had made with him, David was sure that it would continue in the lives of his descendants.

The abiding thought from this psalm is God's sovereignty shown in delivering the afflicted, coupled with His abasement of the proud (cf. 22:28). Though David has been prominent throughout (for he has been recounting his personal experiences), he wanted to assure us that God's blessings are not reserved for a select few. His strength and resources are available to all who call upon Him in sincerity and truth.

Some will raise an objection. As with Little Faith in John Bunyan's insightful book *The Pilgrim's Progress*, they will claim that, on account of the numerous buffetings and beatings they have had throughout their lives, their faith is insufficient for the trials they face. To such (and there are many of them, for they fill the offices of psychologists) we would like to offer some words of encouragement.

One of D. L. Moody's favorite verses was Isaiah 12:2, where we read, "I will trust and not be afraid." He used to point out that a person can travel to heaven either first class or tourist class. Those in first class can hold on to Isaiah 12:2, while those in tourist class can hold on to Psalm 56:3, which states: "At what time I am afraid, I will trust in You." Of course, a first-class passage is preferable, but for those who cannot at this time attain to such a level of spirituality, they can nonetheless trust in the Lord to the best of their ability. And later on, they can upgrade their ticket to first class. The key to such progress lies in the use they are able to make of the Word of God (see Hebrews 5:13-14).

INSPIRING WORDS AND A LASTING TRIBUTE

2 Samuel 23:1-39

At one time, the parting counsel of a dying relative or friend was treasured by those who remained behind. Their admonition or commendation was taken seriously. And perhaps there still are situations where this is true today.

In saying good-bye to friends and loved ones, those who are soon to depart from this earthly scene experience a mixture of emotions. On the one hand they may want to pass on information they believe is vital to the future happiness of those who are near and dear to them, and on the other hand they may also wish to express their gratitude to those whose love and companionship has enriched their lives.

We are given examples of such admonitions in the Bible. One is to be found in Genesis 48:1–49:33. There, for example, we read of Jacob calling for his sons to his bedside so that he could bless them. Then, in John chapters 14 through 16 we learn of Christ's parting counsel to His disciples. In 2 Timothy 4:1-8, we note Paul's final charge to his young protege, Timothy. In 2 Peter 3:1-7 and 14-18, we take note of encouragement and hope with which Peter concluded his letter. And the apostle John, in 1 John 2:7–5:21, gives those whom he had won to faith in Christ his parting counsel.

Although 2 Samuel 23 begins with the phrase, "These are the last words of David," (23:1), we need to realize that this does not mean David never spoke again. These were his last words to the nation. They are not his final utterances because, before his death, he will give a charge to young Solomon (see 1 Kings 2:1-9). What we have here, therefore, is a unique address to the people whom David has served in one capacity or another for approximately fifty-five years.

David's "last testament" needs to be processed carefully if its truths are to be properly understood. In this prophetic (*ně'ūm*, "oracle, utterance") psalm, he expresses his confidence in the Lord. He believes that He has fulfilled His promise to him, and will continue to do so to his descendants after him.[1]

When this chapter is compared with the preceding one, it will at once become evident that, while 2 Samuel 22 is concerned with the past, this psalm looks to the future. The earlier hymn of praise extolled God's goodness to David in hearing his prayers, delivering him from his enemies, and blessing him above and beyond anything he could have requested. This psalm speaks of David's house (i.e., dynasty) and, in its descriptive statements, anticipates the reign of David's Son, the Lord Jesus Christ.[2]

OUTLINE

An outline of this chapter must include an understanding of David's prophecy as well as his commendation of those who had helped him gain and retain the throne. These men had showed uncommon courage and devotion, and it is fitting that their contribution be remembered. David's tribute to his "mighty men," therefore, is most apropos, and its place after his words to the nation brings two related thoughts together. As we read through the list of names, we find that some of these brave champions had already passed on to their reward. But their deaths did not stop David from remembering their deeds. Their names rightly belong in this special "hall of fame."

The material may be outlined as follows:

- The Last Words of the King (23:1-7)
    The Identification of the Prophet (23:1-3*a*)
    The Description of the Ruler (23:3*b*-4)
    The Assumption of the Prophet (23:5)
    The Condemnation of the Wicked (23:6-7)

- The Loyal Warriors of the King (23:8-39)
    The First Triad (23:8-12)
    The Actions of David's Friends (23:13-17)
    The Second Triad (23:18-23)
    The Roster of the Rest (23:24-39)

THE LAST WORDS OF THE KING (23:1-7)

The poetic imagery of David's parting thoughts is such that each figure of speech or expression is important. At no time can the Bible student become complacent, for should this happen, some important truths are sure to be lost.

The Identification of the Prophet (23:1-3a)

In much the same way that the Song of Moses (Deuteronomy 32) is followed by the blessing of the people, so David's great song of triumph is followed by this, his last inspired message to the nation. It is noteworthy that David does not allude to his human achievements but dwells instead on his relationship with his God. This, in the final analysis, is all that counts when one knows that he or she is soon to take leave of this life.

As we read these verses, we are at once struck by the formality and solemnity of David's remarks. God had elevated him to the throne of His people and given him the ability to compose hymns of praise. And this he has done. Now, however, the emphasis is not on himself but on what the Spirit of the Lord is saying through him. His words, therefore, become a *māšāl*, "wise saying." They are also God-breathed (cf. Numbers 12:2,6,8 for an example of one other instance when God spoke to His people in this way) and of great significance to David's posterity.

The Description of the Ruler (23:3b-4)

The next part of this prophetic psalm begins in a dramatic way. The original has only six words. They provide the profile of God's ideal King ruling in perfect justice, controlled and guided by the reverential awe of God. Verse 4 depicts in figurative language the benefits of His reign: His appearance will be like the life-giving sunshine of a cloudless morning. And blessings, like the rich foliage that clothes the land as a result of the united influences of both sun and rain, will spread over all the world.[3]

Dr. William Blaikie has drawn attention to the difficulty of believing that this psalm refers solely to David's immediate successors.

> If the prophecy should bear on nothing more remarkable than some earthly successor of David, all this preliminary glorification would be singularly out of place. It would be like a great procession of heralds and the flourishing of trumpets in an earthly kingdom to announce an event of the most ordinary kind, the repeal of a tax or the appointment of an officer.[4]

The emphasis of these words is obviously on a Ruler—One who

will exercise His authority righteously—and who will conduct all His affairs in the "fear of the Lord" (Isaiah 11:2).[5] The description given of the Kingdom (23:4) has to be of the Millennium, for a beneficial influence comes over the whole earth as a result of this King's administration.[6]

The Assumption of the Prophet (23:5)

David sees "his house" (i.e., dynasty) playing a role in Christ's Millennial Kingdom. He knows that he and his descendants will fall short of the ideal, but God's promise is sure (cf. 7:12ff.). The Lord had established an everlasting covenant with him, "ordered in all things and secured."

Then, as Dr. A. F. Kirkpatrick has shown, David expresses his confidence that, in due time, the Lord will bring to completion the salvation He promised to him and his house.[7] Though this verse presents difficulties in translation (and uses the kind of Hebraism in which a positive thought is framed in what seems to us to be a negative way), the thrust is on David's assertion of confidence in God's promise.

The Condemnation of the Wicked (23:6-7)

These verses contain a powerful corrective that adequately answers those who think of Christ's rule as showing only mercy. Isaiah predicted the "day of vengeance of our God" (Isaiah 61:2; see also Isaiah 34:8; 35:4; 59:17; 63:4). He also saw another vision of the Messiah marching triumphantly from Bozrah with His garments stained with blood (Isaiah 63:1-6; see also Isaiah 34:6, 8-10). And in the Book of Revelation the apostle John described Christ as clothed for battle with blood staining His robe (Revelation 19:1-6, 11-21).

Those who will be excluded from the Kingdom are described as "worthless" (*belīya'al*, "evil [men]." Cf. 2 Timothy 3:13). They are likened to thorns (i.e., thorny scrub or, in parts of the U.S., tumbleweed) that a farmer gathers and burns (cf. Matthew 3:10; 13:30. See also Malachi 4:1-3; Luke 19:27; Hebrews 6:8). So as not to injure himself, the farmer uses one kind of implement to dislodge the bush from its place, and another to carry it and throw it into the fire (23:7).

Being burned to ashes is the only thing that can be done with thorn bushes, for they are good for nothing else (and so it is with the wicked, cf. Isaiah 33:12). All of this impresses upon us the fact that people cannot be neutral toward Christ. In this life they either own His right to rule over them, or in the life to come they will forever be separated from Him (cf. Matthew 13:40-43).

As we summarize this psalm we find that the Lord has given us a retrospective explanation of David and his house (dynasty), with the prospective hope of Christ's eventual return.[8] The temporary application is found in the way those who do justice and walk in reverential awe of the Lord will be blessed. Then they, in turn, will become a means of blessing to others. But those who love what is evil (i.e., who are "men of belial") will have their works burned up.

THE LOYAL WARRIORS OF THE KING (23:8-39)

From the last words of David to the nation we pass on to consider his lasting tribute to those who gave so willingly of themselves through all the difficult years of his life. In a sense, these men prefigure the kind of leaders Christ will bring with Him when He returns to earth, puts down His enemies, and sets up His Kingdom.

The inspired writer of Chronicles introduces those included in this "hall of fame" with the following explanation:

> And these [were] the heads of the warriors who [were] to David (i.e., whom David had), who made themselves strong with him in his kingdom, with all Israel, as the word of Yahweh (i.e., according to the word of Yahweh), over Israel (1 Chronicles 11:10).

A knowledge of who these men were and what they did enables us to "understand the human instrumentality by which [David] achieved so brilliant a success." We are then able to gain an understanding "of the kind of men by whom [David] was helped, the kind of spirit by which they were animated, and their intense personal devotion to [him]."[9]

One point must not be overlooked: Joab is *not* in mentioned in this list!

The First Triad (23:8-12)

When David penned the words of his prophecy and gave oversight to the compilation of this list, he was secure in his position as the nation's leader. This is seen from the way he readily delegated authority to those under him.

If the three mentioned in 23:8-12 were his "four star" generals, then Abishai, Benaiah, and Ittai the Gittite would have been his "three star" generals, and those included in verses 24-39 would have been in the "two star" category.

The first group, called "the Three," consisted of Josheb-basshebeth (most often referred to as Jashobeam, 1 Chronicles 11:11), Eleazar, and Shammah. They probably served in a similar capacity to the U.S. president's "joint chiefs of staff." As such they were an integral part of David's war cabinet and were responsible for the security of the nation.

Rising Above the Crowd (23:8). Josheb-basshebeth had joined David in Ziklag (1 Chronicles 12:1,6; see also 1 Chronicles 27:2),[10] while David's movements were still restricted on account of King Saul. Josheb-basshebeth, and those who accompanied him, were equipped with bows and slings, and used both right hand and left to sling stones and shoot arrows. They were from the tribe of Benjamin (1 Chronicles 12:1-3*a*,6), and at one time had been numbered among Saul's elite guard. This special relationship entitled them to be called "Saul's kinsmen."

Josheb-basshebeth is identified as the son of Hachmon in 1 Chronicles 11:11, but he is spoken of as the "son of Tachemon" in 2 Samuel 23:8. He is also referred to as the "son of Zabdiel" in 1 Chronicles 27:2. The apparent discrepancy between Hachmon and Tachemon can easily be explained. In Hebrew the letters T (ת) and H (ח) are very similar. It would have been easy for a copyist to make a mistake and take the one letter for the other.

Hachmon was of the line of Korah (1 Chronicles 12:6). How, then, could he also be a descendant of Zabdiel? Zabdiel had settled in one of the cities of northern Judah. In the course of time, he became prominent in the area, and his name was given to the territory in which he lived (cf. 1 Chronicles 27:32). In keeping with Semitic custom, those born in this area were spoken of as his "sons." Because the border between Judah and Benjamin was constantly changing, Josheb-basshebeth grew to manhood within the territory of the tribe of Benjamin.[11] There he trained to become a soldier and in time achieved recognition as a skilled warrior (cf. 1 Chronicles 12:2). He must have been quite young when he was included in Saul's army, and he most likely saw action against the Philistines. He also took part in the several hunts for David, whom he had been told was a dangerous insurrectionist. But when David twice spared the king's life, Josheb-basshebeth's attitude began to change.

Ultimately, Saul's harsh policies caused him (and several others with him) to defect to David. When he arrived in Ziklag, he found it full of defectors who, like himself, had fled the tyranny and oppression of Saul's rule.

Of course, Josheb-basshebeth shared with David and the rest all of the fluctuating fortunes that were a part of the insecurity of an outlaw's life. Included was the abortive march to Aphek, the return to Ziklag, and the pursuit of the Amalekites (1 Samuel 30:1-26). It is highly possible that, when David and his four hundred tired men attacked the Amalekites, Josheb-basshebeth killed the eight hundred enemy warriors mentioned in 23:8.

It is also true that in 1 Chronicles 11:11 we are informed that "he lifted up his spear against three hundred whom he killed at one time." The context there has to do with the wars against the Philistines, so the two incidents do not refer to the same battle.

Josheb-basshebeth then gave David "strong support" as he organized his kingdom. In addition to his valor on the battlefield, he was also a good administrator. He was assigned a division of twenty-four thousand men with which to safeguard the kingdom for one month each year (1 Chronicles 27:1). He not only proved to be a capable leader of men, but he also modeled for those under him the principles of integrity, loyalty, courage, perseverance, and versatility.

Making a Difference (23:9-10). The second "four star" general within this triad was Eleazar (cf. 1 Chronicles 27:4, where he is named Dodai). The information given us about him illustrates the benefit of a godly heritage, the value of his fearless courage, and concludes with the significance of his notable victory.

We consider first his heritage. It is easy to pass over the name Eleazar. It is foreign to us and does not have the familiar sound of Brad or Jeff, Scott or Wayne. It points, however, to something significant in the lives of his parents.

Eleazar means "God has helped." Apparently, in naming their son, Eleazar's parents did so in grateful recognition of the way the Lord had helped them. The precise circumstances are not known to us. His parents, however, chose him to be the perpetual reminder of God's past goodness. And his life was molded by their attitude and Godward relationship. What he perceived in them exerted an influence upon him, and this had a direct impact upon all he did.[12] Eleazar grew up to trust in the Lord as the One who helps us in all the many trials of life.

Second, Israel's battles against the Philistines were all hard fought (cf. Psalm 60). Victory rarely came easily. On one occasion, following an initial engagement, David's men were forced to withdraw (cf. 1 Chronicles 11:13). They retreated into the hills where the Philistine chariots could not follow them.

It was while they were engaged in a hasty withdrawal that Eleazar found himself fighting alone. Refusing to be intimidated by the opposition, he took his stand in a field of ripened barley (cf. 1 Chronicles 11:13b-14) and completely devastated all who came against him. For some reason, the Philistine chariots could not come up to the small plateau where the barley was growing, so the infantry was forced to engage him in hand-to-hand combat.

"And Yahweh saved them by a great victory" is the Biblical writer's way of reminding us of the sovereignty of God in human affairs (23:10*a*). After the battle, the people who had fled returned to the scene of the fracas but only to take the spoils of war from those who had been slain (23:10*b*).

So hard did Eleazar fight that his hand became "weary" of holding his sword. He then suffered from painful muscle spasms so that he could not release his sword when the fighting was over. Only then could others help him by prying open his fingers. After this they had to massage the stiffened muscles so that the pain was eventually eased and he regained the use of his hand.

Eleazar was also made the leader of a band of twenty-four thousand men (1 Chronicles 27:4), showing that his administrative gifts developed alongside his military prowess.

Overcoming Formidable Odds (23:11). The third "four star" general to be included in the first triad is Shammah. The notable deed that caused his name to be enshrined in God's Word took place at Lehi on the border of Philistia and Judea (cf. Judges 15:9-20). The Philistines had come up to plunder the crops of God's people and destroy all that they could not carry away.

As we look briefly at this passage, we note Shammah's personal integrity, the pressing necessity that suddenly faced him, and how he handled external threats. The writer once again records Israel's flight before their enemies. As with Eleazar, Shammah found himself fighting alone. He took his stand in the midst of a field of lentils, and completely repulsed each and every Philistine attempt to overpower him. The sacred historian once again reminds his readers of the Lord's activity behind the scenes: "And Yahweh brought about a great victory" (23:11-12).

What was the response of the people to such valor? We do not know, but if the experience of David and his men in 1 Samuel 23 is any indication, the public were probably quick to praise him and then just as quick to forget what he had done.

In summary, it has been said that each of us is three people: "Who we think we are, who our friends think we are, and who we really are." It often takes a crisis to reveal a person's true character, and in the case of Shammah it was a Philistine invasion. The crisis revealed him to be a man of courage, determination, and perseverance.

The Lessons of History. In thinking of this brave trio, I am reminded of something Winston Churchill once said. These were the dark days of World War II, and the hope of the British had almost faltered on account of the Nazi war-machine that was sweeping across Europe like a huge tidal wave. Everything was being enveloped in its path.

Mr. Churchill had gone to high school at Harrow, and the principal and faculty members decided to invite him back to speak to the students. The date was October 29, 1941. After a boring and loquacious introduction, Mr. Churchill rose to his feet and walked to the podium. Everyone was expecting an equally long address. What they heard that night was unexpected. The great orator's words were brief but weighty. All he said to the assembled group was,

> "Never give in, never give in, never, never, never, never—in nothing, great or small, large or petty—never give in except to convictions of honour and good sense."

And he sat down. The convocation was over. The impact of his words, however, remained. And what he advocated the schoolboys do was what Josheb-basshebeth, Eleazar, and Shammah had done. These men did not know what it was like to give in. They never gave up no matter how formidable the opposition. The only things to which they yielded were principles of righteousness and honesty, devotion to duty and loyalty to David. And God worked through them to achieve His purpose for His people.

The Actions of David's Friends (23:13-17)

Having introduced us to the inner circle of David's "mighty men" (known as "the Three"), the writer now provides a vignette of the faithfulness and affection that was characteristic of "the Thirty." The incident took place when the Philistines were so well entrenched in the land that they had even taken possession of Bethlehem.

In these few verses we find illustrated for us the freedom friendship inspires (23:13); the loyalty friendship shows (23:14); the desire friendship expresses (23:15); the kind of deeds friendship accomplishes (23:16); and the love friendship acknowledges (23:17).

David's men had freedom to return to their homes and farms as occasion required. No compulsion was laid upon them. His relationship with them was non-possessive. On the occasion preserved for posterity by the inspired penman, David and some of his followers were in a cave (probably Adullam). It was summer, and the streams from which they usually drew water had dried up.

In Israel, the drought ends in late November/early December. This is a time for sowing wheat and barley. It is followed by the winter rains, which provide the necessary moisture for the generation of the seed. These "latter rains" occur in March/April (cf. Deuteronomy 11:17; see also Deuteronomy 28:12,24; 2 Chronicles 6:26-27; Psalm 84:6; Jeremiah 3:3; 5:24; etc.). At the time of our story, David and his men would have had to draw water from springs at some distance from the cave.

It is estimated that each person needs a *minimum* of a gallon of water per day. More is required for washing. The difficulty of sustaining life had been increased because the Philistines had overrun the land. They had taken possession of the strategic valley of Rephaim and had penetrated into the hill country. David and his men were between the Philistines (to the east) and Philistia (to the west). They ran the risk of being detected by reinforcements going up the valley or patrols from Socoh looking for them or soldiers on furlough going down the valley toward Gath or Ekron.

Late one afternoon, when the sun's rays had baked the surrounding land so that the air shimmered in the heat and the day's water supply had been used up, David happened to express the wish that he would like a drink from the well at Bethlehem (23:15).

During his boyhood, he must often have refreshed himself at this well, and the remembrance of those experiences made him appreciate what he had then taken for granted. In verbalizing his thoughts, David had no idea anyone would act upon them.

Without saying a word to him, three of his close associates decided to try to get him a goatskin of water from the well. It was a hazardous task, for it necessitated breaking through the enemy lines in order to get to the well and then having to face a hornet's nest of activity on their way back.

These determined men not only broke through the enemy ranks and drew the water, but also fought their way past the Philistines on their return. Then they brought the water to David. His surprise when they gave him the skin of cool water must have been great! But at once he saw beyond the water to their love and sacrifice, and in deep gratitude he poured out the water "before Yahweh," saying:

> "Far be it from me, O Yahweh, that I should do this (i.e., drink the water). [Is this not] the blood of the men who went with their lives (i.e., who took their lives in their hands)" (23:17).

His friends understood his actions. They realized that he was moved to worship as a result of their gift—of which he believed himself to be unworthy—and they did not take offense.

There are those, however, who might have misunderstood the motive of one such as David. Some might have thought him too pious, and others might have concluded that he did not adequately appreciate what his friends had done for him. Such misunderstanding might easily lead to a breakdown in the relationship.

If this seems improbable, think of how easily this kind of situation can arise at Thanksgiving or Christmas or a birthday party. A grandparent or spouse or child gives a gift of intrinsic worth to which the recipient attaches little value. Inadequate appreciation is shown, and the giver feels slighted. He or she may then climb a mifftree and nurse a grievance. And such misunderstanding might blight a relationship for years to come.

David's friends understood his motives. Their hearts were in tune with his. They also realized that, in pouring out the water before the Lord, he was in fact honoring them.

Why is it that we are seldom able to form such friendships today?

Dr. Ignace Lepp, in *The Ways of Friendship*,[13] believes that many of us have an inability to develop deep, meaningful friendships because, in part at least, we lack the ability to sustain meaningful communication. In his book, he points out that all of us derive satisfaction from *emotional* communication through the giving of ourselves in dialogue and other expressions of warmth and intimacy. It is this kind of human communication that enables us to share with another our hopes and needs, problems and disappointments, and find in our friend a sympathetic ear, a wise counselor, and a source of continual encouragement.

True friendships are built upon a foundation of shared beliefs, values, and goals (cf. John 13:34; 17:21). With *acceptance* there should be reciprocal loyalty (cf. Job 17:5; Psalm 122; Proverbs 16:28; 17:17; 18:24); the ignoring of generation gaps (2 Samuel 3:8; Proverbs 27:10); the expectation of consistency (contrast 2 Samuel 16:16-17); the exclusion of slander (Psalm 7:4; 15:3); the demonstration of devotion (2 Samuel 15:32ff.; Acts 24:23; 2 Timothy 1:16); and the promise of prayerful support (Job 42:8-10). Sharing—giving and receiving—is an integral part of friendship.

In Scripture we are told to exercise prudence in choosing friends. We also take note of the fact that true friendships become more intimate and more enduring than natural relationships. And as friendships mature, we realize the need to speak the truth in love (Proverbs 27:6).

The Second Triad (23:18-23)

From the story of the love of David's friends we move to consider the second triad of generals. It is made up of those who did not attain to the first group (23:19*b*, 22-23). Only two men are named, Abishai and Benaiah. The Biblical text reads:

> And Abishai, the brother of Joab, the son of Zeruiah, he [was] the head of the three; and he lifted up (i.e., brandished) his spear against three hundred, [and] killed [them], and he had a name among the three. Was he not honored more than the three? And he was to them (viz., the Thirty) for a commander (i.e., he became their commander), but he did not come to the [first] three (23:18-19).

Harnessing the Power Within (23:18-19). Abishai's life exemplifies the importance of loyalty, zeal, and devotion. He was possibly the oldest of Zeruiah's three sons (1 Chronicles 2:16) and must have joined David in the Cave of Adullam, even though we do not read of him until he accompanied David into Saul's camp one night (1 Samuel 26).

Saul and his elite corp of three thousand men had come into the land of Ziph looking for David. They had gone to sleep, and this gave David and Abishai the opportunity to creep in among them. It required great daring, but Abishai was equal to the challenge. He wanted to kill Saul, but David restrained him.

Later, after David had become king in Hebron, Abishai was a representative of the southern tribes in the battle that took place at the "Field of Daggers" near the pool of Gibeon (2:16-23). It was at this time that his younger brother, Asahel, was killed.

After David had been crowned king over all Israel the Ammonites began preparing for war with them. David did not wait to be attacked but sent Joab to engage them in battle. When David's forces found themselves caught in a pincers movement, the army was divided into two, and Abishai was given command of one division (10:7-14).

Many years later, in the battle associated with Absalom's rebellion (18:1-8), Abishai was again honored with command of one third of David's army. And finally, he distinguished himself in David's last battle by killing the giant who was intent upon killing his sovereign (21:15-17).

It was fitting that Abishai should be accorded a place with David's "mighty men."

No Room For Compromise (23:20-23). The second of David's "three star" generals was Benaiah. He exemplifies the importance of developing the right attitudes (23:20*a*). The Biblical record gives two illustrations that show the value of being proactive (23:20*b*-21). Then it concludes by subtly hinting at the need to handle disappointments wisely (23:22-23).

Benaiah's attitudes were developed in a godly home. His grandfather and father were warrior-priests (1 Chronicles 27:5) who lived in Kabzeel, a small village on the border between Judah and Edom (see Joshua 15:21). They honed Benaiah's beliefs, values, and goals by setting him an example of active righteousness. Their fearless dedication to duty made a lasting impression upon him.

Life was hard in this arid, semi-desert area. Bands of raiding Bedouin would descend unexpectedly upon the village at night or attack shepherds in an outlying area. It became necessary for each man to defend what little he had. And young boys in the village, as they grew toward manhood, had to acquire skill in self-defense and hand-to-hand combat.

Benaiah's perseverance in acquiring these skills is noteworthy. As he attained manhood, he became known for his "mighty deeds." He did not become great all at once. There was methodical growth that eventually led to acts of bravery. These paved the way for the feats of daring that are forever associated with his name.

Earlier in our study of 2 Samuel, we read of an act of bravery that earned Benaiah renown. It probably occurred when Israel was forced to defend its border against the Moabites. Benaiah showed real courage when he tackled the "two Ariels" and killed them. My late friend, Dr. Ray C. Stedman, believed that these "Ariels" were two crack battalions. This is possible. I am inclined to believe that, based upon the derivation of the word, they were most likely powerful lion-like warriors (from *'ari*, "lion," and *el*, "god," lit. "lion of god"). There is every probability that they were aided by demonic forces when they went to war, for they were thought to be invincible. Their presence boosted the morale of the Moabite soldiers who felt that, with them augmenting their forces, they could not be conquered.

These two Ariels had most likely gone through an initiation that probably included killing a lion and perhaps drinking some of its blood (for this was thought to contain the strength of the lion and in this way the lion's strength passed on to its killer). If this is so, then their cultic belief was similar to Mithraism, which involved the drinking of the blood of a bull. Benaiah killed these two Moabites and achieved a remarkable victory for Israel.

Another illustration is of Benaiah's ability to be proactive. It also involved a lion and occurred one wintry day. Driven by hunger, this lion had left the hills and come down to a village. Snow was lying on the ground, and it blurred visual distinctions. Roaming about in search of food, the lion had fallen into a pit. It would have been easy for Benaiah to walk by and ignore the danger this trapped animal posed for the women and children of the village. Furthermore, no one was standing on the sidelines to either goad him into an act of reckless bravery or cheer him on to success.

Disregarding any danger to himself, Benaiah jumped into the pit and single-handedly took on this hungry, frightened, and angry beast. It was not an easy task in such cramped quarters, and in all likelihood no one would have known of what he had done had they not seen the claw marks on his body.

The next incident illustrating Benaiah's ability to size up a situation and take appropriate action concerns his single combat with an Egyptian. This man was of impressive stature—about seven and one-half feet tall. His spear was about ten feet long and exceeded in thickness the size of a rounded four-by-four. By contrast, all Benaiah had was a short club.

Once again Benaiah acted decisively. Possibly avoiding the Egyptian's first lunge, he wrested the spear from the Egyptian's hand and then killed him with it. His training had developed his skills, and these were now used in the service of his God and his king.

The final point brought before us concerns the way in which he handled disappointment. He "had a name as well as the three" but he did not attain to "the first three." He was not included in the inner circle of David's advisors. Benaiah, however, did not allow disappointment to detract from his devotion to duty. When it was found that he could be trusted, he was placed over David's bodyguard (comprising the Cherethites and Pelethites).

Completing the Triad. But who was the third person of this triad? Several individuals (e.g., Amasa) have been named, but none of them are truly viable. The only one worthy of serious consideration is Ittai of Gath. If Abishai was over "the Thirty," and Benaiah over the Cherethites and Pelethites, the only remaining group of warriors not mentioned so far were the Gittites. It seems logical, therefore, that Ittai of Gath, as the leader of the Gittites, should be honored as the third member of the second triad (cf. 15:18b-22; 18:1-2).

Little is known of Ittai. He most likely joined forces with David during his outlaw years and went with him to Ziklag. In time he came to command a special army of six hundred Philistines who were loyal to David. He also came to trust in Yahweh, David's God. Such was his devotion to Israel's king that he was prepared to endure the changing fortunes of life as an exile rather than serve with anyone else.

That someone's name needs to be added to the second group of three is evident from the total given in 23:39. Only thirty-six names are listed, yet we are told that all together there were thirty-seven. It seems logical to regard Ittai as the third "three star" general because of his captaincy of a group of men not otherwise included in this summation of David's fighting force.

Verses 18-23 underscore for us the privilege of serving even in a secondary capacity. Not everyone can be "Number One." The late Dwight D. Eisenhower used to tell a story that illustrates the point of serving competently in whatever capacity we are in. During his White House years, he had as an assistant a man of unusual competence. On one occasion he offered him a more responsible position that carried with it a considerable increase in salary. It was a tempting offer. After giving the matter serious thought, Eisenhower's aide declined the position, saying:

> "I am a No. 2 man—and I think a good one—but I am not a No. 1 man. I am not fitted for such a job."[14]

This assistant, like David's able subordinates who "did not attain to the first three," continued to serve well in a secondary capacity.

The Roster of the Rest (23:24-29)

The final group shows David's ability to captain men of varied backgrounds—Israelites from different tribes, some from the north and some from the south; and foreigners from Ammon, Anatolia, and Philistia.

Asahel, of course, was David's nephew, the son of his sister, Zeruiah. He had been killed by Abner soon after David became king in Hebron. For one month every year, he had exercised leadership over twenty-four thousand men. During this time he had the responsibility of protecting Israel's borders (1 Chronicles 27:7).

Elhanan was from Bethlehem and may have been a lifelong friend of King David.

Shammah and Elika were Harodites and were most likely from a small village near Bethlehem. As with Asahel, Shammah was also entrusted with the responsibility of maintaining the nation's independence one month each year (1 Chronicles 27:8).

Helez the Paltite may have been a descendant of Caleb, for Pelet was of the extended family of Caleb (1 Chronicles 2:47). Ira the Tekoaite was of equal rank with Asahel and Shammah. He, too, was placed in charge of the sixth division of the army (1 Chronicles 27:9).

Little or nothing is known of most of the men who served David so loyally (23:27-38), and often the town from which they came was an insignificant one. And certain names were borne by more than one person (e.g., Ittai, Benaiah, Shammah).

Eliam (23:34), the son of Ahithophel, was Bathsheba's father (though some commentators dispute this). And David was not forgetful of his friend Uriah. Far from wanting his name to be forgotten, he insured that it be remembered!

Very capable men need a very capable leader. David was described by his own men as "the lamp of Israel" (21:17). He was valued by those who served under him because of his godliness, vision, and courage. Without him, the people would have been bereft of a vital source of illumination and inspiration (*viz.*, his creative impulse, imagination, military genius, and originality). It was precisely because Israel realized the value of the leadership provided for them by God that they were prepared to follow David wherever he led them.

23

TURNING TIMES OF TESTING INTO TRIUMPHS OF GOD'S GRACE

2 Samuel 24:1-25

In her autobiography, *One More Time*, comedienne Carol Burnett relates a story that illustrates for us the nature of guilt and the grace of forgiveness. She describes that, as a child, she spent a lot of time with her grandmother. Together they would visit a diner where "Nanny" would order sodas and, when no one was looking, put her arm on the counter and sweep knives, forks, spoons or whatever was within reach into her bag.

With such modeling, Carol tried some shoplifting of her own. One day, while in a dime store, she saw some "ruby red lipstick" on a makeup counter. Following her grandmother's example, she lifted it off the counter, made her way out of the store, and ran all the way home with the lipstick hidden in her pocket. On reaching her home, she ran inside, slamming the door behind her. So terrified was she of being caught that she looked under her bed to make sure no one was there.

Going into the bathroom, Carol locked the door, and then took the lipstick out of her pocket. She was just about to unscrew the tube and apply it when her grandmother banged on the door, demanding to know what she was doing. Carol nearly died of fright. She promptly opened the door, fled past her grandmother, and ran back to the store. There she confessed what she had done and "turned herself in." Although her guilt was prompted by fear, her repentance was real. As a result of her confession, she was forgiven. The manager treated her graciously, and Carol went home "feeling cleansed."[1]

Confession is a good way to handle feelings of guilt, but what happens when it is not possible to make amends? Or, after having done so, to still feel inwardly condemned? When this happens, a deeper understanding of the varieties of guilt is needed.

There are four different kinds of guilt. The first is *theological guilt.* We all share in this, for it is part of what Biblical scholars call "the Fall" (cf. Romans 3:10-18; 5:12-21). It causes us to feel inwardly unworthy. We realize that none of us is fit for the presence of God.

The second is *legal guilt.* This arises when we transgress the law (e.g., by exceeding the speed limit). We are caught and experience inner condemnation. No matter how sorry we are for breaking the law, there is a penalty to be paid. Only after that are we free from reproof and disapprobation.

The third is *psychological guilt.* This is a false form of guilt and is sometimes referred to as an "internalized parent." It arises whenever our conduct conflicts with internalized norms or standards. For example, our parents may have set a high premium on hard work. As adults, we may feel guilty each time we relax, for this goes against the strong emphasis of continuous diligence that was instilled in us as children.

Finally, there is *Biblical guilt.* This takes the form of a "godly sorrow" that leads us to repentance (see 2 Corinthians 7:9-11). When we have repented of our sinful act(s) and confessed whatever we have done to the Lord, we need no longer feel guilty (see 1 John 1:5–2:2). And with forgiveness comes restoration to God's favor.

Of course, these types of guilt may be experienced singly or in combination. Those who have sinned grievously often feel that God's punishment will follow them to their grave (cf. Numbers 32:23). They may have heard preachers say, "God can forgive sin, but He cannot remove the consequences," or statements like that. What is implied is a never-ending series of misfortunes brought on by our sinfulness.

It is at a time like this that I am profoundly thankful for a chapter such as 2 Samuel 24. It reaffirms God's grace and points the way out of our fears to a life of confident trust in the Lord.

OUTLINE

The word *again* in 2 Samuel 24:1 links this story with the one in 21:1-14 as a record of God's punishment of sin. It is also implied (though not expressly stated) that the famine of chapter 21 was an expression of the Lord's displeasure, and chapter 24 opens on a similar note. Furthermore, 21:14 resembles 24:25 in word and concept, and this further links these chapters together.

There is no intimation of time to show when the events recorded here took place. It seems reasonable to conclude that it was a period

of peace, for Joab and the captains of Israel were able to spend almost ten months taking the census. During this interval, the nation
must have been enjoying freedom from all forms of oppression and
harassment. Two possible eras suggest themselves: (1) After the
events of chapter 9, and (2) in the interval after Absalom's coup had
been crushed.[2] The former is the most likely.

Here is the outline we shall follow:

- The Numbering of the People (24:1-9)
    God's Intention to Punish His People (24:1)
    David's Instructions to His Officers (24:2-9)

- The Judgment of the People (24:10-17)
    Confession of Sin (24:10)
    Choice of Punishment (24:11-14)
    Grief for the People (24:15)
    Intercession for the People (24:16-17)

- The Sparing of the People (24:18-25)
    The Prophetic Announcement (24:18)
    The Prompt Response (24:19)
    The Generous Offer (24:20-23)
    The Acceptable Sacrifice (24:24-25)

Historically, the importance of this chapter centers in the threshing floor that David purchased from Araunah the Jebusite. It will eventually become the site of Solomon's Temple (1 Chronicles 21:28–22:1).
Experientially, this chapter is of value to us for it points the way out
of the quagmire of guilt and fear and enlarges our understanding of
God's grace.

THE NUMBERING OF THE PEOPLE (24:1-9)

God's Intention to Punish His People (24:1)

The chapter begins with a surprising announcement:

> And again the anger of Yahweh burned against Israel, and [He]
> moved David against them, to say, "Go, number[3] Israel and Judah"
> (24:1).

The text reads simply enough, and yet there are several matters
of importance that have a bearing upon our interpretation of this

chapter. First, while David appears prominently in the story, it is God's people who have incurred His anger. If the events of this chapter took place after Absalom's attempted coup, then the Lord may have been punishing the nation for their sin in turning against His anointed. Whatever the cause, their sin must have been persistent in nature to bring on them the kind of judgment that is described in these verses.[4]

Second, Israel and Judah are designated as separate entities in verse 1. (But it is plain that the whole nation is in view in the use of "Israel" in verses 2 and 4). A temporary division of the kingdom occurred at the time Absalom's coup failed, but the major division of the tribes would not take place until after the reign of Solomon. Care, therefore, needs to be exercised in determining exactly who is involved by the term "Israel."

Third, in Chronicles we are told that it was Satan who stirred up David to number the people (cf. 1 Chronicles 21:1). Some writers have seen a conflict between this assertion and 24:1. Others look upon the change as indicative of progress in the evolution of the religious understanding of God's people. Both of these views, though held by capable Bible scholars, tacitly deny the doctrine of inspiration (2 Timothy 3:16). God is sovereign. His activities in the experience of people and nations is improperly understood (cf. 1 Kings 11:14, 23). Because we compartmentalize our thinking ("This is good," "That is bad"), we expect God to do the same. We expect Him to fit into one or other of our categories. And when He does not accommodate Himself to our limited perceptions, we flounder in the rising surf of our own misunderstanding. We fail to realize that He can use evil to accomplish His purpose.

The seemingly contradictory statements of 2 Samuel 24:1 and 1 Chronicles 21:1 may be harmonized as follows: God saw that the nation's persistent sin needed to be corrected. In His sovereign will he allowed an adversary (*sāṭān*, lacks the article) to tempt David to number the people (cf. James 1:13-15).[5]

Fourth, the numbering of the people was not in itself sinful. Moses had twice conducted such a census (see Numbers, chs. 1 and 26). God had stipulated, however, that atonement money was to be taken from those numbered (Exodus 30:12-16). There is no record in the text of it being collected by Joab and his captains.[6] Was this an instance of David's ignorance of Scripture, or was the money collected and paid into the Tabernacle treasury without being mentioned by the Biblical writer?

Fifth, the question, "Why did David number the people?" needs to be answered. William J. Deane, who dates the census in the interval between the wars of 2 Samuel 8,9 and 15 says:

> [David's action was not] wholly alien from the spirit of the theocratic king…. He looked around, and saw other empires, with natural resources not greater than his own, become mighty and celebrated by foreign conquests; [and he thought] why should [Israel] not be as one of these world powers?[7]

William Blaikie, who dates the census after David's prophetic psalm (23:1-7), explains the king's rationale differently.

> The project of David appears at first the more extraordinary in that it was conceived after the prophecy of the Ruler—after [David's] mind had been divinely filled with the vision of Christ's kingly glory. But it is not difficult to suppose that that very vision of the universal empire of Christ had something to do with the numbering of the people. David knew that there was a certain connection between his kingdom and Christ's…may not, then, the vision he had just received, have led him to think of the gigantic effort to enlarge the typical empire over which he himself presided?[8]

Whatever view we choose, we must take note of the fact that David was only tempted. When he fell it was as a result of a decision that he made. He, therefore, took responsibility for his actions.

David's Instructions to His Officers (24:2-9)

The king's instructions to Joab are explicit:

> "Go about now through all the tribes of Israel, from Dan to Beersheba, and number the people that I may know the number of the people" (24:2).

The word translated *host* (24:2,4) in some versions is really the word for "people." In this context it carries the idea of "soldiers" (including all men of military age).

Joab objects to David's plan. In the past he had exerted influence over King David, and he presumes to do so again.

If this census was conducted after the events of 2 Samuel 9, we are hard pressed for an explanation as to why David would refuse to listen to him. We would expect David to listen to the "commander of the host" as formerly.

If, however, the numbering of Israel's fighting force took place after the insurrection of Absalom, then the answer comes easily. Joab had mortgaged his credibility. He had deliberately disobeyed the king by having Absalom killed, and he had assassinated Amasa in order to reinstate himself as commander of the army. In David's eyes he was now *persona non grata*—a person without standing before him. He had forfeited the right to be heard.

Joab does not take David's refusal lightly. Such is his arrogance that he solicits the help of "the captains" to try to overrule the king. At this David's resistance hardens. In the end, Joab and the leaders of the different divisions of the army have no option but to carry out their sovereign's command.

With little or no enthusiasm, they set about taking the census. First, they cross the Jordan and commence where the River Arnon forms Israel's southern border.[9] Aroer, one of the chief cities of this region, is situated "on the edge of the valley of the Arnon" (cf. Deuteronomy 2:36). Reuben is the first tribe to be enrolled, followed by Gad (whose territory includes the city of Jazer, cf. Joshua 13:25) and the district of Gilead. The goal of these captains is to work their way northward toward Dan and then circle to the west, turn south, and so take in Israel's western border as far as Beersheba.

The entire census takes nine months and twenty days (24:8). Then Joab comes before David and gives his report.

Once again Bible critics have imagined a discrepancy between the account in 2 Samuel and the one in the Book of Chronicles. According to Joab, the total fighting force under David is said to be 1,300,000 (24:9), whereas in 1 Chronicles 21:5-6 it is said to be 1,570,000 that drew the sword. How then may the apparent discrepancy be harmonized?

The tribes of Benjamin and Levi were not included in the census Joab conducted. If the number of these tribes were obtained later on and were available to the Chronicler, then this may account for the discrepancy. On the other hand, some Bible scholars have looked for a solution in the word *'ălāphîm*, translated "thousand." Depending upon the context, it may have more than one meaning. It is capable of being used as an actual number (i.e., one thousand), but it can also be used of a "military contingent" that could be comprised of either more or less than a thousand men.

THE JUDGMENT OF THE PEOPLE (24:10-17)

Confession of Sin (24:10)

After receiving the figures from Joab (and not realizing that Joab had not completed the task), David believes that he has compelled

Joab's compliance. That being the case, there is no longer any need for him to maintain a hard-line posture. Having gained this tacit victory, his conscience is no longer stifled by the need for self-assertion. It is now free. And with a sudden wave of guilt, he becomes acutely aware of the nature of his *'āwôn*, "iniquity." He knows of only one thing to do: Confess it to the Lord and ask for forgiveness.

> And David says to Yahweh, "I have sinned greatly [in] that which I have done, and now, O Yahweh, take away I pray the iniquity of Your servant, for I have acted very foolishly" (24:10).

His humiliation and contrition are real. His confession is honest and complete.

Choice of Punishment (24:11-14)

The next morning, the prophet Gad[10] comes before the king. He has not been summoned by David but rather has been sent to him by Yahweh, Israel's Suzerain. His words to the king are painfully direct:

> "Thus says Yahweh, three [things] I am imposing upon you; choose for yourself one of them and I will do [it] to you. Shall there come to you three years [of] famine, upon the land? Or shall you flee [for] three months before your adversaries while he pursues you? Or shall there be three days plague in your land? Now consider and see what I shall take back to Him who sent me" (24:12-13).

These are hard choices. In David's response, however, we see the transparency of his soul. He has nothing to hide. His reply is devoid of all hypocrisy. He says to Gad,

> "Great distress [has come upon] me; let us now fall into the hand of Yahweh, for many [are] His mercies; and into the hand of man let us not fall" (24:14).

I am so thankful for this story. I am often called upon to counsel a person who has had an affair, or has chosen to have an abortion, lied to or misrepresented facts about another, or stolen something. Their guilt lies heavily upon them. They fear God's judgment and they wonder how long His punishment will last. After they confess and try to set things right, I am able to point them to this chapter and encourage them to do as David did. I advocate that they commit themselves and their future to the Lord (cf. Psalm 55:22; 1 Peter 5:7), knowing that His mercies are great. Then, once they have made this decision, I encourage them to continue to serve the Lord faithfully as David did. Their confidence can then lie in the fact that the Lord will deal with them graciously even as He did with David and the Israelites.

In discussing the choice David made, William Deane pointed out that,

> [David] chose not war, for he knew the cruelties and hardships inflicted therein by man on man, and he shuddered now, under his better feelings, to think whither his ambition unchecked might have led. He choose not famine, for that would have fallen upon his people, while he himself would have been spared the infliction; and he selected the pestilence as the punishment, in which his danger was as great as that of the lowest of his subjects.[11]

With David having made his choice, Gad goes back to his home where he relates to the Lord the king's decision.

Grief for the People (24:15)

Next we read: "And Yahweh gave (i.e., sent) a plague upon Israel from the morning even to the time appointed." The angel responsible for carrying out God's directive seems to have worked in a circular fashion (24:16), perhaps following the same route taken by the captains of the army when they conducted the census. If so, then he began in the east, moved northward, then circled around to the west, moved south, and from Beersheba turned northward again so that he came at last to Jerusalem.

But who is this "angel" who brings death to the people in response to the command of the Lord? This is not the first time we have heard of him. In the Book of Exodus, where he is called "the destroyer" (Exodus 12:23), we are told of how he killed the firstborn in Egypt in a single night (Exodus 11:4-5; 12:12-13, 29). And later on, during the period of the divided kingdom, we will again learn of his activities when a large portion of the army of Sennacherib will be wiped out (2 Kings 19:35).

The means used on Israel is a plague of unprecedented virulence. In retrospect, the people recognize it as a supernatural visitation.

Though it continues for only a part of one day,[12] in that short time seventy thousand people die.

God in His grace does not punish the people for the full three days. In fact, a careful reading of the text will reveal that even before David began to pray for the people, the Lord had told the angel, "It is enough" (24:16).

Intercession for the People (24:16-17)

Toward mid-afternoon, at the time when wives and mothers begin to prepare the evening meal and the priests in the Tabernacle commence the evening sacrifice, David is given the ability to see the angel as he approaches Jerusalem. He has no means of knowing what has been happening throughout Israel. He did not even know that the plague had started.

Imagine his surprise, therefore, when he sees the angel approaching Jerusalem. He probably believes that the plague is about to begin. His first thought is for his people, and he immediately begins to intercede for them.

> "Look, *I* have sinned! Yes, *I* have acted perversely; and these—, the flock, what have they done? Let now Your hand be on *me*, and on the house of *my* father" (24:17).

His prayer is remarkable for several reasons. First, the pronouns are emphatic. There is no sanctimonious rhetoric in what he says. He is sincere. His request is that the Lord will punish him instead of His people.

Second, he takes all the blame upon himself. His attitude is devoid of pretense. Had David been insincere, the Lord would not have heard him (Psalm 66:18). David, however, is utterly transparent in his intercession for his people.

Third, he refers to the people as sheep—defenseless, unable to guide themselves, and vulnerable. He is their "shepherd" and charged with the responsibility of caring for them.

From our understanding of the passage, we know that in this instance the "sheep" were guilty of a greater sin than the "shepherd," but David did not know that. The anger of the Lord had been kindled against them for their evil deeds (24:1). It was with a view to chastening them that He removed His hand and allowed David to be tempted to number the people. Since both are now guilty, both will be punished: The sheep in their persons, the shepherd in the tenderest feelings of his heart.

It is beautiful to see a man willing to take upon himself more than his share of the blame! What a contrast to the spirit often encountered in the world, where people appear eager to take more of the credit than is their due and often are ready to lay any blame on another's shoulders rather than their own![13]

THE SPARING OF THE PEOPLE (24:18-25)

The Prophetic Announcement (24:18)

Following his prayer, David waits. He has asked the Lord to spare his people and to punish him instead. Matters are now in God's hands.

Once again the prophet Gad is sent to David. He instructs the king to go up to the threshing floor of Araunah[14] the Jebusite and there offer sacrifices to the Lord.

The Prompt Response (24:19)

David obeys promptly. He does "according to the saying of Gad, as Yahweh has commanded" (24:19). He ascends to this raised elevation where the slightest breeze is used to separate the wheat from the chaff.

As he climbs the hill, he may have reflected inwardly on the significance of God's words to him, for this was the spot where, a thousand years earlier, Abraham had built an altar on which to offer up Isaac (Genesis 22:2-18).[15]

Whatever his thoughts, it is his actions that are important. His desire to have his sins and the people's blotted out before harm comes to the city is noteworthy.

The Generous Offer (24:20-23)

Imagine Araunah's surprise as he looks down the slope and sees the king walking up to meet him. He has no idea what has been taking place, nor can he see the angel of death with sword drawn ready to strike down the people within the city. He walks toward the king and bows before him with his face toward the ground. His attitude is respectful. He asks: "Why has my lord the king come to his servant?" (24:21).

When David explains the reason for the visit, Araunah offers to give him the threshing floor as a gift. Not being a Hebrew, he is not bound by the same laws of inheritance as God's people (Deuteronomy 25:23; Numbers 36:7. cf. 2 Kings 21:1-3). He is free to dispose of the property as he sees fit. He also offers the king the oxen (that have been walking over the ripened grain so as to separate the wheat from the husk) and the implements for use as firewood. It is a most gracious offer.

The Acceptable Sacrifice (24:24-25)

As king, David could easily have accepted the threshing floor and its contents as a gift. In replying to Araunah, however, he says:

> "No, for I will surely buy it from you for a price, and I shall not offer to Yahweh my God burnt offerings for (i.e., of that which cost me) nothing" (24:24).

And this same kind of attitude should characterize our giving to the Lord!

So David buys the threshing floor for fifty shekels of silver, and the site of the future Temple becomes the property of David and his heirs. In Chronicles it is stated that David paid Araunah six hundred shekels of silver (1 Chronicles 21:25). Rashi, the Jewish commentator, sought to harmonize the two accounts by arguing that David paid fifty shekels for each tribe.[16] The discrepancy is slight and is better explained as a copyist's error.

The transaction completed, David quickly makes an altar and sacrifices the bullocks as burnt offerings and peace offerings to the Lord. This done, he prays for his people. And Yahweh hears his prayer, and the plague is stayed. It stops as suddenly and mysteriously as it had broken out.

OF GOD AND MAN

Playing Games with God

There is a sense in which the Bible is a very contemporary book. In the events that it describes, as well as in the lives of the people, it reveals what we too are like. We have all been in the place of either David or the Israelites. There have been times in our lives when unconfessed, long-forgotten sin has brought its inevitable chastisement. We have been like Israel, who aroused the Lord's anger so that He has sent some sudden calamity upon us as He did on them. The purpose of such discipline is to bring us back to Himself.

In these times of bewilderment, we may have taken belated inventory of our soul's condition and asked the Lord to bring to our remembrance those things which we have done that have been displeasing to Him. Or we have confessed ourselves sinners and have asked Him to graciously pardon our iniquities and restore to us the joy of our salvation.

One of the subtlest forms of error for conscientious Christians may be the sin of presumption. We may have been enjoying a life free from trial and begun unwittingly to abuse our liberty. Or we may have taken God's kindness for granted. Or we may have engaged in actions of which He does not approve (note Psalm 50:21). Or we may have been guilty of thanklessness and perhaps even a failure to fulfill some promise or vow made to Him (Psalm 50:14-15).

Others may have neglected His Word and, by their actions, aligned themselves with those who "hate instruction." In acts of self-will, they may even have "cast His Word behind their backs." But such practices do not make the Bible less convicting or less relevant. They merely shut the practitioner off from the source of truth and light that God intended for their blessing (Psalm 50:16-17).[17]

Then there are those who compromise with evildoers, fail to stand for what is right, become slanderers of the good, and seldom give much thought to how God views their sins (Psalm 50:18-20). They are then surprised when He chastens them for the error of their ways (Psalm 50:22-23).

But these are not the only kinds of presumptive sins. There are other kinds of sin. They may flow from good intentions and worthy motives. An example of this kind of behavior is illustrated for us in David's decision to number the people. At no time did he ask counsel of the Lord or seek to know His will. He acted then as some in Christian work do now. If the church needs a larger sanctuary, they presume it is God's will for them to have one. So a building program is launched, whether God wants His people to have one or not.

Another example comes in the kind of spouses people choose. I have counseled scores of wives and a few husbands who married unbelievers, confident that after the wedding they would be able to influence their unsaved spouse for the Lord. Years later they have had to admit that life has become "a living hell"...and in desperation, and as a last resort, they have asked if I will pray for them and their family.

In recent years our religious magazines have carried two stories of Christian entrepreneurs who each claimed that God told them to start a university. One of these men, knowing that certain property outside a large city had been zoned as a future greenbelt, nonetheless went ahead with plans to purchase it. A sum of several million dollars was paid to the owner of the land, and a promissory note was given for the rest. The interest on the note was about $250,000 every three months. This Christian leader felt sure he could pressure the city fathers into re-zoning the land. He could then approach a developer to build his university and apply to a bank for the loan and pay off the promissory note.

After several years of fruitless negotiation and literally millions of dollars wasted in interest, he had to scrap his plans. But what of his presumptuous claim, "God told me to start a university"?

The other entrepreneur was more successful. However, as time went by, the resources of his wealthy backers were drained, and he was forced to close the school he had started. As a final face-saving device, he sought for a merger with another institution. Each of these men was guilty of the sin of presumption.

We too are often equally guilty. We commit this same sin when we come together to discuss the Lord's work and then conclude our meeting by asking God to bless the decisions we have made. Or we engage in a business venture, buy a house, or invest some money and then, when difficulties arise, ask God to bail us out of our dilemma. Such sins are the same in kind as David's sin in numbering the people.

Right Use of Guilt

A second dimension to this story needs to be underscored in our minds. It is seen in David's response to guilt once he become aware of his sin. His godly sorrow drove him to repentance (24:10).

Brenda Poinsett, in her book *Understanding a Woman's Depression*, chided counselors for all too often focusing attention on the bad effects of guilt while ignoring the positive side of this emotion. She pointed out that this imbalance is unfortunate because guilt serves as a safeguard against unacceptable behavior. "True guilt," she affirms, "is a valuable asset for living." She then continued:

> [Guilt] helps us when we hurt others or betray our own standards and values. God uses guilt to influence us to change our minds about what we are doing, leading us to repentance. If we never felt guilty, we would not follow difficult rules or standards, obey the law, or have good relationships with loved ones.[18]

But if guilt is so valuable, why does it so often lead to depression? Depression arises whenever we feel that we have lost something of intrinsic worth to us, and we must not forget that depression has a physiological component as well as a psychological/spiritual one. David did not allow his breach of fellowship with the Lord to continue unchecked. He kept short accounts of his sins with God. His feeling of alienation from God was quickly remedied through confession. And with fellowship restored, he could face the future.

The Israelites, however, may have continued under a false sense of guilt for a long time after the plague. They did not have Bibles in their homes as we do today and were dependent upon the ministry of the priests for their knowledge of God's will. Often, the priests who lived among them were unspiritual, and they could not and did not give adequate guidance to those who were unsure of their spiritual state.

We, however, do have Bibles, and the daily meditation on some portion of Scripture is a sure way to correct our feeling of false guilt and lift our depression. Then we, like David, can rejoice in God's forgiveness and, as a result, maintain a positive attitude toward the ups and downs of life.

The Magnanimity of God's Grace

Finally, we must take note of God's grace. He mercifully reduced the length of the punishment from three days to about nine hours. In Psalm 103:8-14 we read these words:

> Yahweh [is] merciful and gracious, slow to (lit. of) anger and much (i.e., full of) mercy. He will not always strive [with us] nor keep [His anger] forever. He has not done to [us] according to our sins, and [He has] not rewarded us [according to] our iniquities. For as high [as] the heavens [are] (lit. is) above the earth, [so] is His mercy over [those who are] fearers of Him (i.e., to those who fear Him). As far [as] the east [is] from the west, [so] far has He put our transgressions from us. As the pity of a father over [his] sons (i.e., As a father pities his sons), [so] Yahweh pities over [the] fearers of Him (i.e., pities those who fear Him). For He knows our form; remembering that we [are] dust.

We often take His grace for granted. We are inclined to think of His love only when He gives us the things we want. And unanswered prayers are looked upon as indications of His disfavor, disinterest, or seeming distance from us. Only as we meditate on what He has chosen to reveal can this materialistic and self-centered view of reality be corrected (cf. Psalm 139:1-24).

IS THIS THE END?

But what of David? Were his fighting days over? Did he live on to a ripe old age? Surely the story does not end here. It seems incomplete.

The primary focus of our study has not been David and his exploits but rather God and His ways with His people. The emphasis is on God's *sovereignty* and the responsibility of all God's people to live in subjection to His will.

In our consideration of the two parts of the Book of Samuel, we have had occasion to note numerous instances of God's sovereignty. We have found that each chapter contains some information of importance to us. Such knowledge should help us understand what is going on in our lives and relate to the Lord in positive ways. As we grow in our relationship with Him, we are able to rest in His lovingkindness toward us. Then, no matter what happens, we will see in the affairs of life reminders of His love and grace.

No, the story of David is not over. It continues into the Book of Kings (which likewise falls into two parts). And there, as one generation follows another, we will find *a record of God's righteousness.*

NOTES

Introduction

1. W. G. Blaikie, *The First Book of Samuel* (Minneapolis: Klock and Klock, 1978), 388. (Emphasis added).
2. D. M. Gunn, "2 Samuel," *Harper's Bible Commentary*, ed. J. L. Mays (San Francisco: Harper and Row, 1988), 287. Used by permission. In spite of the value of Gunn's insights, he adheres to many of the tenets that have become identified with theological liberalism.
3. Ibid., 287.
4. Beginning with *Judges: The Power of God* (1990), I have attempted to interpret the historic books of Judges through 2 Chronicles from the perspective of the theocracy. Strictly speaking, a theocracy is a society ruled by God. In ancient Israel Yahweh was His people's King (Deuteronomy 33:5), Israel was His army (Exodus 7:4), and the wars they fought were His wars (Numbers 21:14).

   The concept of a theocracy is not only a military one, it is legislative and judicial as well. The authority to administer justice in these different realms resided in God alone. He delegated some of His power to those whom He had chosen; and they, in turn, could elect others to positions of responsibility (cf. Exodus 18). Even the king was only God's vice-regent (Deuteronomy 17:15). He was responsible for defending God's people and promoting faith in Yahweh, the one true God.

   Closely bound up with these duties was the Covenant God had entered into with Israel. Its basic essence can be traced to the simple statement: "I shall be your God and you shall be My people." See also T. C. Vriezen, *An Outline of Old Testament Theology* (Oxford: Clarendon, 1960), 229.
5. Cf. J. D. Pentecost, *Things to Come* (Grand Rapids: Zondervan, 1964), 65-94, for a clear presentation of the Biblical covenants as these apply to God's progressive revelation. The discussion by G. N. H. Peters in his *The Theocratic Kingdom* (Grand Rapids: Kregel, 1988), 3 vols., is also relevant. Volume I: 290-351 is especially deserving of careful reading.
6. The scope of the Biblical covenants (extending through this present day of grace and on into the Millennial Kingdom and the Eternal State) has been surveyed in J. D. Pentecost's excellent book *Thy Kingdom Come* (Wheaton, IL: Victor, 1990), 360pp., and its serious study is recommended.

Chapter 1

1. W. Bridges, *Transitions: Making Sense out of Life's Changes* (Reading, MA: Addison-Wesley, 1980, 90. Used by permission. I have profited greatly from a study of this book, and many of the concepts applied to David and his men have been drawn from Bridges' discussion.
2. Ibid., 112.
3. Ibid., 134.
4. Ibid., 141.
5. T. Ishida, ed., *Studies in the Period of David and Solomon* (Winona Lake, IN: Eisenbrauns, 1982), 27-54; A. A. Anderson, *2 Samuel*, Word Biblical Commentary (Dallas: Word, 1989), 5-6; P. M. McCarter, Jr., *2 Samuel*, Anchor Bible (Garden City, NY: Doubleday, 1984), 60; K. W. Whitelam, *The Just King* (Sheffield, England: Journal for the Study of the Old Testament, 1979), 104-05. Whitelam believes that in the exchange between David and the Amalekite, there are traces of formal judicial language. His views have not gained a wide following. What is more likely is that David, having virtually been a petty king, was accustomed to acting with judicial authority.

6. H. C. Alleman and E. E. Flack, eds. *Old Testament Commentary* (Philadelphia: Muhlenberg, 1948), 397.
7. The Amalekites were the descendants of Esau (cf. Genesis 36:12; 1 Chronicles 1:36). Cf. R. deVaux, *Ancient Israel: Its Life and Institutions*, trans. J. McHugh (New York: McGraw-Hill, 1961), 74-76. They usually inhabited the Negev or south land and the area today known as Saudi Arabia. Enmity had existed between Israel and the Amalekites from the time of the Exodus (Exodus 17:8-16; Numbers 14:43-45). God had decreed their total extermination first through Moses and then through Samuel (1 Samuel 15:1ff.). Cf. J. H. Gronbaek, *Studia Theologica* 18 (1964), 26-45.
8. A rich corpus of literature has grown up about the signs and symbols of mourning. Information is to be found in M. Jastrow, Jr., *Journal of the American Oriental Society* 20 (1899), 133-50; E. F. de Ward, *Journal of Semitic Studies* 23 (1972), 1-27 and 145-66; and deVaux, *Ancient Israel*, 59.
9. This is the conclusion of most scholars, J. Mauchline (*1 and 2 Samuel*, New Century Bible [Greenwood, SC: Attic, 1971], 196-98), being a notable exception. Cf. C. E. Hauer, Jr., *Catholic Biblical Quarterly* 31 (1969), 153-67. A careful comparison of these verses with 1 Samuel 31:1-2 points to an important contrast. In 1 Samuel Saul is said to have died. The Amalekite said he came upon Saul leaning upon his spear, but *without* a sword in his abdomen. The supposed exchange between Saul and the Amalekite is reminiscent of Saul's request of his armor bearer, but Saul's words to his armor bearer could have been overheard by the Amalekite and adopted to exonerate himself from all blame. Cf. Josephus, *Antiquities of the Jews*, VII:1:1.
10. deVaux, *Ancient Israel*, 59-61.
11. S. R. Driver (*Notes of the Hebrew Text of the Books of Samuel*, 2d ed. [Oxford: Clarendon, 1966], 233) objects to this view.
12. J. G. Baldwin, *1 & 2 Samuel*, Tyndale Old Testament Commentaries (Downers Grove, IL: InterVarsity, 1988), 176.
13. The *hannēzer*, "coronet," was part of the royal insignia (cf. 2 Kings 11:12). It intimated the sacred nature of the king's office (cf. Exodus 39:30; Psalms 21:3; 89:39).
14. The *haṣṣĕ'ādâ*, "armlet," would appear to be a large, flat bracelet worn on the forearm. Cf. J. B. Pritchard, *The Ancient Near East in Pictures* (Princeton, NJ: Princeton University Press, 1954), plates 441-42, 617, 626.
15. The *gēr*, "sojourner, resident alien," indicates that the Amalekite was living legally within the borders of Israel and was not absolved from adhering to the Mosaic law (Leviticus 24:22. See also Leviticus 20:2; 24:16; etc.). Some writers believe that he may have been a proselyte like Doeg (cf. 1 Samuel 21:7; 22:17-19). David's questions were probably with a view to determining whether or not the Amalekite came under the jurisdiction of the law. Cf. G. C. Macholz, *Zeitschrift für die alttestamentliche Wissenschaft* 84 (1972), 163-64.
16. McCarter, *2 Samuel*, 60. Used by permission. Cf. deVaux, *Ancient Israel*, 74-76; and *Theological Dictionary of the Old Testament*, G. J. Botterweck and H. Ringgren, eds.; trans. J. T. Willis. In process (Grand Rapids: Eerdmans, 1974-), II:443-48.
17. Blaikie, *Second Samuel*, 6-7; cf. H. W. Hertzberg, *I and II Samuel, a Commentary*, Old Testament Library, trans. J. J. Bowden (Philadelphia: Westminster, 1964), 237.
18. Ishida, *David and Solomon*, 75; T. N. D. Mettinger, *King and Messiah* (Lund, Sweden: Gleerup, 1976), 185-232.
19. C. Westermann, *Zeitschrift für die alttestamentliche Wissenschaft* 66 (1945), 46. Westermann has identified two main kinds of literary laments. The former is a dirge or funerary lament, and the latter is a general or distress lament. Funerary laments would naturally take place in the house of the deceased. David's elegy, due to circumstances beyond his control, was uttered in Ziklag, a town on the very border of Philistia and Judah. Cf. E. Oren, *Biblical Archaeologist* 45 (1982), 155-66.
20. Cf. Anderson, *2 Samuel*, 14-15.
21. W. F. Albright in *Old Testament Commentary*, eds. H. C. Alleman and E. E. Flack, 398. Used by permission. See also J. P. Fokkelman, *Zeitschrift für die alttestamentliche Wissenschaft* 91 (1979) 290-92; D. N. Freedman, *Ex Orbe Religionum*, eds. C. J. Bleeker, S. F. G. Brandon, and M. Simon, 2 vols. (Leiden, The Netherlands: Brill, 1972), I:141ff.;

W. L. Holladay, *Vetus Testamentum* 20 (1970), 153-89; W. H. Shea, *Bulletin of the American Schools of Oriental Research* 221 (1976), 141-44; and J. Wozniak, *Biblische Zeitschrift* 27 (1983), 213-18.

22. Blaikie, *Second Samuel*, 9-13.
23. Albright, *Old Testament Commentary*, 398.
24. Ibid., 398.
25. J. P. Fokkelman, *Narrative Art and Poetry in the Books of Samuel*, Vol. 1: *King David, II Samuel 9–20, and I Kings 1–2* (Assen, The Netherlands: Van Gorcum, 1982), 670-71.
26. The false theory that the "love" of David and Jonathan was the result of a homosexual relationship is too absurd to require refutation. Cf. T. Horner, *Jonathan Loved David* (Philadelphia: Westminster, 1978), 163. It should be remembered that, while sexual deviants may look to this poem for support to excuse their lifestyle, the whole tenor of the Old Testament is against such a view. Both David and Jonathan had healthy heterosexual relationships with their wives, and to propose a homosexual relationship (elsewhere condemned in God's Word!) places the burden of proof on the proponent. Cf. Anderson, *2 Samuel*, 19.
27. Albright, *Old Testament Commentary*, 398.

Chapter 2

1. L. J. Wood, *Israel's United Monarchy* (Grand Rapids: Baker, 1979), 92ff. Wood describes the smallness of the territory ruled by David and the difficulties he faced when he ascended the throne. Cf. *Macmillan Bible Atlas*, by Y. Aharoni and M. Avi-Yonah, rev. ed. (New York: Macmillan, 1977), 98.
2. G. A. Larue, *Journal of Bible and Religion* 33 (1965), 337-39; P. C. Hammond, *Revue Biblique* 72 (1965), 267-70; idem, *Revue Biblique* 73 (1066), 566-69; idem, *Revue Biblique* 75 (1968), 253-58; idem, *Princeton Seminary Bulletin* (1965), 19-28. Cf. J. Lindblom, *Vetus Testamentum* 12 (1962), 164-78.
3. A. Alt, *Essays on Old Testament History and Religion*, trans. R. A. Wilson (New York: Doubleday, 1968), 190. Cf. Anderson, *2 Samuel*, 22; McCarter, *2 Samuel*, 83.
4. Hebron is higher in elevation than any other city in Israel, being about 3,000 feet above sea level. For a description of the ancient city, see E. Lipinski, *Vetus Testamentum* 24 (1974), 41-55.
5. Cf. J. A. Soggin, *Das Köngtum in Israel* (Berlin: Topelmann, 1967), 65. Other views are presented by A. Weiser, *Vetus Testamentum* 16 (1966), 325-54; and J. J. Jackson, *Canadian Journal of Theology* 11 (1965), 183-95.
6. J. D. Levinson and B. Halpern, *Journal of Biblical Literature* 99 (1980), 507-18, overstate the political importance of David's wives. They further err in regard to Ahinoam (the wife David took when he was in the Cave of Adullam) by claiming that she had been the wife of Saul. At the time of David's marriage, Saul still had approximately ten years to reign. It is preposterous to see in this marriage a fulfillment of 2 Samuel 12:8.
7. Levinson and Halpern further err in regard to Abigail. They believe that she was David's (half) sister. Nothing in the text supports this view. For a different interpretation, see C. J. Barber, *You Can Have a Happy Marriage* (Nashville: Nelson, 1990), 93-108.
8. Cf. R. deVaux, *Early Israel* (Philadelphia: Westminster, 1978), 547; Ishida, *David and Solomon*, 65-66; H.-J. Zobel, *Vetus Testamentum Supplement* 28 (1975), 253-77.
9. Mettinger, *King and Messiah*, 198-208. Cf. L. K. R. R. Gros, *Semeia* 8 (1977), 15-33; D. M. Gunn, *Semeia* 3 (1975), 14-45; B. Halpern, *Harvard Theological Review* 72 (1979), 316; N. P. Lemche, *Journal for the Study of the Old Testament* 10 (1978), 2-25.
10. Cf. A. D. Baly, *The Geography of the Bible* (San Francisco: Harper and Row, 1974), 148, 170, 198; N. Glueck, *The River Jordan* (New York: McGraw-Hill, 1968), 93-95, 130-36, 139; E. B. Smick, *Archaeology of the Jordan Valley* (Grand Rapids: Baker, 1973), 31, 84.
11. It is possible that this idea is furthered by the words *teḥĕzaqnâ yĕdēkem*, "let your hands be steady" (2 Samuel 2:7). David called upon the people to act courageously

and with confidence. It was a tactful way of showing that he (David) was now the
authority in the land by the will of God. He promised to act with *'asa toba*, "good
friendship" toward them. Cf. Mettinger, *King and Messiah*, 147; D. R. Hillers, *Bulletin
of the American Schools of Oriental Research* 176 (1964), 46-47; W. L. Moran, *Journal
of Near Eastern Studies* 22 (1963), 173-76; and T. R. Preston, *Journal for the Study of
the Old Testament* 24 (1982), 27-46.

12. Anderson, *2 Samuel*, 29; McCarter, *2 Samuel*, 84-85.
13. Ish-bosheth is assigned different names in Scripture (1 Chronicles 8:33; 9:39).
    For a discussion of this phenomenon and the significance of these names, see
    McCarter, *2 Samuel*, 86; M. Noth, *Die Israelitischen Personennamen im Rahmen der
    gemeinsemitischen Namengebung* (Hildesheim, Germany: Olms, 1980), 138-39; E.
    Lipinski, *Orientalia lovaniensia periodica* 5 (1974), 5-13; and M. Tsevat, *Hebrew Union
    College Annual* 46 (1975), 71-87. For a discussion of his reign, see J. A. Soggin, *Biblica
    et Orientalia* 29 (1975), 31-49.
14. The age of Ish-bosheth is disputed, with most biblical scholars of the opinion that
    his age in the Masoretic Text has been made to conform to the maturity of other
    monarchs when they assumed the throne. The opinion of Anderson (*2 Samuel*, 33-
    35), Driver (*Hebrew Text*, 240) and McCarter (*2 Samuel*, 85-86) should be weighed
    carefully.
15. Blaikie, *David*, 140.
16. Ibid, 139-41; idem, *Second Samuel*, 27.
17. Most preachers I have heard, when preaching on 2 Samuel 12, are quick to inveigh
    against David for not being with his troops in battle. They ignore the evidence of
    this passage and blithely sidestep the fact that affairs of state most likely required
    David's presence at the capital. In 2 Samuel 2, Joab is the one who repulses the
    planned invasion of Abner. These same preachers do not criticize David when they
    discuss that passage. It seems evident, therefore, that they have a special agenda
    that they resort to when discussing chapter 12.
18. Cf. *Encyclopedia of Archaeological Excavations in the Holy Land*, M. Avi-Yonah and E.
    Stein, eds., 4 vols. (Englewood Cliffs, NJ: Prentice-Hall, 1975-77), II:446-50; A. Negev,
    The Archaeological Encyclopedia of the Holy Land, rev. ed. (Nashville: Nelson, 1986),
    157-58; W. L. Reed, *Archaeology and Old Testament Study*, ed. D. W. Thomas (Oxford:
    Clarendon, 1967), 237-38; E. Robinson, *Biblical Researches in Palestine*, 3 vols. (Lon-
    don: Murray, 1856), I:455; J. Blenkinsopp, *Vetus Testamentum* 24 (1974), 1-7; A. Demsky,
    Bulletin of the American Schools of Oriental Research 212 (1973), 26-31; J. B. Pritchard,
    Biblical Archaeologist 19 (1956), 66-75.
19. R. deVaux, *The Bible and the Ancient Near East* (New York: Doubleday, 1971), 127-31;
    Y. Yadin, *The Art of Warfare in Bible Lands*, 2 vols. (New York: McGraw-Hill, 1963),
    II:266-67; W. L. Batten, *Zeitschrift für die alttestamentliche Wissenschaft* 26 (1966), 90-
    92; W. Bruggemann, *Journal of the American Academy of Religion* 40 (1972), 96-109; F.
    C. Fensham, *Vetus Testamentum* 20 (1970), 356-57; Y. Sukenik, *Journal of the Palestine
    Oriental Society* 21 (1948), 110-16; Y. Yadin, *Journal of the Palestine Oriental Society*
    21 (1948), 110-16.
20. C. Gordon, *Hebrew Union College Annual* 23 (1950-51), 131-36.
21. Y. Yadin, *Journal of the Palestine Oriental Society* 21 (1948), 110-16; idem, *Art of War-
    fare*, II:266-67.
22. A. F. Kirkpatrick, *The Second Book of Samuel*, Cambridge Bible for Schools and Col-
    leges (Cambridge: University Press, 1930), 63.
23. Josephus, *Antiquities of the Jews*, VII:1:3.
24. *Macmillan Bible Atlas*, 99.
25. *Zondervan Pictorial Encyclopedia of the Bible*, M. C. Tenney, ed. (Grand Rapids:
    Zondervan, 1969), I:422, 628. Cf. H. C. Trumbull, *The Blood Covenant* (Minneapolis:
    James, n.d.), 209-93.
26. C. F. Keil and F. J. Delitzsch, *Biblical Commentary on the Books of Samuel*, trans. J.
    Martin (Grand Rapids: Eerdmans, 1968), 235. Cf. Hertzberg (*I and II Samuel*, 252) for
    a differing view.
27. *Macmillan Bible Atlas*, 99. Cf. M. Greenberg, *Journal of Biblical Literature* 76 (1957),

34-39; M. R. Lehmann, *Zeitschrift für die alttestamentliche Wissenschaft* 81 (1969), 83-86.

28. *Zondervan Pictorial Encyclopedia of the Bible*, II:760-62.
29. Baly, *Geography*, 206-09; Aharoni, *Land and the Book*, 35-36, 54-60.
30. J. R. W. Stott, *Understanding the Bible*, rev. ed. (Grand Rapids: Lamplighter, 1979), 187. In addition to Stott's work which is worth reading in its entirety, here are a few others that treat methods of Bible study, interpretation, and application: C. J. Barber, *Dynamic Personal Bible Study* (Neptune, NJ: Loizeaux, 1981), 191; W. M. Dunnett, *The Interpretation of Holy Scripture* (Nashville: Nelson, 1984), 210pp.; and J. Kuharschek, *Taking the Guesswork out of Applying the Bible* (Downers Grove, IL: InterVarsity, 1990), 163.
31. D. Bonhoeffer, *Letters and Papers from Prison*, ed. E. Bethge (New York: Macmillan, 1972), 64. Used by permission.
32. R. B. Graham, in *Living Quotations for Christians*, eds. S. E. Wirt and K. Beckstrom (San Francisco: Harper and Row, 1974), 151 (#2024). Used by permission.

Chapter 3

1. E. M. Forster, *A Passage To India* (London: Arnold, 1953), 335.
2. P. Tournier, *The Person Reborn* (London: SCM, 1975), 74. Used by permission.
3. Baldwin, *1 & 2 Samuel*, 187.
4. W. G. Blaikie, *First Samuel*, 39-43; A. Redpath, *The Making of a Man of God* (Westwood, NJ: Revell, 1962), 195-96, 198. Cf. C. Plautz, *Zeitschrift für die alttestamentliche Wissenschaft* 65 (1963), 3-27.
5. E. Neufeld, *Ancient Hebrew Marriage Laws* (London: Longmans, Green, 1944), 118ff.
6. Almost without exception, commentators and preachers have denounced David as a poor father. They move ahead of the narrative twenty or more years and show how some of David's sons acted unwisely or selfishly. We do not wish to gloss over the faults of David's sons. We believe, however, that the condemnation of David is unwarranted. To be impartial, those who indict David should also indict God, who bore a Father-son relationship to Israel. His "sons" turned out badly (cf. Isaiah 1:2)! Are the same criteria to be applied to Him too? Let preachers and commentators be careful in their application of the text to the lives of people. I have met many godly parents who are crushed over their children's attitudes and lifestyles. They reared their sons and daughters as wisely as they could, and the choices of their grown children are now a continuing source of grief. Cf. K. Ham, "Where Are All the Godly Offspring?" *Institute for Creation Research* (December 1989), a-c.

   Michal is not mentioned in this list of David's wives because she had borne him no children. *Amnon* was David's eldest son and, in the eyes of most people, the one likely to succeed his father on the throne. For a consideration of the term "first-born" see *Theological Dictionary of the Old Testament*, II:121-27. His name means "faithful" (see Noth, *Personennamen*, 128). *Chileab* was the son of the godly Abigail. He is called Daniel in 1 Chronicles 3:1. This may have been a second name by which he was known. (Or if Chileab died while still young, the chronicler may have included the name of a second son born to Abigail and David.) Nothing more is recorded of Chileab. Some have argued that the original of the word was *Kil'āb* (a shortened form of *ykl-'b* or *ykl-yh*, meaning "the Father [i.e., God] prevails"). Still others adhere to the theory that *Kil'āb* is an abbreviation of "Caleb," since Abigail possibly descended from the family of Caleb. Little is to be gained from such speculation. *Absalom* was born to a princess, the daughter of the king of Geshur. He dominates chapters 13–19. His name comes from two Hebrew words, *Abi*, "my father," and *shalom*, "peace." The question is, Who is the "father," David or God? Cf. *Theological Dictionary of the Old Testament*, I:16; Noth, *Personennamen*, p. 222. For the location of Geshur, see B. Mazar, *Journal of Biblical Literature* 80 (1961), 17. For a discussion of the political significance of the marriage of Maacah to David, see J. D. Levenson and B. Halpern, *Journal of Biblical Literature* 99 (1980), 518; and A. Malamat, *Journal of Near Eastern Studies* 22 (1963), 8. *Adonijah* is the first son of David to be given a Yahwistic theophoric name (i.e., one ending in *Jah*). Cf. Noth, *Personennamen*, 117-21. *Shephatiah* and *Ithream* are unknown apart from their inclusion in the this genealogy. The former means "God has judged," but the meaning of the latter is uncertain (cf. Noth, *Personennamen*, 197). Ithream's mother is specifically designated as being the "wife" of David. Perhaps with a growing harem, and Eglah lacking anything significant in her background, it was too easy for her to be treated as a concubine (cf. Noth, *Personennamen*, 230). A court recorder would be likely, therefore, to specify her true status. The proposal of H. P. Smith, *A Critical and Exegetical Commentary on the Book of Samuel*, International Critical Commentary (New York: Scribner's, 1902), 274, that she was David's half-sister is unwarranted and introduces more problems than it solves. For the value to God's people of these genealogies, see M. D. Johnson, *The Purpose of the Biblical Genealogies...*, New Testament Studies Series (Cambridge: Cambridge University Press, 1969), 310; R. R. Wilson, *Genealogy and History in the Biblical World* (New Haven, CT: Yale University Press, 1977), 222; B. B. Warfield, *Princeton Theological Review* 9 (1911), 1-17; and M. Tsevat, *Journal of Semitic Studies* 3 (1958), 237-43.

7. The LXX mistakenly refers to Ish-bosheth as "Mephibosheth." Cf. Kirkpatrick, *Second Samuel*, 264.

8. Cf. McCarter, *2 Samuel*, 112.

9. C. E. Macartney, *Chariots of Fire* (New York: Abingdon, 1951), 150-59. To take the wife or concubine of a deceased king was tantamount to assuming the right to the throne (cf. the conduct of Absalom and Adonijah in 2 Samuel 16:22 and 1 Kings 2:22, respectively, and the consequences of their actions).

10. Cf. Anderson, *2 Samuel*, 56; McCarter, *2 Samuel*, 112-23.

11. Neufeld, *Ancient Hebrew Marriage Laws*, 123-24.

12. *Rōʾš keleb*, "dog's head," has been explained by Kirkpatrick (*Second Samuel*, 264) as follows: "In the East in ancient times as at the present day, dogs although used for guarding flocks and houses (Job 30:1; Isa. 56:10), were chiefly seen prowling about towns in a half-wild condition, owning no master, living on offal and garbage. Cp. Ps. 59:14,15; I Kings 21:19,23,24; 22:38. Hence the aversion with which they were regarded, and 'dog' became (1) as here, a term of reproach and contempt (cp. I Sam. 17:43; 24:14; 2 Sam. 9:8; 16:9; 2 Kings 8:13): (2) an expression for fierce and cruel men (Ps. 22:16): (3) a name for impure persons (Matt. 7:6; Phil. 3:2; Rev. 22:15)." Cf. H. B. Tristram, *The Natural History of the Bible* (London: Society for Promoting Christian Knowledge, 1889), 78-81;

13. Cf. Anderson, *2 Samuel*, 56.

14. Cf. Kirkpatrick, *Second Samuel*, 264.

15. *Macmillan Bible Atlas*, 90, 106. Cf. *Encyclopedia of Archaeological Excavations in the Holy Land*, I:313-21.

16. J. Perrot, *Israel Exploration Journal* 5 (1955), 17-40, 73-84, 167-89; R. B. K. Amiran, *Israel Exploration Journal* 5 (1955), 240-45; T. Josien, *Israel Exploration Journal* 5 (1955), 246-6; M. Dothan, *Israel Exploration Journal* 6 (1956), 112-14; and Y. Aharoni, *Israel Exploration Journal* 8 (1958), 26-38.

17. Anderson, *2 Samuel*, 56; Hertzberg, *I & II Samuel*, 258; and Kirkpatrick, *Second Samuel*, 69.

18. The term *Lō'-tir'eh 'et-pānay*, "You will not see my face" emphasizes David's authority. It was a privilege or favor granted to only a few to "see the king's face." Cf. the discussion in Blaikie, *Second Samuel*, 44; McCarter, *2 Samuel*, 114.

19. Blaikie, *Second Samuel*, 45-46. For an evaluation of the laws of the time, see Z. Ben-Barak, *Vetus Testamentum Supplement* 30 (1979), 15-29.

20. Cf. *Your Marriage Can Last a Lifetime* (17-28), in which I stress monogamy as God's original intent for marriage. In *You Can Have a Happy Marriage* (Nashville: Nelson, 1990), 77-89 and 93-108, I have commented on some of David's marriages.

21. A careful consideration of different legal codes in force during this period supports the suggestion made in the discussion of verses 13-16. Cf. G. R. Driver and J. C. Miles, *The Babylonian Laws* (Oxford: Clarendon, 1955), I:50-53; C. Edwards, *The Hammurabi Code and the Siniatic Legislation* (Port Washington, NY: Kennikat, 1971),

46; *Ancient Near Eastern Texts Relating to the Old Testament,* ed. J. B. Pritchard (Princeton, NJ: Princeton University Press, 1955), 171-73, 180-85, 190, 196; G. R. Driver and J. C. Miles, *The Assyrian Laws* (Darmstadt, W. Germany: Scientia Verlag Aalen, 1975), 36-55, 386-97; E. Neufeld, *The Hittite Laws* (London: Luzac, 1951), 146-53.

Adultery was to be severely punished, see R. Patai, *Sex and Family in the Bible and the Middle East* (New York: MacGibbon and Kee, 1960), 80-91; S. Greengus, *Hebrew Union College Annual* 40/41 (1969-70), 33-44. If nothing else, public opinion would have weighed heavily against David. But the people did not look upon reunion with Michal as an adulterous relationship. Cf. F. W. Falk, *Hebrew Law in Biblical Times* (Jerusalem: Wharmann, 1964), 154-57; and H. J. Stoebe, *Von Ugarit nach Qumran* (Berlin: Toplemann, 1958), 224-43. The different viewpoints have been summarized by Z. Ben-Barak in *Studies in the Historical Books of the Old Testament* (Leiden, The Netherlands: Brill, 1979), 15-29.

22. Paltiel is called Palti in 1 Samuel 25:44. He was from Bahurim, a village northeast of Jerusalem (cf. 2 Samuel 16:5; 19:16).

23. A. Malamat, *Biblical Archaeologist* 27 (1965), 34-65.

24. Abner had come into Judah under what amounted to a "flag of truce." He had been entertained in lavish style by the king and sent away in peace. H. C. Trumbull, in *The Salt Covenant* (New York: Scribner's, 1899), 182, describes some of the customs of the ancient Near East that would have given Abner further assurance of protection. See also J. Cunningham, *A Way Through the Wilderness* (Grand Rapids: Chosen Books, 1983), 87-94.

25. For a discussion of the role of the elders in Israeli life, see *Theological Dictionary of the Old Testament,* IV:122-31.

26. There is some confusion over the identity of this well, see Josephus, *Antiquities of the Jews,* VII:1:6; Anderson, *2 Samuel,* 61; McCarter, *2 Samuel,* 117; W. M. Thomson, *The Land and the Book,* 3 vols. (New York: Harper and Brothers, 1886), I:194-95, 201-02.

27. Hertzberg (*I and II Samuel,* 261) is in error when he proposes that Joab had concocted a secret understanding with David whereby Abner was to be recalled and killed, and that Joab would take the blame.

28. J. Pedersen, *Israel, Its Life and Culture,* 4 vols. in 2 (London: Cumberlege, 1959), I-II:388.

29. A. P. Stanley, *Scripture Portraits* (London: Allen, n.d.), 70-71.

30. *Wĕdan... yāhōl 'al-rōʾš Yôʾāb,* "may the blood come down upon the head of Joab," is a strong curse. It is possible that, in spite of all David did to avoid having his name connected with Abner's murder, there were still people who slandered him and pointed out how much he had to gain from Abner's death. Contemporary examples are N. P. Lemche, *Journal for the Study of the Old Testament* 10 (1978), 17-18; J. C. Vanderkam, *Journal of Biblical Literature* 99 (1980), 532.

31. *Zondervan Pictorial Encyclopedia of the Bible,* V:192.

32. H. A. Brongers, *Oudtestamentische Studien* 20 (1971), 20.

33. N. Stinnet and J. DeFrain, *Secrets of Strong Families* (Boston: Little, Brown, 1986), 196.

Chapter 4

1. W. F. Albright, *Archaeology and the Religion of Israel* (London: Penguin, 1954), 206, note 62; E. M. Blaiklock, *Today's Handbook of Bible Characters* (Minneapolis: Bethany, 1979), 156. J. Bright, *A History of Israel,* 3d ed. (Philadelphia: Westminster, 1981), 191, states: "Eshbaal [another name for Ish-bosheth] was never acclaimed by the people (cf. II Sam. 2. 8f), never rallied the tribal levies about him, plus the fact that even in his lifetime people were considering going over to David (cf. 3:17-19), shows that his claims [to the throne] had little basis in the popular will." Cf. A. Soggin, *Old Testament and Oriental Studies* (Rome: Biblical Institute Press, 1975), 31-49; M. Tsevat, *Hebrew Union College Annual* 46 (1975), 71-87.

2. Blaikie, *David,* 151-52.

3. Ibid., 152-53: "The two men that murdered [Ish-bosheth] seem to have been among those whom Saul enriched with the plundered spoils of the Gibeonites. They were men of *Beeroth*, formerly one of the cities of the Gibeonites, but now reckoned to Benjamin. Saul appears to have attacked and killed or driven away the Beerothites, and given their property to his favourites (comp. 1 Sam. 22:7, and 2 Sam. 21:2). A curse rested upon the transaction; Ishbosheth, one of his sons, was murdered by two of those who were enriched through the unhallowed deed; and many years after, his bloody house had to yield up seven of his sons to justice, when a great famine showed that for this crime the Divine wrath still rested on the land." Cf. P. K. McCarter, Jr., *Interpretation* 35 (1981), 355-67.

4. J. Kitto, *Daily Bible Illustrations* (Grand Rapids: Kregel, 1981), I:761-62.

5. *Bě'ērōt*, "wells," has been identified with modern Khirbet el-Biyar, approximately 5 miles northwest of Jerusalem. Cf. *Macmillan Bible Atlas*, 130; Y. Aharoni, *The Land of the Bible*, trans. A. F. Rainey, rev. ed. (Philadelphia: Westminster, 1979), 212.

6. T. Veijola, *Revue Biblique* 85 (1978), 338-61. Josephus (*Antiquity of the Jews*, VII:2:1) omits mention of Mephibosheth. Cf. Driver, *Hebrew Text*, 254; M. Tsevat, *Hebrew Union College Annual* 46 (1975), 75-83.

7. Aharoni, *Land of the Bible*, 35-36, 40-41, 54-60; F.-M. Abel, *La Géographie de la Bible*, 2d ed. (Paris: Gebalda, 1933), I:423-29; Robinson, *Biblical Researches*, I:169; II:186-87.

8. S. Talmon, *Textus*, Annual of the Hebrew University Bible Project I (Jerusalem: Magnus, 1960), 144-84.

9. J. C. VanderKam, *Journal of Biblical Literature* 99 (1980), 521-39; N. P. Lemche, *Journal for the Study of the Old Testament* 10 (1978), 2-25; Kirkpatrick, *Second Samuel*, 275; and Ch. Mabee, *Zeitschrift für die alttestamentliche Wissenschaft* 92 (1980), 89-107.

10. Since the crime was self-confessed, no witnesses were needed. David, as judge, merely pronounced sentence in accordance with the law. Cf. S. Mendelsohn, *The Criminal Jurisprudence of the Ancient Hebrews* (New York: Hermon, 1968), 38-44; deVaux, *Ancient Israel*, 10-12, 158-59. It is most unlikely that Rechab and Baanah were executed *in* the palace. It is probable that they were taken to a place of execution.

11. The Pool of Hebron is often identified as Birket es-sultan. Cf. Abel, *Géographie*, I:454; Robinson, *Biblical Researches*, II:74; and Thomson, *The Land and the Book*, I:275-77.

12. Cf. *Theological Wordbook of the Old Testament*, I:158-59 (#343); *New International Dictionary of New Testament Theology*, ed. C. Brown (Grand Rapids: Zondervan, 1976), II:208-09; *Theological Dictionary of the New Testament*, ed. G. Kittel and G. Friedrich, trans. G. W. Bromiley (Grand Rapids: Eerdmans, 1964), I:657-58; R. A. Stewart, *Rabbinic Theology* (Edinburgh: Oliver and Boyd), 157-60.

13. *New International Dictionary of New Testament Theology*, III: 564-69. Cf. J. J. Gluck, *Vetus Testamentum* 13 (1963), 144-50; E. Lipinski, *Vetus Testamentum* 24 (1974), 497-99; W. Richter, *Biblische Zeitschrift* 9 (1965), 71-84.

14. Saul's reign is said to have lasted for forty years. This included Ish-bosheth's occupancy of the throne (inasmuch as he was the last of the Saulide dynasty). David is said to have reigned for seven and a half years in Hebron, and for 33 years in Jerusalem. It seems likely that the six month overlap occurred during which time the northern tribes debated the viability of having David as their king.

15. McCarter, *2 Samuel*, 131.

16. Blaikie, *David*, 157-58.

17. W. Bruggemann, *Catholic Biblical Quarterly* 3 (1970), 532-42; G. Fohrer, *Zeitschrift für die alttestamentliche Wissenschaft* 71 (1959), 1-22; M. Weinfeld, *Biblica* 56 (1975), 120-28; idem, *Journal of the American Oriental Society* 90 (1970), 184-203; D. R. Hillers, *Zeitschrift für die alttestamentliche Wissenschaft* 77 (1965), 86-89; and J. F. Walvoord, *Bibliotheca Sacra* 110 (1953), 97-110.

18. M. B. Hodge, *Your Fear of Love* (Garden City, NY: Doubleday, 1967), 270pp.

19. C. J. Goslinga, *Gereformeerd Theologisch Tijdschrift* 59 (1956), 11-16; D. M. Gunn, *Semeia* 3 (1975), 14-45; idem, *Vetus Testamentum* 26 (1976), 214-29; J. J. Jackson, *Canadian Journal of Theology* 11 (1965), 183-95.

20. For a few of the less well-known examples of retribution, see Hosea 9:1, 3-4, 8, 11-13,

15; Amos 1:3–2:16; 4:6-13; Micah 3:1-12; 6:5, 10-16; Habakkuk 1:46; 2:6-8; Haggai 1:6, 9-11; Zechariah 7:9-14; Malachi 2:2, 6-9; 3:5; 4:2-3.

Chapter 5

1. Cf. Blaikie, *David*, 159.
2. B. Mazar, *The Mountain of the Lord* (Garden City, NY: Doubleday, 1975), 41; H. T. Frank, *An Archaeological Companion to the Bible* (London: S.C.M., 1972), 117, 124-27; K. M. Kenyon, *Digging Up Jerusalem* (London: Book Club Associates, 1974), 34, 41-42, 46-48. 50; J. J. Simons, *Jerusalem in the Old Testament* (Leiden, The Netherlands: Brill, 1952), 35-194; G. A. Smith, *Jerusalem*, 2 vols. (New York: Armstrong, 1908), I:154fff.; II:39ff. See also R. K. Harrison, ed., *Major Cities of the Biblical World* (Nashville: Nelson, 1985), 139-41; *Ancient Near Eastern Texts* 329, 489; *Archaeology and Old Testament Study*, 3-15.
3. A. P. Stanley, *Sinai and Palestine In Connection With Their History* (London: Murray, 1889), 176f.
4. Kenyon, 33, 99; Smith, *Books of Samuel*, I:154ff.; II:39ff.; C. E. Hauer, Jr., *Catholic Biblical Quarterly* 32 (1970), 571-78; E. L. Sukenik, *Journal of the Palestine Oriental Society* 8 (1928), 12-16.
5. Bright, *History of Israel*, 200.
6. C. Herzog and M. Gichon, *Battles of the Bible* (New York: Random, 1978), 77-78.
7. G. Brunet, *Vetus Testamentum Supplement* 30 (1979), 65-86; Yadin, *Art of Warfare*, II:269.
8. Josephus, *Antiquities of the Jews*, VII:3:1.
9. The meaning of *sinnor* has attracted the attention of scholars for decades. Cf. Anderson, *2 Samuel*, 84; Mazar, *Mountain of the Lord*, 168; *Theological Wordbook of the Old Testament*, II:771 (#1942); W. F. Albright, *Journal of the Palestine Oriental Society* 2 (1922), 286-90; G. Bressan, *Biblica* 25 (1944), 346-81; G. Brunet, *Vetus Testamentum Supplement* 30 (1979), 73-86; J. Shiloh, *Biblical Archaeologist* 44 (191), 170. Interpretations of *ṣinnôr* vary. Some of the most common translations of the word are "weapon," and "grappling iron." The most satisfactory explanation, however, still is "water shaft" (cf. Simons, *Jerusalem*, 45-67; and L. H. Vincent, *Revue Biblique* 33 [1924], 357-70).
10. Thomson, *The Land and the Book*, I:514-18; N. Avigad, *Discovering Jerusalem* (Nashville: Nelson, 1983), 235-37.
11. For a further discussion of *ṣinnôr*, see Josephus, *Antiquities of the Jews*, VII:3:1. Cf. Mettinger, *King and Messiah*, 41; W. C. E. Watson, *Vetus Testamentum* 20 (1970), 501-02.
12. Josephus, *Antiquities of the Jews*, VII:3:1.
13. For other references to the "Lord of Hosts" see W. Gesenius, *Hebrew and English Lexicon of the Old Testament*, eds. F. Brown, S. R. Driver, and C. A. Briggs (Oxford: Clarendon, 1962), 838-39; *Theological Wordbook of the Old Testament*, II:750-51 (#1865).
14. Ishida, *David and Solomon*, 212-14. This event, and others like it, foreshadows the people of the world coming to Jerusalem to receive God's blessing during the Millennium, and the kings of the nations bringing gifts to the Lord's Anointed (Isaiah 2:2-3; 49:6-7, 22-23; 60:3-14; Zechariah 8:22).
15. Bright, *History of Israel*, 201 (see also Charts IV and V); Anderson, *2 Samuel*, 86; Josephus, *Against Apion*, 1:18.
16. D. A. Anderson, *All the Trees and Woody Plants of the Bible* (Waco, TX: Word, 1979), 16, 44-46.
17. M. Henry, *Commentary on the Whole Bible* (New York: Revell, n.d.), II:469. Emphasis in the original.
18. David has many critics who are unsparing in their censure of him. As competent a Bible scholar as J. C. Laney indicts him for breaking the Law. He writes: "The multiplication of David's wives and concubines (5:13-16) was in direct violation of Deut. 17:17. These verses reflect David's involvement in international treaties and alliances that were sealed by the marriage of a king's daughter to the other

participants in the treaty" (*First and Second Samuel* [Chicago: Moody, 1982], 94). Such a belief places the burden of proof on Laney's shoulders, for only Maacah was a king's daughter. If preachers and teachers would only interpret David's actions in light of the culture of his times, we would not need to defend him against such charges.

19. Attention focuses on *Solomon*, and the following articles present differing views concerning him and whether or not he was the firstborn of David and Bathsheba after the death of their child who was a result of their adulterous relationship. G. Gerleman, *Zeitschrift für die alttestamentliche Wissenschaft* 85 (1973), 13; A. M. Honeyman, *Journal of Biblical Literature* 67 (1948), 23; J. J. Stamm, *Theologische Zeitschrift* 16 (1960), 296. T. Veijola, *Vetus Testamentum Supplement* 30 (1979), 230-50, conjectures that *Solomon*, whose name means "peace," may have been looked upon by his parents as a substitute for Uriah or his brother who died a week after he was born. This view, however, seems unlikely. (It is likely that at least six weeks had passed between the birth and death of Bathsheba's firstborn, not a single week.)

It is unwise to read too much into the names given each child. *Shammua*, "Yahweh has heard" (cf. Noth, *Personennamen*, 185). *Shobab*, meaning uncertain (cf. Noth, *Personennamen*, 258). It has been conjectured that *Nathan* may be an abbreviation of Jonathan or some other name ending in "nathan" (see Noth, *Personennamen*, 170). *Ibhar*, may express the idea "May God choose" (cf. Noth, *Personennamen*, 209). *Elishua*, similar to the well known "Joshua," means "God is salvation." *Nepheg*, meaning uncertain. *Japhia*, possibly "May [God] shine" (cf. Noth, *Personennamen*, 204). *Elishama*, "God has heard." *Eliada*, "God knows." And finally, *Eliphelet*, "God is deliverance" (cf. Noth, *Personennamen*, 156).

20. *Macmillan Bible Atlas*, 100. Cf. Robinson, *Biblical Researches*, I:219.
21. Herzog and Gichon, *Battles of the Bible*, 79-82; C. E. Hauer, Jr., *Catholic Biblical Quarterly* 32 (1970), 571-78.
22. Anderson, *All the Trees... of the Bible*, 16, 44-46.
23. Ibid., 44-46.
24. Many scholars believe Gibeah was meant instead of Geba. Cf. *International Standard Bible Encyclopedia* (1982), II:706ff.
25. *Encyclopedia of Archaeological Excavations in the Holy Land*, II:428-43; *International Standard Bible Encyclopedia* (1982), II:458-60.

Chapter 6

1. *Zondervan Pictorial Encyclopedia of the Bible*, IV:360-66. Cf. A. F. Key, *Journal of Biblical Literature* 83 (1964), 57-58; G. von Rad, *Studies in Deuteronomy* (London: SCM, 1953), 37-44; Pedersen, *Israel*, I-II:245-59.
2. J. P. Ross, *Vetus Testamentum* 17 (1967), 76-92. W. Eichrodt refers to the Ark as Yahweh's "dynamic presence" in the midst of Israel (see his *Theology of the Old Testament*, trans. by J. A. Baker [Philadelphia: Westminster, 1967], II:190-94, noting in particular p. 193). See also A. B. Davidson, *Theology of the Old Testament* (Edinburgh: Clark, 1961), 164-69.
3. *Macmillan Bible Atlas*, 90, 100. Referred to variously as Kiriath-baal (Joshua 15:60; 18:14) or Baale-judah (as in the present passage), Kiriath-jearim (1 Samuel 6:21; 7:1-2) lay half way between Jerusalem and Gezer. Cf. Keil, *Samuel*, 258; N. H. Tur-Sinai, *Vetus Testamentum* 1 (1951), 275-86. See also W. G. Hupper, *An Index to Periodical Literature on the Old Testament and Ancient Near Eastern Studies*. In process (Metuchen, NJ: Scarecrow, 1987-), II:432.
4. W. J. Deane, *David: His Life and Times* (London: Nesbit, n.d.), 108.
5. Blaikie, *David*, 165.
6. Many of the festivals in ancient Israel were connected with the people's agrarian economy. See G. A. Smith, *Historical Geography of the Holy Land* (New York: Armstrong, 1902), 63, who says: "The ruling feature of the climate [of the Near East] is the division of the year into a rainy and a dry season. Toward the end of October heavy rains fall, at intervals, for a day or several days at a time. These are

what the Bible calls the *early* or *former* rains (Heb. *yoreh*) literally the *pourer*. It opens the agricultural year. The soil, hardened and cracked by the long summer, is loosened, and the farmer begins plowing. Till the end of November the average rainfall is not large, but it increases through December, January, and February, begins to abate in March, and is practically over by the middle of April. *The later rains* (Heb. *malqosh*) of Scripture are the heavy showers of March and April. Coming as they do before the harvest and the long summer drought, they are of far more importance to the country than all the rains of the winter months, and that is why these are passed over in Scripture, and emphasis is laid alone on the *early* and *latter* rains. This has given most people to believe that there are only two intervals of rain...the vernal and autumnal equinox; but the whole of the winter is the rainy season, as indeed we are told in the well-known lines of the Song of Songs:

> Lo, the winter is past,
> The rain is over and gone.

Hail is common, and is often mingled with rain and with thunderstorms, which happen at intervals throughout the winter, and are frequent in spring. In May... till October not only is there no rain, but a cloud seldom passes over the sky." See also Baly, *Geography*, 47-59, 84-86.

7. Cf. G. H. Davies, *Annual of the Swedish Theological Institute* 5 (1967), 30-47; Davidson, *Theology of the Old Testament*, 112.
8. The term *'ărôn hā'ĕlōhîm*, "the Ark of God," in verse 2 is surprising. We would have expected "Ark of the Covenant." Cf. *Hebrew and English Lexicon* (eds. Brown, Driver and Briggs), 1027-28; E. Nielsen, *Vetus Testamentum Supplement* 7 (1960), 61-74.
9. Blaikie, *Second Samuel*, 86ff.
10. M. Haran, *Eretz Israel* 5 (1958), 83-89; idem, *Israel Exploration Journal* 9 (1959), 30-38; W. F. Albright, *Biblical Archaeologist Reader*, Vol. 1 (New York: Doubleday, 1961), 95-97; deVaux, *Ancient Israel*, 295-302, 319-20. See also *The Minister's Library* (Neptune, NJ: Loizeaux, 1985-87), I:451-56 and II:488-92, for works on the Tabernacle.
11. G. R. Driver, *Journal of Theological Studies* 34 (1933), 34-38; M. Gorg, *Zeitschrift für die alttestamentliche Wissenschaft* 89 (1977), 115-18; R. Nicole, *Westminster Theological Journal* 17 (1955), 117-57.
12. *Zondervan Pictorial Encyclopedia of the Bible*, IV:311-24. Cf. Hupper, *Index to Periodical Literature*, I: 242-46; *New International Dictionary of Biblical Archaeology*, eds. E. M. Blaiklock and R. K. Harrison (Grand Rapids: Zondervan, 1983), 322-23; D. R. Hillers, *Catholic Biblical Quarterly* 30 (1968), 48-55; S. B. Finesinger, *Hebrew Union College Annual* 3 (1926), 21-75; J. A. Soggin, *Vetus Testamentum* 14 (1964), 374-77.
13. *Hebrew and English Lexicon*, 1030. Cf. Mauchline, *1 and 2 Samuel*, 224.
14. Cf. Hertzberg, *I and II Samuel*, 279; Kirkpatrick, *Second Samuel*, 291; Mauchline, *1 and 2 Samuel*, 224.
15. Keil, *Samuel*, 261; *Theologisches Wörterbuch zum Alten Testament*, eds G. J. Butterweck and H. Ringgren (Stuttgart: Kohlhmmer, 1970-), III:188.
16. Baldwin, *1 and 2 Samuel*, 208.
17. Ibid., 208.
18. Keil, *Samuel*, 262; Josephus, *Antiquities of the Jews*, VII:4:2. Cf. Kirkpatrick, *Second Samuel*, 293. Cf. Noth, *Personennamen*, 137-39.
19. W. F. Albright, *Archaeology of Palestine* (New York: Penguin, 1956), p. 140. Cf. E. G. Krealing, *Journal of Biblical Literature* 47 (1928), 156.
20. J. Hall, *Contemplations on the Historical Passages of the Old and New Testaments* (London: S.P.C.K., n.d.), 214.
21. Blaikie, *David*, 168.
22. Ephods of fine twined linen, and colored gold, blue, purple, and scarlet, were customarily (though not exclusively) worn by priests. They were sleeveless vests that fitted closely around the shoulders, being held in place by two straps under the armpits. A hole at the top admitted the head. Ephods extended down to the wearer's buttocks (cf. Exodus 28:4-40; 35:27; 39:2-29). The ephod could either be worn over a *me'il*, or long "robe" that reached down to the ankles, or over a *kuttonet* or "tunic"

that reached down to the middle of the thighs. Cf. J. Morgenstern, *Hebrew Union College Annual* 17 (1942), 153-265; deVaux, *Ancient Israel*, pp. 349-52. A *mothen* or "loin cloth" (like a short pair of trousers) was worn under the *kuttonet* so that the wearer could work without embarrassment.

It seems most likely that David wore a *kūttōnet* or shorter form of tunic. If this is so, then he would certainly have worn a *mōthēn* (loin cloth) under his tunic.

An idiom of the time, however, referred to a man as "naked" if all he had on was his tunic and "loin cloth" (cf. 1 Samuel 19:24; John 21:7). In our culture this would not raise such a comment. Depending on the setting, being attired in a T-shirt and Bermuda shorts, could be quite appropriate.

For a further discussion see A. Phillips, *Vetus Testamentum* 19 (1969), 485-87; N. L. Tidwell, *Vetus Testamentum* 24 (1974), 505-07.

23.   M. I. Gruber, *Biblica* 62 (1981), 345. Cf. W. E. O. Oesterley, *The Sacred Dance* (Cambridge: Cambridge University Press, 1923), 234pp.; Pedersen, *Israel*, III-IV:759; A. Sendry, *Music in Ancient Israel* (New York: Philosophical Library, 1969), 441ff.

24.   A. Whyte, *Bible Characters: Old Testament* (Grand Rapids: Zondervan, n.d.), 274-75. See also the revealing work by B. Snyder, *Stand by Your Man* (Sisters, OR: Questar, 1990), 221pp., further enlarges upon this theme. For additional discussions on this subject, see Hupper, *Index to Periodical Literature*, I:66.

25.   Cf. Barber, *You Can Have a Happy Marriage*, 77-92. Cf. D. J. A. Clines, *Vetus Testamentum* 22 (1972), 272; J. Morgenstern, *Zeitschrift für die alttestamentliche Wissenschaft* 49 (1931), 54-55.

26.   H. H. Rowley, *Journal of Biblical Literature* 58 (1939), 126-27. Cf. R. E. Clements, *God and Temple* (Oxford: Blackwell, 1965), 163pp.; Campbell, *The Ark Narrative*, 126-40; idem, *Journal of Biblical Literature* 98 (1979), 31-43; J. Morgenstern, *Hebrew Union College Annual* 17 (1942), 153-265.

27.   According to the *Midrash Rabbah* on Numbers (I:134-35) Michal did not come into David's house, but, leaving her house, accosted David in the street and overwhelmed him with reproaches so that those who passed by witnessed a family feud. This conflicts with the Biblical record, for David is specifically said to have entered his house (and was intent upon bestowing the blessing of the Lord on all present) when Michal intercepted him. The Bible also records accurately what transpired between them.

28.   '*Amhôt 'abādāyw*, "servants' wenches," is a derogatory term used by Michal to describe all the women who participated in the celebrations, both slave and free. Some of them were probably the wives of David's high-ranking officials. This shows that she thought all of them to be inferior to herself. She was animated by such a haughty spirit that we are not surprised she was totally out of sympathy with her husband's actions and aspirations. There is no reason to conclude with R. A. Carlson in *David, the Chosen King* (Stockholm, Sweden: Almquist and Wiksell, 1964), 87, 91-96, and J. R. Porter, *Journal of Theological Studies* 5 (1954), 166, that the women to whom Michal referred were "sacred prostitutes."

29.   Henry, *Commentary*, II:477.

30.   For a discussion of *bahur* in God's choice of David, see Z. Weisman, *Vetus Testamentum* 31 (1981), 441-50.

31.   Josephus, *Antiquities of the Jews*, VII:6:3-4 attempts to exonerate Michal. He believes that after this incident she returned to Paltiel and her five children. The *Midrash Rabbah* on Numbers (I:219) confirms this. The *Talmud*, Sanhedrin, 19*b* and 21*a*, however, claims that the children were Merab's and Michal was rearing them for her deceased sister. The *Midrash Rabbah* on Numbers (I:133f.) also states that other women looked down on the procession, saw David dancing, but did not take exception to what he was doing.

32.   Baldwin, *1 and 2 Samuel*, 211.

33.   *The Jewish Encyclopedia*, ed. I. Singer (New York: Funk and Wagnalls, 1906), VIII:541; *Universal Jewish Encyclopedia*, ed., I. Landman (New York: Universal Jewish Encyclopedia Company, 1946), VII:531. The Targum on Ruth 3:3 state that David and Michal "never lived together again." This has given rise to the belief

that he divorced her. Cf. J. Morgenstern, *Zeitschrift für die alttestamentliche Wissenschaft* 49 (1931), 54-55.
34. Mauchline, *1 and 2 Samuel*, 226. Cf. J. R. Porter, *Journal of Theological Studies* 5 (1954), 166.
35. P. Buck, *The Exile* (New York: Reynal and Hitchcock, 1936), 251.
36. Whyte, *Bible Characters: Old Testament*, 276-77.
37. Cf. W. W. Wiersbe, *Real Worship* (Nashville: Nelson, 1986), 191pp.
38. Cf. M. R. Littleton, *Submission Is For Husbands, Too* (Denver, CO: Accent, 1987), 189pp.
39. Two helpful books on codependence are M. Beattie's *Codependent No More* (San Francisco: Harper and Row, 1987), 229pp., and R. Hemfelt's *Love Is A Choice* (Nashville: Nelson, 1989), 284pp.
40. Cf. C. J. Barber and G. H. Strauss, *The Effective Parent* (San Bernardino, CA: Here's Life, 1980), 147pp.
41. G. Inrig, *Quality Friendship* (Chicago: Moody, 1981), 223pp.
42. G. A. Getz, *A Biblical Theology of Material Possessions* (Chicago: Moody, 1990), 438pp.
43. W. W. Wiersbe, *The Integrity Crisis* (Nashville: Nelson, 1988), 142pp.

Chapter 7

1. Cf. J. B. Phillips, *Your God Is Too Small* (New York: Macmillan, 1967), 140pp. This is an excellent book. Phillips was one of the first pastor/theologians to draw attention to the correlation between the manner in which one was reared and the later development of his/her Godward relationship. Other good works are S. Brown's *When Being Good Isn't Good Enough* (Nashville: Nelson, 1990), 222pp., and J. VanVonderen's *Tired of Trying to Measure Up* (Minneapolis: Bethany, 1989), 171pp.
2. In theology, *transcendence* means that God is above and independent of the material universe. He is different from the rest of Creation. He is "wholly other," infinite, and without a beginning. Because God is transcendent, nothing can transcend Him. We may experience His love and faithfulness, but God's love in all its fullness transcends time and space and exceeds our ability to comprehend it.
3. Theologically speaking, *immanence* means that God, through sovereign and transcendent, is also present and active in both creation and human history. The Biblical teaching on God's nearness, presence, and indwelling keep the believer from the errors of Deism on the one hand, and Pantheism on the other. God's immanence is seen in His sustaining the whole world order, and energizing the souls and wills of His creatures.
4. J. P. Sartre, *Being and Nothingness*, trans. H. E. Barnes (New York: Washington Square, 1969), 811pp.
5. Pentecost, *Things to Come*, 65-94; idem, *Thy Kingdom Come* (Wheaton, IL: Victor, 1990), 51-64; Peters, *Theocratic Kingdom*, I:292-311; II:137, 144; III:309ff.
6. Pentecost, *Things to Come*, 95-99; idem, *Thy Kingdom Come*, 101-8; Peters, *Theocratic Kingdom*, I:311-12; J. F. Walvoord, *Israel in Prophecy* (Grand Rapids: Zondervan, 1962), 80-131. Cf. A. Gelston, *Zeitschrift für die alttestamentliche Wissenschaft* 84 (1972), 92-94.
7. Peters, *Theocratic Kingdom*, I:313-19; Pentecost, *Things to Come*, 100-15; idem, *Thy Kingdom Come*, 137-58. Other studies include K. Baltzac, *The Covenant Formulary in Old Testament, Jewish, and Early Christian Writings*, trans. by D. A. Green (Philadelphia: Fortress, 1964), 121ff.; P. J. Calderone, *Dynastic Oracle and Suzerainty Treaty* (Manila, Philippines: Loyola House of Studies, 1966), 80pp.; A. Malamat, *Prophecy: Essays Presented to Georg Fohrer...* (Berlin: deGruyter, 1980), 68-82; M. Noth, *The Laws in the Pentateuch and Other Studies* (London: Oliver and Boyd, 1966), 250-59; M. Ota, *A Light Unto My Path*, ed. H. N. Bream. Gettysburg Theological Studies (Philadelphia: Temple University Press, 1974), 403-08; C. C. Ryrie, *The Basis of the Premillennial Faith* (New York: Loizeaux, 1953), 48-61, 70-73, 94-95.

Journal articles treating the Davidic Covenant include: G. Cooke, *Zeitschrift für die alttestamentliche Wissenschaft* 73 (1961), 202-05; J. Coppens, *Ephemerides Theologiche Louvanienses* 44 (1968), 489-91; P. deRobert, *Vetus Testamentum* 21 (1971), 116-18; W.

J. Drumbell, *Reformed Theological Review* 39 (1980), 40-47; H. Kruse, *Vetus Testamentum* 35 (1985), 139-64; O. Loretz, *Catholic Biblical Quarterly* 23 (1961), 294-96; W. E. Marsh, *Interpretation* 35 (1981), 397-401; J. Muilenburg, *Vetus Testamentum* 9 (1959), 347-65; D. J. McCarter, *Journal of Biblical Literature* 90 (1971), 31-41; J. L. McKenzie, *Theological Studies* 8 (1947), 187-218; P. V. Reid, *Catholic Biblical Quarterly* 37 (1975), 17-20; M. Tsevat, *Hebrew Union College Annual* 34 (1963), 71-82; idem, *Biblica* 46 (1965), 353-56; J. F. Walvoord, *Bibliotheca Sacra* 110 (1953), 97-110; A. Weiser, *Zeitschrift für die alttestamentliche Wissenschaft* 77 (1965), 153-68; Y. Yadin, *Israel Exploration Journal* 9 (1959), 95-98.

8. This is the first mention of Nathan in Scripture. Those who believe that he was a Canaanite from Jebus who had stayed with David after the fall of that city, err in their understanding of Scripture. What is probable is that he was a protege of Samuel's and a "graduate" of one of the Schools of the Prophets. Cf. 1 Chronicles 29:29; 2 Chronicles 9:29.

    For relevant literature on Nathan, see G. W. Ahlstrom, *Vetus Testamentum* 11 (1961), 113-27; P. W. Pruyser, *Pastoral Psychology* 13 (1962), 14-18; C. E. Macartney, *The Woman of Tekoa* (New York: Abingdon, 1955), 133-47, and Blaiklock, *Bible Characters*, 161-62.

9. O. T. Allis, *Prophecy and the Church* (Philadelphia: Presbyterian and Reformed, 1945), 32.

10. G. L. Murray, *Millennial Studies* (Grand Rapids: Baker, 1948), 26-27.

11. The word used in the Masoretic Text is not the usual *mishkān*, "tabernacle," (cf. 6:17), but *'ohel*, "tent," (cf. Exodus 26:1; 36:8) where the plural occurs. Cf. *Theological Wordbook of the Old Testament* I:118-30; F. M. Cross, *Biblical Archaeological Review* (Garden City, NY: Doubleday, 1961), I:201-08 (noting esp. 224-26).

12. B. S. Childs, *The Book of Exodus*, Old Testament Library (Philadelphia: Westminster, 1974), 512ff.

13. Some confusion exists because, in 1 Samuel 1:9, mention is made of a temple and this appears to be contradicted in the present passage (cf. Jeremiah 7:12, 14). Later, however, in the parallel passage in 1 Chronicles 23:32 it is referred to as the "tent of meeting"–the same designation used of God's dwelling place during the wandering of the Israelites in the wilderness. See V. W. Rabe, *Catholic Biblical Quarterly* 29 (1967), 230; F. M. Cross, *Canaanite Myth and Hebrew Epic* (Cambridge, MA: Harvard University Press, 1973), 73 (footnote 114); Hertzberg, *I and II Samuel*, 285; Ishida, *David and Solomon*, 96.

14. *Theological Dictionary of the Old Testament*, V:44-64; *Theological Wordbook of the Old Testament*, I:305-06 (#698).

15. See the excellent treatise by W. W. Barndollar, *Jesus' Title to the Throne of David* (Findlay, OH: Dunham, 1963), 151.

16. J. I. Packer, *Knowing God* (Downers Grove, IL: InterVarsity, 1973), 22.

17. The Pauline teaching on *adoption* is treated in *A Greek-English Lexicon of the New Testament*, by W. Bauer, trans. and adapted by W. Arndt and F. W. Gingrich, rev. by F. W. Danker (Chicago: University of Chicago Press, 1979), 833. Cf. J. D. Dunn, *Romans*, Word Biblical Commentary (Dallas, TX: Word, 1988), I:460-62; H. G. T. Shedd, *Commentary on Romans* (Minneapolis: Klock and Klock, 1978), 246-47; R. Y. K. Fung, *Epistle to the Galatians*. New International Commentary on the New Testament (Grand Rapids: Eerdmans, 1988), 182-88; J. B. Lightfoot, *Epistle of St. Paul to the Galatians* (Grand Rapids: Zondervan, 1969), 168-73.

18. J. D. Woodbridge, ed., *Renewing Your Mind in a Secular World* (Chicago: Moody, 1985), 24-35.

Chapter 8

1. J. F. Walvoord, *Daniel: Key to Prophetic Revelation* (Chicago: Moody, 1971), 239-48; M. F. Unger, *Biblical Demonology* (Wheaton, IL: Scripture, 1963), 181-200.

2. R. C. Stedman, *Spiritual Warfare* (Waco, TX: Word, 1975), 11-12.

3. J. A. MacArthur, Jr., *The Charismatics* (Grand Rapids: Zondervan, 1978), 224pp.

4. Tristram, *Natural History of the Bible*, 306-18; J. D. Whiting, *National Geographic*

Magazine 28 (December 1915), 512-50; T. Chapelle and D. Chapelle, *National Geographic Magazine*, 103 (April 1953), 545-62; T. A. M. Conley, *National Geographic Magazine* 136 (August 1969), 202-27.

5. *Macmillan Bible Atlas*, 9.
6. *Zondervan Pictorial Encyclopedia of the Bible*, II:501.
7. Kirkpatrick (*Second Samuel*, 306) states that this is "a general formula of transition and connection." A. Alt (*Zeitschrift für die alttestamentliche Wissenschaft* 54 [1936], 149-52) sees 8:1 as a summary statement (an epitome of 5:6-26).
8. Baldwin, *1 & 2 Samuel*, 219-20.
9. McCarter, *2 Samuel*, 251-52. Cf. Wood, *United Monarchy*, 235-36; and M. Tsevat, *Hebrew Union College Annual* 34 (1963), 71-82.
10. Keil, *Samuel*, 355; Blaikie, *Second Samuel*, 111.
11. *Peoples of Old Testament Times*, ed. D. J. Wiseman (Oxford: Clarendon, 1973), 53-78; Aharoni, *Land of the Bible*, 291, 294, 297, 312; *New International Dictionary of Biblical Archaeology*, 205-07.
12. *Peoples of Old Testament Times*, 229-58; *New International Dictionary of Biblical Archaeology*, 319-20.
13. Aharoni, *Land of the Bible*, 293, 296-97, 332-37.
14. Kirkpatrick, *Second Samuel*, 307.
15. Keil, *Samuel*, 357; Hertzberg, *I and II Samuel*, 291.
16. *Macmillan Bible Atlas*, 101, 102, 104. Cf. *Peoples of Old Testament Times*, 134-55; *New International Dictionary of Biblical Archaeology*, 147-48; Harrison, *Major Cities of the Old Testament*, 86-106.
17. For a description of the area see Robinson, *Biblical Researches*, III:443ff.; and Stanley, *Sinai and Palestine*, pp. 414ff. For a critical examination of the events described in the text, see A. Malamat, *Journal of Near Eastern Studies* (1963), 2-25; B. Mazar, *Biblical Archaeology Reader* (Garden City, NY: Doubleday, 1964), II:131. McCarter (*2 Samuel*, 247) believes David intended to establish *his* supremacy at "the River" and that Hadadezer opposed him. McCarter makes a claim for David intending to leave a stela or *yado*, "hand" (i.e., monument) there. The weakness of his position is that, after the victory had been won, there is no record of David having erected a monument. If this was his original intent, then we may be sure the Biblical writer would have mentioned the accomplishment of his aim.
18. Anderson, *2 Samuel*, 132-33; McCarter, *2 Samuel*, 249; Yadin, *Art of Warfare*, II:285. Cf. A. Malamat, *Biblical Archaeologist* 21 (1958), 96-102.
19. There is some confusion over the meaning of *nĕṣîb*, "prefect" or "garrison." We prefer the latter meaning as being more in keeping with David's intentions at this time. To place "prefects" in Syria would have served no useful purpose unless they had soldiers under them. Cf. Anderson, *2 Samuel*, 133; Mauchline, *1 and 2 Samuel*, 235.
20. Cf. R. Borger, *Vetus Testamentum* 22 (1979), 397-98. He argues that what is meant by *šilṭê hazzāhāb* is "golden quivers" not "golden shields." Yadin, *Art of Warfare*, II:360 has a picture of a basalt orthostat showing cavalrymen with a round bossed shield over one shoulder. McCarter (*2 Samuel*, 250) rejects this idea in favor of "golden bow case" or "quiver." The context where *šilṭê* is used elsewhere in the Old Testament favors "shields" (cf. 2 Kings 11:10; Song of Solomon 4:4; Ezekiel 27:11).
21. Hebrew *Tebab*, "Tibath." According to Genesis 22:24, this was the name of Abraham's nephew. It is possible that he achieved renown and his name was given to the region.
22. *New International Dictionary of Biblical Archaeology*, 225-26; Aharoni, *Land of the Bible*, 297.
23. *Peoples of Old Testament Times*, 229-58; *New International Dictionary of Biblical Archaeology*, 170-71.
24. *New International Dictionary of Biblical Archaeology*, 394 (commonly, though erroneously, identified as the Wadi el-Milh).
25. For the different views to account for the number of Syrians/Edomites killed, see P. R. Ackroyd, *Second Book of Samuel* (Cambridge, Cambridge University Press, 1977),

88; Driver, *Hebrew Text*, 282-83; Hertzberg, *I and II Samuel*, 292; Mauchline, *1 and 2 Samuel*, 236.

26. Blaikie's excellent discussion (*Second Samuel*, 122-27) should be noted.
27. *Theologisches Worterbuch zum Alten Testament*, II:999-1009; *Theological Wordbook of the Old Testament*, II:947-48 (#2443); D. A. McKenzie *Vetus Testamentum* 17 (1967), 118-21.
28. Mauchline, *1 and 2 Samuel*, 236-37; McCarter, *2 Samuel*, 255; J. Begrich, *Zeitschrift für die alttestamentliche Wissenschaft* 58 (1940/41), 1-29; H. G. Reventlow, *Theologische Zeitschrift* 15 (1959), 161-75.
29. Reference to 2 Samuel 20:23-26 states that Zadok and Abiathar were priests (cf. 15:24, 35; 19:11; 1 Kings 4:4). Abiathar was the son of Ahimelech and the only one to escape the massacre of Nob (1 Samuel 22:20-23). It is possible that a copyist inadvertently reversed the names. For other explanations, see Anderson, *2 Samuel*, 137; Keil, *Samuel*, 356-66; Mauchline, *1 and 2 Samuel*, 237; McCarter, *2 Samuel*, 255-56; R. Begrich, *Zeitschrift für die alttestamentliche Wissenschaft* 58 (1940/41), 5-8. For material on Zadok, see C. E. Hauer, Jr., *Journal of Biblical Literature* 82 (1963), 89-94; H. H. Rowley, *Journal of Biblical Literature* 58 (1939), 113-41.
30. *International Standard Bible Encyclopedia*, III:962, 967.
31. *Soper* literally means "remembrancer." Cf. J. Begrich, *Zeitschrift für die alttestamentliche Wissenschaft* 58 (1940/41), 1-29.
32. C. E. Armerding, *Current Issues in Biblical and Patristic Interpretation*, ed. G. F. Hawthorne (Grand Rapids: Eerdmans, 1975), 75-86.
33. H. H. Rowley, *Worship in Ancient Israel, Its Forms and Meanings* (Philadelphia: Fortress, 1967), 95-96.
34. Stedman, *Spiritual Warfare*, 46. Cf. J. A. Robinson, *Commentary on Ephesians* (Grand Rapids: Kregel, 1979), 130-33, 212-15; and R. E. Pattison and H. C. G. Moule, *Exposition of Ephesians*, 2 vols. in 1 (Minneapolis: Klock and Klock, n.d.), I:217-26.

Chapter 9

1. *The Random House Dictionary*, ed. J. Stein (New York: Random, 1966), 787. Italics in the original. Used by permission.
2. Shakespeare, *Macbeth*, I:5:17.
3. A. Pope, *Moral Essays* (San Marino, CA: Henry E. Huntington Library, 1926), I:109.
4. *Theological Wordbook of the Old Testament*, I:305 (#698); M. Sakenfeld, *The Meaning of Hesed in the Bible* (Missoula, MT: Scholars, 1978), 88.
5. Blaikie (*David*, 134-35) says: "Even Michal, Jonathan's sister, does not seem to have known that a son of [her brother] had survived" the massacre. Had David been aware that a child of Jonathan was living, we may be sure he would have taken steps as soon as he became king to fulfill his vow to his friend. The fact that about ten years had passed since making Jerusalem his capital (or approximately 17.5 years since becoming king in Hebron) indicates that he believed the family of Jonathan had been killed at the time of Israel's defeat by the Philistines (1 Samuel 31).
6. Anderson, *2 Samuel*, 141-42; Kirkpatrick, *Second Samuel*, 315; McCarter, *2 Samuel*, 260.
7. H. W. Robinson, *Corporate Personality in Ancient Israel*, rev. ed. (Philadelphia: Fortress, 1980), 40pp.
8. Blaikie, *David*, 135.
9. Kitto, *Daily Bible Illustrations*, I:739-45.
10. *Macmillan Bible Atlas*, 109, 138.
11. Mephibosheth is referred to as Meri-baal in 1 Chronicles 8:34 and 9:40. Cf. Kitto, *Daily Bible Illustrations*, I:761ff.
12. Blaikie, *David*, 138-40.
13. J. MacDonald, *Journal of Near Eastern Studies* 35 (1976), 147-70.
14. Cf. Fokkelman, *Narrative Art and Poetry*, 30; Mauchline, *1 and 2 Samuel*, 244. According to 1 Chronicles 8:35-40 and 9:41-44 Micah had an impressive line of descendants.
15. A. Stevens, *The Women of Methodism* (New York: Carlton and Lanahan, 1869), 145-73;

[J. K. Foster ?], *The Life and Times of Selina Countess of Huntingdon* (London: Painter, 1841), 2 vols.

16. See the recent work on the life of Charlotte Bronte by M. Peters, entitled *The Unquiet Spirit* (New York: Pocket, 1975), 340pp.; and E. C. Gaskell, *The Life of Charlotte Brontë* (New York: Dorsett, 1982), 432pp.
17. *The Autobiography of Henry Morton Stanley*, ed. D. Stanley (Boston: Houghton, Mifflin,, 1937), 1-125.
18. Source unknown.

Chapter 10

1. Fokkelman (*Narrative Art and Poetry*, 415) has a most interesting outline of this section. Sufficient to note is the fact that most modern commentators have abandoned the heretofore widely accepted outline, viz., that 2 Samuel 1–10 deal with *David's triumphs*, and chs. 13–25 deal with *David's trials*, with the fulcrum being his affair with Bathsheba and Nathan's indictment of his sin (chs. 11–12). Approaches now are based more directly upon the structure of the text.
2. Blaikie, *Second Samuel*, 146.
3. Baldwin, *1 & 2 Samuel*, 228.
4. W. L. Moran, *Catholic Biblical Quarterly* 25 (1963), 80; Anderson, *2 Samuel*, 146; McCarter, *2 Samuel*, 270.
5. Edersheim, *Bible History*, IV:185. The usage of *ûlĕhopkāh*, "turn [over], destroy" (10:3), has led recent translators to paraphrase the thought of the writer "and overthrow it (i.e., the city)." This creates a problem, however, for the idea of "to overthrow or destroy it" is only used in contexts where Yahweh is the subject.
6. Kitto, *Daily Bible Illustrations*, I:1:762-65.
7. Cf. Numbers 13:21. Beth-rehob is also listed among the cities conquered by Thutmosis III of Egypt. See *Ancient Near Eastern Texts*, 243. Micah, according to Judges 18:28, controlled the valley in which Dan had been built. See *Macmillan Bible Atlas*, 101-02, 104, 106.
8. Cf. 1 Chronicles 19:6. B. Mazar, *Journal of Biblical Literature* 80 (1961), 16-28;
9. Tob is identified with modern et-Taiyibeh. The Hebrew text reads *ʾîš ṭôb*, "man of Tob" (evidently the king) who brought his twelve thousand followers (soldiers) with him. Tob is situated twelve miles southeast of the Sea of Galilee. Cf. *New International Dictionary of Biblical Archaeology*, 455.
10. From 2 Samuel 3:22ff. we realize that there were times when David did not go out with the army. Affairs of state (i.e., acting as the chief judge and magistrate of his people) necessitated his presence in Jerusalem. No stigma, therefore, should be attached to the fact that David remained in Jerusalem.
11. The Biblical text of 1 Chronicles 19:6-7 states that the Syrians and the forces under the king of Maacah camped "before Medeba," about twenty miles southeast of Rabbah. Anderson (*2 Samuel*, 147) claims that this is unlikely, for they would be too far from Rabbah to be of any good. If, however, they camped outside of Medeba until after Israel had passed en route to Rabbah, and then moved up toward Rabbah under cover of darkness to lie concealed in a field, then it is easy to see how Joab was taken by surprise when he found himself caught in a pincers movement.
12. Cf. Mazar, *Biblical Archaeologist Reader*, II:131; Y. Yadin, *Biblica* 36 (1955), 349-50; H. J. Stoebe, 93 *Zeitschrift der deutschen Palästina-Vereins*, (1977), 243f.
13. *Bahir*, "chosen" (as distinct from the rest).
14. Cf. R. Giveon, *Journal of Biblical Literature* 83 (1964), 416.
15. Fokkelman, *Narrative Art and Poetry*, 48. Cf. Josephus, *Antiquities of the Jews*, VII:6:1; and Whyte, *Bible Characters: Old Testament*, 303ff.
16. *Macmillan Bible Atlas*, 102. Apart from this reference, Helam is unknown as far as the Biblical record is concerned. It is probable that this out-of-the-way place was chosen to prevent for as long as possible word of their activities getting back to David. Cf. Josephus, *Antiquities of the Jews*, VII:6:2.
17. Cf. A. Malamat, *Journal of Near Eastern Studies* 22 (1963), 2.

18. Blaikie, *Second Samuel*, 151.
19. By focusing on Hanun, we tend to forget David's ambassadors.
20. Blaikie, *Second Samuel*, 155.
21. "An appeal to God, invoking his curse upon (1) either one's self or (2) another," see *Near Eastern Religious Texts Relating to the Old Testament*, ed. W. Beyerlin, Old Testament Library (Philadelphia: Westminster, 1978), 99ff., 129-34.

Chapter 11

1. Fokkelman, *Narrative Art and Poetry*, 51-52. His outline is also of interest to us. It is based upon a structural analysis of the text. He does not find a unifying theme in the text but rather seeks to show the literary symmetry of the writer. Cf. M. Augustin, *Biblische Zeitschrift* 27 (1983), 145-54, who presents a view contrary to the one adopted in this chapter.
2. The opening clause *litšûbat haššana*, "at the return of the year" (11:1), has been interpreted by McCarter (*2 Samuel*, 284-85) as implying "at the same time of year when the ambassadors were first sent to Hanun...."
3. The article with "kings," *hammĕlākîm*, "the kings," indicates specific individuals. Some look upon this verse as a flashback to 10:15 when Syrian monarchs joined Ammon to fight against Israel (10:19b). The text of 10:19b, when read in conjunction with 11:1 *and the seige of Rabbah* (which did not take place when Israel first attacked the Ammonites, [cf. 10:14b that describes the end of Israel's campaign]), implies that these "kings" must have been vassals of Ammon and rulers of "city-states" (but not Syrians. Syria always posed a greater threat than Ammon, and these kings were defeated quickly. Furthermore, the text reads "and [Joab's army] destroyed the sons of Ammon" (not Syria). Those who believe that the reference to "the kings" is to Syrian monarchs err in their interpretation of the text.
4. H. B. Trisham, *Land of Israel* (London: SPCK, 1865), 533ff. Cf. L. Oliphant, *Land of Gilead* (Edinburgh: Blackwood, 1880), 251ff.; Thomson, *The Land and the Book*, III:607-24.
5. Kirkpatrick, *Second Samuel*, 325 (emphasis added). Cf. U. Simon, *Biblica* 48 (1967), 209; H. J. Stobe, *Biblica* 67 (1986), 388-96.
6. *New Unger's Bible Dictionary*, 1058.
7. Kirkpatrick, *Second Samuel*, 325.
8. Mauchline, *1 and 2 Samuel*, 248.
9. Many writers have drawn attention to the usage of the *hithpael* in verse 2 (cf. Baldwin, *1 & 2 Samuel*, 232). It obviously implies pacing back and forth. It is probable that some affair of state brought on this lack of inner ease. If David had wrestled with the matter of considerable importance for some time, then he would be even more likely to welcome a distraction that would give him respite from whatever responsibility had occupied his thoughts.
10. There is absolutely no reason to conclude with Augustin and others that the woman wanted to be seen by David. There is no evidence that she even knew he was on the roof of his palace. Cf. M. Augustin, *Biblische Zeitschrift* 27 (1983), 145-54.
11. Kirkpatrick, *Second Samuel*, 325.
12. D. Bonhoeffer, *Creation and Fall and Temptation* (New York: Macmillan, 1959), 116-17. Cf. R. Gilpin, *Daemonologia Sacra: or a Treatise of Satan's Temptations* (Minneapolis: Klock and Klock, 1982), 58-83; and D. MacDonald, *The Biblical Doctrine of Creation and the Fall* (Minneapolis: Klock and Klock, 1984), 394-488.
13. It is most unusual for a married woman to be identified by the name of her father. The mention of Eliam in this context must indicate something special. According to 2 Samuel 23:34 there was an Eliam who was the son of Ahithophel, David's trusted friend and advisor (cf. Psalm 41:9). If Bathsheba was the daughter of Eliam (as seems likely), then she was Ahithophel's granddaughter (cf. *Talmud*, Sanhedrin, 69b, 101a). Not to be overlooked is the fact that Uriah was one of David's "Mighty Men" (23:39).
14. Cf. Neufeld, *Ancient Hebrew Marriage Laws*, 163-75; deVaux, *Ancient Israel*, 36-37; Z.

C. Hodges, *Bibliotheca Sacra* 136 (1979), 318-32; M. Fishbane, *Hebrew Union College Annual* 45 (1974), 25-45; Barber, *You Can Have a Happy Marriage*, 109-22.

15. Deane, *David: His Life and Times*, 138. Cf. Blaikie, *Second Samuel*, 160-61. Jewish writers try to excuse David's actions. The *Talmud*, (Shabbath, 55:6) denies the adultery of David on the ground that every warrior, before going to the field of battle, had to give his wife a divorce. This, they conclude, freed Bathsheba and so the sin was one of fornication, not adultery (and all David had to do to cover his sin was to marry Bathsheba).

    We do not accept this view. Three lines of evidence may be advanced: (1) David wished to cover his tracks and so tried to induce Uriah to make love to Bathsheba, concluding that he would then believe the child to be his. If she had been legally divorced, David could have taken her into his harem. (2) Throughout this chapter and the next, Bathsheba is specifically referred to as "the wife of Uriah" (and this continues into the New Testament as well [cf. Matthew 1:6b]. Such repeated mention would be ludicrous if Uriah had divorced her. And (3) God did not see David's actions the way the Jewish Rabbis did, cf. 2 Samuel 11:27b.

16. *Talmud*, Niddah, 31b. Cf. Driver, *Hebrew Text*, 289; Hertzberg, *I and II Samuel*, 309f.; Smith, *Books of Samuel*, 317-18.

17. Fokkelman, *Narrative Art and Poetry*, 51-53. Cf. G. Bush, *Notes Critical and Practical on the Book of Leviticus* (Minneapolis: Klock and Klock, 139; R. K. Harrison, *Leviticus, an Introduction and Commentary*, Tyndale Old Testament Commentaries (Downers Grove, IL: InterVarsity, 1980), 163; S. H. Kellogg, *The Book of Leviticus* (Minneapolis: Klock and Klock, 1978), 305-312; and G. J. Wenham, *The Book of Leviticus*, New International Commentary on the Old Testament (Grand Rapids: Eerdmans, 1979), 219-25.

18. *Ancient Near Eastern Texts*, 173, 182; L. M. Epstein, *Sex Laws and Customs in Judaism*, 194-215; E. Neufeld, *Ancient Hebrew Marriage Laws*, 163-75; deVaux, *Ancient Israel*, 36-37; Cf. M. Fishbane, *Hebrew Union College Annual* 45 (1974), 25-45; P. Davies, *Christian Century* 95 (1978), 360-63; Z. C. Hodges, *Bibliotheca Sacra* 136 (1979), 318-32. See also Bush, *Leviticus*, 192-98, 217; Harrison, *Leviticus*, 206; Kellogg, *The Book of Leviticus* (Minneapolis: Klock and Klock, 1978), 418-31; and Wenham, *The Book of Leviticus*, 278-86.

19. Some have taken the words "and wash your feet" as a euphemistic expression for sexual intercourse (cf. Deane, *David*, 139; Hertzberg, *I and II Samuel*, 310-11; U. Simon, *Biblica* 48 (1967), 214.

20. According to Deuteronomy 23:9-10 and 1 Samuel 21:4b, men on active service were to abstain from sexual intercourse. Uriah seems to imply that to have conjugal relations with Bathsheba would be a breach of the sacramental law. Cf. G. H. Jones, *Vetus Testamentum* 25 (1975), 656.

21. Cf. Fokkelman, *Narrative Art and Poetry*, 71-96.

22. Shakespeare, *Macbeth*, III:4:137.

23. Hall, *Contemplations*, 223; R. O. Corvin, *David and His Mighty Men* (Freeport, NY: Books for Libraries, 1970), 153-63.

24. Homer, *Iliad*, VI:168-69. Cf. Gunn, *Story of King David*, 46.

25. Deane, *David*, 140.

26. Oliphant, *The Land of Gilead*, 260.

27. Cf. Genesis 50:10; 1 Samuel 31:13; and in the Apocrypha, the Books of Judith (16:24) and Ecclesiasticus (22:12). In exceptional cases thirty days were spent mourning the dead (Numbers 20:29; Deuteronomy 34:8). See also E. F. deWard, *Journal of Jewish Studies* 23 (1972), 1-27; deVaux, *Ancient Israel*, 59; Petersen, *Israel*, I:241, 295ff., 494f.

28. Blaikie, *David*, 219-28; Blaiklock, *Bible Characters*, 161; C. Gulson, *David: Shepherd and King* (Grand Rapids: Zondervan, 1980), 135-42; F. W. Krummacher, *David, King of Israel* (Minneapolis: Klock and Klock, 1983), 356-72; C. E. Macartney, *The Way of a Man with a Maid* Grand Rapids: Baker, 1974), 116-29; I. Powell, *David, His Life and Times* (Grand Rapids: Kregel, 1990), 237-42; D. Zeligs, *Psychoanalysis and the Bible* (New York: Bloch, 1974), 206-16; et cetera.

29. C. F. H. Henry, *Baker's Dictionary of Christian Ethics* (Grand Rapids: Baker, 1975), 665ff.
30. J. R. W. Stott, *The Epistles of John* (Grand Rapids: Eerdmans, 1964), 98-101; and J. J. Lias, *First Epistle of John* (Minneapolis: Klock and Klock, 1982), 113ff.
31. A. Liversidge, *Omni* (November, 1990), n.p.
32. Lias, *First John*, 118.
33. D. J. Levenson, *The Seasons of a Man's Life* (New York: Ballantine, 1978), 191-259.
34. Lias, *First John*, 118-19. See also note 2 on p. 118.
35. Ibid., 119-20.

Chapter 12

1. A self-fulfilling prophecy is a prediction of belief that serves to bring about its own fulfillment. The person believing it acts in such a way as to make the prophesied event more likely. Cf. R. K. Merton, *Antioch Review* 8 (1948), 193-210; R. Rosenthal, *Experimental Effects in Behavioral Research* (New York: Irvington, 1976), 129-33, 138, 407-13; R. Rosenthal and K. L. Fode, *Behavioral Science* 8 (1963), 183-89; R. Rosenthal and L. Jacobson, *Pygmalion in the Classroom* (New York: Holt, Rinehart and Winston, 1968), 240pp.
2. From 2 Samuel 12:14*b* and 15*b* we realize that David and Bathsheba's child had already been born. From 12:24 we know that at least six weeks had elapsed after her son's birth or else both would have contravened the law of purity and become ceremonially defiled (cf. Leviticus. 12:2-4).
3. Cf. A. D. Hart, *Counseling the Depressed*, Resources for Christian Counseling (Waco, TX: Word, 1987), 44-100. Those who say that David's sins of adultery and murder incapacitated him from leadership err in their judgment (1) of the teaching of this passage, (2) of human nature, and (3) of God's grace. It is depression that renders a person less decisive and less inclined to take effective action. And when depression is compounded by guilt and/or anger or fear, the result can be detrimental to one's leadership ability.
4. U. Simon, *Biblica* 48 (1967), 207-42. For a fuller discussion of verses 1-15*a*, see G. Altpeter, *Theologische Zeitschrift* 38 (1982), 46-52; G. W. Coats, *Interpretation* 35 (1981), 368-82; idem, *Interpretation* 40 (1986), 170-75; P. W. Coxon, *Biblica* 62 (1981), 247-50; A. Phillips, *Vetus Testamentum* 16 (1966), 242-44; A. Rofe, *Vetus Testamentum Supplement* 26 (1974), 143-64; W. M. W. Roth, *Semeia* 8 (1977), 1-13; S. Schill, *Zeitschrift für die alttestamentliche Wissenschaft* 11 (1981), 318; H. Seebass, *Zeitschrift für die alttestamentliche Wissenschaft* 86 (1974), 203-22; and W. S. Vorster in *Text and Reality: Aspects of Reference in Biblical Texts*, eds. B. C. Lategan and W. S. Vorster (Atlanta, GA: Scholars, 1985), 95-112.
5. *Talmud*, Baba Bathra 15*b*. Cf. 1 Kings 20:39-40; Isaiah 5:1-7. See also U. Simon, *Biblica* 48 (1967), 220-25; Gunn, (1978), 40-42; G. W. Coats, *Interpretation* 35 (1981), 368-80.
6. Henry (*Commentary*, II: 500) lays justifiable stress on the fact that it was a "traveler" who came to David, not a frequent "guest." His sin, therefore, was neither habitual nor premeditated.
7. Animals that had become family pets were excluded from those that could be slaughtered and eaten. Cf. A. al-'Ārif, *Bedouin Love, Law, and Legend*, trans. H. W. Tilley (Jerusalem: Cosmos, 1944), 146.
8. David's descriptive phrase, *ben-mắwet*, "son of death," is difficult to interpret. It normally means "one who is as good as dead" or "one who deserves to die." It appears as if David is characterizing the man's behavior, not condemning him to death. This seems to be the meaning, for he goes on to impose the usual penalty of the Law, *viz.*, fourfold restitution. Cf. A. Phillips, *Vetus Testamentum* 16 (1966), 243-44; H. Seebass, *Zeitschrift für die alttestamentliche Wissenschaft* 86 (1974), 204-05; Anderson, *2 Samuel*, 162; Hertzberg, *I and II Samuel*, 312-13; Mauchline, *1 and 2 Samuel*, 253-54; Smith, *Books of Samuel*, 322-23.

   McCarter (*2 Samuel*, 299) compares *ben-mắwet*, "son of death" with *ben-bĕlīya'al*, "son of Belial," that he renders "son of hell." It appears, however, as if he exceeds the linguistic evidence. Exceptions can be found, and as a consequence caution must be used in translation (16:7. Cf. 1 Samuel 20:31-32; 26:16).

9. Exodus 22:1; Proverbs 6:31. W. Coxon (*Biblica* 62 [1981], 250), follows a textual emendation that reads "sevenfold" (*šib'ātayim*). He then points to a possible play on words using the name Bathsheba, which may mean "well of the seven" (or "well of the oath"). Cf. deVaux, *Ancient Israel*, 160.

The *Talmud* (Yoma, 22b) follows the Masoretic Text in advocating fourfold compensation. Cf. al-'Ārif, *Bedouin Love, Law, and Legend*, 147. We reject the Talmudic idea that the fourfold restitution is somehow to be correlated with the deaths of four of David's children: the son of Bathsheba, Ammon, Tamar, and Absalom. (Tamar, as we shall see in the next chapter, did not die.)

10. Cf. Fokkelman, *Narrative Art and Poetry*, 77.

11. "Into your bosom" is a euphemism for sexual intercourse. The obvious implication of the verse embarrasses us. Some have sought to obliquely sidestep the issue by claiming that we have no evidence David actually took Saul's wives into his harem. But the words "and if [these things had been] too little, I would have *added to you many more things like these!*" (12:28b, emphasis added) only increase their dilemma. Baldwin (*1 & 2 Samuel*, 237) writes:

> "[David] had inherited the kingdom and [his] *master's wives*. Evidently the custom was that the harem of the dead monarch was inherited by his successor, and by this rule David had already added to his household. In no respect could he claim that he had been deprived; he was a rich man. Moreover, if he had asked for more he could have had more, such is the extent of the Lord's generosity towards him" (Emphasis in the original).

12. As McCarter (*2 Samuel*, 300) has pointed out, David's sanctimonious words of reassurance to Joab (11:25) will come back to haunt him. The sword will indeed devour, sometimes in one way and sometimes another.

13. Anderson (*1 and 2 Samuel*, 163) reminds us that there is a blank space in the Hebrew text after verse 13a. He believes it may at one time have contained a cross-reference to Psalm 51. Cf. Gunn, *Story of King David*, 97.

14. Cf. G. Gerleman, *Beitrage zur alttestamentliche Theologie:*, ed. H. Donner, R. Hanhart, and R. Smend (Gottengen: Vanderhoeck und Ruprecht, 1977), 133-34; J. W. Rogerson, *Journal of Theological Studies* 21 (1975), 5. See also Anderson, *1 and 2 Samuel*, 163; Hertzberg, *I and II Samuel*, 314-15; Mauchline, *1 and 2 Samuel*, 254-55; and McCarter, *2 Samuel*, 301.

15. Blaikie, *Second Samuel*, 182.

16. R. P. Lightner, *Heaven, For Those Who Can't Believe* (Schaumberg, IL: Regular Baptist Press, 1977), 64pp.

17. Blaikie, *Second Samuel*, 191.

18. David named Bathsheba's second son Solomon. In the Old Testament the naming of a child was usually done by the mother (cf. Genesis 29:32; 1 Samuel 1:20; 4:21), but it could also be done by the father (Genesis 16:15; Exodus 2:22).

19. The name Solomon has generally been identified with *šālōm*, "peace" (cf. 1 Chronicles 22:9, 18. Keil, *Samuel*, 306).

More recently this has been thought to be an "Ersatzname" for Bathsheba's first son. Cf. T. Veijola (*Vetus Testamentum Supplement* 30 [1979], 248) who believes that Solomon was Bathsheba's firstborn. In this, of course, he is mistaken for Bathsheba's firstborn died a few weeks or months after its birth. Solomon's birth was a sign from God of His forgiveness of both the father and the mother.

20. McCarter (*2 Samuel*, 303) is of the opinion that Solomon's name comes from *šēlōmōh*, "the replacement" or "to make amends, replace, restore."

21. N. Wyatt, *Biblica* 66 (1985), 112-25.

22. *Encyclopedia of Archaeological Excavations in the Holy Land*, IV:987; J. H. Stoebe, *Zeitschriften deutschen Palastina-Vereins* 93 (1977), 236-46; *New International Dictionary of Biblical Archaeology*, 382-83.

23. McCarter (*2 Samuel*, 313) believes the weight to be 75 pounds.

24. Baldwin, *1 & 2 Samuel*, 245-46. Baldwin also points out that the words "their king" (*malkām*) could be read as the name of the Ammonite deity (cf. Jeremiah 49:1, 3; Zephaniah 1:5). While some have rejected this on the grounds that David would never take and wear the crown of an idol, Baldwin believes that he might have done so if the crown showed the superiority of Yahweh to Milcom.
25. Driver (*Hebrew Text*, 227-29) refers to the writings of G. Hollmann, *Zeitschrift für die alttestamentliche Wissenschaft* (1882), 53-72, who argues that the real meaning of *malken* is "brick-mould," not "brick kiln." The verb "made to pass through" (AV) could better be rendered "made to labor at" (though this would require the change of *r* (ר) to *d* (ד). The preposition "under" is not the usual rendering of *b* (ב), for which "at" is to be preferred.

    Baldwin, who has placed the whole world in her debt as the result of the publication of her commentary, draws attention to the rendering of the NIV which incorporates these points "consigning them to labor with saws and with iron picks and axes, and he made them work at brick-making." Cf. McCarter, *2 Samuel*, 313.
26. G. C. O'Ceallaigh, *Vetus Testamentum* 12 (1966), 184 (cf. 2 Kings 25:10). Others believe that David set the Ammonites to work "with stone-saws and brick molds."
27. God's grace does not make Him lax in dealing with sin. He will do so, but only when a sinner has refused to respond positively to His lovingkindness (cf. 1 Timothy 5:24-25; Hebrews 9:27). Because we are finite we want to see the Lord punish speedily those who do wrong. He is not limited by time as we are and so can afford to be patient.
28. L. L. Morris, *The Apostolic Preaching of the Cross* (Grand Rapids: Eerdmans, 1965), 224-74 and 125-185; and C. R. Swindoll, *Growing Deep in the Christian Life* (Portland, OR: Multnomah, 1986), 233-45. Swindoll (418 and 420) defines *justification* as "The judicial act of God whereby He declares righteous the believing sinner at the moment of salvation" (Romans 3:24-28; 5:1), and *propitiation* as "The doctrine of the satisfaction of all God's righteous demands for judgment on the sinner by the death of Christ" (Romans 3:25; 1 John 2:2).
29. S. Mendelsohn, *The Criminal Jurisprudence of the Ancient Hebrews* (New York: Hermon, 1968), 131-39.
30. O. Wilde, "De Profundis," *The Works of Oscar Wilde* Leicester, England: Bookmart, 1990), 857.
31. Idem, "The Ballad of Reading Goal," *Works*, 830, 835-36.
32. C. Nimmo, *Power for Living* (May 4, 1980), 2-3.

Chapter 13

1. N. Webster, *Webster's New Universal Unabridged Dictionary*, 2d. ed. (New York: Dorset and Baber, 1979), 317. Used by permission.
2. For information on the laws of consanguinity, see Neufelt, *Ancient Hebrew Marriage Laws*, 191-212; deVaux, *Ancient Israel*, 31-32; Pedersen, *Israel*, I:65f.
3. G. J. Wenham, *Vetus Testamentum* 22 (1972), 342-43. Cf. *Theological Dictionary of the Old Testament*, II:338-43; *Theological Wordbook of the Old Testament*, I:137-39 (#295).
4. Cf. *Talmud* (Sanhedrin, 21*a*) refers to Jonadab as "wise for doing evil."
5. These *lĕbîbôt* were "dumplings," not cakes. They may perhaps have been heart-shaped from *lĕbab*, "heart." Some scholars deduce from *libbēb*, "enhearten" (i.e., give strength, add vigor) that they were either believed to be good for sick people or had aphrodisiac properties. Cf., M. H. Pope, *Song of Songs* (Garden City, NY: Doubleday, 1972), pp. 382-83 who believes the words are erotic and mean simply "to arouse, excite." David certainly did *not* attach such a meaning to Amnon's use of *lebibot*.
6. Baldwin, *1 & 2 Samuel*, 247.
7. Hertzberg, *I and II Samuel*, 323; McCarter, *2 Samuel*, 322. For a contrary opinion, see G. R. H. Wright, *Numen* 28 (1981), 61. Wright also believes that these "cakes" were thought to be aphrodisiacs or to have had therapeutic properties.

8. Anderson (*2 Samuel*, 174) reminds us that a cognate verb to *lēbāb*, "heart," is rendered "make." The polysemantic pun, therefore, can mean "to make (dumplings)" and also "to arouse" (Song of Solomon 4:9).
9. *Theologisches Worterbuch zum Alter Testament*, II:26-30; *Theological Wordbook of the Old Testament*, II:547-48 (#1285).
10. A. Phillips, *Vetus Testamentum* 25 (1975), 241. Cf. W. M. W. Roth *Vetus Testamentum* 10 (1960), 394-409 (note esp. p. 406). A "fool" in Scripture denotes not only the person who is lacking in sense, but more specifically the one who has cast off restraints of decency and morality because he or she has abandoned the "fear of the Lord" (cf. 13:13; Psalm 14:1). The usage of the word here is designed to show Amnon's lack of fitness to rule God's people.
11. D. Daube, *Studies in Biblical Law* (New York: Ktav, 1947), 77-79; deVaux, *Ancient Israel*, 19-20.
12. Cf. Anderson (*2 Samuel*, 177), says: "... the whole incident was part of Amnon's self-assertion over against Absalom and his family."
13. *Theologisches Worterbuch zum Alten Testament*, II:341-50; *Theological Wordbook of the Old Testament*, II: 682-84 (#1652).
14. Various explanations have been offered for the basic shift in his emotions. Cf. *Talmud*, Sanhedrin, 21a; Hertzberg, *I and II Samuel*, 324.
15. The Hebrew text of 13:16 is difficult to translate (cf. G. R. Driver, *Alttestamentliche Studien*, eds. H. Junker and J. Botterweck (Bonn, W. Germany: Hanstein, 1950), 46-61 (noting esp. pp. 48-49). Many versions rely heavily upon the Lucianic version of the LXX and the Old Latin version of the Bible.
16. Baldwin, *1 & 2 Samuel*, 249. Cf. Tacitus, *Agricola*, 100:42. For a discussion of *samen*, "desolate," see *Theological Wordbook of the Old Testament*, II:936-37 (#2409); and deVaux, *Ancient Israel*, 59.
17. *Macmillan Bible Atlas*, 98, 107-08. There is debate over whether the text should be read *'prym*, "Ephraim" (2 Chronicles 13:19) or *'pr*, "oprah" (cf. Joshua 18:23). No vowels are included in the original. The majority of modern scholars favor Oprah. H. Seebass (*Vetus Testamentum* 14 [1964], 498) has shown that the preposition *'im* means "near, in the vicinity of" and not "within." We prefer to retain the reading of the Masoretic Text–"Ball-hazor which is *near* Ephraim." See also K.-D. Schunck, *Vetus Testamentum* 11 (1961), 188-200.
18. *Walo* conveys the idea of "if not you, then at least...."
19. *Macmillan Bible Atlas*, 90, 98, 101-02.
20. McCarter (*2 Samuel*, 333), in commenting on Jonadab's "wisdom" (13:3), says: "[He] seems to have been 'wise' enough to stay home" and not to attend Absalom's party.
21. *Macmillan Bible Atlas*, 71, 73.
22. Fokkelman, *Narrative Art and Poetry*, 109.
23. Driver, *Hebrew Text*, 235.
24. Anderson, *2 SAmuel*, 178, 182.
25. *Macmillan Bible Atlas*, 101-02.
26. J. R. Lowell, *The Complete Works of James Russell Lowell* (Boston, Houghton Mifflin, 1925), 67.
27. T. Archer, *Decisive Events in History* (London: Cassell, Petter, Galpin, n.d.), 11-10.
28. *Suetonius*, trans. J. C. Rolfe, Loeb Classical Library (London: Heinemann, 1951), I:1-119; *Plutarch's Lives*, trans. B. Perrin, Loeb Classical Library (London: Heinemann, 1949), VII:442-609 (noting esp. pp. 523ff.);
   See also Plutarch, *The Lives of the Noble Grecians and Romans*, trans. by J. Dryden, rev. by A. H. Clough (New York: Modern Library, n.d.), 854-89 (noting esp. pp. 874ff.).
   The Rubicon has been identified with the Fulminico River and was the northern most border of Italy.
29. Archer, *Decisive Events in History*, 115-25.
30. R. B. Morris, *Witness at the Creation* (New York: H. Holt, 1985), 279pp. He discusses in particular the contributions of Alexander Hamilton, John Jay, and James Madison.

Chapter 14

1. T. Jefferson, *Writings*, X:304.
2. J. Kieran and A. Daley, *The Story of the Olympic Games* (Philadelphia: Lippincott, 1973), 107-110; S. Magnusson, *The Flying Scotsman* (London: Quartet, 1981), 50-56; C. Swift, *Eric Liddell* (Minneapolis: Bethany, 1990), 89-104.
3. I value highly the writings of the late C. E. Macartney. The position taken in this chapter differs from his interpretation of the incident (see his *The Woman of Tekoa* [New York: Abingdon, 1955], 9-23). For other approaches, see C. V. Camp, *Catholic Biblical Quarterly* 43 (1981), 14-29; J. Hoftijzer, *Vetus Testamentum* 20 (1970), 419-44; G. G. Nicol, *Studia Theologica* (1982), 97-104; and L. A. Schokel, *Biblica* 57 (1976), 192-205.
4. Cf. E. Bellefontaine, *Journal for the Study of the Old Testament* 38 (1987), 47-72; W. M. Clark, *Journal of Biblical Literature* 88 (1969), 266-78; H. McKeating, *Vetus Testamentum* 25 (1975), 46-68; and A. Phillips, *Journal of Jewish Studies* 28 (1977), 105-26.
5. Cf. Anderson, *2 Samuel*, 252-53. See also J. J. Jackson, *Canadian Journal of Theology* 11 (1965), 183-95; H. McKeating, *Vetus Testamentum* 25 (1975), 46-68; A. Phillips, *Journal of Jewish Studies* 28 (1977), 105-26.
6. Baldwin, *1 & 2 Samuel*, 252-53. Cf. Fokkelman, *Narrative Art and Poetry*, 126; McCarter, *2 Samuel*, 344. Josephus (*Antiquities of the Jews*, VII:8:4) holds that David planned Absalom's return from the beginning. If this were the case, there would have been no need for the woman from Tekoa.
7. *Macmillan Bible Atlas*, 94, 119, 130, 133. Cf. Baly, *Geography*, 89, 182; Thomson, *The Land and the Book*, I:486-87. See also M. Marcoff and D. J. Chitty, *Palestine Exploration Quarterly* (1929), 171-74.
8. From 14:16 and 19 it is evident that Joab threatened this widow and her son. His actions give us further insights into his personality.
9. H. Hagan, *Biblica* 60 (1979), 301-26. Cf. W. M. Clark, *Journal of Biblical Literature* 88 (1969), 266-78.
10. deVaux, *Ancient Israel*, 39-40; Pedersen, *Israel*, I-II:77ff., 227; III-IV: 550, 583, 593. See also F. C. Fensham, *Journal of Near Eastern Studies* 21 (1962), 129-39.
11. Kirkpatrick (*Second Samuel*, 350) writes: "The surviving son, who is the least hope for the continuance of his family, is compared to a live coal still left among the embers, by which the fire, almost extinct, may be rekindled. If this son was put to death, her husband's family will be extinct (cf. Num. 27:4). Their conduct was actuated not so much by a wish to execute justice as by covetousness and a desire to share the inheritance among themselves. Cf. Matt. 21:38."
12. Ibid., 350. Cf. Hertzberg, *I and II Samuel*, 331-32; Mauchline, *1 and 2 Samuel*, 265-66.
13. Cf. J. Hoftijzer, *Vetus Testamentum* 20 (1970), 427 for a different interpretation to the one presented here.
14. E. Bellefontaine, *Journal for the Study of the Old Testament* 38 (1987), 48. For a fuller explanation of 14:4-21, see pp. 47-72.
15. Cf. W. M. Clark, *Journal of Biblical Literature* 88 (1969), 266-78; A. Jepsen, *Vetus Testamentum* 8 (1958), 293-97.
16. Cf. Whitelam, *The Just King*, 135.
17. Cf. J. MacDonald, *Journal of Near Eastern Studies* 35 (1976), 147-70. See also *Theological Wordbook of the Old Testament*, II:585-86 (#1389a).
18. Cf. *Encyclopedia Judaica*,I: 133-34; A. F. Rainey, *Bulletin of the American Schools of Oriental Research* 179 (1965), 34-36; R. B. Y. Scott, *Biblical Archaeologist* 22 (1959), 34; A. Segre, *Journal of Biblical Literature* 64 (1945), 357-75.
19. In 18:18 it is explicitly stated that Absalom had no heir. Many writers have presumed that there must be a discrepancy in the text. This is presumptuous, given the Bible's amazing accuracy in other areas. All that is implied is that at the time of the events described in chapter 18 Absalom had no male heir. His sons could have died before these events took place. Perhaps that is why they are not named. Cf. T. W. Rosmarin, *Journal of Biblical Literature* 52 (1933), 261-62.
20. Fokkelman, *Narrative Art and Poetry*, 147.

21. Anderson, *2 Samuel*, 191.
22. P. Hoare, *Memoirs of Granville Sharp* (London: H. Colburn, 1820), 524pp. Cf. E. M. Howse, *Saints in Politics* (London: Allen and Unwin, 1971), 20-21, 25-26, 30-31, 45-46.
23. Later, when the Federal Government required the issuing of contracts covering the publication of all original works (e.g., books, poems, music, etc.), Loizeaux Brothers naturally complied. In their personal dealings, however, they continue the highest principles of Christian ethics.
24. Corrie ten-Boom, *Tramp for the Lord* (Fort Washington, PA: Christian Literature Crusade, 1974), 192.

Chapter 15

1. N. Webster, *Webster's New Universal Unabridged Dictionary* (New York: Dorset and Baber, 1979), 56. Used by permission.
2. Cf. C. K. Barrett, *A Commentary on the First Epistle to the Corinthians* (New York: Harper and Row, 1968), 217-18; G. D. Fee, *The First Epistle to the Corinthians*. New International Commentary on the New Testament (Grand Rapids: Eerdmans, 1987), 433-41; and F. L. Godet, *Commentary on First Corinthians* (Grand Rapids: Kregel, 1977), 471-78, for a few examples of Paul's use of athletic metaphors.
3. Cf. Anderson, *2 Samuel*, 212; Fokkelman, *Narrative Art and Poetry*, 414ff.; Gunn, *King David*, pp. 115-16; and Ishida, *David and Solomon*, 31-38.
4. Anderson, *2 Samuel*, 193-94, 197. For a discussion of Absalom's ambitious scheme, see C. J. Barber, *God Has the Answer...* (Grand Rapids: Baker, 1974), 124-34; Blaiklock, *Bible Characters*, 165-68; and Whyte, *Bible Characters: Old Testament*, 309ff.
5. The speculation of Blaikie (*Second Samuel*, p. 217) and Deane (*David*, 159) that King David paid for Absalom's equipage and retainers is just that–speculation. The Biblical text states that *"[Absalom] provided for himself..."* and that should be sufficient proof that David played no part in his son's self-aggrandizement. Furthermore, Absalom had wealth of his own and could easily afford such expenditure.

   For the use of chariots and horses, see Whitelam, *The Just King*, 141; Yadin, *Art of Warfare*, II:284-86.
6. Deane, *David*, 159. Cf. Blaikie, *Second Samuel*, 217-18.
7. There is little consensus on the part of scholars as to whether "Israel" in this context means only the northern tribes or included people from the south as well. It seems likely that the whole nation was involved, perhaps with a greater number from the north becoming disenchanted with King David (cf. 19:8b; 20:1ff.). We may also be sure that Absalom took care not to confide in any who were loyal to David. For a discussion of this and other matters pertaining to the rebellion, see M. A. Cohen, *Studies in Jewish Bibliography, History, and Literature*, ed. C. Berlin (New York: Ktav, 1971), 91-112; Z. Kalli, *Israel Exploration Journal* 28 (1978), 251-61; and McCarter, *2 Samuel*, 357-58.
8. For a discussion of the *šōfĕṭîm*, "judges," in Israel, see H. J. Becker, *Law and the Administration of Justice in the Old Testament and Ancient Near East*, trans. J. Moiser (London: SPCK, 1980), 224pp. ; M. S. Rosenberg, *Eretz-Israel* 12 (1975), 77-86; M. Weinfeld, *Israel Oriental Society* 7 (1977), 65-88; and J. Weingreen, *Vetus Testamentum* 19 (1969), 263-66.

   We may be sure that when the wise woman from Tekoa was shown into David's presence, Joab had already told those responsible for insuring that all interested parties were present that the plaintiffs would not be coming.
9. A. Maclaren, *Life of David Reflected in His Psalms* (Grand Rapids: Baker, 1955), 234-44.
10. Deane, *David*, 159.
11. The Masoretic Text reads "forty" years. This is plainly an error. If Absalom killed Amnon when he was about 18 or 19, spent three years in exile and two more under house arrest, and then devoted *forty* years to stealing away the hearts of the people, he would have been about 65 years of age at the time of his rebellion. And David would have been about 95. We know from 2 Samuel 5:4 (see also 1 Kings 2:10-11 and

1 Chronicles 29:27-28) that David died at age 70. He was thirty when he began to reign and his reign lasted for forty years. David was about sixty at the time of Absalom's coup, and he reigned for a further ten years after Absalom had been defeated. It is preferable to read "*four*" in place of "forty." Absalom would be about 27 or 28 years old, and this fits better David's statement in 18:5 "[Deal] gently for my sake with the *young man*, with Absalom." Cf. J. J. Davis, *Biblical Numerology* (Grand Rapids: Baker, 1968), 174pp.; Josephus, *Antiquities of the Jews*, VII:9:1.

12. Henry, *Commentary*, II:537-38.

13. Cf. Abel, *Géographie*, II:338; A. Mazar, *Israel Exploration Journal* 31 (1981), 1-36.

14. For a Biblical example of how to handle rejection, see the writer's exposition of *First Samuel* (chap. 8). Cf. B. Mazar, *Vetus Testamentum* 13 (1963), 310-20. And for a contemporary statement of the pain and possible injustice of rejection, see *Tom Landry: An Autobiography* (San Francisco: HarperCollins, 1990), 240-65. Landry had coached the Dallas Cowboys for many years and had the finest winning record of any coach in the NFL.

15. Cf. M. Delcor, *Vetus Testamentum* 28 (1978), 409-22. And for a discussion of David's elite soldiers, see B. Mazar, *Vetus Testamentum* 13 (1963), 310-20.

16. B. Mazar, *Vetus Testamentum* 13 (1963), 314.

17. Biographical sketches of Ittai are few and far between. Cf. Barber, *God Has the Answer...*, 32-40.

18. Cf. Sakenfeld, *The Meaning of Hesed in the Bible*, 31-32.

19. Cf. Hupper, *Index to Periodical Literature*, I:82.

20. Fokkelman, *Narrative Art and Poetry*, 455.

21. Blaiklock, *Bible Characters*, 170.

22. Ibid., 169.

23. For a discussion of "the friend of the king" see deVaux, *Ancient Israel*, 22-23; J. Bright in *The Organization and Administration of the Israelite Empire*, 203-04; H. Donner, *Zeitschrift für die alttestamentliche Wissenschaft* 73 (1961), 269-77; H. Schmidt, *Zeitschrift für die alttestamentliche Wissenschaft* 67 (1970), 180-81, 187; A. van Selms, *Journal of Near Eastern Studies* 16 (1957), 121-22.

24. *Macmillan Bible Atlas*, 109. For a discussion of Shimei, see Blaiklock, *Bible Characters*, 168-69; and Whyte *Bible Characters: Old Testament*, 297ff.

25. Cf. H. C. Brichto, *The Problem of "Curse" in the Hebrew Bible*, JBL Monograph Series (Philadelphia: Society of Biblical Literature, 1968), 232pp.; and W. Brueggemann, *Catholic Biblical Quarterly* 36 (1974), 175-92.

26. Cf. J. A. Emerton, *Vetus Testamentum* 37 (1987), 214-17.

27. It is generally agreed that Psalms 3 and 4 belong together. Similarity of style and content cause them to fit well into this period of David's life when he fled from Absalom. For a discussion of these psalms, see Maclaren, *Life of David*, 245-61.

28. Shakespeare, *King Lear*, 1:4:310.

29. Idem, *Hamlet*, III:1:56.

Chapter 16

1. A partial answer to this dilemma is found in the work of Q. J. Schultz, et al, *Dancing in the Dark* (Grand Rapids: Eerdmans, 1990), 347pp.

2. J. Dryden in *Seventeenth Century English Poetry*, eds. J. T. Shawcross and R. D. Emma (Philadelphia: Lippincott, 1969), 523 (lines 39-44). (I am aware that Dryden, as well as many preachers of his day, saw a remarkable parallel between the aspirations and actions of Absalom and the unsuccessful uprising against Charles II by his bastard son, James Scott, the Duke of Monmouth. This may have caused Dryden to allow the tinge of contemporary events to govern his choice of words, or to embellish a particular scene in the Biblical narrative with factual data from his own time.)

3. *Yehî hammelek*, the equivalent of "Long live the king," also involved an oath of allegiance. Cf. P. A. H. deBoer, *Vetus Testamentum* 5 (1955), 225-31; E. Lipinski, *La Royalte de Yahwe dans la poesie et le culte de l'ancien Israel* (Brussels: Paleis der Academein, 1965), 352; and Mettinger, *King and Messiah*, 131-37.

4. Cf. H. Donner, *Zeitschrift für due alttestamentliche Wissenschaft* 73 (1961), 269-77; A. van Selms, *Journal of Near Eastern Studies* 16 (1957), 118-23.
5. Baldwin, *1 & 2 Samuel*, 264.
6. Dryden, *Seventeenth Century English Poetry*, 529 (lines 303-312). Cf. Isaiah 14:12-15 for the background of Dryden's "angelic" comments.
7. Ibid., 525-26 (lines 150-155).
8. Some indication of the sanctity of the husband-wife relationship may be gleaned from *The History of Herodotus*, trans. G. Rawlinson (New York: Tudor, 1928), 3ff., where Gyges, though invited by Candaules to watch from concealment as Candaules' wife undressed, does not want to do so as this is against the customs of the times. And Sophocles, who in his *Works*, ed. F. Storr, Loeb Classical Library (London: Heinemann, 1956), I:6-139, records the unwitting incestuous relationship of Oedipus and Jocasta, also records their respective reactions when they found out. Jocasta committed suicide, and Oedipus plucked out his own eyes that had in innocence looked upon his mother's nakedness. The apostle Paul tacitly confirms this kind of attitude in 1 Corinthians 5:1.
9. F. Langlamet, *Revue Biblique* 83 (1976), 321-79. Cf. Gunn, *King David*, 116.
10. Baldwin, *1 & 2 Samuel*, 265.
11. Ibid., 266-67. Italics in the original.
12. Probably located at the confluence of the Kidron Valley and the Valley of Hinnom (cf. Joshua 15:7; 18:16). See also Robinson, *Biblical Researches*, I:268-73; Thomson, *The Land and the Book*, II:8; Mazar, *Mountain of the Lord*, 156ff.
13. The verbs "would come and give" and "would go and repeat" imply that communication with David was regularly maintained. We have recorded the first of such relays in order for us to understand the danger involved.
14. Baldwin, *1 & 2 Samuel*, 268. The *Mishnah* (trans. H. Danby [London: Oxford University Press, 1933]), Sanhedrin, 10:2, preserves the rabbinic tradition that Ahithophel will not have a part (in the blessings of) the world to come.
15. Milton, *Paradise Lost*, V:893.
16. Maclaren, *The Life of David*, 245-61.
17. Blaiklock, *Bible Characters*, 167-68.
18. Anderson, *2 Samuel*, 390.

Chapter 17

1. *Talmud*, Yoma, 8:6.
2. Webster, *Webster's New Universal Unabridged Dictionary*, 56. Cf. *International Encyclopedia of the Social Sciences* (New York: Macmillan, 1968), I:27-33.
3. Shakespeare, *Julius Caesar*, III:2. Cf. Appian, *Appian's Roman History*, trans. H. White, Loeb Classical Library (London: Heinemann, 1928), III:4:137; Dio Cassius, *Dio's Roman History*, trans. E. Cary, Loeb Classical Library (London: Heinemann, 1954), IV:327-43; *Plutarch's Lives*, "Caesar," 523ff.; Suetonius, *Works*, I:76ff.

   See also T. Mommsen, *History of Rome*, 4 vols. (London: Bentley, 1862-66), IV:450ff.; and E. D. S. Bradford, *Julius Caesar: The Pursuit of Power* (New York: W. Morrow, 1985), 312pp.
4. *Encyclopedia Britannica*, 11th ed., X:829; XIII:291, 865; XXIII: 1017ff. Cf. *Memoirs of Marguerite de Valois* (New York: Collier, 1910), 364pp.
5. J. R. Green, *History of the English People*, 4 vols. (New York: Harper, 1877-80), IV:41. See also the exemplary work of J. H. Merle D'Aubigne, *The Reformation in England* (Edinburgh: Banner of Truth, 1963), II:425-34, 441-46, 448-50. Shakespeare's *Henry VIII*, III:2 also makes interesting reading.

   God's involvement in the lives of His people has been discussed by J. M. M. Roberts in *Vetus Testamentum* 21 (1971), 244-52.
6. Cf. H. Kohut, *The Analysis of the Self* (New York: International Universities Press, 1971), 368pp.; idem, *The Restoration of the Self* (New York: International Universities Press, 1977), 345pp.; and M. S. Mahler, *On Human Symbiosis and the Vicissitudes of Individuation* (New York: International Universities Press, 1968), 271pp.

7. Some versions read "Ishmaelite." Cf. Anderson, *2 Samuel*, 223; Baldwin, *1 & 2 Samuel*, 268; Hertzberg, *I and II Samuel*, 357; McCarter, *2 Samuel*, 393-94, 420.

8. We hear no more of Hanun, Shobi's brother, and we are left to presume that he had either been killed when Rabbah fell or else deposed. Shobi collaborates with the others to bring David sorely needed essentials.

    We have not heard of Machir since reading about Mephibosheth. He had been a loyal Saulide. Now he is numbered among those who bring food and other items to the exiled king. Apparently, David's sincere regard for Mephibosheth had removed all trace of animosity.

    The third contributor to David's needs is Barzillai, whom we will read about again in our next chapter.

9. Blaikie, *Second Samuel*, 270.

10. Cf. P. Haupt, *Journal of Biblical Literature* 45 (1921), 357. See also J. MacDonald, *Journal of Near Eastern Studies* 35 (1976), 147-70.

11. It is obvious that Absalom could not remain in Israel, but he could be sent into exile (most likely to his grandfather, Talmai, in Geshur). Cf. B. Mazar, *Journal of Biblical Literature* 80 (1961), 16-28.

12. The "Forest of Ephraim" was probably named by Ephraimites who, during the reign of Saul, fled eastward to escape Philistine incursion. Cf. Hertzberg, *I and II Samuel*, 358-59.

13. It is probable that losses among David's men were very slight because they had Gileadites from the area serving as guides for each division of one hundred men.

14. McCarter (*2 Samuel*, 405) disputes the Biblical record and claims that Absalom lost between 100 and 280 of his men. His views are contrary to Josephus, *Antiquities of the Jews*, VII:10:2.

15. The word used is *śôbek*, "entangle, entwine." The sentence structure implies that the branches were intertwined, not that Absalom's hair became entangled in the tree.

16. *Talmud*, Sotah, 9*b*.

17. Josephus, *Antiquities of the Jews*, VII:10:2.

18. Cf. F. Langlamet, *Revue Biblique* 84 (1976), 355 (with his full discussion of this passage covering pp. 321-79 and 481-529); Smith, *Books of Samuel*, 357-58.

19. G. R. Driver, in *Studies and Essays in Honor of Abraham A. Newman*, eds. M. Ben-Horin, B. D. Weinryb, and S. Zeitlin (Leiden, The Netherlands: Brill, 1962), 133-34.

20. Hertzberg, *I and II Samuel*, 359. Cf. Baldwin, *1 & 2 Samuel*, 270.

21. Blaikie, *Second Samuel*, 273-74.

22. Josephus, *Antiquities of the Jews*, VII:10:3. Cf. Keil, *Samuel*, 439-40; U. Cassuto, *Revue des etudes juives* 105 (1939, N.S. 5), 126-27; M. Delcor, *Journal of Semitic Studies* 12 (1967), 230-34.

23. *New International Dictionary of Biblical Archaeology*, 187-88; *People of Old Testament Times*, 79.

24. Cf. E. F. deWard, *Journal of Jewish Studies* 18 (1967), 230-34; idem, *Journal of Jewish Studies* 23 (1972), 1-27, 144-66.

25. Blaikie, *Second Samuel*, 279-82. Cf., W. Bruggemann, *Journal of the American Academy of Religion* 40 (1972), 96-109; C. C. Conroy, *Absalom! Absalom!* Rome: Pontifical Biblical Institute, 1978), 191pp. The most common view offered by commentators is that David blamed himself for Absalom's actions (that eventually led to his son's death). They refer back to the Bathsheba incident and claim that God was punishing David for his adultery. If this is so, then he carried with him a neurotic form of guilt that completely nullified the forgiveness he claimed to have received when he wrote Psalms 32 and 51. But such was not the case. David's forgiveness by God was genuine. He had not lived under a cloud of fear for the past ten years wondering when God's punishment would fall. Those who believe otherwise show how little they understand of grace, and their unwillingness to allow for David's sin to be forgiven. In reality, what they imply is an affront to God (for, in their view, following his repentance the Lord kept David in suspense wondering when the judgments would fall). Absalom made his own choices and the result of these decisions was a "grave" in a pit in the Forest of Ephraim.

26. Kirkpatrick, *Second Samuel*, 389.
27. A. Tennyson, *The Complete Poetical Works of Tennyson*, ed. W. J. Rolfe (Boston: Houghton Mifflin, 1898), 551. My wife and I passed by Romney's house in Kendal, Westmoreland, when we visited England's famous Lake District. His old home has been converted into a (small) hotel.
28. Henry C. Morrison, *Lectures on Prophecy* (Louisville, KY: Pentecostal, 1915), 47.

Chapter 18

1. McCarter, *2 Samuel*, 423.
2. Blaikie, *David*, 297.
3. Blaiklock, *Bible Characters*, 179-80. See also J. C. Geikie, *Old Testament Characters* (New York: J. Pott, 1903), 244-51; and Whyte, *Bible Characters: Old Testament*, 303-08.
4. *Madon*, "quarrels." See *Theological Wordbook of the Old Testament*, I:188 (# 426).
5. Cf. P. V. Reid, *Theologische Zeitschrift* 16 (1960), 1-4.
6. Joab was apparently replaced because of his disobedience in the death of Absalom.
7. The reference is, strictly speaking, to the tribes of Ephraim and Manasseh. The context of Shimei's statement, however, implies all the northern tribes. Cf. Z. Kallai, *Israel Exploration Journal* 28 (1978), 251-61; deVaux, *Early History*, 643.
8. Cf. Brichto, *The Problem of "Curse" in the Hebrew Bible*, 138-41.
9. The various uses of the word "today" need to be understood in light of their usage. Cf. S. J. DeVries, *Yesterday, Today, and Tomorrow* (London: S.P.C.K.), 1975), 221.
10. Cf. Mettinger, *King and Messiah*, 119. McCarter (*2 Samuel*, 421) states that "a coronation was accompanied by a general amnesty." See also G. C. Macholz, *Zeitschrift für die alttestamentliche Wissenschaft* 84 (1972), 170. Anderson (*2 Samuel*, 242) adds the weight of his scholarly understanding by affirming that Absalom's coronation ("anointing" 19:10) had effectively deposed David, and he needed to be publicly reinstated as Israel's king.
11. Mettinger, *King and Messiah*, 119. Cf. Whitelam, *The Just King*, 145; and D. M. Gunn, *Semeia* 3 (1975), 14-45.
12. Anderson, *2 Samuel*, 242.
13. Cf. Josephus, *Antiquities of the Jews*, VII:11:3; and the *Talmud*, Yebamot, 48a. The reference to Mephibosheth's "moustache" probably includes his beard. The importance of one's beard in the ancient Near East has been described in *First Samuel* (see commends on 21:10-15) and in the present volume where the affront of David's ambassadors highlighted the significance of a man's beard (10:4-5).
14. This seems ludicrous, for when Absalom (having stolen the hearts of the people of Israel) established his throne in Jerusalem, it was most unlikely that he would turn it over to a descendant of the late King Saul. Ziba's words might be true only (1) if Absalom's plan failed, and (2) if both Absalom and David were killed in battle. Then, and only then, might the northern tribes exert their power and demand that a member of Saul's family be seated on the throne.
15. McCarter (*2 Samuel*, 421) believes that Mephibosheth went down to the River Jordan to meet David. Because of the many people there, the conversation recorded here did not take place until after the ceremony at Gilgal. It is possible that the men of Gilgal wanted to hurry David off to Gilgal and on that account Mephibosheth did not have the opportunity of speaking with the king.
16. Baldwin, *1 & 2 Samuel*, 277.
17. *Me'od 'îš gādôl*, "very great man." Cf. *Theological Dictionary of the Old Testament*, V:309. See also Josephus, *Antiquities of the Jews*, VII:11:4.
18. Cf. J. R. Bartlett, *Vetus Testamentum* 20 (1970), 257-77.
19. Blaikie, *Second Samuel*, 303.
20. Whyte, *Bible Characters: Old Testament*, 330-34.
21. It is unusual in a context such as this for mention to be made of one's mother.
22. There are certain expressions (e.g., "do not know right from wrong") that need explanation. A discussion of them is to be found in Anderson, *2 Samuel*, 292-93; Hertzberg, *I and II Samuel*, 367-68; Mauchline, *1 and 2 Samuel*, 292-93; and McCarter,

2 Samuel, 422-23. I have not dealt with them in the exposition because to do so would disturb the flow of the narrative.

23. Blaiklock, *Bible Characters*, 176, 180-81.
24. It is interesting to note the way in which defense mechanisms block the work of the Holy Spirit. See Barber, *Dynamic Personal Bible Study*, 129ff.
25. Cf. *Baker Encyclopedia of Psychology*, ed. D. G. Penner (Grand Rapids: Baker, 1985), 869-70.
26. Cf. *Baker Dictionary of Theology*, ed. W. A. Elwell (Grand Rapids: Baker, 1984), 874.

Chapter 19

1. Kirkpatrick, *Second Samuel*, 401. The Targum cited by Kirkpatrick is plainly in error. Absalom was dead. For the different views, see F. Langlamet, *Revue Biblique* 83 (1976), 321-79; M. Tsevat, *Journal of Semitic Studies* 3 (1958), 237-43.
2. G. B. Caird, *Interpreter's Bible* (Nashville: Abingdon, 1953), II:1149.
3. Z. Kallai, *Israel Exploration Journal* 28 (1978), 251-61.
4. Fokkelman (*Narrative Art and Poetry*, 316) believes David to be wimpish and a "born quitter." In this he plainly errs.
5. Deane, *David*, 181.
6. Cf. Noth, *Personennamen*, 146-47.
7. Bright, *History of Israel*, 210.
8. Cf. J. A. Emerton, *Vetus Testamentum* 37 (1987), 214-17; V. Maag, *Theologische Tijdschrift* 21 (1965), 287-99.
9. B. L. Montgomery, *The Path to Leadership* (London: Collins, 1961), 9. This and all other quotations from this book are used by permission of the publisher.
10. Blaikie, *Second Samuel*, 319-20.
11. Anderson, *2 Samuel*, 240; Baldwin, *1 & 2 Samuel*, 279. Cf. C. Berlin, *Studies in Jewish Bibliography, History, and Literature*, 91-112.
12. J. B. Pritchard, *Vetus Testamentum Supplement* 7 (1959), 6. Ackroyd (*2 Samuel*, 189) believes that the large stone was an altar.
13. Deane, *David*, 183. Cf. Blaiklock, *Bible Characters*, 179-80.
14. Identified as modern Abil el-Qamh. Cf. *Macmillan Bible Atlas*, 124, 147. J. Kaplan, *Israel Exploration Journal* 28 (1978), 157-59; E. C. B. MacLaurin, *Palestine Exploration Quarterly* 110 (1978), 113-14.
15. Baldwin, *1 & 2 Samuel*, 280.
16. G. Rude, ed., *Robespierre* (Englewood Cliffs, NJ: Prentice-Hall, 1967), 182pp.
17. Cf. J. Bright in *Magnalia Dei*, 193-208; and R. deVaux, *Revue Biblique* 48 (1939), 394-405; *Ancient Near Eastern Texts*, 307-08.
18. A. F. Rainey, *Israel Exploration Journal* 20 (1970), 191-202.
19. *Zondervan Pictorial Encyclopedia of the Bible*, III:306.
20. Blaikie, *Second Samuel*, 323.
21. B. Mazar, *The Early Biblical Period*, eds. S. Ahituv and B. A. Levine (Jerusalem: Israel Exploration Society, 1986), 266pp.
22. L. B. Flynn, *When the Saints Come Storming In* (Wheaton, IL: Victor, 1988), 14.
23. Cf. D. L. Kanter and P. H. Mirvis, *The Cynical Americans* (San Francisco: Jossey-Bass, 1989), 1-2.
24. Montgomery, 14.
25. Ibid., 15.
26. Ibid., 18.
27. Ibid., 19.
28. Ibid., 19.

Chapter 20

1. Kirkpatrick, *Second Samuel*, 408. Cf. Blaikie, *Second Samuel*, 326-27.
2. Baldwin, *1 & 2 Samuel*, 282-83. Cf. Anderson, *2 Samuel*, 248.
3. Kirkpatrick (*Second Samuel*, 408) writes: "There is no adverb of time marking

chronological connection with the foregoing narrative. In Palestine a famine was the almost certain consequence of a failure of the winter rains, on which both corn-fields and pasturage depend. See I Kings 17:1, 18:2; Joel 1:8-20, for famine as the result of drought; and compare Gen. 12:10, 26:1, 42:5; Ruth 1:1; 2 Kings 8:1, 2."

4. Blaikie, *Second Samuel*, 328.
5. Joshua 9:23, 27. For Saul's motive in wanting to exterminate the Gibeonites, see *Talmud*, Yebamoth, 78b; J. Blenkinsopp, *Gibeon and Israel* (Cambridge: Cambridge University Press, 1972), 56. Blenkinsopp believes that the Gibeonites constituted a security risk. The situation of these cities effectively cut Israel in half and a Philis-tine-Gibeonite alliance would have had disastrous results to the nation. Cf. McCarter, *2 Samuel*, 441; A. Malamat, *Vetus Testamentum* 5 (1955), 1-12.
6. *People of Old Testament Times*, 126; Hertzberg, *I and II Samuel*, 177-78; Blenkinsopp, *Gideon and Israel*, 67-71.
7. Cf. Anderson, *2 Samuel*, 249; Baldwin, *1 & 2 Samuel*, 283.
8. Blenkinsopp, *Gideon and Israel*, 34, 136.
9. *Ancient Near Eastern Texts*, 394-96.
10. Blaikie, *Second Samuel*, 330.
11. *Talmud*, Sanhedrin, 34b.
12. F. C. Fensham, *Biblical Archaeologist* 27 (1964), 100. Cf. R. Polzin, *Harvard Theologi-cal Review* 62 (1969), 236. Polzin favors dismemberment for covenant breakers (simi-lar to the sacrifices used in the establishing of a covenant, see Genesis 15:10; Jeremiah 34:18).
13. J. B. Mozley, *Ruling Ideas In Early Ages* (London: Rivingtons. 1889), 104-25.
14. J. J. Gluck, *Zeitschrift für die alttestamentliche Wissenschaft* 77 (1965), 72. Gluck be-lieves that Michal did have children. Others conjecture that Merab died while still young and Michal reared her sisters children as her own. No mention is made of them when she rejoined David in Hebron, and this is the kind of item a court re-porter or national archivist would have mentioned, particularly as these five young men could constitute a threat to David's throne.
15. It is surprising that Merab's children were chosen, because they were Saul's grand-children. Furthermore, according to the laws of paternity, they would be reckoned among their father's family, not their mother's. Perhaps they were included because David could not find seven direct descendants of Saul's to hand over to the Gibeonites.
16. S. P. Brock, *Vetus Testamentum* 23 (1973), 100-03.
17. Macartney, *Chariots of Fire*, 150-59. A "concubine" or "wife of secondary rank" be-longed to her husband and enjoyed certain legal rights. Her position differed from a "mistress" in today's world in that a mistress does not legally belong to the man who is keeping her and has no legal rights. She can be dismissed at will. For a dis-cussion of the rights of concubines in the Bible, see Neufeld, *Ancient Hebrew Mar-riage Laws*, 118-34.
18. Kirkpatrick, *Second Samuel*, 414.
19. Baldwin, *1 & 2 Samuel*, 285.
20. Blaikie, *Second Samuel*, 338-39.
21. Considerable debate surrounds the usage of *hārāphāh* and *Raphah*. Most modern writers see in these words some cultic association (cf. C. E. L'Heureux, *Bulletin of the American Schools of Oriental Research* 221 [1976], 83-85; F. Willesten, *Studia Theologica* 12 [1958], 192-240). Mauchline (*1 and 2 Samuel*, 305) makes a case for "Raphah" being a collective noun. The description of the giant's equipment, how-ever, would argue for a man of enormous size. Y. Yadin discusses his javelin in *Pales-tine Exploration Quarterly* 86 (1955), 58-69.
22. *New Unger's Bible Dictionary*, 753-54. Cf. R. H. Smith, *Biblical Archaeologist* 27 (1964), 1-31, 101-24; idem, *Biblical Archaeologist* 29 (1966), 1-27.
23. Cf. C. E. L'Heureux, *Bulletin of the American Schools of Oriental Research* 221 (1976), 83-85; J. D. deMoor, *Zeitschrift für die alttestamentliche Wissenschaft* 88 (1976), 323-45.
24. L. M. M. von Pakozdy, *Zeitschrift für die alttestamentliche Wissenschaft* 68 (1956),

257-59; A. M. Honeyman, *Journal of Biblical Literature* 67 (1948), 13-25 (noting in particular pp. 23-24); J. J. Stamm, *Vetus Testamentum Supplement* 7 (1960), 165-83 (noting in particular pp. 167-68, 182).
25. *The Eerdmans Bible Commentary*, eds. D. Guthrie and J. A. Motyer (Grand Rapids: Eerdmans, 1970), 318-19.
26. K. Menninger, *Whatever Became of Sin?* (New York: Hawthorn, 1973), 52-57.
27. Cf. T. E. Miller, *Portraits of Women of the Bible* (London: Allenson, n.d.), 152-62. Miller exceeds the biblical evidence in places, but preachers will find his thoughts suggestive.

Chapter 21

1. For a comparison of this chapter with Psalm 18, see F. M. Cross, Jr., and D. N. Freedman, *Journal of Biblical Literature* 72 (1953), 15-34. Cf. Anderson, *2 Samuel*, 261; Blaikie, *Second Samuel*, pp. 350-51; Kirkpatrick, *Second Samuel*, 418; Mauchline, *1 and 2 Samuel*, 306-07; McCarter, *2 Samuel*, 463-64.
2. Blaikie, *Second Samuel*, 350-51.
3. Cf. G. von Rad, *Holy War in Ancient Israel*, trans. M. J. Dawn (Grand Rapids: Eerdmans, 1991), 166pp.
4. Blaikie, *Second Samuel*, 350.
5. Ibid., 353-54.
6. Blaikie, *Second Samuel*, 356.
7. A theophany has been defined as "a visible or auditory manifestation of God" (e.g., when God spoke directly to Moses at the burning bush or when His voice was heard at the time of Christ's transfiguration).
8. *Merḥāb*, "broad place." Cf. *Theological Wordbook of the Old Testament*, II:840-41 (#2143).
9. Blaikie, *Second Samuel*, 356.
10. Payne, *Samuel*, 268-69.
11. Baldwin, *1 & 2 Samuel*, 288.
12. The reference to "jumping over a wall" is puzzling. The word used in v. 30 is *sur*, which is normally translated "rock," whereas *homa* or *qir* are the usual words for "wall." David apparently did not have a literal wall in mind.
13. Kirkpatrick, *Second Samuel*, 428.
14. Blaiklock, *Bible Characters*, 167-68.

Chapter 22

1. *English and Hebrew Lexicon*, 610. Cf. Pentecost, *Things to Come*, 69, 104, 107; Peters, *Theocratic Kingdom*, I: 290-91. See also A. B. Davidson, *Old Testament Prophecy*, ed. J. A. Patterson (Edinburgh: Clark, 1903), 347-75 (noting in particular pp. 349f.). Usually *ne'um* is found in the context of "Thus saith the Lord" passages. It is rare to find it connected with the name of an individual (cf. Numbers 24:3-4, 15-16 and Proverbs 30:1 for exceptions). There is similarity of expression between Balaam's opening remarks and those of David (cf. Numbers 24:3, 15 and 2 Sam. 23:1), but it is unwise to push the similarity too far. Cf. McCarter, *2 Samuel*, 379-80. For a discussion of this psalm, see H. N. Richardson, *Journal of Biblical Literature* 40 (1971), 257-66.
2. McCarter (*2 Samuel*, 481) has written: "The expression denotes the awe of the worshipper in the presence of the numinous, but it connotes proper religious devotion in general, even with the suggestion of obedience to divine statutes and customs.
3. Ibid., 509: "The meaning of the metaphor as I understand it is that a just king, ruling in accordance with religious principles, is like the sun on a cloudless morning, which by its light causes the rain-drenched earth to turn green."
4. Blaikie, *Second Samuel*, 364-65. Cf. Tristram, *Natural History of the Bible*, 454.
5. Blaikie, *Second Samuel*, 366; Kirkpatrick, *Second Samuel*, 435.
6. Cf. Pentecost, *Things to Come*, 104-05; Peters, *Theocratic Kingdom*, I:314.
7. Kirkpatrick, *Second Samuel*, 436.

8. Pentecost, *Things to Come*, 554-55. Some students of God's Word are concerned over the fact that the Old Testament predicts the return of Christ *after* the tribulation. A distinction must be maintained between Christ's return for His own and His return to the earth to put down His enemies and set up His Kingdom. The "rapture" was unknown in Old Testament times. The apostle Paul, when he introduces the idea of Christ's return for His own, calls it a "mystery" (not something mysterious, but something previously hidden that has now been revealed). Cf. Romans 11:25ff.; 16:25-27; 1 Corinthians 15:51 and 1 Thessalonians 4:13–5:10; Ephesians 1:9-12; 3:3, 5-9; Colossians 1:26-27. Cf. Pentecost, *Things to Come*, 193-218.
9. Blaikie, *Second Samuel*, 369.
10. *Macmillan Bible Atlas*, 94.
11. J. R. Bartlett, *Vetus Testamentum* 19(1969), 10; Mazar, *Early Biblical Period*, 90; Yadin, *Art of Warfare*, I:277; Corvin, *David and His Mighty Men*, 175pp.
12. Ibid., 25-31.
13. I. Lepp, *The Ways of Friendship*, trans. B. Murchand (New York: Macmillan, 1966), 127pp.
14. D. D. Eisenhower, *Reader's Digest* (June 1965), 54.

Chapter 23

1. C. Burnett, *One More Time* (New York: Random, 1986), 74, 91. Used by permission.
2. Kirkpatrick, *Second Samuel*, 448-49.
3. Cf. McCarter, *2 Samuel*, 509.
4. Blaikie, *Second Samuel*, 377.
5. Cf. *Evangelical Dictionary of Theology*, 428-30; 937-38.
6. Deane, *David*, 186. Josephus, *Antiquities of the Jews*, VII:13:1.
7. Deane, *David*, 187. He is followed by Anderson (*2 Samuel*, 284).
8. Blaikie, *David*, 343.
9. *Macmillan Bible Atlas*, 106. Cf. Baldwin, *1 & 2 Samuel*, 295-96; W. Fuss, *Zeitschrift fur die alttestamentliche Wissenschaft* 74 (1962), 156; G. E. Mendenhall, *Journal of Biblical Literature* 77 (1958), 52-66.
10. Cf. 1 Samuel 22:5. See H. Haag, *Archaologie und Altes Testament*, Festschrift fur Kurt Galling, eds. A. Kuschke und E. Kutsch (Tubingen: Mohr, 1970), 135-43.
11. Deane, *David*, 190. For a similar type of situation, see *Near Eastern Religious Texts*, 122-28.
12. Ibid. But exactly what is the meaning of 24:15? McCarter (*2 Samuel*, 511) has pointed out that in Talmudic Hebrew the nouns *sā'ôd* and *sĕ'udâ* mean "meal, dinner." The expression, then, probably refers to the time of the evening meal. Thus the plague raged for one day before it reached Jerusalem. Anderson (*2 Samuel*, 286) affirms this: "The 'appointed time' cannot very well refer to the *end* of the three day period because Yahweh intervened *before* this point was reached (cf. v. 16). It seems that the plague lasted hardly a day (if our interpretation is right), but its severity was very great." So once again we have an illustration of the grace of God in the Old Testament.
13. Blaikie, *David*, 347.
14. H. B. Rosen, *Vetus Testamentum* 5 (1955), 318-20; G. W. Ahlstrom, *Vetus Testamentum* 11 (1961), 117-18; N. Wyatt, *Studia Theologica* 39 (1985), 39-53. Cf. Josephus, *Antiquities of the Jews*, VII:13:4; Smith, *Jerusalem*, I:230; and Stanley, *Sinai and Palestine*, 251.
15. Cf. Mazar, *The Mountain of the Lord*, 52, 96. For a discussion of the significance of the threshing floor, see Blaikie, *Second Samuel*, 382-87; and Blaikie, *David*, 347.
16. Cf. J. M. Myers, *1 Chronicles*, Anchor Bible (Garden City, NY: Doubleday, 1965), 149; and W. E. Lemke, *Harvard Theological Review* 58 (1965), 349-63.
17. Woodbridge, *Renewing Your Mind in a Secular Age*, 3-53;
18. B. Poinsett, *Understanding a Woman's Depression* (Wheaton: Tyndale, 1984), 35-36. Used by permission.

SCRIPTURE INDEX

1 Kings

Proverbs

PERSON AND TITLE INDEX